YALE CLASSICAL STUDIES

YALE CLASSICAL STUDIES

EDITED FOR THE DEPARTMENT OF CLASSICS

by
T. F. GOULD
and
C. J. HERINGTON

VOLUME XXV
GREEK TRAGEDY

CAMBRIDGE UNIVERSITY PRESS

CAMBRIDGE
LONDON · NEW YORK · MELBOURNE

Published by the Syndics of the Cambridge University Press
The Pitt Building, Trumpington Street, Cambridge CB2 1RP
Bentley House, 200 Euston Road, London NW1 2DB
32 East 57th Street, New York, NY 10022, USA
296 Beaconsfield Parade, Middle Park, Melbourne 3206, Australia

First published 1977

Typeset in Great Britain
at the
University Printing House, Cambridge
Printed in the United States of America

Library of Congress Cataloguing Data

Main entry under title:

Greek tragedy

(Yale classical studies; v. 25)

1.   Greek drama (Tragedy) – History and criticism – Addresses,
essays, lectures. I. Gould, Thomas.
II. Herington, C. J. III. Series.
PA25.Y3 vol. 25 [PA3133] 870'.9s [882'.01] 76–8156
ISBN 0 521 21112 3

Contents

Introduction   *page* vii

Septem contra Thebas   I
R. P. WINNINGTON-INGRAM

The dissembling-speech of Ajax   47
JOHN MOORE

The tragic issue in Sophocles' *Ajax*   67
M. SICHERL

Sophocles' *Trachiniae*: myth, poetry, and heroic values   99
CHARLES SEGAL

On 'extra-dramatic' communication of characters in Euripides   159
H. P. STAHL

The infanticide in Euripides' *Medea*   177
P. E. EASTERLING

The *Medea* of Euripides   193
B. M. W. KNOX

On the *Heraclidae* of Euripides   227
ALBIN LESKY

Euripides' *Hippolytus*, or virtue rewarded   239
GEORGE E. DIMOCK, JR

Euripides' *Heracles*   259
JUSTINA GREGORY

Contents

The first *stasimon* of Euripides' *Electra*   *page*   227

GEORGE B. WALSH

Trojan Women and the Ganymede Ode   291

ANNE BURNETT

The *Rhesus* and related matters

H. D. F. KITTO   317

Introduction

THE articles in this volume are all literary studies of Greek tragedy.

As the best scholars of earlier generations have seen – Wilamowitz above them all – the full understanding of Greek tragedy by a modern demands the concerted techniques not merely of the literary critic, but also of the linguist, the metrician, the palaeographer, the philosopher, the historian, and the archaeologist. With this principle we agree entirely, adding only that perhaps there is yet another desirable qualification: to have lived a little; to have contemplated not books only, but also men and women, moral dilemmas, spiritual crises, and both the richness and the cruelty of life. Yet the conditions of human existence as such are unresearchable, at any rate by the techniques of professional scholarship; and there are plenty of classical journals available for the publication of articles on linguistics, metrics, and so forth. A volume on tragedy which was both to possess a certain unity and to interest a fairly wide circle of readers, classical and non-classical, had therefore best confine itself to the most commonly understood and easily communicable of those many approaches, literary criticism. Accordingly, on being asked by the Yale Department of Classics to edit this volume, we decided to invite contributions from a number of scholars whom we knew to be working on the literary criticism of Greek tragedy. As the project became known, several other scholars also submitted contributions. We laid down no rules as to topic or method, requiring only that to be included a paper should be literary-critical in a broad sense, good of its kind, and as accurate as possible in its treatment of the establishable data.

The resulting cross-section of contemporary preoccupations and methods is, we think, interesting in its own right. Most remarkable is the distribution of interests with regard to the three tragedians and their several plays. We received no contributions on the *Oresteia*, the *Prometheus*, the *Antigone*, the *Oedipus Tyrannus*, or the *Bacchae*. One contributor, only, writes on Aeschylus (*Seven Against Thebes*). Three papers concern Sophocles (two the *Ajax*, one the *Trachiniae*). By far the majority of the contributors chose Euripides, and even these, with the exception of one who discussed the *Hippolytus* and two who discussed the *Medea*, concentrated on plays which have not been among the most famous during the last century or so. For our purposes, this distribution may be fortunate. The *Oresteia*, the *Oedipus Tyrannus*, and the other masterpieces mentioned, remain masterpieces, and still deserve our admiration and our comment; but it is always to be regretted when one or two works of a given tragedian are singled out in the public mind as supreme, and as characteristic, so that the full range of his art – and consequently of our own sensibilities – is dangerously contracted. The present volume may do something to correct such an imbalance.

Furthermore the pattern of choice revealed in the contributions we received may not be entirely accidental; for it is not unique in history. A similar pattern emerges from an examination of the editions and translations of Greek tragedy published in Renaissance Europe.[1] In that period, too, the plays of Euripides (and especially the *Medea*) aroused by far the greatest interest. In Sophocles, the *Ajax* attracted most attention. Those few commentators and translators who ventured to approach the still heavily corrupted texts of Aeschylus concentrated on two plays, the *Prometheus* (always the most accessible of the corpus, for stylistic and textual reasons) and...the difficult *Seven Against Thebes*. The parallel between that Renaissance selection and the range of contributions in the present volume is strange; future historians may be tempted to speculate why the closing years of the twentieth century, like the era of the Reformation, seemed able to respond better to a lone hero at his wits' end, or an ancient city threatened by annihilation, than to the codas of the *Coloneus* or of the *Oresteia*.

1. We rely for our data primarily on the as yet unpublished dissertation of Margaret J. Arnold, 'Literary Criticism of Aeschylus and Sophocles in the Editions and Translations published between 1502 and 1664' (University of Texas 1971). For Euripides, vol. II of J. E. Sandys, *A History of Classical Scholarship* (repr. New York 1958) may be consulted.

The critical approaches represented in this book will be found to show a healthy diversity, but even so they seem to permit the drawing of a few tentative conclusions about contemporary tendencies. Predictably, biographical and historicist interpretations are here largely avoided – perhaps too much so, one may speculate, considering that these poets were very influential citizens in a tight-packed, politically and intellectually volatile, argumentative, precariously existing city. (Have the Hellenists now learned all too thoroughly the exciting lessons of a criticism developed primarily through analysis of the alienated modern artist?) The literary scholars even of fifty years ago, let alone of the nineteenth century or the Renaissance, would have raised their eyebrows somewhat at this austere concentration on purely literary and aesthetic phenomena. They would have been still more bewildered, however, by a critical trend which appears in the majority of the essays included here: the preoccupation with *diction*, with verbal themes and patterns, as essential clues to the interpretation of the dramas. It is precisely here, perhaps, that those earlier scholars could have learned most. This is a breakthrough. During the last two generations such methods have already to a great extent transformed our understanding of Aeschylus, and even now – even in this volume – are drastically modifying our understanding of the other two tragedians. There are some latent dangers, of course, in this approach, and it may be that the coming generation of scholars will have to devote itself to counteracting them. The worst is that in less skilled hands the study of Greek tragedy might become merely a matter of cold, static, verbal analysis (as it once did, from very different motives, in the hands of the Byzantines); and that people should forget that one partly subliminal poetic technique is not, after all, the *only* component in the playwright's art. Beyond – no, at the end of – all our critical paths stand dynamic happenings at once of baffling wholeness and of baffling complexity: the live Greek tragedies acted out on the stage.

Septem contra Thebas[1]

R. P. WINNINGTON-INGRAM

THE *Septem* carries the stamp of greatness: in the entrance-song of the chorus (for instance) and in the sombre rhetoric of the so-called *Redepaare*. Indeed, throughout we catch what Longinus called 'the resonance of a great mind'. It has, moreover, a feature which was not to be found in the *Persae* and will not be found in the *Supplices*: the dramatic issues are focused upon an arresting individual figure. Eteocles has been called 'the first Man of the European stage', and the play 'our earliest tragedy of character'.[2] Yet what *is* the character of Eteocles? The question has fascinated recent writers, but no agreement has been reached upon the answer.[3] This great play and this great dramatic figure continue to baffle us.

1. Much of the following article remains more or less as I drafted it in 1964 at the Institute for Advanced Study at Princeton, to which I owe such a debt of gratitude as will readily be understood by all who have had the privilege of membership. I have had the benefit of comments on various drafts from a number of friends.

2. H. D. F. Kitto, *Greek Tragedy*[3], p. 54. 'The first clearly studied individual character in dramatic literature' (Gilbert Murray, in the preface to his translation). 'Der erste "tragische" Mensch der Weltdichtung': O. Regenbogen, *Hermes* 68 (1933), 69, who deliberately avoids the word 'Charakter'.

3. A number of more specialized articles are cited with full details in subsequent footnotes. The following publications (all since 1958) are cited by name of author only or (in some cases) by name and date: H. H. Bacon, 'The shield of Eteocles', *Arion* 3.3 (1964), 27–38; Anne Burnett, 'Curse and dream in Aeschylus' *Septem*', *GRBS* 14 (1973), 343–68; R. S. Caldwell, 'The misogyny of Eteocles', *Arethusa* 6 (1973), 197–231; H. D. Cameron, 'The debt to Earth in the *Seven against Thebes*', *TAPA* 95 (1964), 1–8; '"Epigoni" and the law of inheritance in Aeschylus' *Septem*', *GRBS* 9 (1968), 247–57; 'The power of words in the *Seven against Thebes*', *TAPA* 101 (1970), 95–118; *Studies on the Seven against Thebes of Aeschylus* (The Hague 1971); R. D. Dawe, 'Inconsistency of plot and character in Aeschylus', *PCPS* 189 (1963), 21–62, esp. 31–42; C. M. Dawson, *The Seven against Thebes by Aeschylus*, transl. with comm. (Englewood Cliffs, New Jersey 1970); K. von Fritz, 'Die Gestalt des Eteokles in Aeschylus' Sieben gegen Theben', *Antike und moderne Tragödie* (1962), 193–226; L. Golden, 'The character of Eteocles and the meaning of the *Septem*', *CPh* 59 (1964), 78–89; *In praise of Prometheus* (1966), 42–61; A. Hecht and

There are difficulties. The *Persae* is complete as a single play; the *Oresteia* is a complete trilogy. The remaining extant plays of Aeschylus are truncated works of art which cannot be fully understood in isolation from their lost companions. The *Septem* was the last play of a trilogy; it was preceded by the *Laius* and the *Oedipus*, and of these plays we know little. As though this were not obstacle enough, there is grave suspicion – amounting in the view of many to virtual certainty – that the ending of the play, as we find it in the manuscripts, is not genuine. It seems that, for some later revival, an interpolator has modified the archaic simplicity of the action by adding a theme from the *Antigone* of Sophocles. But, even if we decide to excise the suspect passages, we cannot be quite sure how much of the original ending survived the interpolator's activities. Our approach to the interpretation of this play must therefore be modest, and discussion is bound to be interrogative and discursive. We can afford to neglect no evidence, no suggestion, but must beware of imposing patterns of interpretation. Without the earlier plays, the problem may well be insoluble.

Laius had been warned by the oracle of Apollo that he should die without offspring, if he was to keep his city safe. He disobeyed, and Oedipus was born, to kill his father and wed his mother. Having discovered the truth, Oedipus blinded himself; and then he cursed his sons. They quarrelled. Polynices, in exile, brought a foreign army against his native city. Thebes is besieged and about to be assaulted. Eteocles leads the defenders. It is with the last phase only of this well-known legend that the *Septem* deals, and its action is of extreme simplicity. The play opens, unlike the *Persae* and the *Supplices*, with a spoken prologue. Eteocles addresses the citizens: it is a general's speech before battle. He is joined by a spy, who tells him that the attack is imminent and that seven Argive

H. H. Bacon, *Seven against Thebes*, transl. (London and New York 1973); G. M. Kirkwood, 'Eteocles *oiakostrophos*', *Phoenix* 23 (1969), 9–25; A. Lesky, 'Eteokles in den Sieben gegen Theben', *WS* 74 (1961), 5–17; G. R. Manton, 'The second stasimon of the *Seven against Thebes*', *BICS* 8 (1961), 77–84; Brooks Otis, 'The unity of the *Seven against Thebes*', *GRBS* 3 (1960), 153–74; H. Patzer, 'Die dramatische Handlung des *Sieben gegen Theben*', *HSCP* 63 (1958), 97–119; A. J. Podlecki, 'The character of Eteocles in Aeschylus' *Septem*', *TAPA* 95 (1964), 283–99; T. G. Rosenmeyer, '*Seven against Thebes*: the tragedy of war', *Arion* 1.1 (1962), 48–78; E. Wolff, 'Die Entscheidung des Eteokles in den *Sieben gegen Theben*', *HSCP* 63 (1958), 89–95.

champions will lead their forces against the seven gates of Thebes. Eteocles prays, and the prologue is over. The chorus enters, not sedately marching, but dancing and singing to the excited dochmiac metre. They are the virgins of Thebes, panic-stricken by the sounds of the enemy; and they have come to throw themselves upon the altars of the city's gods in passionate prayer. Eteocles rebukes them for indiscipline (in a scene which we shall have to consider with some care). At the end, saying that he will himself fight at one of the seven gates, he leaves the stage. After a choral ode, the Spy and Eteocles return in haste. The Spy has discovered the order of battle of the invaders: that is, he now knows which Argive champion will assault which gate. Each warrior is described – his bearing, his words, the blazon upon his shield; and against each Eteocles announces the dispatch of an appropriate defender. Six attackers and six defending champions. But at the seventh gate is Polynices. This is the dramatic climax of the play. Eteocles recognizes the working of his father's curse and prepares to fight his brother in single combat. The chorus pleads with him, unavailingly, and he leaves the stage in full armour. They then sing of the Erinys which is accomplishing the curse of Oedipus; they sing of the disobedience of Laius and so place the present crisis in relation to the disastrous history of the house. During their song the battle is decided. A messenger brings the news that the city is saved, but the two brothers have slain one another. Their bodies are brought on, and the play (the genuine play) ends with a lyric lamentation, or *threnos*.

The summary is flat – deliberately flat, to avoid taking issue on matters of controversy. Except that the spuriousness of the closing scene has been assumed. And on this something must be said, though it can be said briefly here. The manuscripts contain, first (861–74), an entry of Antigone and Ismene to lead the lamentations over their brothers and then, later (1005–78), the entry of a herald, who, speaking on behalf of the community, forbids the burial of Polynices. Antigone plays her familiar Sophoclean role and defies the edict, supported by half the chorus, and two separate funeral processions move off. (What fate awaits Antigone we can only surmise.) Here are two separate questions. The first is whether Aeschylus introduced the sisters at all, and it is of minor importance: some critics who reject the Herald accept Antigone and

Ismene. Since this has little effect upon the general interpretation of the play, no words need be wasted on it. It is different with the Herald-scene. The real argument against the genuineness of this scene is not linguistic or stylistic (though such objections have been raised), but dramatic. It has seemed to many in the last degree improbable that at the very end of a trilogy Aeschylus would raise a new issue – and fail to carry it to a proper conclusion. And, since there was motive and opportunity for interpolation, it has seemed preferable to believe that the trilogy was not murdered by its own creator. As it stands in the manuscripts, the close of the trilogy is ragged. The *Oresteia* leaves no loose ends; and such evidence as we have suggests that the Danaid and Promethean trilogies also solved their problems in a rounded conclusion. It is of course an assumption, founded on a subjective judgment, that Aeschylus in 467 was writing trilogies upon the same principles of art and thought as in 458, but it is the assumption one prefers to make.[4]

This view also assumes that, if the interpolated passages are removed, we are left with a conclusion which is artistically satisfactory, consistent with what we know or can reasonably conjecture about the trilogy as a whole. For the content of the lost

4. H. Lloyd-Jones, 'The end of the *Seven against Thebes*', *CQ* 9 (1959), 80–115, sought to demonstrate, not that the suspected passages are undoubtedly genuine, but that the objective evidence adduced against them falls short of establishing that they are spurious. The weight of recent opionion is against their authenticity: cf. esp. E. Fraenkel, 'Zum Schluss der "Sieben gegen Theben"', *MH* 21 (1964), 58–64; R. D. Dawe, 'The end of *Seven against Thebes*', *CQ* 17 (1967), 16–28; P. Nicolaus, *Die Frage nach der Echtheit der Schlusszene von Aischylos' Sieben gegen Theben* (Diss. Tübingen 1967). 'Recent writers agree that the essential question is whether a new theme is likely to have been introduced at the end of a trilogy' (Cameron (1968), p. 249). For me the answer is clearly 'no', certainly not in this way. 'Was folgt aus dem so unerbitterlich formulierten Verbot? Nichts folgt, ganz und gar nichts; nichts geschieht, nichts wird oder kann geschehen' (Fraenkel, 'Zum Schluss...'). As to the sisters, whom W. Pötscher, 'Zum Schluss der Sieben gegen Theben', *Eranos* 46 (1958), 140–54, tried to rescue, I would only say that, if Aeschylus introduced them, he did not do so with the anapaests which stand in the text. It is simply incredible that the lines 854–60 – one of the finest and most moving sustained metaphors in the whole of Aeschylus – were separated from the *threnos* they were written to lead into by this poor stuff. If no sisters, 996f. should be deleted with Wilamowitz and Fraenkel. (Recently, Hecht and Bacon, pp. 7f., have maintained that 'the scene is integrated with the entire design of the play', but I am not convinced.)

plays our most important evidence is in the second *stasimon* (720–91) – the choral ode which intervenes between the departure of Eteocles for the battle and the news of its outcome.[5] In its explicit reference to past generations it is unlike any other feature of the surviving play; and its purpose is, obviously, to place the immediate action in a long perspective, to pull the threads together in preparation for the final act, which closes not this play only, but the trilogy as a whole. The ode is constructed with great care and with characteristic Aeschylean symmetry.

It opens with a word of fear; and fear was the key-note of the chorus' earlier songs – fear for the city and for their fate as citizens. What they now fear is the Erinys, the grim goddess that is like to accomplish the curse of Oedipus upon his sons (720–6). 'I shudder at the destroyer of a *house* (τὰν ὠλεσίοικον)'. At the end (790f.), after the terms of the curse (or something close to them) have been given, the ode concludes with the words: 'I tremble lest the swift Erinys bring it to accomplishment.' This is the familiar ring-composition. But, in addition, rather more than half-way through the ode (764f.) there is a third word of fear (followed immediately by a third reference to curses, a third word of accomplishment).[6] And the fear is different. 'I fear lest along with the princes the city be subdued.' What has intervened to cause this change in the object of fear is the story of Laius and his disobedience. His disobedience to Apollo, who thrice spoke in his Pythian shrine to say that it was by dying without progeny that Laius would keep his city safe (θνᾴσκοντα γέννας ἄτερ σῴζειν πόλιν). We can be sure that in these or similar terms the audience had heard the oracle before (perhaps in the prologue of the *Laius*). The terms were chosen with care, so that neither Apollo nor Aeschylus was committed to the final destruction of the city. Oracles are traditionally ambiguous. This oracle might mean that the city would certainly be destroyed, if Laius had offspring: it was not excluded, however, that, if the family that should never have come into

5. For a careful examination of the ode see Manton, who conducted a series of seminar discussions on the play at the University of London Institute of Classical Studies in May 1960: after this lapse of time it is hard to be sure what I owe to him and to other participants.

6. Curses, 725, 766, 787; fear: 720, 763, 790; accomplishment: 724, 766, 791. The theme of wealth also appears at the beginning, middle and end of the ode: see pp. 33f. below.

5

being perished, the city would be saved.[7] One thing is certain: since the birth of Oedipus, the city has been in jeopardy.[8] Thus, when the Messenger announces that the city has been saved (πόλις σέσωται), the words of the oracle (σῴζειν πόλιν) are clearly recalled.[9] But, if the city has been saved, the princes are dead and their ill-fated family has come to an end.[10] The fates of both city and family have been in the balance; and of this double issue there is a double outcome. There is, as the Messenger says, cause for rejoicing and for tears, and his words are picked up by the chorus (814ff., 825ff.).

The *polis*-theme which runs through the *Septem* – and must have run through the trilogy – is underlined by the metaphor of the ship of state, of the ship in storm (there is no better example of a recurrent metaphor in Aeschylus). It is used with economy, and thus the more effectively, at salient points: in the first words of Eteocles (1ff.); towards the end of the Spy's first speech (62ff.); in the choral ode which follows the departure of Eteocles (758ff.); in the first words of the Messenger (795f.).[11] It is specially associated with Eteocles. Eteocles is steersman of the ship of state; he is lord of the Cadmeians (Καδμείων ἄναξ) and so first addressed (39). But he is also 'son of Oedipus' and so addressed by the chorus (203). Thus the two issues are both focused upon him; his words and actions and decisions affect them both. In the earlier part of the play we see him primarily in his 'political' role. As king of Thebes,

7. Cf. Manton, p. 80. The oracle in this form was no doubt the invention of Aeschylus. What was the question, and in what circumstances was it put? Better than the commonplace enquiry of childless couples, it would suit a consultation on the safety of the city (cf. Herodotus 6. 19). In any case the answer, as Manton points out, is paradoxical, 'since normally a king would regard it as his duty to provide for the carrying on of his own guardianship of the state by begetting a son'.

8. And was certainly jeopardized on a previous occasion by the Sphinx: see pp. 29f. below.

9. The passage 803–21 has suffered dislocation, and scholars are not agreed upon a remedy: see most recently H. Erbse, 'Interpretationsprobleme in den Septem des Aischylos', *Hermes* 92 (1964), 19–22; C. W. Willink, 'A problem in Aeschylus' *Septem*', *CQ* 18 (1968), 4–10. Both 804 and 820 open with πόλις σέσωται, followed by a reference to the fate of the royal brothers. If not both, then at least one or the other is genuine.

10. Line 828 (ἀτέκνους); cf. 690f.

11. The same comparison is used by Eteocles at 208–10. Dawson, pp. 18f., reviews the passages, together with related metaphors of wind and wave. Cf. also Kirkwood, pp. 19–22.

he speaks as the situation requires (λέγειν τὰ καίρια, 1), and his generalship is wise. When he speaks and acts as son of Oedipus, will his words and deeds be as timely? It seems as though Aeschylus may have intended to invite this question. It is perhaps worth noticing a contrast brought out in the earlier part of the play. Note the words of the Spy at the end of his first speech (67f.): 'through my clear reports you will have knowledge of the state of the external foe (τὰ τῶν θύραθεν) and will come to no harm'. As defender of his city against this external enemy, we see Eteocles as vigilant (3), undeceived (38) and well-informed (40, 67), saying as well as doing what is seasonable. May it not be that in his role as the accursed son of Oedipus, caught off his guard, caught in a trap, summoned to deal with a foe internal to his house, internal to himself, he will display a different quality?[12] Perhaps it is no accident that the Spy, as he leaves the stage after announcing that Polynices is at the seventh gate, is made to recall the prologue by reverting to 'the ship of state' (651f.).[13]

His speech (631–52) is the great hinge upon which the structure of the play turns; and his final words round off the whole first portion of the play. The sharp, the shattering, contrast between what has gone before and what comes after is enhanced by the extraordinary way in which Aeschylus has handled the exposition of this play – with a boldness only an 'archaic' poet would have dared to employ. Though the occasion of the war is the quarrel between

12. Cf. Bacon, pp. 29f.: 'there is a danger "outside" which must not be let in, and a danger "inside" which must not be let out'; Caldwell, p. 205. Bacon points out that images of storm and animality are used of both the internal and the external enemy.

The expression τὰ τῶν θύραθεν recurs in 193, contrasted in the following line with ἔνδοθεν; since 194 is so true of Eteocles and his house, Aeschylus may have intended a double meaning. (If, with Headlam, reading ὀφέλλεται, we could translate 193 as 'things outside are going as much as possible in our favour', the point would emerge more clearly, but this is a doubtful sense for the verb.) The contrast recurs at 201f.: the women should leave 'external' affairs to the man, their place is within the house. But the house will be the source of danger, in relation to which Eteocles will need – and will reject – their counsels.

13. It is commonly, and perhaps rightly, held that 619 is spurious. It may seem uncalled-for as a comment on the Delphic oracle. If it was 'dragged in', it was in order to remind the audience of line 1, before the seasonableness of Eteocles' speech is put to the final test. Dawson, *ad loc.*, defends the line, also with reference to 1, but on rather different grounds.

Eteocles and Polynices, and though the climax of the action is to be their single-combat, no word is spoken of the quarrel, nor is Polynices named or his presence in the invading army mentioned, until the play has run more than half its course (576ff.). Though the quarrel and the duel are the working-out of the curse of Oedipus, that curse is only mentioned once in the earlier portion of the play, when Eteocles (69ff.), praying the gods to save the city, joins to Zeus and Earth and the city's gods the name of the Erinys that is his father's Curse. Then the theme drops out until (655) Eteocles recognizes in the conjunction of himself and his brother at the seventh gate the fulfilment of that curse. From then on, it is never out of mind.[14] This arrangement makes for a sheer dramatic effect of great power, for a moment of 'astonishment' (ἔκπληξις) such as Aeschylus loved; and this might be explanation enough. But it has made critics ask in what the unity of the play resides, if it has unity; and what is the relationship between the Eteocles of the first part and the Eteocles of the second part, if they are related. It may be worth while to list some of the views which have been held upon these questions.

Aeschylus has taken from different versions of the myth two themes which are not really consistent and has combined them mechanically to fill out the action of his play (Wilamowitz). He has made Eteocles play different roles as each scene demanded, being interested in the dramatic effect of individual scenes rather than in the consistency of the whole (Howald). There is no inconsistency, no change in the bearing of Eteocles, who is from first to last the unselfish patriot, and who accepts the pollution of a brother's blood as the last and greatest gift he can make his country (Pohlenz). The complete change in Eteocles from the calm patriot of the first half to a man lusting after his brother's blood is the best possible evidence of the power of the Erinys now suddenly working upon him (Solmsen). There are these views and variations upon them.[15] Closely related to this controversy is

14. Lines 655, 695, 700, 709, 720ff., 766, 785ff., 819, 833, 841, 887, 977; cf. 987.
15. U. von Wilamowitz: e.g. *Aischylos Interpretationen* (Berlin 1914), pp. 66f.; *Griechische Verskunst* (Berlin 1921), p. 199. E. Howald, *Die griechische Tragödie* (Munich 1930), p. 73. M. Pohlenz, *Die griechische Tragödie*² (Göttingen 1954), pp. 91ff., 145. F. Solmsen, 'The Erinys in Aischylos' *Septem*', *TAPA* 68 (1937), 197–211 – an article which initiated a generation of debate. Add the view of Golden, for whom Eteocles is from first to last a self-seeking politician with no real belief in the Erinys.

another. To what extent should we regard Eteocles as a free agent? Is the decision that he shall fight his brother at the seventh gate his own or imposed upon him by the gods? Or do his own desires go along with the decrees of destiny? Are we right to speak of a *decision*? What did he decide and when did he decide it? Perhaps it will be best to take this last question first. It involves, for one thing, the effect and significance of the most striking single feature of the play.

Aeschylus liked to build an imposing feature in the middle of his plays (or rather later): the Darius-scene in the *Persae*, the Cassandra-scene in the *Agamemnon*, the great *kommos* in the *Choephori*. So here, in the centre of the play, 300 lines – nearly a third of the whole – are taken up with seven pairs of speeches (with brief lyrics between each pair): the Spy describes one by one the seven Argive champions at the seven gates and Eteocles names a Theban to oppose each one of them. (It is convenient to refer to this scene by the German term *Redepaare*.) The scene is unrealistic (and provoked a jibe from Euripides),[16] but the day is doubtless past when it had to be defended from the charge of being undramatic. The drama resides primarily in the fact that Eteocles does not know, though the audience and the reader foresee, that he will meet his brother at the seventh gate; and, as each Theban champion is posted to meet an adversary who is not Polynices, the more certain it becomes that the brothers will meet, so that we see Eteocles, as it were, being forced down a narrowing tunnel towards his doom. If, as Kitto suggested,[17] there are always good reasons why Eteocles should not post himself at one of the first six gates (and particularly if the sixth chance, because of the virtues of Amphiaraus, proves to be no chance at all), there is a strong effect of dramatic irony. The idea is attractive, but has met

16. *Phoen.* 751f.: cf. *Arethusa* 2 (1969), 139, n. 18.

17. *Greek tragedy*[3], pp. 50f. Kitto is excellent on the general effect of this scene, but goes too far when he speaks of Eteocles as 'a man of acute moral perceptions', who appoints against each attacker 'the man best fitted by his moral character to meet that particular assailant'. Neither the attackers nor the defenders are quite so clearly differentiated as that. A special importance seems to attach to Tydeus (and Kitto may be right that the first person singular in 397 suggests, for a moment, that Eteocles will go against him), and to the virtuous Amphiaraus against whom he cannot go; and it may not be accidental that these, together with the seventh gate, are the three cases in which a future tense is used (see n. 19). (Delete 472, with Fraenkel and Page.)

a powerful challenge.[18] When did Eteocles make his choices? He states (at 282ff.) that he will post seven champions, himself included, to the seven gates 'before the swift and hasty-rumoured words of a messenger arrive and set all ablaze under pressure of need'. This is explicitly said, and (so the argument goes) it should be assumed, in default of evidence to the contrary, that it is carried out and that, therefore, when he meets the Spy, his postings have already been made; and, since the Argive order of battle has been determined by lot (55f., 376), it is the gods, not Eteocles, who have paired the two brothers at the seventh gate; and it is this divine appointment that he recognizes by his outburst at 653ff. This view also has its attraction, but encounters a difficulty. Having described the first of the Argive warriors, the Spy asks: 'Whom will you post against him?'; and in due course Eteocles replies: 'I will post against Tydeus the good son of Astacus.' τίν' ἀντιτάξεις τῷδε;, τόνδ' ἀντιτάξω (395, 408). That the Spy, who cannot know what has been happening, should use the future tense is natural enough. But surely, if Aeschylus wished it to be clear that the postings had already been made, the one thing he should not have done was to make Eteocles use the future tense of the very first posting. In fact different tenses are used in different instances: three futures, two perfects, an aorist and a present; and this has perplexed the commentators. More perhaps than it need have done. Taking the tenses at their face-value, a spectator will suppose that Eteocles has been interrupted at his work, that some champions have been posted and some not. It could even be that, as Lesky suggests, he aimed deliberately to combine two impressions both vital to the effect of the scene – the sense of an inexorable destiny, the sense that something is developing before our eyes. And the second impression *is* vital. Indeed it is hard to see that there is any real advantage, dramatic or religious, in making the conjunction of Eteocles with Polynices arise automatically from decisions taken prior to this scene. The duel is in any case contrived by the Erinys. How much better that the spectator should feel that the Erinys has been working under his very eyes, through words and decisions of a character upon the stage![19]

18. By Wolff and Patzer in *HSCP* (1958).
19. My criticism of the Wolff–Patzer view follows much the same lines as A. Lesky in *WS* (1961) and *Die tragische Dichtung der Hellenen*³ (Göttingen 1972),

And perhaps it does not make all that difference whether Eteocles takes his decisions now or then, for when we come to the seventh gate, his position is the same and equally fatal. He is committed to fight, and now this is the only gate at which he can fight, and it is his brother's gate. On both hypotheses, he has the same alternative – to fight or go back on his word. And that is how the issue of freedom presents itself: is he free – and does he wish – to change his mind, to go back on his decision? He does not change his mind. And, if we ask why, we are not importing a modern speculation, for he gives his reason. He seems to give more than one reason. The whole scene, which begins with the speech of Eteocles at 653ff. and continues up to his final exit, needs – and will receive – close examination, but one dominant factor, one strand in a complex fabric, is his recognition that the curse of Oedipus is being fulfilled, that it is thus futile to struggle, because he and his house are dedicated to destruction by the gods. The Erinys, to which he prayed in the prologue, and of which the chorus will sing, is at her fatal work.

It is often said or implied that, except for the prayer of Eteocles, the curse and the Erinys which embodies it are absent altogether from the first portion of the play and, with that same exception, from the mind of Eteocles. And it is true that Aeschylus has excluded any other direct reference to the curse or the quarrel or even to the presence of Polynices with the invading army. But the explicit is not everything, least of all in Aeschylus. Here, as so

p. 95; see also von Fritz, pp. 200–5, and Kirkwood, pp. 12f., who criticizes Erbse's laboured attempt ('Interpretationsprobleme...', n. 9) to justify the use of future tenses referring to a posting which has already been made, on the grounds that the time referred to is the (future) time of Eteocles' *answer*. 'Ich will deine Mahnung mit folgender Disposition beantworten.' Surely it would have needed a very sharp-witted member of the audience to take the point. As to 285f., the lines are certainly preparation for the simultaneous entries of Eteocles and Spy at 369ff., being clearly recalled by the language of 371 and 373f. Surely, this cuts both ways. It could indicate that Eteocles has fore-stalled the situation envisaged, but it could equally mean that that situation has in fact arisen, interrupting Eteocles at his work. This was the view of Wilamowitz, Groeneboom and Italie; and (*pace* Kirkwood and others) I prefer to accept it, not believing Aeschylus used his tenses without precise intention. See n. 17 (futures used for the most significant choices) and n. 41 (a special point about Hippomedon and Hyperbius). For a recent defence of the Patzer-view, see Burnett, pp. 346f. (with notes 12 and 13).

often, we suffer from the loss of the preceding plays. It is, however, tolerably certain that the *Oedipus* contained the curse; and that the audience listened to the *Septem*, from the start, with the curse in their minds.[20] We then must read it so and remember, when the first speaker introduces himself as Eteocles, that this is a man who has been cursed by his father. Whatever the terms of the curse, and in whatever sense they were understood, for a man to lie beneath a father's curse was to the Greek a most terrible thing: it had the force of an Erinys and was recognized by Eteocles as 'great in power' (70; cf. 977). The mental state of such a man might well be abnormal and show itself in his words. Of course, Aeschylus often frustrates modern expectations, but, supposing that he wished to convey such a hint, he would be likely to do it early. It is thus worth considering the words of Eteocles, when first he gives his name. 'If we should fare well, god's is the credit; but, if...disaster should befall, the name of Eteocles – and of Eteocles alone – would be loudly sung throughout the city by the citizens, with muttering preludes and with groans' (4ff.).[21] Do the words express an attitude of mistrust, a sense of isolation, not only from other men but also from the gods, such as a man under a curse, the member of a doomed family, might feel? It is a hint, no more, but it prepares us for the equally strange tone of other references

20. Having the curse in mind, an audience might be alert to the double aspect in which Earth is presented in the prologue as in the whole play (see Cameron (1964), and Dawson, pp. 19–22). A kindly mother to be defended (16ff., cf. 415f.), she is also associated with death, drinking shed blood, and receiving the bodies of the dead. Hence the ironical fulfilment of the curse: the brothers, who have quarrelled over their share in earth as the giver of wealth, receive equal shares of earth in burial. Perhaps the idea of the world of the dead as 'all-hospitable' (860, cf. *Suppl.* 156f.) was so familiar that πανδοκοῦσα at 18 conveyed a double meaning (cf. Dawson, p. 21, n. 45).

21. The sentiment can be paralleled, with progressive secularity, from Thuc. 2. 64. 1–2 (cited by Dawson, p. 4, n. 10) and Dem. *de Corona* 212, discussed by E. Fraenkel in *MH* 18 (1961), 37, who suggests that Aeschylus may be using a familiar form of contemporary oratory. The phraseology of our passage is, however, remarkably suggestive. (i) There is the relationship of Eteocles to the *polis* (6, 9) – and his potential isolation from it. (ii) There is his relationship to the gods, brought out by the hymn-and-prelude metaphor. (There will be a hymn indeed, but directed *against* Eteocles – and Eteocles alone. It will have a prelude in groans and mutterings, prior to something worse.) The preceding plays might have thrown light on this theme. (iii) There may be a play on the name of Eteocles. On this – and on the drama as a whole – see J. T. Sheppard, *CQ* 7 (1913), 73–82, which is still valuable.

by Eteocles to the gods. But Eteocles, in his civic capacity, must pray to them. About the terms of his prayer there has been much debate.

And the debate turns on a particle. 'O Zeus and Earth and the city-gods, and the Erinys-Curse of my father that has great power, do not utterly uproot the city in total destruction by enemy-sack...' The word for city is followed by the particle γε, which can have limiting or restrictive force: 'the city at least'. And, if it has limiting force, it can hardly fail to suggest a distinction between the city which is to be saved and the house which is to be destroyed, and to the destruction of which the terms (πρυμνόθεν πανώλεθρον ἐκθαμνίσητε) are so appropriate.[22] It would be blindness to deny that this distinction is deliberately suggested by Aeschylus. The doubt is whether the distinction is in the mind of Eteocles or whether his words, by the familiar device of dramatic irony, convey more than he means. Much has been built on this particle. For, if Eteocles is in effect saying: 'Destroy me and my house, if you must, but spare the city', this prepares the way for an act of un-selfregarding sacrifice on his part at the climax of the play. Decision on this issue is precarious and bound to be subjective. In Aeschylus, the word is apt to be more important than the man (the word with a life of its own), which should make us lean towards an interpretation in terms of the theme (and the action) rather than in terms of psychology. But the principle must not be pressed too far. If there is other evidence for the mental state of Eteocles in this earlier phase of the play, we should perhaps say that, with these words, he vaguely forebodes the destruction of his house and of himself: to say that he offers himself as a willing sacrifice to save the city seems more than should be read into the words.[23]

We must now turn to the scene between Eteocles and the women of the chorus. Nowhere in the play have critical judgments been more sharply opposed. It seems to be a matter of temperament

22. As the text stands, Eteocles goes on to couple with πόλιν the expression δόμους ἐφεστίους, which, if it means anything, must mean houses where dwells a group united by common worship at the hearth. This is a prayer that, as regards houses, cannot be answered in respect to the house of Oedipus. R. D. Dawe, *The collation and investigation of manuscripts of Aeschylus* (Cambridge 1964), pp. 180f., has launched so powerful an attack on the genuineness of 73 that it may be unsafe to base interpretation upon it. Page, in his Oxford Text, deletes with Dawe, but the line is defended by Lloyd-Jones in *CR* 16 (1966), 20f.

23. Cf. Lesky, pp. 10f.

whether or not one finds an excess of violence in the abusive words with which Eteocles rebukes the frightened women. Clearly a commander is entitled to restrain those who, he fears, will spread panic among his troops; a religious – or superstitious – man might well fear words of ill-omen, even when they are addressed to the gods;[24] a Greek, in either case, is likely to base himself upon a general principle. Yet, this sweeping condemnation of the female sex! 'Neither in trouble nor in prosperity may I share my house with the female sex. When a woman is dominant, her confidence [her criminality?] is intolerable; when she has become afraid, she is an even worse evil to house and city.' The double reference to the *house* (188, 190) in this *political* context should perhaps be noted; and it is not surprising that a French critic leans towards a psychological interpretation and regards the violence of Eteocles as a reaction to his accursed state. 'C'est la maternité qu'Étéocle haït, car il ne l'a connue, dans sa famille, que souillée par l'inceste.'[25] The point is well taken – may indeed have been obvious to those who had seen the *Laius* and the *Oedipus*. One may agree that Eteocles was affected by the horror of the relationship between the sexes in his family, linked as it was to his accursed state. But did Aeschylus ever write a speech of twenty lines mainly for the purpose of characterizing a personage? Here too the words may be more important than the man. And perhaps we shall never seize the significance of the words without the help of the lost plays, in which, probably, a woman played a role. But to this we will return.[26]

In the scene which follows (203–44), the chorus plead against the threats of Eteocles their fears and the piety which leads them to place all their hopes in the gods. Their piety as such he cannot rebuke (236), but urges them to discipline: they should stay at home and keep quiet and leave the required religious observances to the men. On the realistic plane this is reasonable enough, but the tone of much that he says arouses question. Words such as 'pragmatism', 'cynicism' and 'insincerity' have been used by critics.[27] Or is it rather that disillusionment of a man who has

24. Cf. Cameron (1970), p. 99, but see n. 30 below.
25. G. Méautis, *Eschyle et la trilogie* (Paris 1936), pp. 108f. Cf. Patzer, p. 103, Podlecki, p. 284, and others.   26. See pp. 35f. below.
27. Dawe (*Collation*, p. 142) speaks of 'Eteocles's half-cynical, half-pessimistic religious attitude (cf. *vv*. 4ff., 217–18, 719)'. Cf. Golden, *passim*; Podlecki,

himself no hope in the gods which we found (rightly or wrongly) in the early lines of the play? The ephirrhematic scene is followed by *stichomythia*, which resumes and concentrates the earlier themes: the fears of the chorus; the abuse of women; the appeal for discipline. The chorus yield compliance (263). Their compliance comes suddenly rather than by a gradual process of persuasion;[28] and the terms they use may be more significant than the fact that they comply. 'I keep silence'; says the coryphaeus (263), 'along with others I will suffer what is fated'. But what is fated for the city? What is fated for Eteocles? It is of sinister import, when he says: 'I choose that word of yours instead of those' (264) and (by ring-composition) closes the main section of his speech by a return to their word: 'None the more shall you escape what is fated' (281). Immediately he announces his intention of fighting, the seventh with six others at the gates.[29]

When Aeschylus emphasizes a theme by the repetition of words, we should take note. The theme is silence. Four times, with the same word, Eteocles urges silence on the chorus (232, 250, 252, 262); and the *stichomythia* comes to its climax with: 'Be silent', 'I am silent'.[30] But can silence alter facts? The chorus *are* afraid, and with good reason (and they *do* hear the horses neighing, 245f.); and in fact, despite their promise, they do go on singing about fear,[31] though, on the realistic plane, it was the part of a prudent general to make them desist. It may, however, be suggested that

pp. 287ff. (who speaks of 'insincerity'); Dawson, p. 5 ('sardonic irony'), p. 7 ('a very pragmatic view of the gods'). At 236, his δαιμόνων... γένος has been seen as derogatory: this is doubtful, but his 256, after 255, approaches blasphemy.

28. Cf. *Eum.* 892ff.

29. The expression used does not necessarily imply that he will be seventh in order, i.e. at the seventh gate, though it was doubtless chosen to suggest it.

30. At 258 παλινστομεῖς is explained by a scholiast with δυσφημεῖς: see the notes of Tucker and Rose, who puts the point as follows – 'If you cannot speak properly, say nothing at all.' One is reminded of the familiar double sense of εὐφημεῖν, εὐφημία: well-omened speech or (to be on the safe side) silence. For the employment of this theme in the *Agamemnon*, see *CQ* 4 (1954), 23–30, esp. p. 28. Either kind of evasion is futile; and I suspect that this is the real significance of the passages examined by Cameron (1970).

31. In metre – and no doubt in music and dance – the first *stasimon* is calmer than the *parodos*. The *parodos*, while envisaging the sack of the city, was concentrated upon the immediate sounds and sights which threatened battle. The *stasimon* is devoted to a vivid evocation of the sack itself – the fate from which the champions of the *Redepaare* are to save the city and its inhabitants.

there is another kind of silence about another kind of fear. It has already been pointed out how remarkable it is that, in the earlier part of the play, except for one line, silence is preserved about the curse of Oedipus – unbroken silence about the presence of Polynices in the invading army. Yet these are facts which will determine the outcome of the action, and silence cannot alter them. The fact of the Erinys is a ground for fear; and Mme de Romilly has shown, in a brilliant book,[32] how intimate is the association in Aeschylus between the idea of an Erinys and the idea of fear – an association which is developed, with formal art, in the choral ode (720ff.) we have already studied. This association has not yet been made explicit in the play, but the audience of Aeschylus may have been ready to assume that a man who is the object of an Erinys is a man in fear. It may be suggested, then, that throughout the first part of the play Eteocles is in fear, which is not fear of battle or of death (for in human affairs he is courageous), but fear of the Erinys. This fear, except for one outburst, he conceals in silence, but the excessive character of his reaction to the fears of the chorus derives from his own – and different – fear. This fear is vague and intermittent; it does not prevent him from using words which imply his survival and victory in the struggle (271ff.) or enable him to see the sinister implications of the references to fate. But the words of Aeschylus cannot be silenced.

If it is indeed true that the Eteocles of the prologue and the first episode is shown, behind the façade of a resolute king and general, to be filled with a vague sense of doom, with fear of the Erinys, with despair in his relation to the divine world, we shall not see this aspect of him in the earlier part of the *Redepaare*. The outburst at 653ff. will be the more effective, the more completely Eteocles is calm and *sophron* in the preceding phase. It is now his function to do and to say what is timely (τὰ καίρια), to interpret the accounts of the Spy, to turn the arrogant words and symbols against the boasters and, with the right words, to send against each the right man.[33]

32. *La crainte et l'angoisse dans le théâtre d'Eschyle* (Paris 1958).
33. On this process of 'verbal magic' see Bacon, p. 32; Rosenmeyer, p. 68; Cameron (1970), pp. 97, 100ff.

On the broad dramatic effect of this scene something has already been said. A tension is generated which justifies the suspension of all obvious dramatic action during nearly one-third of the play. But Aeschylus had set himself a technical problem in giving ordered variety to an episode which, prior to the seventh gate, consisted merely of six pairs of speeches. The over-riding pattern is that of boasters on the one side, men of modest courage on the other. This pattern he was enabled to break by presenting the prophet Amphiaraus as a good man fatally involved with evil companions. He was still left with five boasters; and all the resources of his rhetoric, all his command of visual and auditory images, might – without his constructional skill – have left a monotonous impression. It is worth studying how he dealt with this problem, and more may emerge than mere technical skill.

First is Tydeus, and against him Melanippus. Tydeus lusts for battle, and abuses the prophet who will not let him fight. So is first introduced the sixth champion Amphiaraus; and in the Spy's sixth speech Amphiaraus answers Tydeus in kind – and then passes judgment on Polynices (his first mention in the play); looking backward and forward, the speech rounds off the first phase and introduces the second. Tydeus is blood-thirsty, a cruel and barbaric figure, arrogant (or unfortunate?) in his choice of blazon for his shield,[34] but he does not blaspheme against the gods. He is in a sense more human than those that follow, as he is closer to the story. (And, as will be seen, his description bears on Eteocles.) Between him and Amphiaraus stand the figures of Capaneus, Eteoclus, Hippomedon and Parthenopaeus. Capaneus is the very paradigm of blasphemers, notorious for his Zeus-inflicted punishment, which Eteocles foretells. Eteoclus is a minor figure under the shadow of Capaneus; he blasphemes, not against Zeus, but merely (on his shield) against Ares; and Eteocles can deal with him briefly. With Hippomedon Zeus returns, but in a skilful variation. As Capaneus was the human being who challenged the thunder of Zeus, so Typhon was his great super-human adversary. Hippomedon has Typhon upon his shield; and this is shown to be ill-omened for him, since, by a lucky chance, his opponent has Zeus upon his. Parthenopaeus – an enigmatic figure, by whose legend the imagination of Aeschylus had perhaps

34. Cf. Bacon, p. 32

been caught[35] – has the Sphinx for blazon, and with it we move back a step towards the present story and are ready for Amphiaraus and his comments upon Tydeus and Polynices. It seems, then, that these four figures move upon a different, a remoter, plane than Tydeus, Amphiaraus, Polynices – and Eteocles. Their defeat is certain, if the gods are just and moral (though their opponents may not escape death),[36] but it is Tydeus and Amphiaraus – the first and the last – who stand closest to the story.

The significance of Tydeus is clear: that, as he lusts after the blood of his enemies, so Eteocles will lust after the blood of his brother. This is so, if verbal reminiscences mean anything.[37] Against Tydeus was sent Melanippus, a man who worshipped the 'throne of Shame' and shrank from shameful deeds and from such deeds alone. So was Eteocles pre-occupied with his honour.[38] Blood-lust and honour are two of the themes which complicate the judgment of the scene to which we must now turn.

When Eteocles hears that his brother is at the seventh gate, threatening to kill him or drive him into exile, as he claims to have been driven, claiming, with no boastful words[39] but through the modest figure of Justice on his shield, that he has right on his side,

35. On the Parthenopaeus-speeches see the interesting discussion of Cameron (1970), pp. 104–6. At 532 Διός and δορός are ancient variants (for the evidence see Dawe, *Collation*, pp. 152–4, and Page's apparatus). βίᾳ with a dependent genitive elsewhere in Aeschylus has the sense of 'despite', and most modern editors favour Διός. It seems strange, however, in view of the care with which Aeschylus has patterned his blasphemers, that this supreme blasphemy should be thrown out so casually and then dropped, picked up by neither Eteocles nor the chorus. Looking at *Sept.* 47, one may suspect that the sense was complete at the end of 531, and the first word of 532 was illegible, both Διός and δορός being reasonably intelligent attempts to supply the missing word, which will have been an adverb or neuter adjective connoting terror or arrogance.

36. Some members of the audience would remember that Melanippus and Megareus – both *spartoi* (412, 474) and so a special class of Thebans with a special relationship to their native soil – died in their defence of Thebes (cf. C. Robert, *Oidipus* (Berlin 1915), pp. 131ff., 247).

37. 380: μαργῶν καὶ μάχης λελιμμένος; 392: μάχης ἐρῶν. Compare the phraseology of 686–8, 692.

38. See pp. 23ff. below. At 415f. we cannot be sure whether ὁμαίμων is a nominative adjective agreeing with Δίκη or a genitive plural (as maintained by K. Wilkens, *Hermes* 97 (1969), 117–21). In any case, the combination is bound to make us think not only of Polynices, who is attacking his native land on a claim of right, but of him and Eteocles, blood-kinsmen between whom an issue of right has risen.

39. Cf. Otis, p. 164; Dawson, p. 10.

what will Eteocles say and what will he do? The Spy, whose function was in relation to the external enemy and has been performed, now leaves the stage. And we are at the heart of the difficulty of interpreting the piece. What will Eteocles say? In a long speech (653–76) he will reject the claims of Polynices, identify himself as the proper adversary of his brother, and will send for his armour. When the coryphaeus pleads with him, he will answer in terms of his honour (677–85). When the full chorus takes up the plea with the power of song, he remains obdurate, speaking bitterly of his father's curse and the hostility of the gods (686–711). All this time, it seems, his panoply is being brought out by slaves and his arming for battle takes place before the eyes of the audience.[40] A fine visual effect of the kind that Aeschylus loved. As each piece of armour is put on, the more impossible that he should withdraw. In a final *stichomythia*, when he speaks as a hoplite (717), he is fully armed – armed as a soldier against the possibility of withdrawal. The coryphaeus shoots her last bolt. 'Will you reap the harvest of a brother's blood?' And Eteocles replies: 'When the gods give, evil cannot be escaped.' He leaves the stage; and the chorus goes on to sing of the Erinys. Every aspect and every theme in this densely-written sequence must be examined.

In his long speech (653–76), when he has spoken of his father's curse, the fulfilment of which he recognizes in this conjunction of his brother and himself, he turns to Polynices and his claims. What has Polynices to do, what has he ever in his life had to do, with Justice? If Justice associates with this criminal, she will be falsely so called (670f.). It is in this confidence (672) he announces that he will fight his brother. As in every other case an appropriate champion has been matched with an invader, so now he finds

40. Cf. H. J. Rose's commentary, pp. 217f.; W. Schadewaldt, 'Die Waffnung des Eteokles', *Eranion* (Festschrift H. Hommel), 105–16; Bacon, pp. 27ff. Opinions differ as to the points in the text at which the various pieces of armour are brought out, and this is something which can hardly be determined. If the shield of Eteocles is brought out, did it have a blazon which was visible to, and recognizable by, the audience? Bacon suggests that it bore an Erinys. Another possibility might be the figure of Dike, the iconography of which can be carried back farther than that of Erinyes. But would either – or any – blazon have been clearly recognizable in the theatre?

himself the proper adversary. 'I will stand with him, ruler with ruler, brother with brother, enemy with enemy.'[41]

The tone of his speech has been differently judged – particularly the tone in which he rejects the claims of Polynices. His words have a tense vehemence: but does he pronounce as a judge the verdict of impartial truth or speak as a personal enemy, in whom bitterness is welling up out of a long history of antagonism? If the answer depended merely upon subjective impression, critics would have to agree to differ. We must look for any relatively objective grounds that we can find. We need help; and the help that the *Oedipus* might have given us is not at our disposal. So some writers have turned to the reported words of Amphiaraus (580ff.), and not without reason. An impartial judge roundly condemns Polynices for bringing a foreign army against his native land; and it is as certain as such things can be that this condemnation is endorsed by Aeschylus. But it does not settle the question of the rights of Polynices or the mood of Eteocles when he rejects them. 'What right shall quench the mother's fount?' says the prophet in his oracular style (584).[42] That is to say, whatever rights Polynices might claim (and however well they might be founded), this did not justify him in ravaging his native land. But Eteocles' condemnation of his brother goes back, hyperbolically, to the very moment when he left his mother's womb: neither then nor as

41. The word is ἐχθρός, expressive of personal enmity and feud; the notion has already been introduced at 509. The aptness of the conjunction of Hippomedon and Hyperbius, ascribed to Hermes, consists not only in their respective blazons, but in a pre-existent personal enmity. Note that in this case at least it is clearly implied that Hyperbius had already been assigned his gate, not only by the tense of ἡρέθη, but because it would be futile to ascribe to Hermes what was Eteocles' own doing.

42. Lines 580–6 are of course an answer in advance to 639–48, where Polynices calls to witness the kinship gods of his father's land (cf. 582, 585f.) and claims that Dike will give him back his father's city. Lines 584–6 are taken by Hermann, Rose and Fraenkel as a paratactic comparison, but, whether this is correct or not, the first element has independent validity. The earth is itself a mother and fount of nourishment, which will be quenched when the invading army ravages the land. The behaviour of Polynices is thus the exact opposite of that of Melanippus, who, prompted by Dike, defends the earth his mother. One might perhaps say that 584 and 585f. look at the same situation, the first in terms of a mystical bond, the second in more realistic terms (σύμμαχος). But there is nothing to deny that Polynices may have a claim of right. In fact the phrasing of 584 rather implies that he has or may have.

a child nor as a youth nor as a young man did Justice deign to look on him.[43]

If Amphiaraus cannot help us, can the chorus? We must of course beware of assuming that, because they are a chorus, they are necessarily right – that they necessarily express a view which the poet intends us to accept. In this scene it may well be that their view of the gods is too simple, but it is surely likely that their view of the mind of Eteocles is correct. (Why should Aeschylus make them mislead the audience on such a point? Why should we presume to know better than they?) We must therefore pay close attention to what they say – and also to the form in which they say it.

The form of the scene between Eteocles and the chorus is epirrhematic, that is to say, it combines song and speech in alternation; the chorus sings short lyric stanzas, after each of which Eteocles speaks three lines. It has often been observed that, though slightly shorter (by a pair of stanzas), this scene has the same form as that which follows the first rebuke of Eteocles to the chorus. The similarity of form might have suggested that Aeschylus wished the two scenes to be considered together, even without the similarity – and contrast – of subject-matter. Each is a scene of persuasion, an appeal for the restraint of ungoverned emotion. In the first Eteocles rebukes the women of the chorus for their hysterical fears and tries to reduce them to calm; in the second the roles are reversed – it is Eteocles who is now seen by the chorus as filled with a mad lust for blood – and for the blood of his brother, from which they seek to restrain him.[44]

Their judgment is first given in the first words of the coryphaeus. 'Dearest of men, son of Oedipus, do not show yourself like in wrath' (or 'in temper') 'to him who has the worst of names.'

43. This hardly sounds to me an 'analytical and deliberate rejection' (Kirkwood) of his brother's claim, nor do I detect (with one critic) 'the undertone of regret and disappointment at a life of promise steered in the wrong path'! One would like to believe that Eteocles and Polynices were twins, that Polynices the younger twin had behaved like Jacob to Esau, but such a story would probably have left a trace!

44. The inconsistency in the role of the chorus, who turn from panic-stricken virgins into counsellors of moderation (even addressing the king as 'child', 686), is mitigated – if Aeschylus would have felt that mitigation was necessary – by the fact that in both situations they take the line of piety: in the earlier scene placing all their hopes in the gods, in the present scene seeking to dissuade Eteocles from an act of impiety (cf. 831).

This is probably the best way in which to take the Greek expression (τῷ κάκιστ' αὐδωμένῳ),[45] with a reference – one of several in the play – to the etymology of the name of Polynices: 'the man of much contention'. In any case, the coryphaeus is saying: 'do not show yourself like Polynices'. If this stood alone, it might justify us in interpreting the mood of the speech of Eteocles as one of hatred and contention. But it does not stand alone. The first two lyric stanzas of the chorus speak of a 'spear-mad infatuation filling the heart', of 'an evil lust', of 'a longing' (like the longing to eat raw flesh) which is driving him 'to accomplish a man-slaying which will bear a bitter fruit in unlawful blood'. The expressions are not only unequivocal in themselves, but reminiscent of the description of Tydeus, who was seen by the Spy 'raging madly and longing for battle'. The same blood-lust that showed itself in the cruel and barbaric Tydeus now shows itself in Eteocles, but the blood is that of a brother.

What then does Eteocles say to this? Does he deny his fierce lust for a brother's blood, his ὠμοδακὴς ἵμερος? No, he explains it (695-7):[46] he explains it in terms of the curse. Now we can look back to the first word which he spoke when the Spy withdrew: 'maddened by the gods' (θεομανές), spoken of the family of Oedipus, that is to say, of himself and of his brother. Much later in the play, after they are dead, the chorus will sing of their 'mad strife' (ἔριδι μαινομένᾳ, 935); and that will be a word they have already used of the heart of Oedipus when he blinded himself and cursed his sons (μαινομένᾳ κραδίᾳ, 781).

The family is 'maddened by the gods' and 'greatly hated by the gods'; and in the following scene Eteocles comes back again and again to his conviction that the gods have decreed the destruction

45. Elsewhere in Aeschylus αὐδᾶσθαι is middle: *Eum.* 380, *P.V.* 766 and (ἐξαυδᾶσθαι) *Cho.* 151, 272; but we find the passive sense 'to be called' in Sophocles: *Trach.* 1106, *Phil.* 240, 430. Corrupt and difficult as 576-8 are (cf. Cameron (1970), p. 106, n. 35), Amphiaraus is clearly playing on the name of Polynices, as does Eteocles at 658. It is not unlikely that the etymology of 'Eteocles' is in mind at 683-5 (see p. 28 below) and possibly at 5ff. (see n. 21); and that, at 830, καὶ πολυνεικεῖς was preceded by a similar reference. Hecht and Bacon, pp. 14f., suggest a double etymology, from *kleos* but also from *klaio*.

46. Lesky, p. 14, rightly called attention to the vital significance of that γάρ (695); and before him Regenbogen in *Hermes* (1933) (see n. 2 above).

of his race.[47] He regards the position as hopeless, delay as futile (704). He speaks of the gods in general (702), of Phoebus that hates the whole race of Laius (691), and of his father's curse, which he knows to be an Erinys (70, cf. 700). (It is such a convergence of upper and nether powers driving a man to an impious act as we shall meet again in the *Choephori*.) It is fair to say – and was said with great emphasis by Solmsen in his influential article – that the mind of Eteocles is now, in some sense, dominated by the Erinys. This does not, however, exclude the attribution to him of other mental states – or one had better say, the description of his mental state in other terms. It does not exclude, but entails, hatred of his brother. It is in terms of the curse that he explains this hatred; it is through this hatred that the curse fulfils itself. If curse and hatred are two strands in the fabric, they are much of a colour. But there is a third strand – and perhaps a fourth.

The third strand is that of shame and honour, glory and disgrace. When the coryphaeus begs him (677–82) not to be contentious like his brother and refers to the pollution of fratricide,[48]

47. Eteocles knows from the beginning that he is under a curse which is likely to be fulfilled and could mean the destruction of the family. When he learns that his brother is at the seventh gate, it is a moment of revelation in which vagueness is turned into clarity (cf. Lesky, pp. 10f.). Though at 672, as at 271–8, he speaks as if he might survive, he really knows that he and his brother will die. Cf. Dawe, p. 41, n. 1. Burnett, pp. 356ff., has recently put forward an interesting suggestion. There were two sources of information about the future, the Curse and the dream (see n. 60 below). The Curse was bitter, speaking of an iron-bearing hand; the dream, of a foreign mediator, was less discouraging. Eteocles has now come to realize (710f.) that the dream was no less sinister than the curse. In the following *stasimon*, as in the concluding *threnos*, the terms of the Curse and the imagery of the dream are fully integrated. This hypothesis, developed in great detail by Burnett, would clarify a number of obscurities, though it can hardly be established with certainty in the absence of the preceding play.
The attitude of the chorus, until they sing their *stasimon*, is not so clear – or so important. Line 681 need not imply both deaths (see Cameron (1970), p. 111 on αὐτοκτόνος), though it is so worded as to suggest them; 718 implies the death of Polynices only.

48. There is a difficulty about the reference to *miasma* (and about the precise meaning of καθάρσιον at 680 and καθαρμούς at 738, which has been much, and inconclusively, debated). The earlier plays may or may not have thrown light on this. The killing of Laius by his son must have caused such a pollution, and in Sophocles it leads to the plague and so to the revelation of Oedipus' identity. Whether this theme was used by Aeschylus is quite uncertain. Perhaps we should assume that *miasma*, so far as it affected the city, was extinguished by the death of Oedipus; and that the *miasma* of fratricide was extinguished by the

Eteocles replies, not – or so it would appear – in terms of hatred, not in terms of the curse, but on the grounds of honour (683–5). 'If a man is to suffer evil (κακόν), let it be without shame (αἰσχύνης ἄτερ).[49] For that is all that profits among the dead. But no good repute (εὐκλείαν) is won from things which are both evil and shameful (κακῶν τε κἀσχρῶν).' The text of 685 is in doubt, but not the general sense of the passage or the word *eukleia*. And in the use of this word Eteocles (or Aeschylus) may well be playing on his name 'the man of true glory' as the coryphaeus had played upon the name of his brother 'the man of much contention'. When he speaks of evil – objective evil (κακόν) – he may mean pollution or death, but, when he speaks of good repute as 'gain among the dead', he clearly envisages that he may die. When he speaks of shame and glory, it is generally supposed that he is thinking of his honour as a soldier and a ruler; and we may recall – may be meant to recall – the words with which he dispatched Melanippus against Tydeus (407ff.).

A third strand has been identified – and perhaps a fourth: but what is the pattern? What is the relationship between curse and blood-lust on the one hand, honour and patriotism on the other? Or has Aeschylus just laid the two double-strands side by side in an attempt – a crude early attempt – to suggest a mixture of motives within the same personality? This could be so, and much of the controversy which the decision – and the character – of Eteocles have evoked could be attributed to the crudity of Aeschylus and the unwillingness of modern scholars to believe him crude. But it may be worth looking at the scene again – and at three lines in particular, three difficult lines which have not yet been taken into consideration.

deaths of both brothers (cf. Cameron (1970), pp. 109ff.). There is no hint of a persisting pollution in the closing scene: even if 843 is taken to imply that the city is still in danger, this is not linked with the notion of *miasma* (and in the 'spurious' portion ἄγος attaches only to Polynices, 1017f., and for a different reason). Aeschylus, while accepting notions of pollution and purification as part of traditional religious belief, may not himself have been happy within this range of ideas. L. Moulinier, *Le pur et l'impur dans la pensée des Grecs*, pp. 193–5, finds different standpoints in the *Oresteia*; and E. R. Dodds, *PCPS* 186 (1960), 23, argues convincingly that, in the *Eumenides*, the importance of the formal purification of Orestes is 'deliberately *minimized*'.

49. Or: 'If a man should suffer evil without shame, then let it be.' It is not easy to choose between the two punctuations.

The chorus has sung that an excessive cruel desire is driving
Eteocles towards fratricide. Instead of denying it, he identifies
the driving force with his father's curse which haunts him, and
whose words he quotes. In answer the chorus sings: 'Yet do not
you be driven.' The general connection of thought is thus clear,
but in the three lines spoken by Eteocles (695–7) there is uncertainty of text and interpretation.[50] It matters little that we
do not know what was the penultimate word of 695, what contribution it made to this astonishing personification. Nor does
it matter greatly how we take the following line. Whose eyes are
dry? Does the Curse haunt the dry eyes of Eteocles or haunt him
with dry eyes? It does not matter, because at this point the line of
distinction between the Curse and the mind of Eteocles is hard to
draw, because the Curse is working on him and in him. At least
it is certain that what the Curse says to Eteocles is also what
Eteocles is saying to himself. What then does the Curse say? (Even
this is disputed, but argument can be left to a footnote.)[51] The
Curse speaks of 'gain (profit, advantage) first; death (fated death)
afterward'. Either there is a gain which will be followed by death;
or there is a gain which ranks superior to death; the meanings are
not mutually exclusive, and both could be intended. The word
for 'gain' is *kerdos*; and it occurred thirteen lines previously, also
in a context of death. We might expect it to have the same meaning here. Since there it meant freedom from disgrace, a good

50. In Page's text the lines read as follows:

φίλου γὰρ ἐχθρά μοι πατρὸς †τελεῖ† ἀρά
ξηροῖς ἀκλαύτοις ὄμμασιν προσιζάνει
λέγουσα κέρδος πρότερον ὑστέρου μόρου.

In 695 Weil's μέλαιν' is excellent in itself, contributing visually to the personification, but, despite 832, there is no compelling reason to believe that Aeschylus
wrote it here. One is as reluctant to jettison the τελει (with varying accentuation)
of the manuscripts as one is incapable of accommodating it. In 696, the
eyes are perhaps more probably those of the Curse, in which case Butler's
ἄκλαυτος is attractive, if not requisite.

51. So good a commentator as Groeneboom took the words as meaning that
an earlier death is preferable to a later one, i.e. better die quickly and get it
over. But how can πρότερον be other than an epithet of κέρδος as ὑστέρου is
of μόρου? It is equally intolerable, with Verrall and Rose, to take πρότερον
of value and ὑστέρου of time. Pauw and others emend the text to read: κέρδος
πρότερον, ὕστερον μόρον – an easy correction, but, in view of the Greek
tendency towards correlative expressions, an unnecessary one. (Dawe is far too
scornful of the received text.)

reputation after death, and since here the chorus replies that Eteocles will *not* be called base (κακὸς οὐ κεκλήσῃ), if he complies,[52] it might indeed seem that the meanings are the same. But there is an objection, which is not so much that in this latter passage the gain is spoken of as prior to death (since the act which gains post-humous glory is, in time, prior to death). The objection is that the words are put into the mouth of the Curse and it is, at first sight, no proper function of the Curse to speak to Eteocles of his honour – of his honour as a soldier. The interest of the Curse is in the mutual fratricide, and its means of bringing it about is the mutual enmity of the brothers. The gain, therefore, that it would be proper for the Curse to hold before the eyes of Eteocles is the death of Polynices; and it is his fierce desire for that death he is seeking to explain. But, if we take *kerdos* of the death of Polynices, we seem to be opening up a breach between its meaning here and its meaning thirteen lines above. The conclusion seems as inevitable as it is unwelcome. On reflection, however, how large is the breach? And indeed does it exist? It all depends on what honour means to Eteocles – or rather on what meaning is, in this context, intended to be conveyed by such words as αἰσχύνη, αἰσχρός, εὔκλεια (which we translate by 'shame', 'shameful', 'good repute'). The answer to this question could have some importance for the interpretation of the play and of the trilogy.

Aeschylus was writing in the fifth century, in a city-state, for an audience of men who had fought the Persians. It has therefore been natural to assume that, when he speaks of shame and glory, using terms of praise and blame so characteristic of Greek morals, the terms were intended to bear the connotations which they had acquired within the city-state. But he was writing about the heroic world. In that world the hero prized his honour above everything – his honour and his prestige. And his prestige de-

---

52. One cannot feel happy about βίον εὖ κυρήσας, least of all with an interpretation which refers the phrase merely to the preservation of life. The scholia have: καλῶς πράξας, εὐτυχήσας, εὖ πράξας. Tucker could be on the right lines: 'The word [βίον] includes material prosperity, which will enable him to offer the (liberal) sacrifices next mentioned.' This suits the reply of Eteocles at 703, the meaning of which is established by 772ff. Oedipus was respected by the gods for his lavish sacrifices: the only gift (χάρις) that the gods will welcome from his sons is their death. Still, one cannot feel quite happy about the phrase.

pended upon his ability to maintain his status and privileges; to resent, retort and retaliate a slight; to humiliate and destroy his enemies. This was his virtue, his excellence, his *arete*. If he failed, his prestige was gone; he was despised and felt the shame it was the main object of his existence to avert. The only 'failure' countenanced by the code was an honourable death in battle. In due course this heroic ideal of *arete* was modified, by addition rather than by subtraction. Courage in battle had always been cardinal to it, but, as the city-states developed, the important context of courage became the defence of the community, not, as in the relatively anarchic world of heroes, defence of one's prestige, property, family and friends. But the old emotional attitudes died hard, if they died at all.[53] If justice became a virtue in the city-state, it could still be formulated in the late fifth century as 'doing good to your friends and harm to your enemies', though the application of this principle was limited by various factors and particularly by the existence of legal process under the aegis of the state.

There was an issue of justice between Polynices and Eteocles – an issue which could not be settled in any court. The 'rights and wrongs' of it we do not know, but each thought that he was in the right. Polynices claimed that he had been dishonoured – deprived of his τιμή – by the brother who had driven him into exile;[54] and he was determined to avenge this injury by death or by repaying him in kind. The image of Justice on his shield says (647f.): 'I will bring back this man, and he shall have the city of his fathers and the range of his house.' The city, like the house, is a patrimony; Polynices (like Orestes in the *Choephori*) is deprived both as son and as ruler (or so he claims). What he has lost (rightly or wrongly, for we do not know) Eteocles enjoys; and the return of Polynices is a menace to his enjoyment. Hence their enmity – the personal enmity conveyed by the word ἐχθρός; hence the appropriateness that (673ff.) ruler should fight against ruler, brother against brother, enemy against enemy.[55]

53. Cf. A. W. H. Adkins, *Merit and responsibility* (Oxford 1960), *passim*.

54. The text of 637 is quite uncertain, but must contain the idea that Eteocles had deprived Polynices of his τιμή by driving him out.

55. ἄρχοντί τ' ἄρχων (674). The fact that Adrastus and not Polynices was in command of the invading army is disregarded here, as it is at 816 and 828. It was the easier to do so that both brothers claimed the rule in Thebes.

When, therefore, Eteocles speaks at 683–5 of shame and honour, what has he in mind? What is it that would destroy his fair fame in the eyes of men and, should he die, deprive him of the only *kerdos* among the dead? Cowardice, of course. So he must go out against the foe, full of rage for battle like a Homeric hero; and it is no accident that, in the stanzas which the chorus sings at 686ff. and 692ff., some of the vocabulary – and much of the spirit – are Homeric.[56] But, by heroic standards, he would lose his honour, not only by cowardice, but also by not resenting a wrong, by not standing up for his rights, by not taking vengeance, by not inflicting upon his enemy the ultimate harm. Since his gaze is now fixed upon his personal quarrel, it is surely not unreasonable to suppose that this is what he has in mind by shame and good repute. (And that is the view of a scholiast, who, being a Greek if late in time, understood these things, and who wrote: ἒν κέρδος τὸ αὐτὸν ἐκδικῆσαι ἀδικούμενον). If that is so, there is no essential difference between the two 'gains', between honour after death (684) and the destruction of Polynices (697), since it is by the pursuit of effective vengeance that Eteocles will establish his good fame – and, one might add, will justify his name. Seen in the light of the present argument, the two names which seemed so far apart – the man of much contention, the man of true glory – come close together.

This line of interpretation simplifies the pattern of the scene we have been considering. It is not merely that hatred and honour converge towards the same result: they are motives so closely related as to be almost identical, both serving the Erinys that now dominates the mind of Eteocles. The pattern is simplified. Has it become too simple? It is perhaps time to insist again on the disadvantages from which we suffer in interpreting this play. We do not know the rights and wrongs of the quarrel: we do not even know how important it would have been to know them. In the Danaid trilogy the rights and wrongs of the quarrel between Danaus and Aegyptus seem to have been left, deliberately, vague.

---

56. Cf. μέμονας (686), ἀνδροκτασίαν (693) and – later (698) – ἐποτρύνου. On ὠμοδακής (692) Tucker cites *Il.* 4. 35; 24. 212, 347; he also refers to Soph fr. 799.5 P for the cannibalism of Tydeus. Did Aeschylus expect his audience to recollect this feature of the legend? See also p. 38 for a possible, but uncertain, act of 'cannibalism' on the part of Oedipus. Such points are not to be pressed.

It could have been so in the Theban trilogy, but this is not so probable, since there was a play which will have demanded a handling of the relationship between the brothers. It may be useful at this point to consider what we know or can without extravagance conjecture about the earlier plays.

Our fragments of the *Laius* and the *Oedipus* are inconsiderable. Our most valuable piece of evidence for the content of these plays is the choral ode in the *Septem* which relates the impending fratricide to the past history of the house (720ff.), but it has to be used with caution. It is easy to list the series of events.[57] The oracle; the disobedience; the birth of Oedipus and his exposure; the killing of Laius; the marriage of Oedipus to his mother (presumably following his victory over the Sphinx). Then a long interval of time. Oedipus discovers the truth, blinds himself, curses his sons. His sons quarrel; Polynices makes friends abroad and plots his return from exile. Oedipus and Jocasta (if she was called Jocasta) are dead before the *Septem*. There is altogether too much, and some of these events must have lain outside the economy of the two lost plays. One of our difficulties is that, while we know the *Oresteia* and can form a fair idea of the Danaid and Promethean trilogies, we do not know quite how Aeschylus may have constructed a trilogy in 467. The *Agamemnon* is much longer than either the *Choephori* or the *Eumenides*, but it would be rash to assume that either the *Laius* or the *Oedipus* had a length or an action out of scale with the brevity and simplicity of the *Septem*.

In any case, some unity of time is likely to have been preserved in both plays. If Laius was a character in the *Laius*, the action will have included his death, in which case the oracle and the birth of Oedipus lie well to the past. A scrap of papyrus has now made it highly probable that Laius spoke the prologue to this play. Prologue and *parodos* between them (the chorus being Theban elders) will have put the audience in possession of the facts, including the oracle and the disobedience. Perhaps Laius announced his intention of leaving – but why and whither? – and left, never to return. Later, a narrative of his death and the advent of Oedipus. (But in which order?) Oedipus can hardly have

57. It is just conceivable that the oracle was motivated by the Chrysippus episode, but there is no hint of this in the extant play.

arrived without vanquishing the Sphinx[58] and winning the hand of Jocasta. Did Jocasta play a part? Laius, Messenger, Jocasta and Oedipus would hardly be too large a cast; and the action would not be out of scale. In reading the second *stasimon* of the *Septem*, we are tempted to assume that 742–57 cover the action of the *Laius*, while 772–90 cover that of the *Oedipus*. But this is too facile. The second of these passages refers to the honours paid to Oedipus 'when he had removed the man-seizing *Ker* from the land'. A long interval of time must have elapsed between the first and the second play, long enough for sons to grow to manhood. Lines 772–7 could well give us the close of the *Laius*: a triumphant Oedipus celebrating his victory, his marriage and his kingship, with lavish sacrifices to the gods and feasts for the people. A saviour whose sons will bring a deadly threat.

It could have been so. The real difficulty is with the *Oedipus*. The *stasimon* (fifth strophe and antistrophe 778–90) gives us the revelation, the self-blinding and the curse. *Stasimon* or no, one feels that, without the curse in the preceding play, the development of the *Septem* would have been barely intelligible to an audience, however familiar with the myth. One may doubt too whether Aeschylus would have dared to withhold all reference to Polynices until 576, unless there had been something about the quarrel, some hint of his activities abroad. (Is the death of Oedipus tacitly assumed? And that of Jocasta?) Revelation, blinding, curse, death, quarrel. Almost too much for a short play; and certainly little room is left for the means of revelation, whatever those may have been. Teiresias – and Apollo? Or a recognition by tokens? A plague?[59] We shall not know, but the revelation may even have taken place before the play began. The characters? Oedipus for certain. Did Jocasta (again?) have a role? Both sons? And did Polynices have a role which balanced that of Eteocles in the *Septem*? Eteocles on Polynices (662ff.) sounds allusive: were the audience in a position to judge for themselves? Was the curse on stage: a big central feature?

These – and many more – questions can be asked and not

58. The fact that Aeschylus used the Sphinx story for his satyr-play might suggest that it was not given detailed treatment in the trilogy, but it must have come in (as it comes into the second *stasimon*, 776f.), doubtless in the form of a narration.

59. Fr. 691 M may or may not come from the *Oedipus*.

answered. It might seem hopeless to proceed farther. If we cannot settle the broad action of these plays, what can we know of their character and their themes? Except that in the Aeschylean trilogy (to judge by what evidence we have) themes tend to persist from play to play. The second *stasimon* seems intended to be a drawing together of threads. It gives us the oracle (the thrice-given oracle) and the involvement of the city with the progeny of Laius: the threat. The threat comes to fulfilment in the *Septem*. Not for the first time. The Sphinx had been a threat to the city and its population (775f.). Oedipus saved the city from this danger; perhaps it was the danger from the Sphinx that prompted the mission of Laius, so that the trilogy began with the city in danger and the first play ended with the city saved. Ironically, because Oedipus who saved Thebes from the Sphinx endangered it when he cursed his sons.

The city was endangered by the disobedience of Laius and by the curse of Oedipus; and, though both come into the *stasimon*, in neither case (because of difficulties of text and interpretation) can we be sure why the act was committed. But we know (roughly) what the curse was: that they should divide their inheritance sword in hand. With iron (σίδηρος). We can be fairly certain that this word was used, together with a reference to lots or shares. The chorus sing first of the iron sword under a riddling image (characteristic of archaic poetry); since iron came from the Black Sea region, it is a Chalybian foreigner that casts lots and distributes the shares equally between the sons, to each so much of the ancestral land as burial required. It is possible that this image was an echo from the *Oedipus*, and was first the image of a dream.[60] But this we cannot know for certain.

60. Only 787ff. purport to give the terms of the curse (cf. Manton, pp. 78f.). What then was the source of the riddling image at 727ff. (picked up at 941ff.)? Cameron (1970), p. 116, following Tucker, holds that the language of the curse itself 'must have said that the sons would have to submit the question of the division of their inheritance to a foreign arbiter from over the sea, born of fire, and who would give them exactly equal shares'. But this, which does not sound quite like a bitterly-worded curse, is difficult to reconcile with the fairly specific 787ff. Manton suggests that the source of the image was a dream; and Eteocles has just referred to dreams (710f.). Hermann saw that the dream or dreams *must* have been in the preceding play. If Eteocles had merely said 'the dreams were all too true', it might have stood on its own, but, when he describes their content as πατρῴων χρημάτων δατήριοι, it becomes intolerably obscure,

Nor do we know what version of the quarrel between the brothers was followed – or devised – by Aeschylus. It is certain that it was a quarrel over inheritance and over shares.[61] What should they have done? Perhaps they should have been joint rulers and held the wealth in common, in which case the 'monarchy' of Eteocles (883) should have been no monarchy at all.[62] Failing that, perhaps they should have shared out the wealth equally; and in the end, ironically, they get equal shares. Unless it was a question of dividing inheritance, why say that they shall divide it *with iron*? It should have been done by the casting of lots (as Zeus, Poseidon and Hades cast lots for theirs, and in the image lots are cast by the Chalybian foreigner. Or by an arbitrator, himself casting lots, if the parties could not agree; and it is in this capacity that the sword (or Ares) is seen to act. Who, then, was to blame? Eteocles or Polynices or both? By no word does the chorus support one claim against the other; and in the closing *threnos* the two brothers are treated upon an equality. This might be easier to understand, if Eteocles had been at fault in driving his brother into exile, just as Polynices was at fault in seeking redress the way he did.[63]

unless the dreams had been reported in the *Oedipus*. Who dreamt the dream or dreams? Eteocles, according to the scholiast, but this could be a guess, if a good one. Conceivably Jocasta. See Manton and, most recently, the full discussion by Burnett (cf. n. 47 above). There seems little doubt that the dream-figure was seen casting lots; and Burnett relates this to frequent occurrences of the lot-theme earlier in the play. H. Engelmann, 'Der Schiedsrichter aus der Fremde', *RhM* 110 (1967), 97–102, provides an interesting review of the evidence for foreign arbitrators.

61. Cameron (1968) argues that the issue was between two contrasted systems of inheritance, by primogeniture and by division of the property – and that this issue had a topical relevance. This seems a great deal to extract from 902f. (where Cameron finds a clue to the sense of ἐπιγόνοις in Plato's *Laws*, i.e. younger sons who do not inherit). If this was a prime issue, it is rather extraordinary that there is no hint of it in the *Redepaare*, 631–76.

62. Joint rule, as envisaged at Eur. *Phoen.* 69f. (cf. the joint rule of the Atridae at Argos, much stressed in the *parodos* of the *Agam.*, e.g. 43f., 109f.). In which case, at the outset of our play (6), the emphasis on Eteocles as sole ruler might be calling attention to a situation which ought not to have existed. Cf. also 674, 816, 828, and esp. 882f. (rival claims to 'monarchy'). Cf. Golden (1964), p. 83.

63. On 923ff. (ἐρξάτην πολλὰ μὲν πολίταις, ξένων τε πάντων στίχας πολυφθόρους ἐν δαΐ) Page justly observes 'phrasis perobscura'. However, the dual verb and the notion of much harm done to citizens and foreigners seem authentic. 'What follows is collectively, not individually true' (Rose). The

However this may be, one thing is clear. Power and wealth were too tempting; and the emphasis is upon wealth. Wealth and the rich land from which it was derived. 'They have their share allotted of the god-given apportionments.[64] Under their bodies there shall be earth's unplumbed wealth' (947ff.). They will lie in their graves 'without share in the great plains' (733). The treatment of this theme in the second *stasimon* may be particularly instructive. The reference to the great wealth-giving lands is led up to by the double stress of κτεάνων χρηματοδαίτας (and the quantitative ὁπόσαν: so much and no more). In the last stanza, returning to the curse and rounding off this theme, the word κτήματα stands alone. But in the middle of the ode comes another emphatic reference to wealth. The chorus has been singing of the successive waves of trouble – and the towering wave that now threatens the city also, so that they fear it may perish with the princes. From this they pass to a general reflection on the dangers of wealth. 'Destruction passes by the poor,[65] but, when the prosperity (wealth) of gain-getting man has waxed too great, it brings a jettisoning from the stern' (769ff.). Then comes the particular application. 'For (γάρ) what man was so admired by the gods who share the city's hearth and by the great throng of mortals[66] as then they honoured Oedipus when he had banished the man-seizing Monster from the land?' By banishing the Sphinx Oedipus had gained the wealth of Thebes. Sacrifice and feast. For what should the gods admire a man except for the lavish scale of his offerings?[67] But wealth is dangerous, when it grows too great.

Wealth at the beginning, middle and end of this ode. Dangerous wealth. We might guess that the wealth which went with the royal

dual suggests, however, that both limbs of the statement were true of both, which would be the case, if they were jointly responsible for the war. Cf. Podlecki, p. 299.

64. Reading λάξεων (E. Fraenkel).

65. There is great uncertainty about the text, and πενομένους is merely a plausible suggestion.

66. Weil's ἀγών (αἰών codd.) is virtually certain and πολύβατος highly probable (see Page's apparatus). The text of 773 is doubtful.

67. It could be of course that the gods admired him for his cleverness (as the gods at Plato, *Symp.* 180a, admired Achilles for his devotion to Patroclus – the word is ὑπεραγασθέντες). Taking 772 and 703 together, it seems more likely that in both cases there is a context of sacrifice, hinted at perhaps by ξυνέστιοι.

power of Thebes had been a leading theme of the trilogy; and it might be a good guess. There caution would stop, with the observation that it was the lure of wealth that ruined the sons of Oedipus. But the generalization about wealth stands between the lyric handling of two crucial episodes. The disobedience of Laius; the cursing of his sons by Oedipus. Why did the one disobey, the other curse? Thanks to obscurities and corruptions in the text (and to our ignorance of the earlier plays), we do not know.

Or rather, as to the disobedience, we are told that Laius 'overmastered by ill counsels begat his own death, Oedipus the fatherslayer, who endured to sow the pure field of his mother where he grew and raise a bloody stem; it was madness that brought together man and wife, their wits destroyed' (750–7). Which man and wife? The point is controversial. If the language (παράνοια... φρενωλής) seems too strong for those who, like Jocasta and Oedipus, came together in ignorance, it is fair to say that, on the other hypothesis, 'the plural form of νυμφίους applied to Laius and Jocasta would suggest that both were responsible' (Manton).[68] But it was Laius who consulted and disobeyed the oracle. Add that Jocasta's role in the preceding sentence is to be impregnated by Oedipus, and the argument seems little short of decisive. It is virtually decisive, unless there is reason to attribute responsibility to Jocasta.

In the translation given above, one Greek word has been omitted: the first line runs κρατηθεὶς ἐκ φίλων ἀβουλιᾶν. All attempts to take φίλων as an epithet (perhaps in the form φιλᾶν) founder in one way or another.[69] If it is a dependent genitive, then Laius was over-persuaded by the bad advice of 'friends', which at first sight gives a poor meaning. But a scholiast suggests

68. Manton, p. 81, lists a number of considerations which he holds to favour a reference to Oedipus and Jocasta. This is the most weighty. Cf. *BICS* 13 (1966), 92, n. 12. In that article I have examined in greater detail *Septem* 187–90 and 750–7 and the bearing the two passages may have upon one another and I refer the reader to it. The same evidence is discussed by Caldwell, whose Freudian interpretation of 'the misogyny of Eteocles' I do not feel competent to criticize.

69. Cf. *BICS* 13 (1966), 90f. The popular view that φίλων/φιλᾶν here is used in the supposedly Homeric sense of 'own' is quite unacceptable, in the light of A. W. H. Adkins, *CQ* 13 (1963), pp. 30ff., esp. 32f. (With ἀβουλίᾳ or ἀβουλίαις, which are possible readings, φίλων is clearly a noun.)

that the reference is to his wife (ἢ ἀντὶ τῆς γυναικός).[70] The stanza immediately gains coherence. If Jocasta shared the guilt, then, as Laius was punished by death at the hands of his son, so she suffered the incestuous marriage. The interior of the stanza deals with the double punishment, the role of Oedipus within it being subordinate to that of his parents; the madness at the end balances (on the principle of ring-composition) the ill counsels at the beginning. Certainly the case for taking the closing sentence of Laius and Jocasta is much strengthened.

But, apart from these phrases of doubtful interpretation, what reason have we to suppose that Jocasta played such a role? Let us return to Eteocles rebuking the chorus (181ff.). We have already noted with surprise the sweeping abuse of the female sex and – most surprising of all – a generalization (a *gnome*), half of which seems quite inappropriate to the context.[71] Which is one of fear. Why, then, is Eteocles made to say to the frightened virgins of Thebes that woman, when she holds the upper hand (κρατοῦσα), is an intolerable *thrasos*, a word which connotes arrogance or criminal boldness? One answer might be that, early in the story, a woman had over-persuaded her husband to a criminal act. Had given him bad counsel. 'Let not a woman give counsel (βουλευέτω): that is the man's affair' (200). 'Laius, overmastered (κρατηθεὶς) by the ill counsels (ἀβουλιᾶν) of his near ones...' (750). We know from other evidence that Aeschylus was much interested in the relationship between the sexes; we know that he chose to depict Clytemnestra as a women of 'manly-counsel' and to display the appalling consequences of her desire for mastery.[72] Did he, then,

70. The suggestion is by no means obvious, and one would like to believe it was made by someone who knew the lost plays. There is, however, no clear evidence of such knowledge elsewhere in the scholia. On 710 it is implied that Eteocles was the dreamer, but this could be a guess.

71. It is closely examined by H. Friis Johansen, *General reflection in tragic rhesis* (Copenhagen 1959), pp. 106ff. It belongs to a type which he classifies as foil-antithesis, in which the generalization consists of two contrasted elements, one of which (generally the former) has no relevance – or no immediate relevance – to the situation illustrated. He compares other Aeschylean examples, but if anything emerges from the comparison it is the exceptional lack of relevance in this case and the choice of κρατοῦσα for emphasis (cf. *BICS* 13 (1966), 88f.). Tucker writes: 'κρατοῦσα is at first sight a peculiar antithesis to δείσασα, but the real opposition of the latter is with θράσος'. Yes, but why put it that way?

72. Cf. *JHS* 68 (1948), 130–47, where I seek to bring out the importance in this connection of words for mastery (κρατεῖν, κράτος) and counsel (e.g.

depict Jocasta as a proud and masterful woman playing a harmful role? No wonder in that case that Eteocles was determined to keep women in their place! Clearly, no certainty could be claimed for this suggestion, though it does help to explain a troublesome feature. Suppose it were true, one is led to ask: if Jocasta over-persuaded Laius to beget a son in defiance of the oracle, what was her motive? It could have been the natural desire of a woman for children, playing on the natural desire of a man (and a king) for heirs. Or she too may have had dynastic thoughts.[73] If the theme of wealth was, as one would like to think, carried back to the beginnings of the story, perhaps it was tolerable to neither king nor queen that the royal wealth of Thebes should go out of the family for want of an heir.

The two fatal moments – fatal decisions – crystallized in the second *stasimon* are the disobedience and (after the blinding) the curse. There is a distinct possibility that the first was linked to the theme of wealth. What was the motive of the curse? In the study of Aeschylus we have to steel ourselves against the obstructions of a corrupt text, but it is really too bad that the text should

ἀνδρόβουλος). Johansen, *Tragic rhesis*, p. 106, n. 17, shows how elaborately the notion of 'counsel' is developed in *Sept.* 182–202, with echoes of political terminology. I would add two further points of a speculative character. (i) What is at issue between Eteocles and the chorus is a question of discipline and obedience. When he speaks in praise of πειθαρχία (224), an audience might well remember Laius' failure to obey – and might be encouraged to do so by the way in which he is made to express himself, in terms of a family of abstractions. It is possible that, in this riddle, the combination μήτηρ γυνή was intended to suggest Jocasta who was mother and wife to the same man. Both her husbands should have been saviours but endangered the city. The mother–wife encouraged the disobedience of a husband and brought to birth the opposite of εὐπραξία. It is conceivable that when Sophocles (*OT* 928) used the same combination to ironical effect he recollected this passage in the *Septem*. (ii) At 196–9 Eteocles threatens any that disobeys: ἀνὴρ γυνή τε χὥ τι τῶν μεταίχμιον (197). The critics are puzzled: what an odd way of putting it! 'The phrase has no specific connotations; he is just too angry to speak with complete coherence' (Dawson, whose explanation is that commonly offered). Eteocles may have been out of control: but was Aeschylus? What does lie between a man and a woman? An effeminate man, but one can hardly suppose a reference to the Laius–Chrysippus story. Or a masculine woman, cf. γυναικὸς ἀνδρόβουλον κέαρ. This is immediately followed by 200 on the male prerogative of counsel. Jocasta as a pilot-model for Clytemnestra!

73. When, at Soph. *OT* 1078f., Oedipus accuses Jocasta of family pride, it is conceivable that he was attributing to her, wrongly, a motive which she truly had in Aeschylus.

have been corrupted at just this point (783–7).[74] Oedipus launched bitter-worded curses upon his children, because he was angry (reading ἐπίκοτος). Angry at what? There is, apparently, a dependent genitive, which in the manuscripts is τροφᾶς, meaning 'rearing' or 'nurture', together with an epithet (though this is less certain) ἀραίας, meaning 'accursed' or (in some way) concerned with a curse. If τροφᾶς is right – and in this play we should be most reluctant to alter it – does it refer to the nurture, the tendance, of Oedipus or to the rearing of his sons? According to some critics,[75] Oedipus cursed Eteocles and Polynices for their mere existence; and a case can be made for this interpretation. In the maddening pain of his discovery, he blinded himself so that he might not see them (another corrupt text) and cursed them so that they might perish. They were reared under a curse, and he cursed them. But the objections too are weighty. 'Wrathful' does not seem the right word (yet ἐπίκοτος echoes περιθύμους in the first stanza) for a curse uttered in sheer disgust. And why, specifically, this curse? If he cursed his sons for their mere existence, one could understand his imprecating upon them an early death: but why that they should divide the property with the sword? It sounds like a punishment to fit a crime. Suffering in Aeschylus is not always deserved, but there is perhaps a difference between suffering because you belong to an accursed family and being cursed by your father for belonging to it. Erinyes are agents of punishment and associated with wrath; and one of the special fields in which they operate is where a parent has been offended. Is there any known case in which the Erinyes of a parent are not called to pursue an offence? There is offence in the epic tradition.

There are two offences, both attributed to the lost cyclic epic *Thebais*.[76] According to one account, Oedipus cursed his sons because, at the feast which followed a sacrifice, they served him with the haunch and not the shoulder (which was the more

74. Not only is the reference to the blinding (783f.) manifestly corrupt, with a tantalizing possibility that it also referred to children, but emendation of some kind is needed either in 778 or in 785, since they fail to correspond metrically. The whole problem is hideously complicated, and I confine myself to the main features only.

75. Schütz, Hermann, Weil and, most recently, H. C. Baldry, 'The dramatization of the Theban legend', *Greece & Rome* 25 (1956), 31, n. 1.

76. Athen. 465e; Schol. Laur. in Soph. *OC* 1375 (frs. II and III Allen).

honourable portion); according to the other, he cursed them because Polynices set before him the silver table and the golden cup of Cadmus which he had forbidden to be used. Aeschylus will have known both versions, but need have used neither. The cup-story has at least this advantage that it is linked to the theme of the fatal wealth of the family: if it was pride of wealth that caused the sons to bring out luxurious articles from the family treasure (τιμήεντα γέρα), this might have revealed that state of mind which brought about their quarrel. But to make the text fit, we must emend it, hazardously.[77] The scholiast to whom we owe the haunch-and-shoulder story refers specifically to the *Septem* (not to the *Oedipus*). He thought the reaction of Oedipus mean and petty, and so may we (though of course we do not know how he was presented in the trilogy). Aeschylus could well have had his own variation on the theme of sacrifice and feast, but in this realm of uncertainties one must be content to review the evidence, with one final comment. Which is that, if the sons were culpable – or thought culpable by their father – Eteocles was presumably no less so than his brother. (To a school of critics for whom Eteocles can do no wrong this is intolerable.)[78]

Once again we come back to the point that in interpreting the *Septem* we are hampered, disastrously, by our ignorance of the earlier plays. Not only of their action, but of the tone and of the roles. We have our idea of Oedipus from Sophocles: the Aeschylean Oedipus, if we knew him, might surprise us. But in what way? Fragments out of context should not be relied upon too much, but there is a testimony which could imply that he tasted and spat out the blood of his victim;[79] we do not have the story of the killing of Laius or its motivation. It is not unlikely that Jocasta had a role, and there is at least one good reason for supposing it was deleterious, but we do not know. Nor do we know whether Polynices and Eteocles – either or both – were presented and

77. We need not only Wilamowitz's ἀρχαίας (printed by Page), which admits more than one interpretation, but also Robert's τρυφᾶς, to which the objection is not so much that the root τρυφ- is not known to be Aeschylean as that, in this play, a word of 'nurture' should not be touched without the most compelling reasons. Cf. Cameron (1964), pp. 2ff.

78. Cf. G. Müller, *Hermes* 94 (1966), 264ff.

79. Fr. 173 Mette.

prominent in the *Oedipus*, though it seems likely. We suffer from blank ignorance on some points tempered by greater or lesser probabilities on others. Yet too many critics courageously assume that we can understand the *Septem* – and Eteocles – without that knowledge of the background at which the play hints again and again, but which is withheld from us by the malignity of fate.

We get at least an impression that the story of this noble family, with its fame of wealth, was a grim one – grim perhaps by reason of the deliberate, as well as the unwitting, acts of its members. Aeschylus is, traditionally, regarded as a writer of tragedies in which impiety and *hubris* are punished, in which, whatever super-human forces may operate, divine and human motivations run in parallel and the individual agent does not escape responsibility for his own decisions. With such a picture would consist a guilty Oedipus. And a guilty Eteocles? For Eteocles also is a member of the family.

We can form more than one picture of Eteocles, as we select – and interpret – the evidence. Sharing with his brother responsibility for the wrong, whatever it may have been, that was done to their father; equally responsible for their disastrous quarrel – conceivably more responsible, if he drove his brother into exile; at the moment of crisis consumed with a passionate hatred indistinguishable from his brother's; preoccupied, like him, with status and power and possessions and the values they dictated to the heroic world; sharing with him an impious disregard of the bond of kinship, so that in the end, justly, they share the narrow territory of their graves. Compatible with the words of Eteocles in the hour of decision (as they have been interpreted above), compatible with the final undifferentiating verdict of the chorus, this picture has a seductive self-sufficiency and a recognizable affinity to Aeschylean tragic thought. One would like to be content with it. But has something been left out? Is there a strand whose place in the pattern has not been identified?

There is another Eteocles, familiar to modern scholarship, about whom little has yet been said. The iron hero, the unselfish patriot, the man of the *Opfertod*. The notion of a sacrificial death, though it has left a legacy in the invincible reluctance of some recent critics to admit any disparagement of Eteocles, has now (in its pure form) been largely abandoned, on the grounds that Aeschylus has given no indication in the text that the fratricidal duel was, as such (and immediately), necessary to the preservation of Thebes. But does not every soldier who dies for his country sacrifice his life? And did not Eteocles, when he went out to fight his brother, go out as a patriot in defence of his city?[80]

At this point we must return, briefly, to the seventh gate and to the Spy, who opens his report (631–8) with the sinister prayers of Polynices. They are complex and revealing.[81] First comes the city (632). No more than Eteocles, it seems, does Polynices envisage a duel as part of the assault. He prays (with a word of cursing) that he may mount the city's defences and raise the paean of capture, and then that he may deal with his brother. Infinitives after participles, this comes as a climax. Either his brother will fight him in single combat to the death (and, extravagantly, he says he is willing to die if only he can first kill) or, if Eteocles prefers to live, he shall be driven into a dishonourable exile.[82] These are the threats – the threat to the city, the threat to Eteocles. To which will the latter respond? We wait to see. And when he perceives his father's curse at work, cries ὤμοι and is close to tears, and then checks his tears 'lest there be begotten a more intolerable lamentation' (657), we wonder if he is thinking of the deaths which will attend the fall of the city.[83] And when, in answer to the

80. Cf. e.g. B. Snell, *Aischylos und das Handeln im Drama*, Philologus Supplb. 20 (Leipzig 1928), p. 83, who, drawing a sharp distinction between the Homeric and Aeschylean views of honour, says that for Eteocles it is not his own fate that stands in the foreground, but that of the city.

81. Von Fritz saw the importance of these lines, and his discussion (pp. 206ff.), including an interesting comparison with Eur. *Phoen.*, is most valuable. I cannot, however, stay with him when he goes on to advance a modified version of the *Opfertod*, which seems to rest on assumptions which Aeschylus could have made clear if he had wished, e.g. that, if Eteocles had survived the duel, he could hardly have lived on, still less continued to rule.

82. I omit reference to the second half of 634, where text and meaning remain extremely dubious. At 636, when Polynices says κτανὼν θανεῖν πέλας, it is an extravagant way of expressing, not a wish, but a readiness to die (parallels in Tucker's note): it is chosen for obvious reasons.

83. The sense of the line must be intentionally elusive, for Aeschylus is clear when he wants to be. γόος *can* be used of sufferings other than death (cf. *PV* 33), and so Eteocles might be thinking of the pain of disgrace, but, since it is most commonly used of lamenting the dead, he might be thinking of his fellow-countrymen. Which is it? In any case, the γόος which actually ensues (and τεκνωθῇ is a carefully chosen word) is that lamentation for the πανδάκρυτον Οἰδίπου γένος which we find in the *exodos* (cf. 853, 917, 967).

coryphaeus, he speaks of disgrace and honour (683–5), we wonder if he is thinking of his honour as a soldier, his duty as a citizen. We wait for a word of the *polis*, and it does not come.[84] Why, if the poet intended us to see the decision of Eteocles in terms of patriotism, has he made things so difficult for us? It would have been so easy – and so clear – if Eteocles had been made to say, like the Sophoclean Oedipus (*OT* 443), ἀλλ' εἰ πόλιν τήνδ' ἐξέσωσ' οὔ μοι μέλει; or if he had taken up the theme of his earlier prayer (71f.) and said that, come what may to him and his house, he will strive to preserve the city at least from destruction. He says nothing of the kind. (Wilamowitz saw this, but drew the wrong conclusion.)[85] Instead, as to tears, we learn that his eyes – or those of the Curse which now inspires him – are dry with a hot longing for his brother's blood; as to honour, that the *kerdos* that it offers and demands is the death of Polynices. This is his answer to the challenge.

Still one ransacks the scene for anything that may bear upon the city.[86] At 717 Eteocles, now in full armour, uses the word *hoplites*. How one would like to know whether the audience, when they watched the arming of Eteocles, remembered their Homer or their hoplites, the Trojan or the Persian War! Did they think of the armed citizens of the contemporary world who marched out to defend their city-states? Without the *Redepaare*, such a suggestion might be dismissed as a fantasy. Yet six such defenders were dispatched, with suitable eulogies; and Eteocles is the seventh. His own references to shame and honour can, as we have seen, be related to his personal quarrel and to the curse. But an

84. Without attaching undue significance to such statistics, I note that, in a play in which πόλις, πολίτης, and other words of the same root, occur on the average once in every 15 or 16 lines, this (648–748) is the longest stretch without such a word. To play fair, one should observe that Eteocles does refer at 668 to his father's land (πατρῷα χθών), mishandled by Polynices.

85. *Aischylos Interpretationen*, p. 67.

86. Dawe, on the same evidence, still argues for an *Opfertod*. 'We continue to get the impression that the death of Eteokles saved Thebes from destruction.' But one must distinguish effect and motive. It is one thing to say (rightly) that the death of the accursed brothers saved the city, another to say that Eteocles died to save the city. The formulation of the prayer at 71f. need not foreshadow an *Opfertod*, but rather (as Dawe himself writes) 'by inserting the particle [γε in 71], Aeschylus implants in the minds of the audience the idea that [the fate of Eteocles and that of the city] are *not* the same, but that one is conditional upon the other'. See p. 13 above and Podlecki, pp. 296ff.

ambiguity remains, since similar terms were used of Melanippus, when Eteocles sent him out to defend his native soil. Does it make *no* difference that, while Polynices attacks their native land, Eteocles defends it? And is this too a strand in the fabric? And is there not perhaps one question we have not yet asked?

Eteocles has two roles, two functions, a two-fold address: he is 'lord of the Kadmeians' and 'son of Oedipus', in virtue of which he is the common focus of a two-fold issue, the destinies of the city and the family, dangerously intertwined. In everything he says or does, he is one or the other. There is a view of the play that sees him as two men, the one suddenly transformed into the other by the arbitrary intervention of a sinister divine force. This is altogether too simple and below the level of Aeschylus. It is too simple because the circumstances in which he found himself lord of the Kadmeians are bound up with his sonship to Oedipus, his emotions and motives as lord are bound up with his brotherhood to Polynices; it is un-Aeschylean because the gods of Aeschylus work through human motive and emotion. Nevertheless, we may yet find a further dimension in the tragedy of Eteocles, if, asking ourselves a question which should be asked of any Aeschylean personage: 'In what situation did he find himself?', we answer that he found himself between two worlds.[87]

Insofar as we can discern a basic pattern in the play – and in the trilogy – it is the entanglement and disentanglement of house and city. At the end, the city which has been in danger since the disobedience of Laius is saved, but the house perishes. Some critics, oddly enough, have found this outcome disconcerting and not what they would have expected in an Aeschylean trilogy; and it has even been greeted as an advance in the thought and theology

87. Cf. V. L. Ehrenberg, *From Solon to Socrates*, p. 207 (with n. 39): 'The individual suffers the tragedy of standing between the demands of family ties and those of the polis, between past and future.' J.-P. Vernant, 'Tensions and ambiguities in Greek tragedy', *Interpretation: theory and practice*, ed. C. S. Singleton (Baltimore 1969), p. 111, writes:

'As the head of Thebes, Eteocles represents these values and attitudes [those of the city] as long as the name of his brother is not pronounced before him. For he has only to hear the name of Polynices to revert from the sphere of the *polis* to another universe: he finds himself once again the legendary Labdacid, the man of the noble *gene*, the great royal families of the past, on whom weigh ancestral defilements and curses.'

of Aeschylus that, in the *Oresteia*, means were found – by him, by the gods, by the myth? – to save a doomed family from utter destruction! Suppose, however, that it was an essential point of the Theban trilogy that the family should be destroyed?[88]

Neither Aeschylus, when he wrote his plays, nor his audience, when it came to the theatre, laid aside all awareness of their contemporary world. The *Persae* was contemporary history, but treated like myth; the *Oresteia* was myth, but had without doubt a relevance to contemporary history, and not least to the troubled political drama which had seen the assassination of Ephialtes.[89] If Aeschylus dramatized the salvation of a city which had been endangered by a *genos*, he could have had in mind a political process which had been carried towards completion in his own lifetime. It had been a result, if not a purpose, of the constitutional reforms of Cleisthenes to disembarrass the political life of the city-state from the dangerous influence of the *gene*, the clans, with their loyalties and rivalries and feuds. The clans were an archaic element in the body-politic, deeply rooted in an earlier world and in its standards of value, inimical to the order of the *polis* and menacing its security.[90] The Theban legend may have offered to Aeschylus the opportunity of dramatizing this process of disentanglement. On the one hand, the *genos*, an archaic relic – a family of dynasts preoccupied with their wealth and privileges – endangering the state. On the other hand, the *polis* that must be saved by the selfless devotion of its citizens, who find their highest excellence in its defence and their greatest shame if they fail to defend it. These are the two worlds between which Eteocles finds himself – the old world and the new. He dies as member of a doomed and disastrous family, despairing of his race, filled with mad hatred, seeing his honour in the ruthless prosecution of a feud. But he also goes out, the seventh, to fight for that city which in the extremity of his hatred he has forgotten, and saves it by a crime.

For, if Eteocles is allowed some footing in a new and more

88. Cf. G. Thomson, *Aeschylus and Athens*[3] (London 1966), pp. 315f.

89. The precise relevance is of course debated. Cf. K. J. Dover, *JHS* 77 (1957), 230ff.; E. R. Dodds, *PCPS* 186 (1960), 19–31; A. J. Podlecki, *The political background of Aeschylean tragedy* (Ann Arbor 1966), pp. 63–100 (on which see *Gnomon* 39 (1967), 641–6).

90. Cf. B. W. M. Knox, *The heroic temper* (Berkeley 1964), pp. 77f.

civilized world, mainly he lives and dies in the old one. Lives and offends and dies. Offends against the religious basis of the family, in a family quarrel. The rights and wrongs of it are never settled; and the theme of justice drops right out of the play as soon as the princes are dead.[91] One might indeed ask whether there is any case in Aeschylus in which an issue of human justice is settled on human terms. It is not claims that matter but conduct, and particularly conduct in relation to the gods.[92] What shocks the chorus, in their piety, is that Eteocles no less than Polynices should disregard the sanctity of kindred blood. When they hear the news, they condemn both brothers impartially with a single phrase. 'They perished with impious mind' (ὤλοντ' ἀσεβεῖ διανοίᾳ, 831). But there was another paramount field of religious obligation – to the wider kinship group, which is how the Greeks conceived the city-state. Whatever his claims of right, Polynices condemns himself, when he attacks his native land. Melanippus and Megareus paid with their lives the debt they owed to the land which nourished them. Perhaps there is one field at least in which Eteocles cannot be deprived of all moral advantage.

This seems at least a possible pattern of interpretation, reconciling some seeming contradictions in the evidence and in the emotional responses which one can, tentatively, assume in an audience of Greeks. There were the city and the family, both in danger. Zeus and the city-gods have saved the city (822ff.); the prayer of Eteocles (69), the prayers of the chorus in the *Redepaare*, have been answered. Thanks must be given, but not yet. The expressions of joy at the salvation of the city are almost perfunctory, before the chorus turns to lamentations for the two brothers upon whom their father's curse has been fulfilled. They address the black accomplishing Curse that Oedipus laid upon his sons (832ff.). The father's prayer has done its work without fail (840f.); no less have the disobedient counsels of Laius had their effect (842). It was an Erinys that ratified the words of Oedipus (885f.); it was Apollo, the Messenger had said (800ff.), who took to himself the seventh gate and 'ratified' upon the family of Oedipus the ill-

91. And one can hardly believe that it was reintroduced, and so oddly, at 1070ff.

92. Cf. D. Kaufmann-Bühler, *Begriff und Funktion der Dike in den Tragödien des Aischylos* (Bonn 1955), *passim*.

counsels of Laius of old. There is a multiplicity of gods in the *Septem*. There is Zeus, and the *polissouchoi theoi* particularized in the frantic prayers of the *parodos*. There is Apollo, with his special concern to punish the disobedience of Laius. There is the Erinys, 'a goddess unlike the gods', a dark power of the underworld to whom the sons of Oedipus are given over. It is the gods who give (719), and the gods by whom Eteocles sees his race as maddened, hated and abandoned (653, 702). It was the simple faith of the chorus that, if the gods received their sacrifices, the black-aegised Erinys would leave the house (699ff.), but the doomed Eteocles had the deeper insight, when he saw that one great sacrifice alone would win the respect of the gods, which was the destruction of his race (703). There are Olympians and Chthonians; divine powers of different and contrasted orders, they are seen in the last analysis – and this is Aeschylean[93] – to converge towards the same end. Eteocles prayed to the Curse–Erinys, along with Zeus and the city-gods, to save the city; and his prayer was answered, paradoxically, by his own impious act, which destroyed the family and liberated the city from its contagion.

This could be true. If we possessed the entire trilogy, we might or might not see it clearly to be true. As things are, a critic can only hope that he has clarified rather than confused the issues.

93. Cf. *JHS* 74 (1954), 22.

The dissembling-speech of Ajax[1]

JOHN MOORE

THIS speech of Ajax (646–92) has been a controversial issue for a little more than a hundred years. As a controversial issue the speech has proved very satisfactory: first because of its crucial importance to the play; and then because so far it has never failed upon re-examination to reveal new intricacies and ambushes. At first the critics naively supposed that only one question existed, namely, whether Ajax spoke with intention to deceive; but a discussion of that point disclosed very soon that other difficulties were present, and indeed the critics have divided sharply over at least one point without apparently realizing that any difference of opinion exists. In order to make the issues as explicit as possible, I shall summarize the leading interpretations.

The speech itself is loaded with verbal ambiguity. In the preceding scene Ajax had made it clear that he intended to kill himself; when Tecmessa begged him to pity her in the name of the gods, he answered brutally and blasphemously, that he was their debtor no longer. Now he comes forth and says quietly, that – even the most steadfast things are overcome...he who was stern before, now feels pity for his wife and child. He will go down to the seashore, wash away his stains, and escape the wrath of the goddess. He will hide his sword, most hateful of weapons, digging in the ground, where no one shall find it. – All this is very two-edged: his hearers understand him to mean that he has changed his mind, taken pity on them, and intends only to seek ritual purification; but his words are equally susceptible of the more sinister interpretation, that he still means to kill himself. He will hide his sword – in his own body: he will yield to the gods and to

1. This paper was left unfinished by the late John A. Moore of Amherst College, who died in 1972. The editors have had to piece together the latter parts (which contain most of what is of interest) from unnumbered hand-written scraps.

47

the Atreidae, as he promises, but only in death. This promise to yield is expressed with grandeur through a series of images from nature, pointing to 'how even dread and intractable things', night, frosts, and tempests, yield in their turn to what comes after them. He gives a few final directions, and starts on his way with the words, 'Unfortunate as I seem now, you may perhaps yet hear of me, that I am saved.' The systematic ambiguity of language, of which I have cited by no means all the examples in the speech, has been variously resolved by the critics according to their general views of the speech and the play.

F. G. Welcker first propounded what we may call the theological interpretation.[2] The audience, he argued, would think of Ajax not merely as an antique figure of epic poetry, but would follow his fate with more immediate concern because he was an Attic hero. This canonization, as it were, is the goal toward which the entire play is moving; and in it Ajax' submission to the gods is a necessary stage. Welcker, accordingly, saw in the speech before us the first recognition by Ajax, after the bitterness and defiance he had maintained throughout the earlier scenes, that the gods are after all supreme and must be obeyed. He will go down to the bathing-places in the meadows by the seashore, and there washing off his stains escape the heavy wrath of the goddess (lines 654-6). The stains are to be washed off in blood; he will escape the wrath of the goddess, by his death. – On this view, the speech before us is of great importance, is in fact the turning-point of the whole play. When Welcker wrote, the generally accepted view was that the speech was intended throughout to deceive – '*tota simulatio est*'. Ajax, it was supposed, deliberately chose the riddling words of which the speech is full, in order to give the impression to Tecmessa and the chorus that he no longer intended to kill himself, while at the same time avoiding verbal falsehood. To Welcker it seemed impossible to give to the speech the tremendous moral and religious significance which he felt it contained, if it were in any way intended to deceive. He attempted to show that the ambiguities of language were such as Ajax could have fallen into if he had not meant to

2. F. G. Welcker, *Kleine Schriften* (Bonn 1845), II, 302-22, reprinted from *Rheinisches Museum* (1829). [The 'theological' interpretation has been recently revived by Peter Burian, 'Supplication and hero cult in Sophocles' *Ajax*', *GRBS* 13 (1972), 151-6. Cf. W. Burkert, 'Greek tragedy and sacrificial ritual', *GRBS* 7 (1966), 87-121. Eds.]

mislead his partisans, but rather, out of a wish to spare their feelings as much as possible, had chosen to speak indirectly and in a veiled manner. They misunderstand him to be sure, but that is no fault of his. Welcker also put forward two other arguments to show that the speech was not a deceit. (1) Ajax says at the first that he pities his wife and child: in this he is surely sincere; but if the rest of the speech is deceitful, then this must be too. (2) In any case, lying would disfigure the character of Ajax, who of all men was least capable of it – as Pindar says, ἦ τιν’ ἄγλωσσον μέν, ἦτορ δ’ ἄλκιμον.[3] Of this second argument we shall hear a great deal.

Welcker's arguments were accepted both in Germany and England, and remained uncontested until Lewis Campbell's edition of Sophocles.[4] He returned to the view that the speech was dissimulation, and by a close examination of the language raised one important detail which made Welcker's theory of unintentional ambiguity very difficult.[5] Campbell's general position was adopted, with more extensive and elaborate arguments, by R. C. Jebb, in his edition of the Ajax.[6] Jebb gave the *coup de grâce* to Welcker's theory of Ajax' intentions by pointing out that lines 658–60, at any rate,

> I'll dig in the ground and hide this sword of mine,
> Hatefulest of weapons, out of sight. May Darkness
> And Hades, God of Death, hold it in their safe keeping,[7]

could hardly have been spoken without an intention to mislead. The language is too studiedly obscure, and while it still escapes being verbally false, it could never have been chosen by anyone

3. *Nemean* 8.24.

4. Lewis Campbell (ed.), *Sophocles* (2 vols., Oxford 1881), *ad loc.*

5. He points out that the words ἐθηλύνθην στόμα (line 651) are ambiguous, since στόμα may mean, not only 'mouth', but also the 'edge' of a sword. 'I, who before was as hard as iron hardened in the dipping, now am softened (ἐθηλύνθην στόμα) as to the edge of my purpose', the audience would naturally understand; but the words could also mean 'only in my speech', and imply a mental reservation on the part of Ajax. It is very hard to believe that this false scent is unintentional.

6. *Sophocles, The plays and fragments*, Part VII, *The Ajax* (Cambridge 1896), introduction, pp. xxxiii–xxxviii.

7. [Here, and throughout the paper, we have inserted Moore's own translation of the *Ajax*, done in Rome 1955–6 and first published by the University of Chicago Press (under the editorship of David Grene and Richmond Lattimore) in 1957. Eds.]

trying to convey his idea rather than to conceal it. Since Jebb wrote, no one has revived Welcker's hypothesis in its original form.

But Jebb's greater contribution was to show that the speech might have all the importance Welcker assigned to it, while still being intended by Ajax to mislead his hearers. Jebb agreed with Welcker fully on the general purport of the play, and on the function of the present scene in particular; but he perceived also that Ajax' speech might contain not one but several strands: 'direct expression of his real mind; irony in a form which does not necessarily imply the intention to deceive; and artifice of language so elaborate as necessarily to imply such an intention, at any rate when addressed to simple hearers'.[8] Ajax really pities his wife and child; indeed his whole mood is changed, from the defiance of his madness and awakening to the calm piety of his end; but his purpose has not changed, and he conceals it beneath this elaborate artifice of language.

These early commentators on the speech, although ranged on opposite sides of what seemed to them the fundamental question (whether the speech was meant to deceive), had much more ground in common than any of the writers since that time: they shared a coherent interpretation of the play as a whole (which I have called the theological); and their interpretations of the present scene were made with a view to that general scheme: where they disagreed on detail, the question was always, is this detail consonant with the tenor of the speech as a whole and the play as a whole?

Of more recent writers only Schadewaldt seems to follow this tradition, and even he does so with reservations. The others divide into two main schools of interpretation: the first, of those who see in the play simply a spectacle of heroic strength shattered by the power of the gods (this is the position of Reinhardt, Perrotta, and von Fritz); the second, of those who abandon the attempt to interpret the play as a whole, and analyze the development of the action not as proceeding from the characters but from the exigencies of dramatic technique. (This is the view of T. von Wilamowitz,

8. *Sophocles*, Part VII, p. xxxviii. Jebb remarks that Ajax would not lose credit in the eyes of Greek hearers by his deceit, which they would condone as a stratagem in war. The English critics seem by and large to have been far less concerned than the Germans with this difficulty.

followed by Pohlenz, and with considerable reservations by Schadewaldt.)

Those who see the play simply as the spectacle of the breaking of Ajax, read the speech before us as a tirade full of bitter sarcasm. For them the question of whether Ajax meant to deceive his partisans becomes one of secondary importance. The real issue – though none of them seems to raise it in any explicit form – becomes, is Ajax sincere in saying that he must learn to yield to the gods: or more precisely, does he conceive that his death will be a yielding to them? This is a point of division as crucial for these recent writers as the question of intent to deceive was for the earlier: in all of them it is evidently felt to be critical, and yet not one of them formulates it. Reinhardt was the earliest of these writers.[9] He apparently does not believe that Ajax intends to deceive, or at least he reduces the element of deceit to a minimum (he admits that the proposal to bury the sword is a 'pretext'); but in any case the function of the speech is far more to express Ajax' feelings than to communicate anything, whether true or false, to the chorus. The *Ajax*, according to Reinhardt, belongs to an early stage of Sophocles' development, in which the characters were singularly unable to communicate their feelings and thereby to influence the action; in which they merely received the blows of fortune and gave poetic expression to their sufferings. That is what Ajax is doing now. His words are uttered with a certain bitterness against the order of the world, in which heroic un-yieldingness can find no place; his concession to the order of nature is expressed with bitter pride and with mental reservations; a certain stiff-neckedness. In his images of how winter yields to summer, and the others, he argues from the law of nature in which every-thing gives way: but he is not reconciled to it. 'Die Verhüllung treibt sein Wesen in die Tiefe: noch einmal rafft er die Hüllen dieser Welt und ihres Hoffens um sich, die ihm fremd und feind geworden.'[10]

K. von Fritz also sees the speech as an expression of Ajax' bitterness: but his interpretation is rather less subtle. Ajax, he thinks, has achieved since the attack of madness a more intellectual penetration of his position than ever before: and seeing his whole

9. *Sophokles* (Frankfurt a. M. 1933), pp. 33–8.
10. *Sophokles*, p. 38.

world in ruins he dies, not because he grasps the necessity of submission, but quite simply because the gods have broken him to
pieces. He does not hesitate to lie to his followers: the heroic
world which he knew has been dashed to fragments, *and its
standards no longer matter*.[11] Von Fritz' interpretation leaves unexplained the calm reflectiveness of Ajax' language in this speech;
it presumably implies that, when he says at the end the chorus
'may hear of him yet as saved', he is merely talking at random to mislead them; and finally it seems to ignore the truly
heroic dignity (whatever else may be said of it) with which he
contemplates and meets his death. For these reasons I find it difficult.

G. Perrotta, I think, has coped with these points more effectively.[12] The play as a whole (up to line 1045) contains the
punishment of Ajax for blasphemy: but the poet has laid most
emphasis on the actual destruction of Ajax and how he bears up
in the face of it, leaving apart the question of his guilt. He too
believes that the speech primarily gives voice to Ajax' bitterness:
quoting the line 'the Atreidae are in power and must be obeyed –
why not?'; the 'why not', he says, is 'piena di finissima amarezza';
and Ajax' promise to yield to the gods is 'undeniable sarcasm'.
Perrotta wrestles with the main difficulty of this position much
better than von Fritz. The supposedly 'sarcastic' offer to yield to
the gods is made through the series of lofty natural similes to
which we have continually recurred. Most critics, and in particular
Schadewaldt and Jebb, have felt that these inspired verses could
not be a mere vehicle of sarcasm or deceit: they must have some
sort of truth. Just so, Perrotta replies; but they are not an expression of Ajax, but of Sophocles. Ajax is only the mouthpiece; he is
used by the poet precisely as Shakespeare uses Banquo the
ambitious general to speak the lines before Inverness Castle about
the martlet and the delicate air. (This is an ingenious answer, but
not, I think, a true one; I shall return to it later.) When, on the
other hand, Ajax comes to apply to himself the parallel from the
great order of nature, a curious *non sequitur* interposes;[13] he turns

11. K. v. Fritz, *Rheinisches Museum* (1934), 113ff. [the italics are Moore's. Eds.].
12. 'L'Aiace di Sofocle', *Atene e Roma* (1934), 63–98. On the question of the
deceit (and whether it would be dishonorable under the circumstances to
a Greek audience) Perrotta agrees substantially with Jebb.
13. First pointed out by U. v. Wilamowitz, *Hermes* (1924), 249–51.

aside to remember an old proverb about the insecurity of friendship, and never returns to give direct expression to what his similes
(or rather the poet's own) had implied. Now it is Ajax speaking
once more, and his mind is not prepared to yield.

The other school of interpretation (T. von Wilamowitz and
Pohlenz are its chief members)[14] accepts the speech as intended
to deceive, and returns to the question raised by Welcker, is such
a deception possible for Ajax, or consistent with his character?
The general thesis of T. von Wilamowitz' work, however, is that
psychological consistency is not to be looked for in a Sophoclean
personage: he speaks what the dramatic situation at the moment
happens to demand, and that is enough. We must not take to our
reading of Greek tragedy the presuppositions of modern psychology. Thus the problem is neatly avoided: but only at the cost, it
would seem, of abandoning many of our strongest impressions
from reading Sophocles: impressions which can hardly arise just
fortuitously from the accident of our reading into his characters
a psychological interest and consistency which for him did not
exist at all.

Schadewaldt,[15] though a sympathetic critic in the main,
answers the view of Wilamowitz with considerable force:

> Henceforth we shall certainly be on our guard against attributing
> each and every word which a character says to some inner law of his
> being – and yet (I appeal to the naive impression of Sophocles that
> each of us bears within himself) when we hear the names of Ajax,
> Oedipus, Antigone, Electra, Deianeira, do not figures sharply de-
> lineated, human beings, each with his own nature and his own will, –
> *characters* in short, come to our minds?[16]

He instances Antigone's brusque answer to Creon, 'How could
I help knowing your command: it was public, wasn't it?'; the
impulse of Deianeira to pity Iole; the quick and suspicious
questioning of Teiresias by Oedipus ('was it Creon or *you* that
invented this?'): the wildness of Antigone, he argues, the gentleness of Deianeira, the keenness of Oedipus are not illusions. And
in the present instance, if this long speech were made by Ajax, as
Wilamowitz supposes, merely to deceive, merely as a pretext; if

14. Tycho v. Wilamowitz, *Philologische Untersuchungen* 22 (1917), 63ff. Max
Pohlenz, *Griechische Tragödie* (Leipzig 1930), pp. 176ff.
15. W. Schadewaldt, 'Aias u. Antigone', *Neue Wege zur Antike* Reihe 1,
Heft 8 (1929), 61ff.   16. *Ibid.*, p. 67.

the fine poetic appeal to the order of nature served merely the needs of the moment; the audience, knowing the traditional character of Ajax and being carried away by the poetry, would miss the point, and the speech would fail of its effect. Rather the speech in these respects must be true, or at least must contain some truth: Ajax, when he veils his purpose in the obscure language of expiation, burial of the weapon, night and Hades, is speaking not merely for the sake of avoiding verbal untruth: the words have for him an emotional meaning which is essentially true; and when he appeals to the alternation of nature, he conceives that he too is about to yield, by death. Essentially Schadewaldt receives the play as Jebb and Welcker did (although ignoring the hero cult): 'das Bild der geistig-ethischen Auferstehung des Menschen'.[17]

In Schadewaldt's view, however, this development is revealed, not as a development of the inner law of Ajax' being, but as a process of adjustment to external and generally valid norms. Hence the development is not continuous: it is presented to us in several distinct stages, first madness, then physical recovery, then spiritual recovery (in the present scene), and finally the translation of his spiritual reorientation into action, in the speech before his death. Nor are the scenes themselves so much an *expression* of the feelings of Ajax at that point, as a *presentation* of the *ēthos* of a personality at that stage: the speeches as Schadewaldt puts it, are less 'aus der Person' than 'über die Person gesprochen'.[18]

In canvassing these interpretations I have tried to show the kind of views which in general have been expressed, and also the main lines of cleavage between them. Some of these differences of opinion are not altogether irreconcilable: for instance, it is conceivable that even in his decision to submit Ajax might chafe at the remembrance of his humiliation; and we can recognize that Ajax' fall is a staggering disclosure of the power of the gods, as Reinhardt says, while still accepting the emphasis of Jebb and Schadewaldt on the ethical significance of these experiences for Ajax.

II

When Welcker decided that Ajax meant his words to convey the truth, he was left to face the question, why then were they capable

17. *Ibid.*, p. 80.   18. *Ibid.*, p. 81.

of being misunderstood? From among all the possible ways of announcing his intentions, including among others the simple blunt words he had used before, what compelled him to choose precisely the one way which could convey another unintended meaning? But, Welcker answered, Ajax' mood is now softened; he does not want to cause his friends unnecessary pain; and so he uses more indirect expressions, by which, as it happens, without intending to, he misleads them altogether. This answer of Welcker's *is* capable of standing as an explanation for the systematic ambiguity; it breaks down only in detail. Here however its lapses are so serious that the theory has now been generally abandoned.

But the very same difficulty, or rather a mirror-image of it, arises for those who think the speech deceitful. Why in the whole course of this long speech is there not a single word which is not verbally true? Why should Ajax manufacture a speech of such systematic *double entendre* when a simple lie would serve? Several answers have been offered: Jebb suggested that the speech would give the audience the kind of pleasure one takes in solving a riddle – a banal and melancholy idea. Much happier is the thought that his words in their true sense are ironical: he will bury his sword – yes, we are meant to understand, but in his body; night and Hades will hide it underground – yes, but in his grave. And undoubtedly there is irony here, and the effect is very fine; but still, if you were deceiving someone, and your feelings about the situation were at the same time very strong, would you make *every* sentence ironical, item by item; or would not some of your words be clearly false, and only here and there the play of irony flicker, where perhaps some random phrase of your deception might suddenly release your true emotion?

But the true *double entendre* of Ajax' speech is of a formidable ingenuity: his phrases are not the natural phrases to convey the desired meaning; and his irony is not the irony that might break through incidentally under stress of emotion; it is too calculated and recondite. Either Sophocles is reaching after effects of irony which can only be described as bizarre, or some other motive is influencing Ajax' choice of words. I can see only one possible solution: Ajax is led into this unnatural language by his desire to avoid verbal untruth.

I need hardly say that I did not reach this conclusion by the process of elimination outlined above. It seemed perfectly obvious intuitively – and indeed I should not be surprised if it were equally obvious to everyone else. But two things have induced me to mention it, first the fact that it is seldom or never explicitly said by writers on the *Ajax*; and secondly, because it has some remarkable consequences.

To begin with, we attain at once far greater clarity as to the character of Ajax. If he intends falsehood, and yet scruples to say anything verbally false, how can we say any longer that he is speaking out of character, or that his words do not arise from any inner law of his nature? On the contrary, the motivation is subtle and also touching. We may not sympathize with his distinction between meaning falsehood and speaking falsehood – intellectually, no doubt, it is quite indefensible; and yet there is pathos in his clinging to such a distinction. We feel a certain difficulty that Ajax should lie; but Sophocles, so far from ignoring the difficulty, has seized on it to secure at once a fine pathetic stroke and a very accurate realization of Ajax' dilemma.

There are those nevertheless who are still unreconciled to a lying Ajax, and are outraged that he should deceive his friends. But it seems to me they are too exacting in their demands for 'consistent characterization'; in fact, they seem to have a detailed *a priori* conception of Ajax' character (derived it appears from the epic literature and a stray phrase of Pindar), which serves as a Procrustean bed for the hero of Sophocles. Then they argue somewhat as follows: Sophocles represents Ajax as lying; lying is against Ajax' character; therefore either (a) Sophocles has blundered; or (b) Sophocles never had any conception of consistent character in the first place. But of course our only knowledge of Sophocles' Ajax must come from this play; and if only we avoid drawing hasty conclusions, and (still more important) making hasty formulations ('Ajax, the simple, blunt soldier', etc.); if instead we allow our impression of the character to accumulate as we read, bearing in mind that different circumstances may elicit different traits in a character; we may be surprised to discover, not the inconsistencies which have perplexed our critics, but instead that degree of flexibility and tact which distinguishes inspired portraiture from 'character drawing' by rules of thumb. To me at least there seems to be some felicity in making Ajax resort to deception because of his tenderness for those he is deceiving. Manifestly he cannot tell them the truth: it would be impossible to make them understand.[19] And yet he must tell them something.

If my explanation is correct, this is no ordinary speech from Ajax, but a very great effort of self-command and intellectual resourcefulness. He must deceive his friends, indeed he must deceive them precisely because he pities them; but because his conscience will not allow him to resort to actual falsehood, he must hit upon such phrases as will be nevertheless, upon some interpretation, true. Reinhardt remarks that the speech has for its purpose far more the expression of Ajax' feelings than to convey anything to the chorus, whether true or false. I cannot believe that this is correct. There is, after all, a concrete dramatic situation, a deception, to be carried out by the most scrupulous means, and demanding great dexterity. Which is not to say that Ajax does not express his true feelings; that is the very instrument of his deception. He so chooses his words that he can always accept the omen, so to speak; and because his heart is full of his own grief, or more exactly of his whole fatal situation, there is a wealth of feeling which is ready to respond to ominous words. Reinhardt is very just in saying that when Ajax speaks of burying his sword and going to a solitary place, 'his thoughts are revolving about his death'. And so is Schadewaldt when he says that some of Ajax' statements, though superficially false, are in a deeper sense again true. But this expression of his true feelings gains in vividness from the dramatic emergency; for since the first necessity is always deception, the ambiguities which reveal his true feeings have an air of providential accident which increases their poignancy.

III

To this point I have discussed the matter only in terms of character and dramatic action; and for the most part writers on Sophocles are accustomed to stop here. We know, though, that these make up only one part of our total impression of the play. The *Ajax* is in

19. Most of Sophocles' other great protagonists are similarly isolated in their moment of crisis. The chorus of the *Antigone* rebuke her for her rashness and unwisdom. The chorus of *Oedipus the King* say of Oedipus that they wish they had never seen him.

reality a poem with its own climaxes and retardations and generally its own manner of unfolding; it has an artistic shape, which more or less subtly affects the way in which we receive the scenes and action. No scene can be felt apart from the weight of what precedes it; and we may even come to estimate the effect of a scene by the emotional reaction which follows it, especially when it brings about a peripety, as this one does.

All the earlier scenes of the play up to the present one seem contrived to build up in us an accumulating sense of the unbearableness of Ajax' position. Athena's mockery of him in the presence of Odysseus, the spectacle of his madness; the well-meaning but completely uncomprehending pleas of the chorus, combined with their chance hints at the anger of the army; the horrible scene in which Ajax comes to himself and sees around him the mangled sheep and cattle which he took for his enemies; his brooding self-absorption, his brutality to those around him, his slow realization of his disgrace (like a trapped animal he hunts for an escape, and each failure increases his desperation – he can neither return home and face his father, nor plunge into the enemy without helping the Atreidae: he is hated by both gods and men): from one end to the other it is an unrelieved nightmare of madness and blood.

Yet nearly everyone feels that by the time the corpse is discovered, these vapors of miasma are completely gone. From then on we tend to forget Ajax' guilt, and think only of the meanness and vindictiveness of his enemies; and it is very far from seeming a false note when Tecmessa says that Ajax' death concerned the gods, not them (line 970). Clearly a great alteration of feeling has taken place; to what shall we ascribe it?

Perhaps to the suicide, to the simple fact of Ajax' death. Undoubtedly it is more difficult to judge a man harshly when he is dead than when he lives; and Ajax' suicide would be sure to produce a reaction in his favor. This, however, is not the difficulty. We are already predisposed in Ajax' favor, and have been from the very first. The madness and guilt of Ajax are oppressive precisely because they cannot be removed merely by his death. For example, if at line 646, instead of Ajax' entrance, a messenger were to come out of the tent and announce his death, the result would be mere confusion and dismay.

58

Or is our changed attitude due to a feeling of pity and terror at the fall of a great man? But Ajax is not fallen only now. We have not seen him except in ruins. The disasters of Oedipus or Othello or Eteocles are sudden, impressive, and terrible, fit to arouse pity and terror; but the end of Ajax is almost an escape from a situation intolerable already.

Or is it Ajax' change of mood before his death, as Jebb and Schadewaldt suppose? Schadewaldt speaks of the suicide as 'propitiation', Jebb of Ajax' recognition that his death is 'an atonement due to Athena'.[20] This seems a strange idea: the conception of sacrifice for propitiation is familiar enough; but suicide for such a purpose is unheard of, so far as I can discover. Suicide in classical Greek poetry is committed with only one end in view, annihilation. Jocasta in Homer and Sophocles, Heracles in Euripides, it is always the same, ᾧ ἄχεϊ σχομένη (λ 279). It is true that Ajax says he will wash his stains away, but that is only an incident to his total annihilation, stains and all; and moreover, he is speaking here ironically. That is to say, his expression is true, but not in its obvious sense, only in a grim manner of speaking. I believe we should take a similar view of his offer to 'yield to the gods and reverence the Atreidae'. Jebb is obliged to say that he means these words, directly and sincerely. Otherwise he would be a Mezentius. But how can he offer to reverence the Atreidae? Jebb replies, he perceives his offence against the social order. Like so many of Jebb's explanations, this one is amazingly ingenious, but it is bound nevertheless to seem forced and unconvincing; by contrast Perrotta's exclamation that the offer is undeniable sarcasm looks like a vivid and spontaneous response. The fact seems to be that here too we have *double entendres*. Ajax will yield to the gods, not through propitiation (as his hearers understand), but through death. He will yield to the Atreidae also, not in the way they expect, but in the way that will embarrass them most. Throughout the speech when Ajax speaks of his death as a 'yielding', he means it only in the sense that whatever is annihilated ceases to resist. I shall try to show presently that it is his attitude toward annihilation that has changed.

It appears that we must look for the answer to our problem, not

20. *Sophocles*, Part VII, p. xxxviii.

in the action, but in some poetic or emotional quality of the intervening scenes. The general effect of this present speech is buoyancy, although much of what Ajax says seems very bitter. For so many scenes the action has stood still, while dismay and helplessness have been accumulating; now at last we are to see Ajax act with resolution. The spirit and virtuosity he displays, and the fortitude with which he covers his strong emotion under impassive and reassuring words, these revive our admiration. But this speech, which is so full of dramatic excitement, is also obliquely a reflective poem. At first its tone would seem to be elegiac – *tempus edax rerum*: the familiar poignant note of reproachfulness because our days are as grass which gentle minds have always loved to utter when in a melancholy mood. But Ajax had always played directly for the great real stakes, prestige, honor, victory; and it comes with the force of an altogether new experience to him, to watch them being now dissolved away.

Usually at the end of a choral song a speaker begins with some simple down-to-earth formula, like 'Friends, it has occurred to me...', or 'I have reached a decision, O sailors', which serves to break the more highly-wrought emotional fabric of music and expedite a return to action. Now, however, Ajax appears from the tent and begins his long and magnificent speech without any such introduction, so that the emotional amplitude of the choral song is not allowed to dissipate, and an impressive elevation is given to his words.

> Strangely the long and countless drift of time
> Brings all things forth from darkness into light,
> Then covers them once more. Nothing so marvelous
> That man can say it will not be –
> Strong oath[21] and iron intent come crashing down.
> My mood, which just before was strong and rigid,
> No dipped sword more so, now has lost its edge –
> And pity touches me for wife and child,
> Widowed and lost among my enemies.

21. ὁ δεινὸς ὅρκος presumably does not mean 'perjury has become fashionable nowadays'. There is a reminiscence of Archilochus, fragment 122 (West),

> χρημάτων ἄελπτον οὐδέν ἐστιν οὐδ' ἀπώμοτον
> οὐδὲ θαυμάσιον...,

that is to say, you would have been ready to swear that such-and-such an event would never happen, but your oath would have proved in vain.

This is no rhetorical commonplace: the lines are full of a sort of wistful amazement, as he feels a different mood come over him. For the moment he merely remarks that his stern will has been softened, and that he pities his wife and child; but the note of acquiescence to a superior power, of willingness to abandon the personal will and forgo the lacerating struggle for self-assertion, recurs and is reinforced as he continues. The purpose of these opening lines ought not to be judged solely in the light of their immediate application to his wife and child: for it very often happens in old Greek poetry, that a general reflection, which seemed to arise first as a comment on the immediate situation, assumes a sort of independent existence: it may be pursued, like a Homeric simile, for its own sake, or it may illuminate other aspects of the present situation, with which it at first had no connection.

In saying that he pities his wife and child Ajax is undoubtedly sincere: and he shows his pity precisely by deceiving them. Manifestly he cannot tell them the truth: it would be impossible to make them understand. And it would outrage both his own feelings and theirs to leave without any further words, particularly in view of the harshness of his last rebuke to Tecmessa. His speech is a sort of farewell, and, as I have said, the necessity of deception enhances its pathos.

> But now I'm going to the bathing place
> And meadows by the sea, to cleanse my stains,
> In hopes the goddess' wrath may pass from me.
> And when I've found a place that's quite deserted,
> I'll dig in the ground and hide this sword of mine,
> Hatefulest of weapons, out of sight. May darkness
> And Hades, God of Death, hold it in their safe keeping.
> For never, since I took it as a gift
> Which Hector, my great enemy, gave to me,
> Have I known any kindness from the Greeks.
> I think the ancient proverb speaks the truth:
> An enemy's gift is ruinous and no gift.

I feel no difficulty in the deception; the real complexity of the speech arises from the elements in it which are not deceptions. While Ajax is finding words to express and yet conceal his true intentions, he continually drifts into language which discloses with great poignancy his sense of the larger context in which he stands.

The purification by the seashore, the almost seventeenth-century curiosity over the fatality of Hector's sword ('If poisonous minerals and if that tree...') which arises so deftly out of the deception; the consignment of the sword to death and Hades; and most of all his lyrical lines on the submission of all intransigent things in nature.

> Well, then,
> From now on this will be my rule: Give way
> To Heaven, and bow before the sons of Atreus.
> They are our rulers, they must be obeyed.
> I must give way, as all dread strengths give way,
> In turn and deference. Winter's hard-packed snow
> Cedes to the fruitful summer; stubborn night
> At last removes, for day's white steeds to shine.
> The dread blast of the gale slackens and gives
> Peace to the sounding sea; and Sleep, strong jailer,
> In time yields up his captive. Shall not I
> Learn place and widsom?

This extraordinary passage is recognized at once as a powerful return to the theme of the first lines of the speech: τὰ δεινὰ καὶ τὰ καρτερώτατα ('all dread strengths', line 669) recalls ὃς τὰ δείν' ἐκαρτέρουν τότε ('my mood, which just before was strong and rigid', line 650); χὠ δεινὸς ὅρκος χαἰ περισκελεῖς φρένες ('strong oath and iron intent', line 649). The tone is as elevated as before and again the question is of yielding. It is of great importance for us to observe the precise emotional inflection of these lines, for as we have seen, one's interpretation of the whole speech very largely depends upon it. Are they a bitter description of a natural order with which the speaker has no sympathy, and from which he felt closed out, as Reinhardt says? Are they a mere irresponsible lyrical interjection by the poet himself, as Perrotta says? Undoubtedly they are preceded by an animadversion to the generals which can only be sarcastic: 'hereafter we shall have to reverence the Atreidae; they are our rulers and must be obeyed, why not?' But the whole speech is a complicated one; Ajax' mood is a response to the complete situation, in which the Atreidae form hardly more than a detail. In short, the reference may merely be a momentary thought. We do not need to assume in advance that he feels inimical to the order of the world; if we listen carefully to the lines I believe we shall not conclude so.

Let us paraphrase: 'If the wintry blizzard yields to fruitful summer, if the wearisome round of night gives way to day's white-ponied cart and lets it shine, and if the blasts of the terrible winds allow rest to the groaning sea, shall not I too yield...?' Always it is the harsh that yields to the desirable, the grim to the gentle and peaceful. It is true that in these lines Ajax makes a direct and explicit argument: 'if these formidable things give way, how much more should I?' But the imagery he chooses serves to reveal the direction in which his thoughts are turning. After the accumulated torture and despair he has experienced since his awakening, he now gives in to a powerful and natural desire to yield: emotionally it seems now the simple and right thing to do. There are no longer any fixed points; everything is loose from its moorings: τὰ δεινὰ and τὰ καρτερώτατα give way. Very forcefully the desire comes over him to abandon the ties and commitments of life.

Ajax' words are thus full of the symbolism and imaginative realization of death. But, someone may object, isn't this interpretation of the imagery capricious or even downright perverse? Ajax makes a perfectly rational argument; first the general proposition, 'time overcomes everything', then the application, 'it has also softened me'. And similarly, 'all stubborn things yield in turn, winter, storms, night; I must yield too'. These are mere arguments whose purpose is to convince. The imagery of their major premise is sublime, and may convince us that Ajax believes the arguments himself; but to rend the images from their context, or to read them as anything but direct illustrations of his point, this, it will be said, is quite unwarrantable. Nevertheless, when one is making an argument the illustrations he chooses and the way he uses them enable us very often to discern his feelings, whether he is resigned to the proposition he is arguing for, whether he regards it as a good thing or a bad, and so forth.

Ajax' feeling is presented to us by what ought to be the most direct and persuasive means: a short piece of imaginative lyric finely keyed to the speaker's mood; and if I am right in my judgment of Sophocles' intended effect in the relentless opening scenes, the present passage should come home to the audience with altogether unusual force. Together with the heightened eloquence of the first words of the speech, which are here recalled, these lines bring about the artistic peripety of the whole play. They cannot be, as Perrotta asserts, an irresponsible lyrical intrusion by the poet in his own person, in this place least of all. No real dramatic poet could be so inept. Perrotta seems unfortunate too in his choice of a parallel: Banquo's lines spoken before Inverness Castle about the 'temple-haunting martlet' is no mere decoration: there is a deliberate irony in this lyrical moment, with its 'delicate air' which, as Duncan remarks only a moment before,

> Nimbly and sweetly recommends itself
> Unto our gentle senses.

This is the castle in which Duncan is to be murdered before morning.

At this point Ajax again breaks off: 'how then shall I not learn moderation?', and his thoughts take a different turn, toward the instability of friendship.

> Shall not I
> Learn place and wisdom? Have I not learned this,
> Only so much to hate my enemy
> As though he might again become my friend,
> And so much good to wish to do my friend,
> As knowing he may yet become my foe?

Most men have found friendship a treacherous harbor. He is musing, 'Yes, the sentence of Bias is right, we must not hate forever or love without reserve. [Hector may be in his mind as an enemy turned friend, the generals as friends turned enemies]; for to most men friendship is a treacherous harbor. . . ' He has returned to the curious mood in which he contemplated Hector's sword. It is important to note that these lines on the 'sentence of Bias' mark a different movement in the speech from the analogy of nature, and must not be confounded with it. The whole speech is a reflective one; there are new departures ever and anon.

After a few final injunctions and some ambiguous words of farewell Ajax leaves.

> Enough: this will be well.
> > You, my wife, go in
> And fervently and continually pray the gods

To grant fulfilment of my soul's desire.
And you, my friends, heed my instructions too,
And when he comes, deliver this to Teucer:
Let him take care for me and thought for you.
Now I am going where my way must go;
Do as I bid you, and you yet may hear
That I, though wretched now, have found my safety.

The chorus is deceived completely – his last word to them was σεσωμένον ('that I...have found my safety'); believing that he has relented they break into a joyful and energetic chorus. These 'hyporchemes' of Sophocles are often said to 'raise our hopes with the expectation of a fortunate issue', so as to make the catastrophe more overwhelming. This can hardly be the purpose here, since everything depends on our realizing that in fact Ajax has gone to kill himself. Rather the chorus is meant to appear pathetic in its hopes; it reminds us of Helen on the walls of Troy, when she notices the absence of her brothers, 'foolish one, for she did not know that the life-giving earth already covered them, in Lacedaemon yonder, their dear fatherland'. This chorus is the climax of the pathetic motif which began with Ajax' deception speech; and technically it forms an important part of the whole cycle of action beginning there. The poet wants an opportunity to give Ajax another long speech. The tension must not, therefore, be allowed to lapse. The pathetic motif, which all during the intricate deception-speech ran parallel with the greater one of Ajax' spiritual reorientation, is now allowed to assume the dominant position, first in the hyporcheme, then in the swift scene of melodrama in which Tecmessa and the chorus discover their mistake. Finally and with complete assurance Sophocles introduces the grand and simple monologue of Ajax before his death, with which this cycle of action is brought to a close.

If I have traced the action correctly, I think it will be agreed that whether or not Sophocles meant us to see Ajax' suicide as a spiritual regeneration, he has framed the scenes and composed the whole motion of the play in such a way that the spectator must feel, at Ajax' suicide, an overwhelming sense of relief (somewhat as though a great weight had fallen into place). This is not the sudden calamity of a great man, like Oedipus or Othello or

Eteocles; but the response of a man already overtaken by calamity; where their disasters appear to us sudden, impressive, and terrible, the end of Ajax is almost an escape. Emotionally the action presents itself as a transition from unendurable misery to resignation in a knowledge of human helplessness.

The tragic issue in Sophocles' *Ajax*[1]

M. SICHERL

THOUGH the *Ajax* is thought to be the earliest of Sophocles' surviving plays, it is certain that the dramatist had already reached the height of his creative powers when it was written.[2] It is equally certain that this play, in the course of its action, exhibits all the distinctive features of Sophocles' particular conception of the tragic world-order. We shall understand this conception best if we start from precisely that part of the play which is most controversial, the famous speech, often called the 'deception speech', which comprises the whole second episode (646–92). Its central position corresponds to its inner significance as the tragedy's heart.[3] One of the most beautiful passages in all Greek tragedy[4]

1. This paper is a revised English version of my article 'Die Tragik des Aias' in *Hermes* 98 (1970), 14–37. I could not use the book of G. Germain (1969), the dissertations of M. H. Shaw (1971) and R. Grutter (1972) and the articles of L. F. Coraluppi (*Dioniso* 42 (1968)), J. Ferguson (*Dioniso* 44 (1970)) and G. A. Markantonatos (Πλάτων 24 (1972)). For translating the greater part of this paper I am indebted to Miss A. Duke, M.A., Lecturer in the University of Cambridge: for correcting my own translation to W. Zukowski. In translating Sophoclean verses Jebb and Lattimore-Grene have provided useful models.

2. On the date of the play cf. C. H. Whitman, *Sophocles: A Study of Heroic Humanism* (Cambridge, Mass. 1951), pp. 42–4; A. Lesky, *Die tragische Dichtung der Hellenen*, 2nd ed. (Göttingen 1964), p. 109; G. Ronnet, *Sophocle, poète tragique* (Paris 1969), pp. 324–8.

3. Welcker (note 5), p. 239 = p. 318; H. Weinstock, *Sophokles*, 3rd ed. (Wuppertal 1948), p. 49; I. Errandonea, 'Les quatre monologues d'Ajax et leur signification dramatique', *LEC* 26 (1958), 23, 29 (a Spanish version in the author's book *Sófocles: Investigaciones sobre la estructura dramática de sus siete tragedias y sobre la personalidad de sus coros* (Madrid 1958), pp. 303–24, a German translation in H. Diller (ed.), *Sophokles, Wege der Forschung* 95 (Darmstadt 1967), pp. 268–95); B. M. W. Knox, 'The Ajax of Sophocles', *HSCP* 65 (1962); I. G. Grossmann, 'Das Lachen des Aias', *Mus. Helv.* 25 (1968) 65–85. In Aeschylus' *Persae* too the play's meaning is revealed in its very center.

4. Whitman, *Sophocles*, p. 74; R. Lattimore, *The Poetry of Greek Tragedy* (Baltimore 1958), p. 70; H. D. F. Kitto, *Form and Meaning in Tragedy* (London 1956), p. 188; Knox, 'The Ajax', p. 2; W. B. Stanford, *Sophocles, Ajax, ed. with Introd., Rev. Text and Comm.* (London–New York 1963), pp. xxxvi, 283, 288.

(thanks to its poetic form and imagery), it is, at the same time, one of the most enigmatic. Since Welcker,[5] in 1829, first recognized the problems it presents, an endless controversy, in which many eminent scholars have participated, has raged about it. However, a few years ago it was rightly said that no one has yet satisfactorily explained why Ajax makes this superb, but ambiguous speech.[6] This is still true today. Interpretation has made little progress. A new approach may, therefore, be justified.

Ajax' honor is deeply wounded by the decision of the Greeks to award the arms of Achilles not to him, as the best of the heroes after Achilles, but to Odysseus. He sets forth in a wild rage, intending to revenge himself by shedding the blood of the army's commanders, Agamemnon and Menelaus, of Odysseus and all the Greek host. But Athena, Odysseus' protectress, deludes[7] him and turns his sword against a flock of sheep which he slaughters in a horrible way, mistaking them for Greeks. When he wakes from his madness, he is conscious of a new disgrace in addition to his earlier dishonor. Through his mad actions, he has exposed himself to the mockery of those very enemies whom he wished to punish. His despair gives rise to a longing for death (361, 387–427). In a monologue (430–80), he comes to the conclusion that death is his only escape from humiliation; for 'a noble man should nobly live, or nobly die'. In a scene (485ff.) inspired by the sixth book of the *Iliad*, his captive-wife Tecmessa begs him to abandon his purpose. However, neither her own misfortunes, nor her plea that he should remember his old parents and his young son, can induce him to change his mind. He has his son brought to him and makes his final dispositions before death (545–82). At the end of the scene, Tecmessa makes a final attempt to restrain him, but he rebuffs her sharply – 'You seem to me to be a fool if you intend to school my temper (ἦθος) now' (549f.) – and withdraws to his tent.

5. F. G. Welcker, 'Über den Aias des Sophokles', *Rh. Mus.* 3 (1829), 43–92, 229–364 = *Kleine Schriften 2* (Bonn 1845), pp. 264–340; here pp. 229ff. = pp. 306ff.

6. D. W. Lucas, *The Greek Tragic Poets*, 2nd ed. (London 1959), p. 136. Errandonea, who examines all previous attempts at interpretation ('Monologues', pp. 22–8), comes to the same conclusion.

7. Lattimore, *Poetry of Greek Tragedy*, p. 67; Knox, 'The Ajax', p. 5; Grossmann, 'Das Lachen...', p. 79.

We must keep this scene clearly before us when we hear the speech (646–92) we propose to consider. After a choral ode that lyrically expresses the gloom and sadness of the moment (596–645), Ajax, sword in hand, comes from his tent and announces that time, which changes everything, has changed him as well. He pities his wife and child, and proposes to bury his sword, which has brought him nothing but misfortune, and to purify himself by washing away his pollution at the sea-shore. He seems resigned to yield to the gods and to honor the Atreidae. His speech ended, he again withdraws.

While the chorus rejoice at this unexpected turn of events (693–718), a messenger appears and announces that the seer Calchas has prophesied that this day will determine whether Ajax lives or dies. Calchas, he says, advises Teucer to confine Ajax to his tent for the rest of the day and not to let him go out if he wishes to see him alive again. Athena's wrath will pursue him this day only.[8]

Tecmessa and the chorus at once set out to find Ajax, and the scene changes abruptly. We discover the hero in a lonely spot on the sea-shore preparing to kill himself. He has so fixed his newly sharpened sword in the earth that 'its cut...should now be deadliest' and 'help me soon and kindly to my death'. In a monologue (815–65), he makes his last requests, calling on Zeus to send a messenger to Teucer with news of his death; on Hermes to conduct him to the underworld, 'when, without a struggle, at one quick bound, I have driven this sword into my side'; on the Erinyes to avenge him on the sons of Atreus and all the Greek host; on Helios to announce his death to his parents. After a moving farewell to the light of day, to Helios, to his homeland, to great Athens, to the fields of Troy, he falls upon his sword.

Thus far, the course of the action. In the succession of events, the speech in question occupies a peculiar position. It seems hardly to fit in the otherwise straightforward development: from Ajax' violence while stricken with madness, to his waking from his delusion, to his consciousness of humiliation, to his resolution to end his life and the fulfillment of that resolution in his suicide.

8. Cf. M. M. Wigodsky, 'The "Salvation" of Ajax', *Hermes* 90 (1962), 149ff. Brief, but excellent, discussion in H. Diller, *Göttliches und menschliches Wissen bei Sophokles*, Kieler Universitätsreden 1 (Kiel 1950), pp. 10ff. = *Gottheit und Mensch in der Tragödie des Sophokles* (Darmstadt 1963), pp. 6f.

After showing himself unapproachable by any attempt to influence his decision, he seems here to have changed. Then, with no motivation, he reverts to his original plan and kills himself. All sorts of questions immediately arise. What is the significance of this apparent change? Is the change real or only pretended? Can we assume that Ajax is lying?[9]

In order to answer these questions, we must consider the speech's position in the development of the play. Before the hero's fate is sealed by death, an unexpected turn of events gives fresh hope to his followers. The chorus express their joy in a *hyporchema*, a dancing song. Their hope, however, proves to be deceptive, and the catastrophe follows soon after. We find similar contrasts in other plays by Sophocles. In the *Antigone*, the chorus sing a hymn of joy when Creon, under the pressure of events, agrees to free Antigone, whom he has condemned, and to allow the burial of Polyneices (1115–54). But Creon's change of mind, like Calchas' warning in the *Ajax*, comes too late. Antigone has already hanged herself and Haimon killed himself over her body. In *Oedipus Tyrannus*, the hero persuades the chorus to share his belief that he is a son of kindly Fortune, while Jocasta, who has already seen through the complexities of the situation, seeks to keep from him the terrible knowledge that he himself is the transgressor for whom he is searching. The catastrophe comes immediately after the *hyporchema* (1086–109). Oedipus discovers that he has killed his father and married his mother. In the *Trachiniae*, which may be close to the *Ajax* in date,[10] we find the situation closest to that of the *Ajax*. Here, the *hyporchema* (633–62) occurs when Deianeira, believing that she could win back Heracles' love with the fatal shirt of Nessus, has sent it to him as a gift. Her gift, however, causes the agonizing death of the man she loves. As in the *Ajax*, the approaching doom is announced immediately after the hymn of joy. Despite certain differences in these scenes, the same intention on the part of the dramatist is evident in all of them. They are designed to achieve retardation. Through contrast with the

9. K. Reinhardt, *Sophokles*, 3rd ed. (Frankfurt 1947), p. 31.

10. *Ibid.* pp. 42ff.; G. M. Kirkwood, *A Study of Sophoclean Drama* (Ithaca 1958), pp. 289–94 = *Wege der Forschung* 95 (1967), pp. 183–9; J. C. Kamerbeek, *The Plays of Sophocles. Commentaries 2: The Trachiniae* (Leiden 1959), pp. 27–9; E. R. Schwinge, *Die Stellung der Trachinierinnen im Werk des Sophokles*, Hypomnemata 1 (Göttingen 1962); Lesky, *Tragische Dichtung*, pp. 117ff.

apparent solution and joyful atmosphere that precede, the cata-strophe will be more devastating in its effect.[11] This is the dramatic purpose of our speech in the *Ajax* as well. Sophocles employed this sudden reversal before the catastrophe to intensify the impact of the disaster, the final 'too late'.

Here, a crucial question arises. How has Sophocles accomplished this purpose? Was the appeal of Tecmessa and the chorus, which Ajax had just so decisively rejected, successful after all? This is the explanation adopted by Sir Maurice Bowra,[12] the chief exponent of this point of view. Bowra, like Welcker, considers it unthinkable that Ajax, a man of upright character, should lie. 'We must', he says, 'take his words to mean what he now thinks. Their poetry is too genuine, their emotion too strong for them to be a calculated piece of deceit.' He claims that 'Sophocles would not send this great being to his death in an unchastened, un-repentant spirit, hated by the gods and hating them in return',[13] and therefore maintains (p. 42) that Ajax 'in modesty and self-denial finds his solution for the conflicts and agonies which have beset him'. 'The lesson of the gods, the human appeal of Tec-messa, have had their effect on him. Sophocles does not show the phases or process of the change, but simply the result.'[14] To explain Ajax' suicide, Bowra supposes that at a later stage, since Athena's anger is still upon him, he returns again to his darker passions and in this mood destroys himself.[15]

11. περίστασις tragica: Donat. in Ter. *Ad.* 297, ed. Paul Wessner, *Aeli Donati quod fertur Commentum Terenti*, vol. 2 (Leipzig 1905), p. 69: 'gaudiorum introductio ante funestissimum nuntium'; cf. Lesky, *Tragische Dichtung*, p. 110, n. 2; E. Schlesinger, 'Erhaltung im Untergang: Sophokles' Aias als pathetische Tragödie', *Poetica* 3 (1970), 373, n. 41.

12. *Sophoclean Tragedy* (Oxford 1944), pp. 39ff.

13. *Ibid.* p. 40; a similar view in Stanford, *Sophocles, Ajax*, pp. xxxivf.

14. Bowra, *Sophoclean Tragedy*, p. 39.

15. *Ibid.*, pp. 43ff. He was preceded by T. B. L. Webster, *An Introduction to Sophocles* (Oxford 1936), pp. 96f. The scholiast on 684 was obviously of the same opinion: ὅρα πόσον ἐπικρατεῖται ὑπὸ τοῦ πάθους ⟨ὁ⟩ λογισμός· ὁ τὰ σοφώτατα γοῦν εἰπὼν ἑαυτὸν ἀναιρεῖ. Similarly on 646: καὶ οἱ ἔμφρονες καὶ παρακολουθοῦντες τῇ φύσει τῶν πραγμάτων ὅμως ὑπὸ τῶν τοιούτων παθῶν ἐπὶ τὸ χεῖρον ἀπολισθάνουσιν. The view of E. Vandvik, 'Ajax the Insane', *Symb. Osl. Suppl.* 2 (1942), 169–75, that Ajax is mad throughout the whole play must be rejected; cf. Kirkwood, *Sophoclean Drama*, p. 87, n. 47; H. Friis Johansen, 'Sophocles 1939–1959', *Lustrum* 7 (1962), 178; Stanford, *Sophocles, Ajax*, pp. 281f. Recently, Vandvik was followed by H. Musurillo, *The Light and the Darkness: Studies of the Dramatic Poetry of Sophocles* (Leiden 1967), pp. 14f.

This view cannot be correct; for it implies that Ajax succumbs to the temptation of avoiding the tragic situation. The main tragic figure of the Sophoclean plays are again and again led into what we may call a temptation. In the *Antigone*, Ismene attempts to save her sister from the catastrophe; in the *Electra*, Electra's sister Chrysothemis counsels her to acquiesce in her situation; in *Oedipus Tyrannus*, Jocasta tries to prevent Oedipus from investigating further; in the *Ajax*, Tecmessa tries to prevent Ajax' suicide. Each time, the dramatist places a non-tragic 'tempter' at the side of the hero in tragic conflict, in order to elucidate the tragic situation by means of contrast.[16] All these 'temptations' come from outside the hero and fail to attain their end; for Sophocles' tragic heroes act according to their own defiant and intransigent natures.[17] There are no inner vacillations in Antigone, Electra or Oedipus, and the same is true of Ajax. The Ajax of the death-monologue is the same Ajax who delivers his final injunctions in the earlier farewell speech. There has been no change, no reversal, in the interval, nor could there have been, since the tragic element would then have been destroyed. Nor is the suicide of a madman, whose powers of intellect and will are suspended, a tragic event. Another weak point in Bowra's theory is that the poet does not even mention (let alone motivate) Ajax' supposed second change of mind. The reason Bowra gives is Webster's invention. It is not supported by the text and involves absurd implications.[18]

If Bowra's theory is wrong, what of those interpreters who maintain that there is no change in Ajax' intentions but only in his mood? For the most part, they suppose that Ajax' inner hardness has been tempered by pity for his wife and child, but while some of them agree with Welcker that Ajax has no intention to deceive and is only misunderstood, the majority, following Jebb,

16. Kirkwood, *Sophoclean Drama*, pp. 99ff.; Lesky, *Tragische Dichtung*, p. 146.

17. Cf. H. Diller, 'Über das Selbstbewusstsein der sophokleischen Personen', *Wien. Stud.* 69 (1956), 70ff.: Lesky, *Tragische Dichtung*, pp. 116, 128f.; id., *Die griechische Tragödie*, 3rd ed. (Stuttgart 1964), pp. 162f.

18. Ronnet, *Sophocle*, pp. 38f., 109; on criticisms of Bowra's view cf. also A. J. A. Waldock, *Sophocles the Dramatist* (Cambridge 1951), pp. 72ff.; Whitman, *Sophocles*, p. 261; H. W. van Pesch, *De idee van de menselijke beperktheid bij Sophocles* (Diss. Leiden, Wageningen 1953), p. 199; Errandonea, 'Monologues', p. 28, n. 24; Friis Johansen, 'Sophocles 1939–1959', p. 177; Stanford, *Sophocles, Ajax*, pp. 281f.

accuse him of deliberate deception. 'He is resolved', says Jebb (p. xxxv), 'to die, and to die in solitude. He also feels a real tenderness for those whom he is leaving. He cannot part from them in silence; nor...can he bring himself to speak openly, and to part from them...by force. He therefore veils his farewell so that it is such only to his own mind, not to their apprehension.' In bitter recognition of his condition and his guilt, he resolves to die. He misleads his friends simply to get away from them.[19] Ebeling[20] thinks that the tragic deception is the consequence of a 'well-intentioned change of expression'. Though his resolve is unaltered, his compassion for Tecmessa leads Ajax to express himself in such a way that his companions are deceived. According to Linforth,[21] he feels that he must die and chooses to do so with resignation, in a deep understanding of his condition, no longer in open rebellion against gods and men. Profoundly moved by pity for his friends, he chooses his words in such a way as to deceive them concerning his intentions. They will learn the truth about him soon enough. Errandonea[22] maintains that Ajax, pitying his wife and son, and wishing to spare them a cruel fate, gives up his original plan of seeking death through an act of open vengeance and contents himself with a humiliating suicide. This change in his mood and the ambiguity of some of his words mislead Tecmessa and the chorus into believing that he no longer intends to kill himself.

All these interpretations are more or less infected by the idea that Ajax compromises with his environment. Such, however, is not the nature of Sophoclean heroes. Though susceptible to feelings of pity, they do not compromise with what contradicts

19. R. C. Jebb, *Sophocles: The Plays and Fragments with Critical Notes, Commentary and Translation, VII: The Ajax* (Cambridge 1907), introd. pp. xxxivff. This interpretation was modified by W. Schadewaldt, 'Sophokles, Aias und Antigone', *Neue Wege zur Antike* 8 (1929), 70f.; cf. F. J. H. Letters, *The Life and Work of Sophocles* (London 1953), pp. 139f.; S. M. Adams, *Sophocles the Playwright*, The Phoenix Suppl. 3 (Toronto 1957), pp. 33f.

20. R. Ebeling, 'Missverständnisse um den Aias des Sophokles', *Hermes* 76 (1941), 297 ('grotesk': Lesky, *Tragische Dichtung*, p. 112); cf. also Stanford, *Sophocles, Ajax*, p. 287.

21. I. M. Linforth, 'Three Scenes in Sophocles' Ajax', *Univ. of Calif. Public. in Class. Phil.* 15, 1 (1954), 10–20.

22. Errandonea, 'Monologues', pp. 36ff.; *id., Wege der Forschung* 95 (1967), 292–4. He was followed in part by Stanford, *Sophocles, Ajax*, pp. 142, 286f. Criticism of this view in Ronnet, *Sophocle*, p. 39.

their nature. If Ajax' attitude towards Tecmessa changed, her main dramatic function as a non-tragic counterpart of the hero, in contrast with whom he is shown to advantage, would be weakened. It is quite unthinkable that Ajax, after having so harshly rebuffed her, would return to the stage to show his feelings softened. Furthermore, if he wished to appease the hatred of his enemies by a conciliatory attitude mingled with subtle irony,[23] he did not succeed, as is shown by subsequent events. The text offers no evidence that will support such a suggestion.[24] Nor can his tender feelings for Tecmessa account for the misleading ambiguity of Ajax' speech. We are left with the apparently inescapable conclusion that, if Ajax has not changed, his speech can only be regarded as deliberately deceitful. Read in this manner, in addition to enabling Ajax, as he wishes,[25] to kill himself unhindered, it also serves the technical purpose of achieving, by means of contrast, an apparent relaxation before the catastrophe. The speech has repeatedly been interpreted in this way and, for this reason, has been called a 'deception' speech. Thus, Ernst Howald claims that the scene, with its deception, exists merely to bring about tension through retardation, an illusory relaxation of tension. This he considers its only significance.[26] The chief exponent of such a purely technical interpretation, which regards the speech as nothing more than a deception, is Tycho von Wilamowitz in his book, *Die dramatische Technik des Sophokles* (1917).

This interpretation, also, raises serious doubts. It is more than likely 'that ancient Greeks would have seen' nothing 'unworthy or unheroic in the use of such deception'.[27] But was Sophocles

23. Errandonea, 'Monologues', p. 39.

24. The opinion of Errandonea and Stanford is contradicted by lines 560ff.: οὔτοι σ' Ἀχαιῶν, οἶδα, μή τις ὑβρίσῃ στυγναῖσι λώβαις, οὐδὲ χωρὶς ὄντ' ἐμοῦ. τοῖον πυλωρὸν φύλακα Τεῦκρον ἀμφί σοι λείψω τροφῆς ἄοκνον.

25. G. Wolff and L. Bellermann, *Sophokles, Aias erkl.*, 5th ed. (Leipzig 1899), p. 62; W. Schmid, *Geschichte der griechischen Literatur* I, 2, *Hdb. d. Altert.* 7, 1, 2 (Munich 1934), p. 337, n. 3; Whitman, *Sophocles*, p. 75; Grossmann, 'Das Lachen...', p. 84; cf. also van Pesch, *De idee...*, p. 199.

26. E. Howald, *Die griechische Tragödie* (Munich–Berlin 1930), pp. 98ff.; cf. G. Perrotta, *Sofocle* (Milan 1935, repr. Rome 1963), pp. 156f.

27. Jebb, *Sophocles*, p. xxxv; F. W. Schneidewin, A. Nauck and L. Radermacher, *Sophokles Aias erkl.*, 10th ed. (Berlin 1913), p. 109; T. v. Wilamowitz, *Die dramatische Technik des Sophokles* (Berlin 1917), pp. 63ff.; Howald, *Griechische Tragödie*, p. 97; Perrotta, *Sofocle*, p. 156; Weinstock, *Sophokles*, p. 45; M. Pohlenz,

really forced to such an expedient simply to give his hero an opportunity of escaping unmolested to the sea-shore? The means are disproportionate to the end;[28] for Ajax could have done as he wished without resorting to such a subterfuge. We feel, moreover, that the superb imagery of the speech cannot have been employed for mere deception.[29] In the *Antigone, Trachiniae* and *Oedipus Tyrannus*, the analogous scenes certainly do not exist solely for the sake of creating or diminishing tension or for any other purely technical purpose. They are motivated as well by the course of the action. Creon breaks down under the burden of disasters that pile up against him, and is forced by them to change his mind, though, tragically, he does so too late. The device by which Deianeira expects to solve her problem backfires and brings disaster instead. Oedipus, misled by the course of events, cherishes the deceptive hope that he is indeed a child of Fortune. In all these cases, the relaxation of tension has an inner motivation. But not only that: in each of these scenes, the essence of Sophocles' tragic vision of human blindness and self-deception is clearly revealed.[30] Each time, the human mind, in its limitations, believes it has finally found a way out of its difficulties: hence, the apparent relaxation of tension. When this belief is shown to be an illusion, the catastrophe follows necessarily.

We must therefore ask ourselves whether this 'deception-scene' has been incorporated into the *Ajax* artificially,[31] simply to serve a technical purpose, or whether it does not more probably represent the flickering of an illusory hope which arises, as in the other

Die griechische Tragödie, 2nd ed. (Göttingen 1954), p. 174; Stanford, *Sophocles, Ajax*, p. 286, with reference to *Hermathena* 75 (1950), 35–48 and his book *The Ulysses Theme* (Oxford 1954), pp. 19–24.

28. Perrotta, *Sofocle*, p. 156; Webster, *Introduction*, p. 96; Weinstock, *Sophokles*, p. 45; Errandonea, 'Monologues', pp. 24 and 28, n. 25; Knox, 'The Ajax', p. 12; A. Maddalena, *Sofocle*, 2nd ed. (Turin 1963); U. Parlavantza-Friedrich, *Täuschungsszenen in den Tragödien des Sophokles*, Untersuchungen z. antiken Lit. und Gesch. 2 (Berlin 1969), p. 20.

29. Jebb, *Sophocles*, p. xxxvi; Schadewaldt, 'Aias und Antigone', pp. 74f.; Reinhardt, *Sophokles*, p. 32; Bowra, *Sophoclean Tragedy*, p. 40; Musurillo, *Light and Darkness*, p. 16; cf. R. Camerer, *Gnomon* 22 (1950), 140.

30. In the *Antigone*, it is Creon's blindness, not Antigone's, that brings about the catastrophe.

31. Perrotta, *Sofocle*, p. 157, who maintains the same view in respect to *Oedipus Tyrannus*; he is rightly opposed by Errandonea, 'Monologues', pp. 29f., n. 25.

plays, out of the situation itself. This relaxation of tension before the catastrophe, the deceptive illusion into which the *dramatis personae* are drawn,[32] must surely be understood, here too, as arising from events. The speech must be seen to have grown out of the fundamental tragic conception of the play and only then to have produced, incidentally, an apparent relaxation of tension.[33] A third interpretation, proposed by Karl Reinhardt in 1933,[34] points in this direction. This has since become a *communis opinio*. Many of the interpretations presented in numerous books and articles since the 1950s are based upon it.[35]

In Reinhardt's view, the speech is admittedly a 'deceptive speech, evidently spoken to deceive another person'. But in it, a deeper truth is revealed. 'Here', he says,

the truly lonely, detached man comprehends the cosmic order as it really is, not only as applying to the community with which he himself is no longer linked; but being himself rooted in nature he sees the cosmic order as valid both in Heaven and on Earth...The eyes of Ajax are suddenly opened, and he comprehends the world, but not as a man who understands and is willing to take his place in it or to submit to its order, or follow the adage 'know thyself', but he sees it as something alien, contrary to his nature, something in which he could have a part only if he were no longer Ajax...In Ajax' words we feel, through the sublime praise of the world-order, an undertone of withdrawal.

Indeed, Ajax – the terrible (205), the intractable (914) – cannot submit to the cosmic law of change. He can never again be the friend of his enemies. But neither can he depend on his friends. By their unjust verdict, they have robbed him of his honor and compelled him to break the oath of fealty he had sworn before setting out against Troy.[36] In such a world, where nothing is permanent, the moral code of the heroic age – to love one's friend and hate one's enemy[37] – becomes meaningless. Ajax cannot

32. Parlavantza-Friedrich, *Täuschungsszenen* (*loc. cit.*), correctly points out that the deception of those on the stage is relevant to the course of the action up to the discovery of Ajax' body.
33. Musurillo, *Light and Darkness*, p. 15.
34. In his book mentioned above, n. 9.
35. Cf. Friis Johansen, 'Sophocles 1939–1959', pp. 177f. This view is seconded by such scholars as Pohlenz, *Griechische Tragödie*, pp. 175f.; Kamerbeek, *Plays of Sophocles*, pp. 133f.; Maddalena, *Sofocle*, pp. 33f.
36. See below p. 82 with n. 59.   37. Knox, 'The Ajax', pp. 3ff.

accept such a world. Like Ivan Karamazov,[38] he must renounce his right of entry to it. 'Here', says Reinhardt, 'the deception has its roots in a deeper level of irony than that we usually define as "tragic": here the irony grows out of a dim awareness of an everlasting clash between the hero and the course of the world.'

But Reinhardt, also, evidently felt that a 'manifest deception', a 'deceitful intention', is incompatible with Ajax' upright nature. 'He no more expresses his resolve by a deliberate deception than he articulates his awareness of the situation by a calculated dissimulation. Rather can it be said that his soul is so much affected by its own deception that he conceals the true issue involuntarily; there is no deliberate attempt to mislead.' Reinhardt contends that, except for the speech's conclusion (684–92), this concealment 'creates its own deeply hidden expression in the recollection of the murderous weapon, the sword.' But it is difficult to see how the hero's soul can be so affected by its own deception that it becomes involved in involuntary concealment at the very moment when his eyes have been opened and he recognizes the nature of the world and his own relation to it. Here, we feel, Reinhardt's interpretation is not wholly satisfactory.

In a penetrating study, B. M. W. Knox has attempted to find a solution that would avoid the difficulties raised by Reinhardt's explanation, but preserve his perception of the conflict between Ajax' comprehension of his situation and the essential immutability of his nature. Knox supposes that, just when conscious reflection has brought Ajax to a recognition of the truth, so that he reaches the right conclusions, his deeper nature breaks through. Irrational impulses arise from his subconscious to frustrate his newly-formed resolves. The very terms in which these resolves are formulated indicate that his deepest instincts reject them.[39] But is this solution adequate? The consistent ambiguity of Ajax' words cannot, it seems to me, be explained by the hypothesis that his conscious decisions are crossed and thwarted by irrational impulses; it must be intentional. Our problem is still unsolved.

The ambiguity of many of Ajax' statements has long been

38. F. M. Dostoievsky, *The Brothers Karamazov*, book 5, ch. 4, in the English translation of C. Garnett (New York s.a.), p. 254.

39. Knox, 'The Ajax', pp. 10ff. (15). Similarly, Stanford supposes that Ajax has been 'converted' to *sophrosyne*, but that his conversion cannot prevail over his *ethos*.

recognized; but in explicating it, some scholars have overshot the mark.[40] As we shall see at once, it is exclusively limited to those portions of his speech in which Ajax alludes to his death, where, indeed, it is remarkably thorough. In these instances, what Heraclitus[41] says of the Delphic oracle may be said of Ajax as well: οὔτε λέγει οὔτε κρύπτει, ἀλλὰ σημαίνει, 'it neither conceals nor reveals, but speaks by signs'. Behind this ambiguity, which is undoubtedly intentional, the key to the riddle must be hidden, yet no one has ever explained it convincingly. Before attempting to do so myself, I will point out those parts of the speech where a double meaning is evident, summarising and indeed supplementing what others have already said.

Ajax says what he intends to do at lines 654ff.:

> ἀλλ' εἶμι πρός τε λουτρὰ καὶ παρακτίους
> λειμῶνας, ὡς ἂν λύμαθ' ἁγνίσας ἐμὰ
> μῆνιν βαρεῖαν ἐξαλύξωμαι θεᾶς.

Well, I will go to the bathing place and the meadows by the sea-shore, to cleanse myself of my stains and thereby escape the goddess' heavy wrath.

We think that he means to purify himself with sea-water.[42] But the cleansing by which he proposes to wash off his stains at the sea-shore, and thus to escape the goddess' terrible wrath, is death. The word *loutra*, which Sophocles uses almost exclusively in connection with death,[43] refers to the hero's blood, which will be shed over his body when he kills himself. The pollution (*lumata*) from which he wishes to cleanse himself is not the blood of the slaughtered animals, nor the murder of the shepherds, nor his treasonous attempt to murder the army's commanders, nor a transgression against the gods, but the dishonor[44] and humiliation that have come to him through the ὅπλων κρίσις and the madness sent by the

40. This is true of the recent commentaries of Kamerbeek and Stanford, which will be cited by preference in the following treatment of the speech.

41. Frg. B 93, *VS* I⁶ 172, 7: cf. Lattimore, *Poetry of Greek Tragedy*, p. 70.

42. On the cathartic power of sea-water see Radermacher, *Sophokles, Aias erkl.*, on 654ff.; H. Erbse, *Hermes* 83 (1955), 424 with n. 3; Guépin (see below n. 120), p. 94.

43. Knox, 'The Ajax', p. 11 with n. 65.

44. Kamerbeek, *Plays of Sophocles*, p. 7; on pp. 654-6 he points out that Ajax calls Odysseus, whom he holds responsible for all his misfortunes, λυμεὼν ἐμός (573).

goddess. He is deeply aware of Athena's wrath (401ff., 450ff.). By dying, he will escape it.

The manner in which Ajax will kill himself is hinted at in the lines that follow (657–60):

And going, where I shall happen upon an untrodden spot, I will hide this sword of mine, the most hateful of weapons, digging out the earth, where no one will see it; but may night and Hades keep it safe below.

The audience remembers the custom of removing polluted objects from the community of men.[45] But the lines predict the hiding of his sword in his body by the act of suicide. Tecmessa later (899) finds him fallen on his hidden sword, κρυφαίῳ φασγάνῳ περιπτυχής ('folded about his hidden sword'), where κρυφαίῳ echoes κρύψω in line 658.[46] κρύπτειν is often used of burial,[47] and may be used so here: Ajax' body will be the grave of his sword. The ambiguity of line 659 has never been fully understood. The clause ἔνθα μή τις ὄψεται depends on κρύψω;[48] γαίας is partitive genitive and depends on ὀρύξας,[49] not on ἔνθα, as is generally assumed. After digging out the earth (in order to fix his sword in place, 815–22), Ajax will bury his sword in his body so completely that no one will be able to see it. Those who hear him, however, think that he will bury it in the earth. Night and Hades are to keep it safe below, because it is to be put into his grave, as he has already implicitly ordained in his farewell speech (577): τὰ δ' ἄλλα τεύχη (except for his shield which his son is to receive) κοίν' ἐμοὶ τεθάψεται; or simply because his body will be the grave in which it is buried. The latter interpretation seems to be supported by the clause ἔνθα μή τις ὄψεται. After his death, he wishes to keep his sword within him.[50] The expression σωζέσθω κάτω is used in the same

45. Wolff–Bellermann refer to Soph. *El.* 435f.; Sen. *Herc. fur.* 1129f.; Radermacher to Apoll. Rhod. 4. 694 and Eurip. *Suppl.* 1205ff.; U. v. Wilamowitz, 'Lesefrüchte', *Hermes* 59 (1924), 250 to Poll. 8. 120. On the latter see Reinhardt, *Sophokles*, p. 248.

46. Jebb and Kamerbeek on 658; Ebeling, 'Missverständnisse...', p. 296, n. 4; Kirkwood, *Sophoclean Drama*, p. 229; Stanford, *Sophocles, Ajax*, p. 145. On *Fernverbindungen* in Sophocles, Ebeling, 'Missverständnisse...', p. 285.

47. κρύπτειν τάφῳ Soph. *Aj.* 1040; *Ant.* 196, 1039; *Skyriai* frg. 501. 5; the same meaning in Soph. *Ant.* 25, 285, 774, 946; *O.C.* 621, 1546, 1552; *El.* 838; Pind. *Pyth.* 9. 81; Hdt. 2. 130.

48. Cf. *O.T.* 1412, 1436f.; *El.* 436f.; *Trach.* 903; similarly *El.* 380; *Trach.* 800.   49. Kühner–Gerth 2, 1 (1898), p. 345.

50. On the sword symbol see below, p. 88.

sense by Electra, when she bids Chrysothemis save her mother's grave-offerings for Clytemnestra's own grave. Elsewhere as well, Sophocles uses κάτω only with reference to the underworld.[51]

The sword, which Ajax had received in an exchange of gifts with his greatest enemy Hector (*Il.* 7. 303f.), has brought him no luck (661–5):

> For since I received this [sword] in my hand, a gift from Hector my greatest enemy, I have never yet had anything worthy from the Argives. But the proverb of mortals is true: an enemy's gift is ruinous and no gift.

Hearing these words, the audience thinks of the slaughter of the flocks, which has exposed him to mockery. But the full meaning of the adage, 'An enemy's gift is ruinous and no gift', will only be realized when Ajax falls upon the sword that was Hector's gift. This is clearly revealed in the death-monologue. Standing before the sword 'fixed firmly in the earth', he is again reminded that it is a gift from Hector, his most hated guest-friend, and that now it is fixed in the hostile soil of Troy 'to help me soon and kindly to my death' (815ff.). The belt which Ajax gave to Hector has been equally deadly. With it Hector was bound to Achilles' chariot and dragged to his death.[52] Ajax' recognition, at the moment of his death, of the evil omen inherent in his enemy's gift is later proclaimed by Teucer (1024ff.).

Since it is destined that Ajax will die by this gift – the gods have willed it so, says Teucer (1034–9) – he will school himself to yield to the gods and revere the Atreidae (666f.):

> τοιγὰρ τὸ λοιπὸν εἰσόμεσθα μὲν θεοῖς
> εἴκειν, μαθησόμεσθα δ' 'Ατρείδας σέβειν.

Wherefore, hereafter we shall know to yield to the gods and learn to revere the Atreidae.

When he says he will yield to the gods, he means that he will resign himself, by dying, to the inescapable fate which the gods, in

51. Knox, 'The Ajax', p. 11 with note 66, with reference to Ellendt–Genthe, *Lexicon Sophocleum*; cf. also Wigodsky, '"Salvation" of Ajax', pp. 155f.

52. In Homer (*Il.* 22. 395ff.), Hector is no longer alive when he is bound to Achilles' chariot with the belt he received from Ajax. According to Jebb (*Sophocles*, p. 235), Sophocles cannot have invented the version found in the *Ajax*. However, Sophocles' treatment may be the source of the epigrams *A.P.* 7. 151 and 152. Cf. Kamerbeek on 1031; Stanford on 1029–31.

their superior power, have appointed for him.[53] At the same time, he acknowledges that victory is with the Atreidae; a victory, however, that will be disastrous for them. The implicit irony in the transposition of the verbs εἴκειν and σέβειν was remarked by the scholiast. σέβειν, he points out, belongs to the gods, while εἴκειν is more appropriate to men.[54] Ajax regards Tecmessa's pleas as a demand to humble himself before the Atreidae. The bitter irony of his words[55] is emphasized by the question τί μή; (668). When we penetrate this veil of irony, we perceive that, while what he says may be taken to imply his humble surrender, it really foreshadows the moral defeat of his adversaries. The double meaning of the whole speech is mirrored in the particle τοιγάρ (666). His companions suppose that Ajax means he will put an end to the misfortunes his sword has brought him by submitting to the Atreidae. But he means no such thing. He is convinced that he cannot escape the unlucky sword and must therefore die by it.[56]

Ajax bases his decision to yield to the gods and the Atreidae on the law of the cosmos. As winter yields to summer, and night to day, he too must submit to change (677):

> ἡμεῖς δὲ πῶς οὐ γνωσόμεσθα σωφρονεῖν;
> And how shall we not learn to be of sound mind?

His hearers believe that he means to yield and subordinate himself to the stronger, the sons of Atreus. But for him, such submission to shame is impossible. He can only surrender to death. His *sophrosyne* is utterly different from that which Menelaus (1075) and Agamemnon (1259) demand. Sound-minded, with true self-

---

53. Schadewaldt, 'Aias und Antigone', pp. 75f.; Lucas, *Tragic Poets, loc. cit.*

54. ἐπιφθόνως ἔφρασεν ἐν εἰρωνείᾳ ἀντιστρέψας τὴν τάξιν· ἔδει γὰρ εἰπεῖν θεοὺς μὲν σέβειν, εἴκειν δὲ 'Ατρείδαις, ὡς τῶν 'Ατρειδῶν οὖν ἤδη καὶ θεομαχούντων. Cf. on this Kamerbeek.

55. This was observed by Jebb, *Sophocles*, p. xxxvi; Radermacher, *Sophokles Aias erkl.*; Schadewaldt, 'Aias und Antigone', pp. 73f.; Dirlmeier, 'Der Aias des Sophokles', *Neue Jahrb. f. Antike u. deutsche Bildung* 1 (1938), 313; Kamerbeek, *Plays of Sophocles*; Errandonea, 'Monologues', pp. 23f., 37, 39; Stanford, *Sophocles, Ajax*; Schlesinger, 'Erhaltung...', pp. 379f.; Ronnet, *Sophocle*, p. 109; and others; but denied by T. v. Wilamowitz, *Sophokles*, p. 65 and Ebeling, 'Missverständnisse...', p. 296, n. 6, and 298, because it does not fit their general view.

56. Cf. Kitto, *Form and Meaning*, p. 194.

knowledge[57] and mastery of himself, he goes to his death, in order to salvage what is most precious to him: his soul's nobility, his honor, his very self. Submission to the world's order requires him to seek death. In this way only can he preserve his honor and avoid disgrace; for longer life could be bought only at the sacrifice of his supreme treasure.[58] Ajax' *sophrosyne* consists in his awareness of his position in the order of things and his decision to occupy it.

According to the law of changes wrought by time, not even the oath, the seal of absolute loyalty between men, is permanent (646–9). By attempting to murder the Greek chiefs, Ajax has broken the oath sworn to Tyndareus.[59] In like manner, he was deceived and defrauded by them (1135, 1137). Neither unconditional friendship nor unconditional enmity lasts forever. Ajax now knows that (679–82):

We should only hate our enemy so much as is due to one who will hereafter be our friend, and as for my friend, I shall only be willing to benefit him with my services so far as is due to one who will not always remain [my friend].

He complies with this law by dying: for when he is dead, he will cease to hate his enemies, and they will cease to hate him. Odysseus will become his advocate (1318ff.) and change from enemy to friend (1377). As for his friends, he will no longer act towards them as though they will remain friends forever, but, regarding all human friendships as unreliable, will qualify his services accordingly. He means by this that he will no longer serve them at all. He is out of place in a world where friends and enemies (because they are κακοί) constantly change,[60] wants nothing further to do with it, and is resolved to leave it. The future tense of βουλήσομαι (though the future of this verb is often used for the present) here has the same enigmatic reference as τὸ λοιπὸν

57. Helen North, *Sophrosyne: Self-Knowledge and Self-Restraint in Greek Literature*, Cornell Studies in Class. Philol. 35 (Ithaca, N.Y. 1966), pp. 50ff.

58. Cf. 470–80; Whitman, *Sophocles*, p. 77. Errandonea failed to recognize this; he draws a distinction between honorable death in open warfare against the Atreidae (hinted at, according to him, in lines 470–80) and humiliating suicide, and concludes from this that Ajax changed his mind (see above p. 73 with n. 22).

59. Cf. Jebb on 1113 and Kamerbeek on 1111, 1112, whereas the latter says on 648, 649, that Ajax has not sworn an oath; Knox, 'The Ajax', pp. 14f.

60. Diog. Laert. 1. 87; cf. the commentaries of Radermacher and Kamerbeek.

εἰσόμεσθα and μαθήσομαι in 666f. and γνωσόμεσθα in 677; all point forward to the time of his death.

Towards the end of his speech, Ajax, turning to his companions, indicates that he means to die in terms that, though enigmatic, are unmistakable[61] to those who can understand. This was remarked by the scholiast in his comment on line 687: 'The intention to commit suicide is clear to the spectator, but hidden from the chorus', for they believe him when he says (684–92):

> But concerning these things all will be well. But you, woman, go within and pray to the gods that in all fullness the desires of my heart may be fulfilled. And you, companions, honor my requests in the same way as this woman does, and give this message to Teucer when he comes: let him take care for me and thought for you. For I am going thither where it is necessary to go. But do as I bid you, and perhaps you will soon hear that, though I am now ill-fortuned, I have been saved (or: found my safety).

Ajax breaks off his meditation with the final remark: ἀλλ' ἀμφὶ μὲν τούτοισιν εὖ σχήσει. This can only mean that death will remedy his misfortunes, but 'his hearers take it as a confirmation of his renunciation of suicide'.[62] Then, turning to Tecmessa, he enjoins her to 'pray to the gods that in all fullness (διὰ τέλους) the desires of my heart may be fulfilled'. Here, his death (τέλος θανάτου)[63] is again hinted at, in the phrase διὰ τέλους. The full significance of τοὐμὸν ὧν ἐρᾷ κέαρ will later be clearly revealed in Tecmessa's mournful reflections over his corpse (967f.): ὧν γὰρ ἠράσθη τυχεῖν ἐκτήσαθ' αὐτῷ θάνατον ὅνπερ ἤθελεν ('For what he longed to obtain, he has gotten for himself, the death which he wanted').

Likewise, only later is it fully apparent what he means by the message he commands his companions to deliver to Teucer on his return (688f.): 'Let him take care for me and thought for you.' It anticipates his prayer to Zeus in the death-monologue: that Teucer will lift his body from the sword and prevent his enemies from throwing it to the dogs and birds of prey (826ff.).[64] Earlier, in his farewell speech (565ff.), he had left instructions for Teucer

61. Even Bowra is compelled to admit this, but he argues that, thanks to tragic irony, Ajax' speech is truer than he himself realizes.

62. Stanford, *Sophocles, Ajax*, p. 150.

63. *Il.* 3. 309; 5. 553 etc. The word *telos* alone is also often used for death, cf. Liddell–Scott s.v. II. 3, p. 1773*b*; Reinhardt, *Sophokles*, p. 35.

64. Kamerbeek is compelled to admit that the instructions to Teucer fall outside the deception.

to remove his son Eurysaces to Salamis. Subsequently, Teucer will protect the boy (983ff., 1171ff.).

Ajax' determination to die rings still more clearly in the next line (690): ἐγὼ γὰρ εἶμ' ἐκεῖσ' ὅποι πορευτέον. While Tecmessa and the chorus suppose that he means he will go to bury his sword and to bathe, the choice of words and the impersonal construction of the subordinate clause (with the verbal adjective πορευτέον) indicate that he has in mind the path to that place where all men go at death.[65] The significance of the causal particle γάρ can only be understood in the light of Ajax' determination to die.[66]

The last two lines of the speech (691f.) forecast Ajax' salvation in death. Soon, his friends will hear that he has found his safety – not only from the vengeance of the Atreidae, but, above all, from a world to which he is irreconcilably opposed and in which he has been wretched (δυστυχῶ).[67] He will be saved, and with him his honor, his better self. It may be that here he also recalls the common thought that life is nothing but sorrow, and regards his fate as confirming the ancient truth that it is better not to have been born or else to depart from this world as soon as possible.[68] Or perhaps his thoughts are of the sort we encounter in Heraclitus and Euripides, echoes of which recur in Plato and, later, in Cicero: that life on earth is death, and death true life.[69] A kindred thought occurs in Ajax' second speech, when he says (581f.) that his malady

65. πορεύομαι of the way to the beyond: Soph. *Ant.* 892f. οἵ πορεύσομαι πρὸς τοὺς ἐμαυτῆς; Plat. *Phaed.* 67 B (enigmatic as here) ἀφικομένῳ οἵ ἐγὼ πορεύομαι; *Menex.* 236 D πορεύονται τὴν εἱμαρμένην πορείαν. In Latin this sense, the word *migrare* is used in this sense, cf. Cic. *rep.* 6. 9, 'antequam ex hac vita migro' and 6. 15, 'ex hominum vita migrandum est' and, on this usage in general, *Thes. L.L.* VIII 936 d. Cf. also Kamerbeek on this line.

66. Kamerbeek on 690.

67. Cf. 925ff. ἔμελλες...στερεόφρων ἄρ' ἐξανύσσειν κακὰν μοῖραν ἀπειρεσίων πόνων. Stanford compares Eurip. *I.A.* 1440.

68. *Cert. Hom. et Hes.* 5, p. 228 Allen; Theogn. 425ff.; Hdt. 1. 31. 3; Soph. *O.C.* 1224ff.: Plat. *Phaed.* 62 A; Aristot. frg. 44 R. (pp. 12f. Walzer); cf. Wigodsky, '"Salvation" of Ajax', p. 158 (Stanford, *Sophocles, Ajax*, pp. 237f.).

69. Eurip. frg. 361, 638, 833 N.; Aristoph. *Ran.* 1082, 1477; Plat. *Gorg.* 492 E; *Crat.* 400 C; Cic. *rep.* 6. 14; *Tusc.* 1. 75; *Scaur.* 4 (all following Plato); Augustine, *C.D.* 12. 21 (probably following Cicero). The thought is Heraclitean as is that of lines 646f. and 669–76 (see below): frg. 62, 77, 88; Sext. Emp. *Pyrrh. hyp.* 3. 230. E. R. Dodds, *Plato, Gorgias, with Introd. and Comm.* (Oxford 1959), p. 300; A. Ronconi, *Cicerone, Somnium Scipionis, introd. e comm.* (Florence 1961), pp. 8of. On Sophocles and Heraclitus, Webster, *Introduction*, p. 51; J. C. Kamerbeek,

craves the surgeon's knife (i.e. death by the sword is the only remedy for his misfortunes).[70] Finally, it is possible that the ἄπιστος ἑταιρείας λιμήν ('untrustworthy harbor of friendship', 683) is meant to evoke the counter-idea of death as a harbor of safety (Eurip. *Bacch.* 903), the λιμὴν Ἄιδου (*Ant.* 1284) or λιμὴν κακῶν (*de sublimi* 9. 7).[71] This would be quite in keeping with the storm-imagery of the earlier part of the speech (674f.).

How are we to account for this pervasive ambiguity? Clearly, it will not admit of the sort of explanation Bowra has proposed.[72] If Ajax wishes to go on living in harmony with the world, his utterances cannot have a veiled reference to suicide. If he has not changed and wishes to deceive his friends for no other purpose than that of gaining an opportunity to carry out his plan, it is not necessary, indeed it would be foolish, to allow them to glimpse his true intention behind his deceitful words. If we assume that he does so, we shall also be compelled to assume that the poet makes his hero speak out of character for his own technical purpose. The argument advanced by some scholars, that Ajax, unable to tell an overt lie, speaks the truth equivocally, is, as we have seen, absurd. 'In order to clear Ajax of this apparent lie', Whitman[73] rightly observes, 'they have involved him in a far more complex

Studia varia Carolo Guilelmo Vollgraff a discipulis oblata (Amsterdam 1948), pp. 84–98 (on the speech of Ajax, pp. 89f.; however there is no reference to these lines); Diller (above n. 8), pp. 26f., 30f.; E. Dönt, 'Zur Deutung des Tragischen bei Sophokles', *Antike und Abendland* 17 (1971), 48ff.; see also Schlesinger, 'Erhaltung...', p. 379. On σεσωμένον as saved from death see 812 and *El.* 59f. λόγῳ θανὼν ἔργοισι σωθῶ and 1229 θανόντα σεσωμένον (Jebb) and Liddell–Scott s.v. 1, p. 1748a.

70. Cf. Plat. *Phaed.* 118 A Ἀσκληπιῷ ὀφείλομεν ἀλεκτρυόνα. 'Socrates hopes to awake cured like those who are healed by ἐγκοίμησις (incubatio) in the Asklepieion at Epidauros': J. Burnet, *Plato's Phaedo with Introd. and Notes* (Oxford 1911), p. 118. This interpretation is rejected by U. v. Wilamowitz, *Platon* 2 (Berlin 1920), 57f. σῴζομαι in the sense of recovering: Liddell–Scott s.v. 1, p. 1748b (Stanford).

71. Kamerbeek on 682, 683, with abundant material to which may be added Joh. Chrysost. *adv. opp. vitae mon.* 2. 9 (*PG* 47, cols. 345f.).

72. Musurillo, *Light and Darkness*, p. 15, following Bowra, *Sophoclean Tragedy*, p. 44, accepts the speech's ambiguity as tragic irony. Grossmann, 'Das Lachen...', p. 84, also assumes tragic irony, though in another way. These interpreters start from the supposition that the ambiguity is not intentional and fail to recognize that death in madness is not a tragic event.

73. Cf. Whitman, *Sophocles*, p. 75; Whitman's reference to Jebb is incorrect; it ought to be to U. v. Wilamowitz, *Hermes* 78 (1924), 251 = *Kleine Schriften* 4 (Berlin 1962), p. 344.

dishonesty.' As we have also seen, the theories of Reinhardt and Knox (that deception and self-deception are linked together, or that conscious reflection is thwarted by irrational drives) do not sufficiently account for the obviously intentional character of the ambiguity. What, then, does it mean?

For all of Sophocles' tragic heroes, there is a point at which they become aware of the tragic nature of their situation. By this means, tragedy rises above situations, such as exist in epic poetry,[74] that are only outwardly tragic. Ajax' speech (as Reinhardt, in fact, perceived) represents such a point. When he first woke from his madness, Ajax was seized with shame and despair and in that state conceived a yearning for death to which he gave lyric expression (360f., 387–427). Later, this yearning was consolidated in his determination to kill himself (430–80). Now, at the heart of the tragedy, in that clarity of vision that comes to those who find themselves between life and certain death,[75] he is fully conscious of the hopelessness of his predicament, the inevitability of his fate, and the insoluble nature of the tragic conflict in which he is involved. By the clear light of reason which shines into the dark depths of his existence, he perceives that change is the law of the world. At the same time, he knows that he himself cannot change as Tecmessa expects him to do.[76] Thus, he can only adapt himself to change by yielding and withdrawing from the world.[77] He compares himself to those natural forces which yield to change. He sees his destiny deeply anchored in the law of the world, which applies to mankind as well as to the cosmos, to moral as well as to physical nature.[78]

The world's demand that he accommodate himself to its laws is answered by his death (669–76):

For even the dread and mightiest things give way to authorities. In this way snow-piled winter retreats before fair-fruited summer. Night's

---

74. A. Lesky, *Gnomon* 21 (1949), 213.

75. F. Dostoievsky, *The Idiot*, book 1, part 1, ch. 2. Cf. R.Camerer, *Gnomon* 22 (1950), 140.

76. On the immutability of the *ethos* (595) cf. Pind. *Ol.* 11. 19f. and Heracl. B 119.

77. This paradox was independently recognized by M. Simpson, 'Sophocles' Ajax: his Madness and Transformation', *Arethusa* 2 (1969), 78ff. While writing this version of my paper, I did not have access to Simpson's article, which coincides with my interpretation in other respects also.

78. Cf. Kamerbeek on 669–77 (*Plays of Sophocles*, p. 140).

dark circle departs for white-horsed day to set her lights ablaze. The dread blast of the gale slackens and gives peace to the sounding sea. Also, sleep which subdues all things, having bound, sets free, nor when it seizes does it hold forever.

As winter must give way to summer, as night must yield to day and sleep to waking, so must Ajax – whose life has become like night, death and fetters[79] – give way to the gods. As 'the dread blast of the gale slackens and gives peace to the sounding sea' (674 ἐκοίμισε), so Hermes Chthonios will bring him peace in the harbor of death, rest from the storms of life (832 κοιμίσαι).[80] He realizes that in the cosmic course of things he is destined to give way, and compares himself – the δεινός (205), the τὰ δεινὰ καρτερῶν (650) – to the καρτερώτατα (669) of the natural world: the δεινὰ πνεύματα (674), the νυκτὸς αἰανὴς κύκλος (672) (where αἰανής can be taken as a synonym of δεινός),[81] the hard-packed snow of winter.[82]

But the great images derived from nature have a light, as well as a dark side. Cold winter is followed by fruitful summer; the darkness of night by the light of day; the fetters of sleep, death's brother,[83] by the freedom of waking; the blast of stormy winds by serene calm at sea. In all of these Ajax finds analogies to his own situation. His death will be summer with plentiful fruit; the light of a bright day; rest in a secure harbor after a stormy voyage; the waking of true life. As early as the *kommos*, after waking from his madness, he had voiced the reversal of day and night, of light and darkness (393ff.): ἰὼ σκότος, ἐμὸν φάος, ἔρεβος ὦ φαεννότατον,

---

79. Death binds: Pind. *Paean* 6. 86: θρασεῖ φόνῳ πεδάσαις; sleep too: Hom. *Od.* 23. 17: ὅς μ' ἐπέδησε φίλα βλέφαρ' ἀμφικαλύψας. Kamerbeek, thinking that λύει πεδήσας means that sleep as the sleep of death 'unbinds by fettering', cannot be right. Line 676 is not ambiguous as are not lines 674f. (see next note). In analogy to these lines the meaning of λύει πεδήσας is that sleep binds and unbinds in turn.

80. Cf. 205–7 νῦν γὰρ ὁ δεινὸς μέγας ὠμοκρατὴς Αἴας θολερῷ κεῖται χειμῶνι νοσήσας and 258 ὀξὺς νότος ὡς λήγει. Kamerbeek's interpretation of lines 674f. cannot be correct because in this context they must mean concrete phenomena to which Ajax refers himself. Stanford is right in following Jebb and Wolff–Bellermann with reference to Hor. *Carm.* 1. 3. 15f.: 'arbiter Hadriae...tollere seu ponere vult freta'; Verg. *Aen.* 3. 69f.: 'placataque venti dant maria' and 5. 763: 'placidi straverunt aequora venti'. Cf. also Radermacher on 674f.

81. Kamerbeek on 672.

82. Diller, *Göttliches...*, pp. 9f. = pp. 5f. Cf. also Schadewaldt, 'Aias und Antigone', p. 74.

83. Hom. *Il.* 14. 231; 16. 672, 682; Hes. *Theog.* 212, 758f.

ὡς ἐμοί, ἕλεσθε, ἕλεσθέ μ' οἰκήτορα ('O darkness, my light, O nether gloom, brightest of things to me, take, O take me to dwell with you'). For him, death is light, and light is salvation.[84] The cosmic comparisons are grounded on the same thoughts which he earlier voiced when speaking of his death.[85] Life and death are interchanged: life is death and death is life. The conflict in which the hero sees himself entangled is the purest form of tragic conflict,[86] since the salvation to be gained through submission to the laws of the world is inextricably connected, indeed identical, with his destruction: death is the very form of salvation.

The tragic paradox[87] that Ajax can only accommodate himself to the world by withdrawing from it, finds its most condensed expression in this ambivalence. Thus, the actions by which he purposes to reconcile himself with the world are actions that lead to his death; or rather, conversely, he regards that course of action which leads to his death as leading also to his reconciliation with the order of things and his proper adjustment in it. He regards his death on the sea-shore as a cleansing from pollution and a liberation from Athena's wrath; as an act of submission to the gods and of accommodation to their divine authority; as an acceptance of the mutability of friendship and enmity; and as his salvation. He regards the driving of the sword into his body as a separation from the fatal gift. The final and paradoxical tragic significance of the sword's deep symbolism[88] is here revealed. Ajax has compared himself to the sword, and now he dies by it. Symbolic, in the first instance, of the conception of friendship and enmity, it becomes, consequently, the hero's own symbol, the embodiment of the heroic friend–foe morality. As such, it is not simply the instrument, but indeed the cause, of his death. Forged by the Erinys (1034) as the agency of his undoing, it acts, as it

84. On φῶς in the sense of σωτηρία cf. E. Fraenkel on Aesch. *Agam.* 522.

85. After writing these lines, I discovered that this interpretation of lines 669–76 had already been given by O. Becker, *Das Bild des Weges und verwandte Vorstellungen im frühgriechischen Denken*, *Hermes* Einzelschr. 4 (Berlin 1937), pp. 205f.; see also his remarks on 654ff., 685 and 690. λύει however cannot be compared with the Homeric γούνατα λύειν and similar expressions.

86. Cf. Lesky, *Die griechische Tragödie*, p. 27: 'geschlossen tragischer Konflikt'.

87. On the tragic paradox in the *Oedipus Tyrannus* see W. C. Helmbold, 'The Paradox in the *Oedipus*', *AJP* 72 (1951), 293–300.

88. Kitto, *Form and Meaning*, pp. 193f.; Knox, 'The Ajax', pp. 3ff.

were, independently and through its own power.[89] Ajax dies because of what he is. His death is ordained by the world-order because he is Ajax. The sword has a significance similar to that of the bed in the *Trachiniae*.[90] Both hint at the tragic possibilities of man's existence as male and female.

From this interpretation, it follows that Ajax' speech is not addressed to his friends, but is a soliloquy designed by the poet to interpret his hero's fate to the spectators.[91] It has long been recognized that the speech is a sort of monologue, but its character as such (up to line 683) has only recently been elaborated by Knox.[92] Still more recent is E. Fraenkel's[93] suggestion that an analogy is furnished by Eteocles' speech at lines 653–76 of Aeschylus' *Seven*. In fact, up to line 683 the speech already has the apparent character of a meditation, in the course of which the speaker forgets his surroundings. He does not address himself to those present, and speaks of Tecmessa in the third person as 'this woman' (652).[94] Since his death is now certain, since he has come to terms with the world, he has nothing more to say to mortal men. He must come to an understanding with himself alone. Only at line 684 does he conclude his meditation and turn to speak to

89. Cf. Hom *Od.* 16. 294; Val. Flacc. *Arg.* 5. 541; Bowra, *Sophoclean Tragedy*, pp. 44f.; J. Dingel, *Das Requisit in der griechischen Tragödie* (Diss. Tübingen 1967), p. 179.

90. P. E. Easterling, 'Sophocles, *Trachiniae*', *Bulletin Univ. of London, Inst. of Class. Studies* 15 (1968), 66.

91. Though the audience may not be able fully to understand the meaning of the speech during the performance, there is certainly a difference between the audience and those on the stage who are deceived. On this question see, besides Perrotta, *Sofocle*, p. 148, Pohlenz, *Griechische Tragödie*, p. 175; G. Méautis, *Sophocle: Essai sur le héros tragique* (Paris 1957), pp. 36ff. and Errandonea, 'Monologues', p. 23; U. von Wilamowitz-Moellendorff, 'Lesefrüchte', *Hermes* 59 (1924), 252 = *Kleine Schriften* 4 (Berlin 1962), p. 344; Howald, *Griechische Tragödie*, p. 99; Kamerbeek, *Plays of Sophocles*, p. 152; Waldock, *Sophocles the Dramatist*, pp. 70f., 74f., 78f.; and especially Parlavantza-Friedrich, *Täuschungsszenen*, pp. 18ff.

92. Knox, 'The Ajax', pp. 10ff. The speech was earlier characterized as a soliloquy by Welcker, 'Über den Aias...', pp. 233f. = p. 313; Ebeling, 'Missverständnisse...', p. 299; Reinhardt, *Sophokles*, p. 35; Weinstock, *Sophokles*, p. 45; and others.

93. 'Zwei Aias-Szenen hinter der Bühne', *Mus. Helv.* 24 (1967), 82f.

94. See the characteristics of soliloquy as given by W. Schadewaldt, *Monolog und Selbstgespräch*, Neue Philol. Unters. 2 (Berlin 1926, repro. 1966), pp. 28f. According to Schadewaldt, solitude is not necessary for a soliloquy; if the speaker imagines himself to be alone, that is sufficient.

those around him. But even here a veil of self-absorption covers the clear references to his death.[95] He is already detached from humanity, and his words come as from another world, which is not that of his companions. Even so, their meaning can only be hidden from those who have let themselves be deceived by what preceded.[96] Tecmessa and the chorus, the witnesses of this oracular speech, fail to comprehend its deeper meaning because of their own human limitations. Hence, they are deceived. 'Seeing, they see not, and hearing, they hear not.'[97]

We must now look at the beginning of the speech and see whether Ajax' words (650–3) support our interpretation:

> κἀγὼ γάρ, ὃς τὰ δείν' ἐκαρτέρουν τότε,
> βαφῇ σίδηρος ὥς, ἐθηλύνθην στόμα
> πρὸς τῆσδε τῆς γυναικός· οἰκτίρω δέ νιν
> χήραν παρ' ἐχθροῖς παῖδά τ' ὀρφανὸν λιπεῖν.

Ajax says that even he, 'erst so wondrous firm – yea, as iron hardened in the dipping[98] – felt the keen edge of my temper[99] softened by yon woman's words'. (Jebb's translation.) Pity, he feels, forbids him to leave her a widow, and his son an orphan,

95. Comparisons with the words of Clytemnestra in Aesch. *Agam.* 973 and Orestes in *Choeph.* 674ff., such as drawn by Méautis, *Sophocle*, p. 40, Maddalena, *Sofocle*, pp. 34f. and Stanford, *Sophocles, Ajax*, p. 287 are therefore incorrect.

96. Cf. the remark of the scholiast on 687 (above p. 83); Ronnet, *Sophocle*, p. 144: 'Trop prompts à prendre leurs désirs pour des réalités et parce qu'ils n'ont pas un instant compris leur chef, ils n'ont pas senti l'amère ironie de ses paroles, ils n'ont pas remarqué que ses derniers mots étaient un adieu'; Jebb, *Sophocles*, p. xxxvii; Schadewaldt, *Aias und Antigone*, p. 70; Linforth, 'Three Scenes', p. 19; Kirkwood, *Sophoclean Drama*, p. 161; Stanford, *Sophocles, Ajax*, p. 287.

97. Soph. frg. 923 Pearson: οὐ κωφοὶ μόνον, ἀλλ' οὐδ' ὁρῶντες εἰσορῶσι τἀμφανῆ. Because of their credulity, the chorus later call themselves (911) κωφός.

98. As iron is hardened by being plunged in water (which generally softens things), so Ajax was first hardened, not softened, by Tecmessa's entreaty. Here also, Kamerbeek has gone too far in his search for ambiguities (as also Wolff–Bellermann). See now Fraenkel, 'Zwei Aias-Szenen', p. 79. With the construction ἐκαρτέρουν βαφῇ cf. Eurip. *Heracld.* 837 ἐκαρτέρει μάχη.

99. In spite of Fraenkel, 'Zwei Aias-Szenen...', p. 80. 4, I take it in that way as denoting the sharp edge of the sword (which is meant by σίδηρος) (cf. Hom. *Il.* 18. 34; 23. 30; *Od.* 16. 294), cf. Linforth, 'Three Scenes', p. 14; Knox, "The Ajax', p. 15; M. Untersteiner, *Sofocle, Aiace* (Milan 1956), p. 139; Errandonea, 'Monologues', pp. 27f. Kamerbeek and Stanford are of the same opinion as Jebb, Wolff–Bellermann and Radermacher; they all regard the word as ambiguous.

among his enemies. We must take these words as a true account of his feelings. Tecmessa's appeal, by which he had first been hardened, has finally softened him; his over-hardened mind has broken like over-hardened steel or an over-bent bow.[100] While he was in the tent, he was touched by pity for his wife and child.[101]

But pity cannot alter his resolve,[102] any more than it altered Hector's in the sixth book of the *Iliad*.[103] Like Hector, he does not succumb to the temptation to be untrue to himself. He rejects such feelings as 'womanish', but they bring him to a deeper understanding of the impossibility of obeying their promptings to save his wife and son by resolving his quarrel with his enemies. As we have said before, he is fully conscious of his place in the world; of his conflict with the cosmic order; and of the tragic paradox that, to fit himself into the world, he must yield and leave it. Consequently, he recognizes that only by dying can he be reconciled with his enemies and satisfy Tecmessa's demands. These are the ends which he magnificently imagines his death as fulfilling:

100. *Ant.* 474ff.: τὸν ἐγκρατέστατον σίδηρον ὀπτὸν ἐκ πυρὸς περισκελῆ θραυσθέντα καὶ ῥαγέντα πλεῖστ' ἂν εἰσίδοις.

101. Welcker, 'Über den Aias', pp. 230f. = p. 311; Jebb, *Sophocles*, p. xxxiii; van Pesch, *De idee...*, p. 200; Linforth, 'Three Scenes', p. 14; Kitto, *Form and Meaning*, pp. 189ff.; Errandonea, 'Monologues', pp. 27, 34, 37, 39; Kamerbeek, *Plays of Sophocles*, p. 134; Knox, 'The Ajax', p. 15; Stanford, *Plays of Sophocles*, pp. 142, 283. I do not agree with Tycho von Wilamowitz, *Sophokles*, pp. 57ff., Schmid, *Geschichte*, p. 337, n. 3, Howald, *Griechische Tragödie*, p. 98, Untersteiner, *Sofocle, Aiace*, p. 139, and Fraenkel, 'Zwei Aias-Szenen', p. 80, who think that there must have been a conversation between Ajax and Tecmessa in the tent during the choral ode. There is absolutely no evidence in the text to support such an opinion (cf. Errandonea, 'Monologues', p. 37, n. 27). Ajax rejects Tecmessa's appeals to his pity so harshly (585ff.) that we may guess that he is not inaccessible to such feelings (cf. Jebb, *Sophocles*, p. xxxiii; Adams, *Sophocles the Playwright*, pp. 32f.; Musurillo, *Light and Darkness*, p. 12) and that there is no need for a renewal of the entreaty. Is it probable that the poet would have imagined as taking place off-stage what was dramatically impossible on the stage itself? Ajax, in fact, expressly says what has moved him to pity: time (i.e. the time while he was alone in the tent). In addition, at Ajax' command Tecmessa had shut the door of the tent from *outside* (579, 581, with the plural at 593!) and must therefore have remained on-stage with Ajax' friends during the subsequent choral ode, expecting her husband's suicide. Only in this way can Ajax' speech, however we interpret it, have the most surprising effect on both those on the stage and the spectators.

102. Whitman, *Sophocles*, p. 77; Knox, 'The Ajax', p. 15; Ronnet, *Sophocle*, p. 39.

103. 6. 440ff. Like Hector, Ajax cannot be κακός.

'Well,[104] I will go to the bathing place...' Through the words οἰκτίρω λιπεῖν,[105] the poet invites Ajax' companions, who are only too eager to believe their chief has changed his mind, to understand what follows. At lines 678ff. he does something similar, making Ajax first say what his friends want to hear (that hatred of one's foes must be kept within certain bounds), and only then what he has come to tell them: that his services to them are at an end.[106] By this means, the poet makes it easy for Ajax' words to be misunderstood on both occasions.

If this interpretation is correct, our dilemma is solved. We are no longer faced with the alternatives that either Ajax is telling the truth but has changed, or has not changed and is lying. He has no intention of deceiving, but is speaking only to himself. The difficulties involved in Reinhardt's interpretation – which is the nearest to the poet's thought – are thus removed: the hero does not deceive, nor is his soul affected by its own deception. In fact, the poet does not allow him to utter a single word that does not arise from the essential nature of the situation. Not a word is aimed at a purely technical end. Rather, the poet accomplishes his purpose, which is to deceive Ajax' companions, through a complete harmony of form and content in Ajax' speech. Here we see Sophocles at the peak of his art; for Ajax' words, while they spring from the heart of the tragic situation, nevertheless accomplish the desired technical effect. Moreover, through an ambiguous speech designed to deceive, the poet paradoxically reveals the tragedy's innermost meaning. All the criticisms of the dramatist's art that emerge from the interpretations we have discussed indicate nothing

104. The commentaries of Jebb, Wolf–Bellermann, De Falco (*Sofocle, Aiace* (Naples 1950)), Untersteiner, Kamerbeek and Stanford don't say anything about the important particle ἀλλ'. In my interpretation of the context it cannot be adversative as is assumed by Ebeling, 'Missverständnisse...', p. 296 (cf. also Ronnet, *Sophocle*, p. 39), but it must be used in the sense of practical consent, expression of willingness to act in a required way; cf. J. D. Denniston, *The Greek Particles*, 2nd ed. (Oxford 1954), p. 17, who refers to *Trach.* 389 πεύθου μολοῦσα...'Ἀλλ' εἶμι. With the word ἀλλ' Ajax' 'inward' answer to Tecmessa's requests commences. Emil Staiger (trans.), *Sophokles, Tragödien* (Basel 1942 = Fischer Bücherei, *Exempla classica* 81 (1963), p. 26) correctly translates 'denn'.

105. There is no ambiguity in these words, as many interpreters (like Jebb, Radermacher, Kamerbeek and Stanford) assume; cf. Kühner–Gerth 2, pp. 6. 2 and 73, n. 3 and Wolff–Bellermann.

106. Cf. Jebb *ad loc.*

more than imperfect understanding on the part of interpreters who have failed to meet its challenge. By having the hero speak the truth in an ambiguous and ironical fashion, the poet makes it possible for Ajax' companions to be deceived, while allowing the real meaning to shine through to the audience.

Defective understanding, it seems to me, is likewise responsible for the theory that in this play a kind of Aeschylean guilt and atonement has not been harmonized with the new Sophoclean view of tragedy.[107] There can be little doubt that the prologue of the *Ajax*, in which Athena condemns human presumption, is influenced by the lost *Niobe* of Aeschylus.[108] Ajax is meant to serve as a deterrent example to Odysseus (127-33). In Calchas' prophecy, the cause of Athena's wrath is expressly stated to be Ajax' hybris towards her (758-77). But is it really true that the Aeschylean conception of avenging justice has remained in the play, as an alien element, side by side with the new Sophoclean view of tragedy as an inescapable conflict grounded in the structure of the world?

This view of the matter is only possible if the scenes discussed above have not been correctly understood. These scenes are not designed to illustrate, in an Aeschylean sense, the punishment of hybris by the gods, but to exhibit Ajax' true nature.[109] His arrogant attitude towards Athena, on the two occasions recounted by Calchas, shows him as a great man who, precisely because of his greatness, fails to recognize his place in the world, but claims an equality with the gods, or even exalts himself above them.[110] His bearing towards Athena in the prologue serves the same purpose. His *hamartia* lies not in single actions (*hamartemata*), but, as Welcker (68 = 286) suspected, in his very nature. Ajax fails to conform to the world, which is divinely disposed. The divine world-order, which seems cruel[111] to those who clash with it, is the dark back-

---

107. Schmid, *Geschichte*, p. 338; Reinhardt, *Sophokles*, p. 38. On the problem, Lesky, *Tragische Dichtung*, pp. 110ff.; Grossmann, 'Das Lachen...', p. 72.

108. Reinhardt, *Sophokles*, pp. 19-23.

109. Whitman, *Sophocles*, pp. 69ff.; Wigodsky, '"Salvation" of Ajax', p. 152; Knox, 'The Ajax', pp. 8f., 18ff.; G. M. Kirkwood, 'Homer's and Sophocles' Ajax', in M. J. Anderson (ed.), *The Classical Drama and its Influences: Studies Presented to H. D. F. Kitto* (New York 1963), pp. 61f.; Grossmann, 'Das Lachen...', p. 80. 110. 777: οὐ κατ' ἄνθρωπον φρονῶν.

111. Sophocles is far from conceiving the gods according to human standards of justice. As Reinhardt, Lesky and Kitto have correctly realized, the gods are

drop against which the action takes place. It is always dimly present as the cause of the hero's sufferings. Three times this backdrop is illuminated, and divine power flashes forth clearly discernible: first, at the beginning of the play, in the Athena-scene of the prologue; then, in the middle, in the seer's message; and again at the end, when Odysseus reappears in a scene that recalls the prologue. In these scenes, Ajax is shown to be a man of such stature that, while he lives, he cannot fit in the world's divinely appointed order. Only when considered in this light does Ajax' declaration that he must give way to the gods reveal its deeper Sophoclean meaning. The new Sophoclean understanding of the tragic nature of existence, already fully developed in this earliest of the surviving plays, replaces the older Aeschylean interpretation; the ultimate justice of divine punishment is replaced by the ultimate justice of the divine order.[112] Only the outline of the story is still Aeschylean.

As in *Oedipus Tyrannus*, so in the *Ajax*, the tragedy reaches its peak with the hero's insight into reality. Ajax, like Oedipus, changes from a blind man to a seeing one. By degrees, he comes to recognize his true position in the world. His attempt to murder the Greek chiefs shows him in complete blindness, since the deed could not have solved his problem. Furthermore, it does not correspond to the nature of his existence and, consequently, cannot succeed. His failure in the attempt is caused by the reality of the divine world-order ('the gods')[113] and by Athena, who keeps him from gaining his object. This, I think, is the deeper significance of Ajax' madness, mental derangement or delusion – whatever we call his state of mind at that moment. At any rate, he is blind when he considers such a deed a practicable solution of his problem.[114] His vain attempt to escape from a hopeless situation naturally causes an aggravation of his condition. Then, in the very

not bound to justify their decisions; their judgements are of an entirely different order from those of men. The divine world-order, though apparently cruel and impenetrable to human understanding, is not absurd. On this background only is Sophoclean tragedy possible. Cf. H. D. F. Kitto, *Sophocles, Dramatist and Philosopher* (London 1958), p. 45 = *Wege der Forschung*, p. 59.

112. Weinstock, *Sophokles*, pp. 59f.; Knox, 'The Ajax', pp. 19f.; Kitto, *Sophocles*, pp. 42ff. = *Wege der Forschung*, pp. 56ff. Cf. also North, *Sophrosyne*, p. 58.

113. Ronnet, *Sophocle*, pp. 178f.

114. Weinstock, *Sophokles*, p. 59.

depth of his suffering, the truth begins to dawn upon him. First, there is a vague yearning for death. This is the beginning of that process of increasing awareness of reality which was hinted at above (p. 86). The process moves from the level of sentiment to that of morals (*ethos*), and ends with clear intellectual insight.[115] Ajax at last fully recognizes his condition; he is expelled from the world, but, at the same time, accepted by it, and finds his appointed place in the scheme of things. The age of *arete* like his is over, but its high value will endure with him as a hero forever.

Ajax' suffering and death are caused by a defect in his nature, by his acceptance of honor (*timē*) as an absolute value. This defect, in turn, arises from an excess of *arete* and greatness, qualities which are part of his essential being.[116] Ajax himself is conscious of his greatness, which is acknowledged also by Tecmessa, by the chorus, by his enemy Odysseus and even by Athena. Nowhere is it more cogently revealed than in the manner in which he faces the ultimate truth in his last moments of life.[117] His greatness, like that of Oedipus, rests upon his conscious decision to embrace the truth that annihilates, but, at the same time, saves and exalts him.

Through his death, Ajax is reconciled with the divine powers of the world, which are represented by Athena. The goddess' wrath will pursue him only on the day of his death, since afterwards he will fit into the world-order and become a *sophron* (and, consequently, an *eusebes*)[118] of the sort the gods love (132f.). The religious significance of Ajax' statement, that he will purge himself of his stains in order to escape the goddess' heavy wrath (655f.), becomes clear only here. By dying, he will purify himself of the stains which his behavior towards the goddess has brought upon

115. Cf. R. Camerer, *Gnomon* 22 (1950), 139f. Simpson (in the article mentioned above, n. 77) is wrong in supposing that the lower degrees of insight are progressively discarded and replaced by the higher. The entreaty of Tecmessa is justified from her point of view, but it is not valid with respect to the situation of Ajax and therefore he is right to reject it; for Ajax there is no alternative. In face of the tragic necessity, the arguments of Tecmessa, the untragic woman, must give way. Again, Ajax' answer to Tecmessa is not superseded by the deception speech; his arguments are not replaced by better ones, but metaphysically enlarged, strengthened and deepened by the fundamental law of reality.

116. North, *Sophrosyne*, p. 51; Grossmann, 'Das Lachen...', p. 85.

117. Cf. W. Schadewaldt, *Sophokles und das Leid* (Berlin 1947), pp. 22ff. = *Gottheit und Mensch* (above, n. 8), pp. 48ff.

118. On the relation between *sophron* and *eusebes* see *Electra* 307f.; North, *Sophrosyne*, p. 65; Dönt, 'Zur Deutung...', p. 52.

him.[119] It seems that the poet wishes to show Ajax' death in another light than we have seen so far. There are many indications that the hero's suicide is to be understood as a ritual sacrifice by which he atones for his offenses against Athena and is reconciled with her.[120] This will not be surprising if we consider the close relation between tragedy and ritual sacrifice that scholars have recently pointed out.[121] Ajax calls himself αὐτοσφαγής (841); the chorus call him νεοσφαγής (898). σφάζω is the technical term for slaughtering a victim. In addition, the sword is not only a weapon, but also does duty as a sacrificial knife.[122] This latter function may be indicated by σφαγεύς (815).[123] Ajax' careful preparations for his cruel death (823 εὐσκευοῦμεν) are reminiscent of a ritual. The newly sharpened sword (820)[124] and the invocation to the gods (824ff.)[125] call to mind a ritual sacrifice. To be sure, he does not name Athena, but calls upon the gods of light and life, of whom he is taking leave,[126] and the gods of death, who are shortly to welcome him. His thoughts are no longer directed towards the meaning of his death, of which he had spoken in the 'deception'

119. Cf. Eurip. *H.F.* 1324; *I.T.* 1039; Méautis, *Sophocle*, p. 39; Maddalena, *Sofocle*, pp. 34, 38; Ronnet, *Sophocle*, pp. 180f.

120. Lattimore, *Poetry of Greek Tragedy*, pp. 75–7; Jebb and Kamerbeek on line 712; Stanford on 815; P. Guépin, *The Tragic Paradox: Myth and Ritual in Greek Tragedy* (Amsterdam 1968), pp. 3f.; cf. Schadewaldt, *Aias und Antigone*, p. 73.

121. W. Burkert, 'Greek Tragedy and Sacrificial Ritual', *GRBS* 7 (1966), 87–121; Guépin *passim*.

122. So repeatedly in Euripides, too: ξίφος *Phoen.* 1091; *Hec.* 436; φάσγανον (as in Soph. *Ajax* 834) *I.A.* 875, 1429; μάχαιρα *Supp.* 1206. As Ajax hides his sword by burying it in the earth (658ff.), so in Euripides *Suppl.* 1205ff. the sacrificial sword has to be hidden in the recesses of the earth (ἐς γαίας μυχοὺς κρύψον) – though this is to be done only after the sacrifice has been completed. The Corinthians too hide the sacrificial sword in the earth after sacrificing to Hera, cf. M. P. Nilsson, *Griechische Feste* (Darmstadt 1957), p. 58; Burkert, 'Sacrificial Ritual', p. 118, n. 71. There it will be found by the victim himself, as Ajax is drawn to death by the sword of ill-omen itself.

123. Eurip. *Andr.* 1134; in the sense of 'sacrificial butcher' *SIG* 1025. 44.

124. Hom. *Od.* 3. 442f. πέλεκυν ὀξύν.

125. Prayer before slaughtering the victim: Hom. *Il.* 1. 458ff.; 2. 421ff.; *Od.* 3. 437ff.; 12. 356ff.; 14. 421ff. Cf. P. Stengel, *Opferbräuche der Griechen* (Leipzig–Berlin 1910), pp. 14f., 40f.; S. Eitrem, *Opferritus und Voropfer der Griechen und Römer* (Kristiania 1915), pp. 277f.; F. Schwenn, *Gebet und Opfer. Studien zum griechischen Kultus* (Heidelberg 1927), p. 124; W. Burkert, *Homo necans*, RVV 32 (Berlin 1972), p. 11.

126. Invocation of light on leaving life: Soph. *O.C.* 1549f.; Eurip. *Alc.* 244; *Hec.* 435; *I.A.* 1506ff. Cf. also Soph. *Ant.* 806ff., 879f.; Aesch. *Agam.* 1323f.

speech, but to the act of suicide itself. If this is correct, then the words of the chorus near the end of the rejoicing hymn tell us, through the medium of tragic irony, what really happened (710–13): 'Ajax, forgetting his trouble, has performed a complete sacrifice with all due rites, in perfection of loyal worship.'[127] Sacrificial priest and victim are here the same.[128]

The religious significance of Ajax' death is confirmed by his consecration as a hero. By accepting the sufferings sent by the gods, man becomes *eusebes* and wins deathless excellence (ἀθάνατον ἀρετήν, *Philoct.* 1420). In the latter part of the *Ajax* there are hints of what occurs in *Oedipus at Colonus*: the man who has come through suffering to truth is finally received by the gods.[129] By sacrificing himself voluntarily, Ajax purges himself of pollution and is reconciled[130] with Athena. Though submitting to change, he retains his immutability (the quality of the gods),[131] and takes his place by the side of Athens' protectress, as a helpful and beneficent hero. Athena herself, at the very moment of his deepest humiliation, hinted (in a general way) at his restoration (131f.): ἡμέρα κλίνει τε κἀνάγει πάλιν ἅπαντα τἀνθρώπεια. His body provides asylum for a suppliant (his son Eurysaces, 1171ff.), and thus has the power of a hero's tomb even before the question of his burial has been settled.[132] Men will remember his tomb forever (1166f.). Neither Ajax' rehabilitation, nor the contrast between the great man and the mean and low-minded, can alone[133] account for the latter part of the play. The chief issue is Ajax' burial, effected despite the opposition of his enemies. Due sepulture is essential for the religious veneration of heroes. Their tombs are the primary shrines of their cults.[134]

127 On ritual vocabulary in scenes of sacrificial death in Euripides cf. Johanna Schmitt, *Freiwilliger Opfertod bei Euripides. Ein Beitrag zu seiner dramatischen Technik*, RVV 17. 2 (Giessen 1921), pp. 78ff.; in tragedy on the whole Guépin, *Tragic Paradox*, pp. 1–5.

128. Cf. Burkert, 'Sacrificial Ritual', p. 112.

129. Dönt, 'Zur Deutung...', p. 55.

130. This 'ontological' reconciliation is different from the moral reconciliation assumed by Jebb, Bowra and their followers; different also from that assumed by the chorus (718f.): Αἴας μετεγνώσθη θυμοῦ τ' 'Ατρείδαις μεγάλων τε νεικέων. (These words are tragic irony, as are lines 710–13.)

131. Knox, 'The Ajax', pp. 18–20.

132. P. Burian, 'Supplication and Hero Cult in Sophocles' *Ajax*', GRBS 13 (1972), 151–6.   133. Reinhardt, *Sophokles*, p. 40, Bowra and others.

134. Jebb, *Sophocles*, introduction, pp. xxviii–xxxii.

The unity of the play, as Jebb observed,[135] rests on Ajax' consecration as a hero. This consecration is guaranteed by his voluntary sacrificial death in accordance with the will of the gods, and finds its expression and seal in the establishment of his cult through his burial, 'so that the latter part of the play is not an arbitrary addition to the former, but a natural, indeed a necessary, development of it'.

135. *Sophocles*, p. xxxii.

Sophocles' *Trachiniae*: myth, poetry, and heroic values

CHARLES SEGAL

T H E monstrous river-god Achelous wooing a tender maiden and defeated amid the crash of fist and horn; the 'beast-man' killed in the river; the poisonous blood of the Centaur mingled with the venom of the Hydra; the tuft of wool flaring up and crumbling ominously in the sunlight; the hideous sufferings of the great hero Heracles as the venom, heated by the sacrificial fires and his own sweat as he slaughters bulls, seeps into his flesh – this is the mythical stuff of which Sophocles made his *Trachiniae*.[1] These

1. I shall cite the following works by author or abbreviated title only: S. M. Adams, *Sophocles the Playwright*, Phoenix Suppl. 3 (Toronto 1957); Adolf Beck, 'Der Empfang Ioles', *Hermes* 81 (1953), 10–21; Penelope Biggs, 'The Disease Theme in Sophocles' *Ajax, Philoctetes*, and *Trachiniae*', *CP* 61 (1966), 223–35; C. M. Bowra, *Sophoclean Tragedy* (Oxford 1944); P. E. Easterling, 'Sophocles, *Trachiniae*', *BICS* 15 (1968), 58–69; Victor Ehrenberg, 'Tragic Heracles' (1943), in *Polis und Imperium*, ed. K. F. Stroheker and A. J. Graham (Zürich and Stuttgart 1965), pp. 380–98; G. H. Gellie, *Sophocles, A Reading* (Melbourne 1972); Johanna Heinz, 'Zur Datierung der Trachinierinnen', *Hermes* 72 (1937), 270–300; T. F. Hoey, 'The *Trachiniae* and the Unity of Hero', *Arethusa* 3 (1970), 1–22; R. C. Jebb, *Sophocles*, Part 5, *The Trachiniae* (Cambridge 1892); J. C. Kamerbeek, *The Plays of Sophocles*, Part 2, *The Trachiniae* (Leiden 1959); S. G. Kapsomenos, *Sophokles' Trachinierinnen und ihr Vorbild* (Athens 1963); G. M. Kirkwood, 'The Dramatic Unity of Sophocles' *Trachiniae*', *TAPA* 72 (1941), 203–11 (henceforth cited as 'Kirkwood, *TAPA*'); *idem, A Study of Sophoclean Drama*, Cornell Studies in Class. Philol. 21 (Ithaca, N.Y. 1958) (henceforth cited as 'Kirkword, *Study*'); H. D. F. Kitto, *Greek Tragedy* (Garden City, N.Y. 1955) (henceforth, Kitto, *Greek Tragedy*); *idem, Poiesis, Structure and Thought*, Sather Classical Lectures 36 (Berkeley and Los Angeles 1966) (henceforth Kitto, *Poiesis*); Albin Lesky, *Die tragische Dichtung der Hellenen*[3] (Göttingen 1972); F. J. H. Letters, *The Life and Work of Sophocles* (London and New York 1953); I. M. Linforth, 'The Pyre on Mount Oeta in Sophocles' *Trachiniae*', *U. Cal. Publ. in Class. Philol.* 14 (1952), 255–67; Marsh McCall, 'The *Trachiniae*: Structure, Focus and Heracles', *AJP* 93 (1972), 142–63; Paul Masqueray (ed.), *Sophocle*, 2, Soc. d'Édition 'Les Belles Lettres' (Paris 1924); Georges Méautis, *Sophocle, Essai sur le héros tragique* (Paris 1957); G. A. Murray, 'Heracles, "The Best of men"', *Greek Studies* (Oxford 1946), pp. 106–26; Gennaro Perrotta, *Sofocle* (Messina and Florence 1935); Max Pohlenz, *Die griechische Tragödie* (Göttingen 1954); Karl Reinhardt, *Sophokles*

elements are not merely pieces of decorative vignettes or 'sensational tableaux'.[2] They are essential elements in one of the boldest and most powerful creations of Greek dramatic poetry. And yet the failure to take these mythical elements and the imagery which surrounds them at full seriousness has led to misunderstanding and undervaluation of this great play.

No other extant Sophoclean play makes use of such intractable mythical material and faces such a gulf between the characters as human beings and the characters as symbolic figures. This gulf creates much of the difficulty of modern response to the play. Sophocles draws Deianeira's domestic tragedy with the fullness and naturalism appropriate to the developed sensibilities of the civilized realm where she belongs, whereas Heracles never emerges entirely from the remote mythology and from the ancient powers of nature which he vanquishes. Of necessity he receives a more schematic, more externalized, less realistic representation. Yet this very difference in characterization reflects the fact that the play places us at the intersection of opposed worlds, at the frontiers between man and beast, civilization and primitive animal drives.[3]

In the *Trachiniae* the humanist view of Sophocles as a dramatist of the emotions and of character meets its greatest stumbling block. This fact has doubtless had something to do with the lack of satisfactory criticism of the play. If, on the other hand, we detach ourselves somewhat from the conventional approach to the play in terms of character and the will of the hero and approach it through its network of symbols and images, the *Trachiniae* takes its rightful place as one of the most original and powerful works of the fifth century.

The relation between naturalism and symbolism is one of the most subtle and distinctive qualities of Sophocles' art. Classical scholarship, prone to stress the former to the exclusion of the latter, has seldom done this subtle relationship justice. A fuller apprecia-

(Frankfurt a. M. 1933); Carl Robert, *Die griechische Heldensage*, 2[4] (Berlin 1921); Gilberte Ronnet, *Sophocle, poète tragique* (Paris 1969); Wilhelm Schmid, in Schmid–Stählin, *Die griechische Literatur*, 1. 2 (Munich 1934); R. M. Torrance, 'Sophocles: Some Bearings', *HSCP* 69 (1965), 269–327; A. J. A. Waldock, *Sophocles the Dramatist* (Cambridge 1951); C. H. Whitman, *Sophocles, A Study of Heroic Humanism* (Cambridge, Mass. 1951).

2. Waldock, p. 102.

3. See Méautis, p. 255; Waldock, p. 102; Reinhardt, pp. 47–8; and especially Letters, pp. 176 and 192.

tion of the *Trachiniae* may, it is hoped, help us achieve a better balance in interpreting the other plays as well.

Not surprisingly the *Trachiniae* has given scandal to critics looking at Sophocles as an embodiment of the classical ideal of harmony and serenity. 'Below Sophocles' usual elevation' ('gewöhnliche Höhe'), August von Schlegel declared, assigning the play to Iophon.[4] Critics as different as Patin in the nineteenth century and Adams in the twentieth have followed Schlegel in doubting Sophoclean authorship.[5] Gottfried Hermann and Bergk did not go quite so far, but suspected two recensions.[6] Those who allowed it to be Sophocles' work have called it 'the weakest of the extant plays' (Croiset) or found it lacking in 'far-reaching generalizations' and issuing from 'no universal apprehension about life'.[7] Inferior, imperfect, 'very poor and insipid', gloomy, dark, puzzling, odd, nebulous, curious, bitter, difficult: these are its standard epithets.[8]

There have been a few voices on the other side. Schiller wrote enthusiastically to Goethe on the 'Tiefe des weiblichen Wesens' depicted in Deianeira and found here what he 'missed elsewhere in Homer and tragedy'.[9] Even critics who objected to the plot admitted the splendor of the poetry and the vividness of the action.[10] Bowra, Pohlenz, Reinhardt, and others have amply demonstrated that the play is worth the effort required to understand it, and recent scholarship has evinced renewed insight into its problems and its poetry.[11]

The enthusiasm of Schiller in the above-quoted passages raises the first hurdle that the interpreter of the *Trachiniae* has to leap. Critics wax eloquent in praise of Deianeira and take the greatest delight in heaping persiflage on the brutality and 'animalistic

4. See Schmid–Stählin, p. 374, n. 3; Jebb, p. ix.
5. H. Patin, *Études sur les tragiques grecs, Sophocle* (Paris 1904), p. 58; Adams, p. 124.
6. Cited in Schmid–Stählin, p. 374, n. 3.
7. Kitto, *Greek Tragedy*, p. 313.
8. For example, Jebb, p. x; Letters, p. 176; McCall, p. 162; Masqueray, p. 4; Méautis, p. 253; Ronnet, p. 48; Schmid–Stählin, p. 318; Waldock, p. 80; Whitman, p. 103.
9. Schmid–Stählin, p. 378, n. 2.
10. E.g. Lewis Campbell (ed.), *Sophocles*, 2 (Oxford 1881), p. 237: 'But it may be confidently asserted that in point of dramatic structure the *Trachiniae* will bear comparison with the greatest of Sophoclean tragedies.'
11. See especially Easterling (the best recent study), Gellie, Hoey, McCall.

rawness' of Heracles.[12] One could compile a choice florilegium of eulogies of the wife and denunciations of the husband. Indeed the contrast has become almost a rhetorical *topos* for criticism of the play.[13] Some critics pay scant attention to Heracles at all, or else find the play redeemed by Deianeira.[14] Jebb suggested that Sophocles let the figure of Deianeira run away with him at the expense of Heracles and the unity of the work, giving us in fact two tragedies, Deianeira's 'of consummate excellence', and Heracles', 'most pathetic..., but produced at a moral disadvantage'.[15]

Jebb's approach raises the celebrated question of who is the hero or whether there is a hero at all. Those who have stressed the interdependence and complementarity of the two figures, as Bowra, Lesky, Reinhardt, and others have done, are probably closest to the truth.[16] But we must here advert to our initial proposition that character is not the best handle by which to grasp this play. Despite the importance of the domestic relationships of Heracles and Deianeira, the play is not the mere 'domestic tragedy' of an unhappy marriage.[17] Both Heracles and Deianeira have their place within a larger pattern which includes also the monstrous figures of phantasmagoric myth, Achelous, Nessus, the

12. Schmid–Stählin, p. 379 ('animalische Roheit'). See also Murray, pp. 119ff.; Masqueray, p. 11; Whitman, pp. 112f.; Perrotta, p. 479.

13. First prize goes to Méautis, p. 256; 'Déjanire est une rose d'automne, alanguie, gardant encore le parfum de sa beauté, mais frissonnant sous le vent du malheur qu'elle pressent.' 'La douce, la naïve, la charmante, la désarmée Déjanire' (p. 276).

14. So G. K. Galinsky, *The Heracles Theme* (Oxford 1972), p. 49; Franz Stoessl, *Der Tod des Herakles* (Zürich 1945), pp. 39–57, especially p. 53; L. Sirchia, 'La cronologia delle Trachinie', *Dioniso* 21 (1958), 70–2; J. A. Moore, *Sophocles and Arete* (Cambridge, Mass. 1938), p. 77. For Heracles as the focus of the tragedy see Adams, pp. 108–9; McCall, pp. 153ff.; Kitto, pp. 178ff.; also Hans Diller, 'Über das Selbstbewusstsein der Sophokleischen Personen', *WS* 69 (1956), 83 and 'Menschendarstellung und Handlungsführung bei Sophokles', *Antike und Abendland* 6 (1957), 168. How divided recent opinion remains may be seen by comparing Ronnet, p. 45 ('La pièce n'a qu'un héros, une héroïne plutôt, c'est Déjanire'), and McCall, p. 161, n. 22 ('There is but one hero in the *Trachiniae*, and it is Heracles').

15. Jebb, p. xxxix.

16. Bowra, pp. 116, 144ff.; Hoey, *passim*; Lesky, p. 217; Reinhardt, p. 47. Also Ehrenberg, pp. 383ff.; Gellie, p. 53; Letters, pp. 187–90; Masqueray, pp. 7–11.

17. See Waldock, pp. 81–2, criticizing Murray; also Kitto's revision, in *Poiesis*, of his earlier view, *Greek Tragedy*, pp. 304ff.

Hydra. Here even the contrast between the so tenderly and humanly drawn Deianeira and the inhuman, thinly characterized Heracles has its significance.

The wide divergence in interpretation and evaluation of the *Trachiniae* has led, as one might expect, to equally wide divergence in dating.[18] Some of those who have advocated an early date see traces of immaturity.[19] Those who have placed it late have found evidence of waning power.[20] The question of the play's relation to the *Alcestis*, *Medea*, and *Hercules Furens* of Euripides is still contro-versial. Reinhardt, Kirkwood, and others have adduced evidence for placing the play in the 440s, that is between the *Ajax* and the *Antigone*. But none of their evidence is decisive, and supposed archaism of style can be due as much to the play's peculiar subject-matter as to early composition.

The poetry of the *Trachiniae* is magnificent with the darkness of destructive passions and the unleashed powers of a primordial beast-world beneath the civilized surface of human life. One might easily be tempted to see in this power the ὄγκος of Sophocles' 'Aeschylean' period; but it may equally be the result of a bold grappling with a myth of unique, awesome force. The static struc-ture and the dramatic 'stiffness' of the long narrative speeches may be the formal rendering of a mythic vision rather than the indication of immature dramaturgy.[21] Sophocles' mythopoeic imagination seems to have been fired by the archaic quality of the material, and hence the unusual tonality of the play.

If we insist on chronological placement, we should keep in mind the two lacunae, of at least ten years each, between *Antigone* and *Oedipus Tyrannus* and between the *Tyrannus* and the *Electra*,

18. Fullest discussion of the dating can be found in E.-R. Schwinge, *Die Stellung der Trachinierinnen im Werk des Sophokles*, Hypomnemata 1 (Göttingen 1962) (before 450 B.C.); see also Kirkwood's Appendix, *Study*, pp. 289–94 (between *Ajax* and *Antigone*); Lesky, pp. 191–3; Kamerbeek, pp. 27–9; Pohlenz, pp. 85–7.

19. So, for example, Ronnet, pp. 41–2; Adams, p. 126; A. Dain and P. Mazon, *Sophocle*, 1, Société d'Édition 'Les Belles Lettres' (Paris 1955), p. 9.

20. See Kitto's salutary remarks, *Greek Tragedy*, p. 323. Perrotta, pp. 473, 526ff. would date the play as late as 410–409 B.C., but see the sharp criticism by F. R. Earp, *CR* 53 (1939), 113–15. The more common late dating is between 420 and 410 B.C., i.e. after the supposed date of the *H.F.*: see M. L. Earle, *TAPA* 33 (1902), 5–29; Jebb, p. xxiii; Masqueray, pp. 14–15.

21. See Reinhardt, p. 72; Sirchia (above, note 14), p. 68; Perrotta, p. 475; Dain and Mazon (above, note 19) p. 8.

two decades in which we do not know what depths Sophocles' mind may have been plumbing. The importance of the oracles, the similarities between the exit of Deianeira and those of Eurydice in the *Antigone* and Jocasta in the *Oedipus Rex*, the close parallels with the *Alcestis*, and perhaps the Euripidean coloring in the theme of female passion would suit a date in the late 430s.[22] But no certainty is, as yet, possible. In addition to its other difficulties the *Trachiniae* also poses problems for the genetic or evolutionary approach to Sophocles,[23] for it has affinities both with his earliest known play, the *Ajax*, and with his latest, the *Oedipus at Colonus*.

II

Like the *Ajax* and the *Philoctetes*, the *Trachiniae* is a play not of cities, but of wild landscape. The city of Trachis never materializes very tangibly, and Heracles' family is not especially well established there: they are 'uprooted', ἀνάστατοι (39), a word which gives a certain restless coloring to the setting from the beginning. One recalls Thucydides' description of the age of the migrations (1. 12). The other city important to the play, Oechalia, is an object of plunder. Instead of cities the violence of the natural world looms everywhere behind the action: the two great rivers of north-west Greece, Achelous and Euenus, the desolate mountain landscape of Trachis and northern Euboea, the great peak of Oeta. Akin in symbolic function to Cithaeron in the *Oedipus Rex*, these settings echo the cries of human suffering (787–8) and suggest the presence of brooding, silent powers. But vaster and more prominent than the setting of the *Oedipus*, the landscapes of the *Trachiniae* throw into relief the question of man's place in a world whose violence he both shares and subdues.

Kitto thought the river-god Achelous an 'un-Sophoclean monster...ill at ease in this setting'.[24] Masqueray, objecting that a fifth-century audience was no longer accustomed to such 'metamorphoses', could only express puzzlement at this detail in this 'most curious of the Sophoclean plays'.[25] Sophocles' Achelous

22. See Heinz, pp. 298–300; McCall, pp. 162–3; Schmid, pp. 361, 374–5, 380, n. 1; Sirchia, pp. 59–68; Whitman, pp. 46–9. Also A. A. Long, *Language and Thought in Sophocles* (London 1968), p. 28, n. 2.

23. For the limitations of this approach in general see Ehrenberg, p. 383.

24. Kitto, *Greek Tragedy*, p. 310.   25. Masqueray, pp. 4–5.

is indeed more 'primitive', in his manner of presentation, than Homer's river-gods in *Iliad* 21.[26] But this primitive aspect is essential to his function and stands at the very center of the play's mood and concerns.

The battle between Heracles and Achelous is virtually our introduction to the story (9–17). It sets the tone for the rest of the play. Achelous' attributes are generally a bull's body and a human head,[27] but Sophocles has endowed him with an even more outrageous monstrosity: he has the triple shape of bull, snake, and man. The fine lines which describe the water pouring down the forest-like tangle of his beard, ἐκ...δασκίου γενειάδος (13), make clear at once that we have to do with a figure who is not yet fully differentiated from the forces of nature.[28] The first *stasimon* returns to this battle in vivid lyrical narration. There are expressively harsh alliterations of *k* and *g* and a swift movement from rapid dactylic and anapaestic meters to excited dochmiacs (516–30).

The long description of Nessus' attempted rape (555–77) continues the theme of elemental violence. This scene begins with a heavy stress on archaic remoteness. Nessus is an 'ancient beast' and his gift too is 'old': ἦν μοι παλαιὸν δῶρον ἀρχαίου ποτὲ θηρός (555–6). The mood is that of remote legend or fairy tale, and it is through these telescopic lenses of the self-consciously legendary and mythical that Sophocles invites us to view the entire action. 'There is an ancient saying...' is the first line of the play (Λόγος μὲν ἔστ' ἀρχαῖος...).

The Centaur, like Achelous, belongs to the elemental forces of nature. Often he is referred to simply as 'the beast' (*ther*).[29] He is

26. See P. Vivante, *The Homeric Imagination* (Bloomington, Ind. 1970), p. 113: 'The representation of Achelous in Sophocles seems much more traditional in the way it accepts the mythical metamorphosis. In Homer, we notice, the river-god never takes a human shape; all we hear is a voice speaking human words – just as the resounding waters suggest the lowing of a bull but never the physical aspect of a bull.' The scholiast Ven. B on *Iliad* 21.237 = Archilochus frag. 270 (Lasserre–Bonnard) observes that Archilochus, unlike Homer, did not dare to represent his Achelous combating Heracles as a river, but only as a bull.

27. See Robert, pp. 570–1.

28. G. Schiassi, *Sofocle, Le Trachinie* (Florence 1953), observes *ad loc.*, 'δάσκιος dà l'idea della boscaglia ombreggiante le rive del fiume.'

29. Lines 556, 568, 662, 680, 707, 935, 1162; cf. also 1059 and 1096. Homer's Centaurs are also 'beasts', φῆρες (*Il.* 1.368). Cf. also φὴρ ἄγριος in Bacchylides(?) frag. 64.27 Snell.

'shaggy-chested', *dasusternos* (557), and his river is 'deep-flowing', *bathurrous* (559), a detail which takes us back to the wild realm and the shaggy beard of Achelous in the opening scene (13–14). In Bacchylides' version of the rape, Nessus' river is lyrically depicted as 'flowery', *rhodoeis* (Bacchyl. 16. 34). Sophocles' 'deep-flowing' is perhaps an intentional criticism of the choral poet's gentler conception of the setting.[30] Similarly Bacchylides presents Nessus' poison in general terms as a 'divinely potent prodigy', δαιμόνιον τέρας (35), whereas Sophocles is specific about its awful ingredients, the coagulated blood and the Hydra's venom (572–4), even though he, like Bacchylides, has omitted the primitive detail of the sperm.[31]

The center of the play is occupied by three long, narrative speeches: Deianeira's presentation of her plight to the chorus, followed by her description of Nessus' attempted rape (531–54 and 555–81); the ominous disintegration of the tuft of wool which reveals to her the horror of what she has done (672–722); and Hyllus' account of Heracles' agonies at Cenaeum (749–806). All of these events have to do with a violent, primitive past encroaching upon and destroying a civilized house with which we identify and sympathize. From that point on, the spectacle before our eyes consists almost exclusively of groans, spasms of unbearable agony, terrible writhings and outcries. Finally the closing movement (1157ff.), as sudden as the onset of the violence in Hyllus' narrative (734ff.), brings a measure of understanding and calm.

Man in this play is vulnerable to the elemental drives and processes of nature: sex, birth, death, and, above all, time – time which brings with it the passage from youth to age, from virginity to nubile status, from mature sexuality to old age. These last themes are Deianeira's main preoccupations (144–50, 547–54). But they have more than a psychological dimension. They are profoundly related to the forces of nature and the instinctual drives

30. A number of scholars have argued for the priority of Sophocles to Bacchylides 16, notably Bruno Snell, *Hermes* 75 (1940), 182; Schwinge (above, note 18), pp. 128–33; Stoessl (above, note 14), pp. 58ff. and Kamerbeek, pp. 5–7. See *contra* Kapsomenos, pp. 5–17. Kamerbeek admits the inconclusiveness of the evidence.

31. Apollod. 2. 7. 6. 6; Diod. 4. 36. 5. See also Kamerbeek, pp. 133–4 (*ad* 580) and Charles Dugas, 'La mort du Centaure Nessos', *REA* 45 (1943), 18–26, especially 24f.

embodied in Achelous and Nessus. It is Deianeira's subjection to time and change and the resultant fear of losing her 'man' (551) because of waning attractiveness which give those mythical figures of her past power over her.

The rhythms of nature, the ever-recurring cycle of birth, sexuality, and death describe a circular pattern over against the linear movement of human life toward transcendence, Heracles' path of ascent to Oeta.[32] The parode views the changeful cycle of human life in the broad perspective of stellar movement (129-31):

But pain and joy circle upon all, like the wheeling paths of the Bear.

At the opening of the parode, however, the cyclical rhythms of nature possess something of the violence which haunts the rest of the action. The passing of night into day and of day into night appears under the metaphors of killing and rebirth (94-6):

Helios, Helios I call upon, whom the shimmering night, as it is slain, brings to birth and then lays to rest blazing with fire.

In those lines the most basic movements of time and nature seem pervaded by the violence of sexuality and death. All of human life is then surrounded by this play of elemental forces. Deianeira's fear of her waning beauty and of Iole's ripeness (547-9) expresses the presence of those forces at work in the human world, and they drive her to the dark magic of the Centaur's blood. Time, sex, birth, darkness, the beast-world and its lusts all form a dense cluster of related themes.

Time, like all of nature's processes in the play, is potentially aggressive and destructive. Iole's ripening youth appears as the onward march of a living creature, ἕρπουσαν πρόσω (547), rather than as the slow unfolding of a blossom.[33] The same verb describes the 'advance' of the deadly sickness upon Heracles (ἕρπει, 1010). The night which, in its death, 'gives birth to and puts to rest the blazing sun' (94ff.) symbolizes the destructive force of time and

32. On the importance of cyclicity in the play see T. F. Hoey, 'Sun Symbolism in the Parodos of the Trachiniae', *Arethusa* 5 (1972), 140ff.; also Ronnet, p. 135.

33. Schiassi (above, note 28) *ad loc.*, for instance, suggests comparison to 'a flower in bud'. Jebb translates 'blossoming'. For the hostile sense cf. *Ajax* 157; *Antig.* 618.

nature. Deianeira, describing the painful changes in a woman's life as she passes from girlhood to maturity (147ff., cf. 547–8), speaks of the cares which trouble her 'in the night' (149). Later in the parode 'shimmering night' (132, cf. 94) recurs as an instance of the transience and instability of human life. The phrasing of 94–6 points ahead to the sinister interplay of light and darkness, fertility and destruction. It suggests even Heracles' extinction in the final blaze of his pyre.[34] If so, the final blaze of this hero as he passes out of the cycles of nature contrasts with the 'blaze' of the sun as it is 'laid to rest' in its 'death' in the rhythmical alternations of day and night.

It is an aspect of Deianeira's helpless subjection to time, part of her tragedy of immanence, that she must wait during undefined, unlimited periods of time. For Heracles, accomplishing exploits with visible, well-defined goals, time is demarcated into distinct units. Heracles 'appoints the time' of his return (χρόνον προτάξας, 164), knows of a 'fulfilment of time' (χρόνου τέλος, 167; cf. 173), and has oracles specifying exact (if conflicting) lengths of time (cf. 164–5, 648, 824–5). But Deianeira must wait out 'the time of days not to be looked for, not to be numbered' (246–7). This time for her is *askopos*, 'not to be understood or looked for', and one wonders whether the word bears a hint of its other meaning, 'inconsiderate', 'heedless of her' (*Il.* 24. 157, A. *Ag.* 462; cf. S. *El.* 864 and 1315). She is totally immersed in time as in a current from which she cannot get free. 'No small time', 'much time', 'slow time', 'long time' (44, 227f., 395, 542): these are the broad, unmarked tracts of months and years which flow by out of her control. When she speaks of time, it is in terms of this unpunctuated duration, *chronos* qualified by one of the adjectives of indefinite extent cited above. The difference between her 'slow' or 'long time' (395, 542) and Lichas' echo of these words in 599 ('With long time we are slow') sums it up with cruel irony: on her side uncomplaining endurance for fifteen months; on his, impatient haste after twenty minutes. With respect to time, as to space (see below, pp. 125ff., 148ff.), the two protagonists live in different worlds.

Related to time as the most powerful and determining of the violent forces surrounding human life is Eros, desire. Not Omphale,

34. See Hoey (above, note 32) *passim*, especially p. 143.

the messenger says, but 'desire for Iole made manifest' (ὁ τῆσδ' ἔρως φανείς, 433) caused the sack of Oechalia. The word φανείς suggests a sudden blazing forth of the power of Eros as in a terrible epiphany[35] and is to be connected with the other ominous associations of 'making visible', light, vision in the play to be discussed later (section VI). The sexual instinct is here all-powerful. It overcomes even Heracles' strength (488–9):

> Champion in all else by force of hands
> He was defeated by love (*eros*) for her (Iole) on every side.

'Fearful desire for her (ταύτης ὁ δεινὸς ἵμερος) rushed through Heracles (διῆλθε)', leading to the sack of the city (476–8).

The figures of Achelous, Nessus, and the Hydra play an important role in connecting Eros with the elemental combat between man and beast. Eros itself is an aspect of the bestial forces in the background. Action and imagery work together to create a series of analogies between the psychological themes centered on Eros and the primordial conflicts of humanity and bestiality, civilization and savagery, which are implied throughout in the background myth of Heracles' labors.

The robe is the clearest link between these two aspects of the tragedy. It spans naturalistically conveyed human emotions on the one hand and mythically presented elemental forces on the other. It is, first of all, a love-charm, the last resort of a desperate woman seeking to regain the love of her husband. But it also harks back to the elemental violence of the Centaur, destructive blood and fire, the Hydra, darkness. The 'seething clotted foam' when the wool is exposed to the sun (ἀναζέουσι θρομβώδεις ἀφροί, 702) recalls the Centaur and his clotted blood in the scene by the Euenus (ἀμφίθρεπτον αἷμα, 572). The 'seething' points ahead to the physical effects of the venom, described in the third *stasimon* as the Centaur's 'deadly, treacherous seething spurs' (φόνια δολιόμυθα κέντρ' ἐπιζέσαντα, 839–40), but also suggests the inward, emotional turbulence of passion (see below, p. 137). The mixed metaphor of this last passage forcibly links the erotic theme with the theme of man's conquest of beasts, here ironically inverted as the horse–man applies 'spurs' or 'goads' (*kentra*) to the human conqueror.

35. 'Like a fire blazing forth', says Jebb *ad loc.*

The poison, this same ode tells us, was 'nurtured' by the Hydra, here called a 'shimmering' or 'wriggling snake' (αἰόλος δράκων, 834). This expression is a verbal recall of another snake-like figure, Achelous in the prologue: αἰόλος δράκων (11–12).[36] Heracles, victorious over a primitive natural force in the first combat, is destroyed, ultimately, in the other. The power of Eros lives in the Hydra's venom, and Eros alone has defeated the hero (431–2, 488–9). Night too, placed within the rhythms of birth and violent death in the parode, is, like the snake-figures, 'shimmering', *aiolos* (94, 132). The nexus linking Achelous, Nessus, the snake-like Hydra, and night is part of a larger complex of associations between darkness, passion, destructive violence which the play makes explicit at a number of points (see below, section VI).

The imagery of heat and fire performs a similar function. The 'heat' of desire is a familar enough metaphor in Greek poetry and appears several times in the play.[37] The meadow of maidenhood, says Deianeira, is protected from the 'sun-god's heat', θάλπος θεοῦ (145). We may compare Zeus' pursuit of the virgin Io in the *Prometheus Bound* (Ζεὺς γὰρ ἱμέρου βέλει | πρὸς σοῦ τέθαλπται, *P.V.* 649–50; cf. 590f.). Heracles has been 'warmed by desire' for Iole (ἐντεθέρμανται πόθῳ, 368). But this metaphorical, emotional 'heat' has a symbolic equivalent in the destructive force of the poison when it is 'warmed', ὡς δ' ἐθάλπετο (697). Among the effects of the poison are the 'spasms of deadly madness' (*atê*) which 'warm' Heracles (*ethalpse* 1082) and his outcry over the 'many hot toils' he has endured (1046), a figurative usage of *thermos* which Kamerbeek finds 'remarkable'.

The blazing altars which activate the poison also mark an affinity between Heracles' own quasi-bestial violence and the forces which destroy him. Those flames of the altar and his sweat (*hidros*) before them (765–7) are symbolically akin to the 'heat' of his own lust (368). His 'offering' at this sacrifice, after all, celebrates his capture of Iole and her train of maidens (cf. 183,

36. The parallelism between the snake-like forms of Achelous and the Hydra is developed by Ovid, *Met.* 9. 68–76.

37. E.g. Sappho frag. 48. 2 LP; Pindar, *Pyth.* 4. 219; Soph. frag. 474. 3 P, with Pearson's note *ad loc.*; see in general Giuliana Lanata, 'Sul linguaggio amoroso di Saffo', *QUCC* 2 (1966), 77–9, with n. 64. See now Dorothea Wender, 'The Will of the Beast: Sexual Imagery in the *Trachiniae*', *Ramus* 3 (1974), 1–17, which appeared while this essay was in press.

244–5, 761). We may recall the 'sweat and warmth' (ἱδρὼς καὶ θερμότης) of Plato's *Phaedrus* (251 A–B), graphic symptoms of erotic desire, behind which stands the even more famous description of Sappho (frag. 31. 10, 13 LP; cf. Theognis 1017). These flames of the victory-sacrifice, therefore, are an essential link in the chain of causality and responsibility which accomplish the vengeance of the 'beast', Nessus: they reflect, ironically, the imperfect nature of Heracles' victory over the 'beast' in himself.

The verb *thelgein*, 'charm', and related words similarly span mythical and psychological reality. When the messenger says that 'Eros alone of the gods charmed' Heracles to sack Oechalia (Ἔρως δέ νιν | μόνος θεῶν θέλξειεν αἰχμάσαι τάδε, 354–5), the verb is a familiar metaphor for the 'spell' of desire.[38] But this 'spell' or *thelxis* is also a part of the mythical apparatus of the tale: the magical love-philter. The philter is once called *thelktra* (585) and elsewhere is described with the related word κηλητήριον, κηλεῖν (575, 998; cf. 1002). Nessus is the *pharmakeus*, both in the sense that the 'charm' of his 'persuasion' leads Deianeira to apply the poison (so 1140–2: φαρμακεύς, ἐξέπεισε, φίλτρον, ἐκμῆναι) and in the sense that his blood is quite literally the 'drug', the *pharmakon* (685, 1142). Hence the *thelxis* which he exercises is both the psychological 'persuasion' of love and the magic of a mythical power.

Peitho, Persuasion, is herself a deity in Aphrodite's entourage (e.g. Pindar, *Pyth.* 9. 39, Sappho 96. 29 LP). The magic of Nessus' initial 'persuasion' of Deianeira, therefore, merges with and prefigures the operation of the darker magic of desire and sexuality.[39]

38. For this erotic sense of *thelgein* cf. *Odyssey* 1. 56–7; 3. 264; 10. 213 and 290–1. In Bacchyl. 5. 175 Kypris has the epithet 'charmer of mortals', *thelximbrotos*. Note that this first reference to Eros in the play describes its power as *thelxis* (354–5).

39. The connections between the ambiguous magic of language and the effect of drugs (*pharmaka*) are interestingly developed, *à propos* of Plato's *Phaedrus*, by Jacques Derrida, 'La pharmacie de Platon', *Tel Quel* 32 (winter 1968), 3–48. See also my essay, 'Eros and Incantation: Sappho and Oral Poetry', *Arethusa* 7 (1974), 139–60, especially 142–4. Professor C. J. Herington calls my attention to θέλκτορι Πειθοῖ in Aeschylus, *Suppl.* 1040, which brings together the 'enchantment' and the 'persuasion' of love in a single expression. See also Gorgias, *Helen* 10 for the association of the power of the *logos* with *thelxis*, *peithō*, and magic (*goēteia*, *mageia*, *epō(i)dai*) and *Helen* 14 for the *logos* and *pharmaka*. See now J. de Romilly, 'Gorgias et le pouvoir de la poésie', *JHS* 93 (1973), 155–62.

The awesome and mysterious force of erotic *peitho* is present in all of its dangerous power when the chorus, thinking that the philter will restore Heracles to Deianeira, joyfully describes him as 'melted by persuasion through the all-anointed beguiling of the beast' (τᾶς πειθοῦς παγχρίστῳ | συντακεὶς θηρὸς ὕπο παρφάσει, 661–2). If this very uncertain text is right (I have given Pearson's version),[40] Sophocles juxtaposes the literal persuasion of Deianeira by deceptive speech (*parphasis*) with the erotic 'persuasion' of the robe (*peitho*), where *suntakeis* is also evocative of love's power (cf. 463). In archaic poetry *parphasis* describes both love's persuasion (*Il.* 14. 217) and the deceitful persuasion of clever speech (Pindar, *Nem.* 8. 32). Both forms of 'persuasion' are equally destructive, and of this common destructiveness the robe is the visible symbol and emblem.

When, fifty lines later, Deianeira understands the treachery of Nessus, she says, 'Wishing to destroy the man who shot him down, he put a spell upon me' (ἔθελγέ με, 710). Here *thelgein* straddles the realm between human emotions and the mythical background. Coming just after the account of the literal magic of the blood, it refers both to the Centaur's manipulation of her emotional needs and the subhuman, irrational forces which he embodies and ultimately calls up in Deianeira. In both cases, on the psychological and on the mythic level, the result is the destruction by the 'beast' of the beast-slayer. Is it mere coincidence that *thelgein* or *thelktron*, which occurs three times in this play, recurs nowhere else in the extant Sophocles, who is elsewhere remarkably restrained in his use of magical devices?[41]

It would be an oversimplification to say that the *thelxis* of the poisoned robe is merely a symbol of lust. Rather to the mytho-

40. For the text see Kamerbeek and Jebb *ad loc.* and Jebb's Appendix, pp. 194–5. Kamerbeek's defense of προφάσει, the manuscripts' reading, is not convincing: there is no evidence for the meaning 'saying beforehand' for πρόφασις, nor does Dain–Mazon's (above, note 19) προφάνσει, with the same meaning ('ainsi que l'avait prédit le Centaure') help any. παρφάσει, on the other hand, gives just the sense required and is well attested in such contexts, as the passages cited in the text show. The choice between συγκραθείς of the manuscripts and συντακείς (Blaydes' emendation) is more difficult. The latter is the more apt for the sense and has some support from 833. Jebb prints συγκραθείς, but he allows that συντακείς is possible. For the erotic significance of τήκομαι see Soph. frag. 941. 7 P, with Pearson's note *ad loc.*
41. See Masqueray, p. 46.

poeic imagination, the robe and the poison *are* the lust, and the plasticity of the symbol allows the poet to conjoin and interweave the psychological and cosmic orders. Hence the 'madness' of desire which the magical drug was to produce (1142) is symbolically one with the 'madness' of the physical 'disease' which it actually effects (999 and cf. 446).[42]

'Disease', *nosos*, is itself one of the most insistent examples of this interchangeability of mythical symbol and physico-psychological affect. Deianeira uses the word in its conventional meaning as a metaphor for the 'disease' of love (445, 491), a disease which she will bear reasonably and not make worse. But after the first *stasimon* on the power of Kypris and the elemental combat between Heracles and Achelous, the metaphorical 'disease' intensifies. That mythic violence awakened, the 'disease' becomes more sinister, less manageable. Hence Deianeira dwells on the word, using it twice in the same line (543–4) in a speech which itself wavers between passion and reason. Now, as she loses the acceptant calm of the earlier scene (note the echo between 445 and 544), the mythical forces in the background begin to come into play, and the 'disease' becomes a more real and vivid power. Her next thought begins, 'I had an ancient gift of a beast of old...' (555–6), and we are launched fully into the remote and the magical. The 'disease' will no longer be merely the inner passion, but it becomes also the physical effect of the magical drug.[43] Heracles, joyfully reported as 'weighed down with no disease' in the first episode (235) is now 'the man diseased', ὁ νοσῶν (784).[44] 'Disease' recurs twice in the next ode (853, 882), and soon after the old man warns about awakening the 'terrible, roving disease' (891).

Heracles' subjection to the 'disease' of love which Deianeira had herself tried to resist appears at the moment when she herself is about to succumb disastrously to the same disease. Speaking of

42. See Easterling, p. 67. Note the play on madness elsewhere, shifting between Deianeira and Heracles: 446 and 982. *Mania* too has erotic connotations (cf. Sappho's μαινόλᾳ θύμῳ, frag. 1. 18 LP) and thus suggests another link between the physical and emotional aspects of Heracles' 'disease'.

43. See Whitman, p. 116: 'One suspects Heracles' new illness of being only a continuation of the old one.' Also Biggs, pp. 223, 228ff.; Easterling, pp. 62–3.

44. Cf. also the 'enormous heaviness' (*baros*) which comes upon Hyllus just as he witnesses the 'rampant terrible disease' (980–2).

Nessus' philter for the first time, she prefaces her fear and sexual jealousy of Iole (547–51) with the disclaimer (543–5),

I cannot be angry with him who is so badly diseased with this disease, and yet to share my house with her...[45]

Hyllus echoes these very words near the end of the play, when the 'disease' of love has reached its full potency, issuing into the terrible physical sufferings of the literal 'disease' inflicted by the robe. Replying to Heracles' command that he marry Iole, he says, 'To be angry at one who is diseased is bad, and yet...' (τὸ μὲν νοσοῦντι θυμοῦσθαι κακόν, τὸ δ'..., 1230–1). The parallel illustrates the violence of Heracles over against the devotion, forbearance, gentleness of those who love him (Heracles has not the least hesitation in 'getting angry'). And yet it echoes the very passage where 'disease' is about to pass from emotional affect to destructive physical power.

Just as the 'heat' which triggers the venom's action is also the heat of Heracles' lust, so the power of the 'disease', like the 'madness' which it produces, is also the power of desire undermining Heracles' victory over the beast. Hence the disease itself becomes a kind of 'beast', identified with the destructive 'beast' whose designs work through it. It bites (770),[46] eats and drinks (1053–5), devours (771, 487, 1084), leaps and rushes forth (1026, 1083, 1089). It is 'wild', *agria*, like a savage creature (1030), 'unapproachable', ἀποτίβατος (1030), like the race of Centaurs themselves (*ameiktos*, 1095). The phrase 'ravening' or 'devouring' disease (διαβόρος νόσος, 1084) takes us back explicitly to the magical setting and the mythical power of the drug, for the same word describes the disintegration of the wool (*diaboron*, 676). As a quasi-personified, bestial force, the disease is the violence of the bestial Nessus living again, but living in the very body of the beast-killer. By imagistically linking the 'bestiality' of the disease with the bestiality which is its immediate cause – i.e. Heracles'

---

45. The sharp juxtaposition of 'anger' and 'understanding' in 543 underlines the fluctuation of Deianeira's emotion. She then returns to the decision 'not to be angry' ('for, *as I said*, it is not well to be angry', 552) after her statement of her fears of Iole's beauty. Within the two enframing statements of rational control over anger (543, 552) bursts forth the woman's natural protectiveness of her 'man' (551) and her sexual rights.

46. See Biggs, p. 230, on the imagery of 'biting' which goes from the anger of Heracles at his supposed insult (254) to the literal violence of the 'biting' disease.

lust – , the poetry breaks through the usual one-dimensionality of our vision and reveals the inward and outward dimensions of reality simultaneously.

In this second third of the play the disease expands to enormous proportions. It becomes almost a mythical power in its own right, a force which, in order to destroy Heracles, must be almost as great as he and in fact a part of his self.

When Heracles finally appears on stage in the last third of the play the power of the disease is visually enacted before our eyes. We see the great hero, the man 'of strength' (*ischuon*, 234), the 'cleanser' (1012, 1061) weak and in pain before us. The great shoulders and arms are helpless now (1089ff.). Repeatedly he is called 'diseased' (1013, 1115, 1120, 1230, 1241). But that 'disease' has a new edge: it poses one of the sharpest visual juxta-positions in Sophocles between heroic strength and human weak-ness, and it raises afresh the question of man's power over nature and nature's power over man. The scene resembles the emergence of Ajax from the tent in the first episode of that play (*Ajax* 333ff.) and also the closing scene of Euripides' *Heracles Mad*. But the effect here, if not more powerful, is at least more concentrated, reduced to the most fundamental contrast of physical strength and physical weakness, triumph and defeat. Unlike the other two heroes Sophocles' Heracles is defined solely in terms of his great physique. That ruined, his loss is total.

The confrontation of Heracles' fantastic past with the more realistically represented present takes place on another level through the analogies between the winning of Deianeira and the winning of Iole. Both women are victims of erotic violence, and both unwittingly cause the destruction of their house through love. The battle between Heracles and Achelous over Deianeira (497–530) finds a close echo in the battle of Heracles and the Oechalians over Iole (856–61). Both battles illustrate the force of Kypris (497, 515 and 862). Both women are prizes of the spear (513 and 860). Of both women it is said that their beauty destroyed them (25 and 465).[47] Both are said to suffer the 'travail' of their woes (*odinas*, 42; *odinousa*, 325). Iole has an ἄзηλον βίον (285); Deianeira perpetrates an ἄзηλον ἔργον (745).

47. See Pohlenz, p. 206; Beck, p. 16. Gellie, p. 237, remarks, 'one battle for a girl in Heracles' world of violence is much the same as another'.

Through these analogies the violence of Eros leaps the limits of time and follows the pattern of cyclical recurrence which is so strongly marked in this play. In pursuing Iole the mature Heracles reactivates his contact with the savage past. He re-enacts with Iole the role of the beast from whom he once 'delivered' Deianeira, but there is no 'Heracles' to deliver Iole from her 'Achelous'. Though he has killed off Hydra, Centaurs, and other fabled monsters, that monstrous world still exists, inwardly, to pull him back. Time, so cruel to Deianeira, seems in this respect to have stood still for Heracles.

By replacing the youthful Deianeira of the traditional legend with an ageing woman,[48] Sophocles gains a temporal perspective which allows him not only to play Heracles' violent past against the supposedly victorious present, but also to set primitive chaos over against an attained stability of familial and social order. The hero who is first shown to us, through the eyes of Deianeira, as the founder of a family, father and husband, still lives among the figures of an anarchic past which undo, in his own personal life, the civilizing achievement of his labors.

Iole, in the youth and innocence of her beauty, becomes the catalyst of the violence of the archaic past. The 'excessive brilliance' of her beauty (*lampra*, 379) is symbolically related to the destructive brightness of the sun and fire which kindle the poison. The word has erotic connotations too, suggesting the luminosity of the love-object, and hence forms part of the constellation of themes linking the fire-imagery of lust to the destructive fires of the action itself.[49] The 'flower' (*anthos*, 549) of her beauty (another sexual metaphor) becomes the savage 'flower of madness' (μανίας ἄνθος, 999) which 'blossoms' (*enthēken*, 1089) to Heracles' ruin.

The first time Heracles is mentioned it is as one who has 'brought release' from a dreadful monster: ἐκλύεταί με (21) says Deianeira, describing Heracles' appearance at the wooing of Achelous. 'I release you from fear', ὄκνου σε λύσω, announces the Messenger confidently when he comes with the news of Heracles' arrival (181). 'Ares, stung to fury (Ἄρης οἰστρηθείς),

48. Schol. on Ap. Rhod. 1. 1212.
49. E.g. Sappho, frag. 16. 18 and 58. 26 LP; cf. Pindar, frag. 123. 2–3 Snell; see Lanata (above, note 37), pp. 76–7.

has brought release (ἐξέλυσε) from the day of suffering', sings the chorus just after Lichas exits with the poisoned robe (653–4). Heracles thought that Dodona's prediction of 'release from toils' (μόχθων...λύσιν, 1170–1) meant happiness, but instead it meant death. 'Release' is what both the main protagonists fervently desire, but the inability to achieve 'release' is a major theme of the play. The Messenger's promise of 'release from fear' turns into the exact opposite for Deianeira. The chorus' hope of 'release' for Heracles in 653 comes at the point in the play when the violence of the savage realm which Heracles thinks he has escaped bursts full upon him. A 'maddened Ares', given the associations of erotic passion and bestiality in οἰστρηθείς,[50] is hardly a likely deliverer. οἰστρηθείς, a metaphor from the animal realm, itself points ahead to the victory of Nessus, which is, in turn, the vengeance of all the monsters that Heracles has slain. The word *oistros*, in fact, recurs at the end of the play when Heracles has obtained a hard-won inward release from this 'maddening sting' of the beast's poison (1254). The hero who, out of lust, 'sacked a city' (πέρσας πόλιν, 244, 750; also 364–5, 433, 467) is himself 'sacked', 'ravaged', by the consequences of his own violence (ἐκπεπόρθημαι, 1104).[51]

Rather than obtaining 'release' from his past, Heracles is in fact trapped in it more fearfully than ever. All of the beast-figures behind the action of the play get a second life as shadowy, yet potent beings that continue to haunt human life, springing forth with renewed virulence from human passions. In the rich and complex poetry of the antode at 831–40 the literal anointing of the poison becomes the work of mysterious phantasms: 'necessity' smeared the robe 'with the aid of the Centaur's deadly cloud' (Κενταύρου φονίᾳ νεφέλᾳ | χρίει δολοποιὸς ἀνάγκα, 831–2). Death, *thanatos*, has begotten the poison, but the 'shimmering snake', that is, the Hydra, has 'nurtured it' (ἔτρεφε δ' αἰόλος δράκων, 834). The poison itself acquires an almost personal existence, as a demonic child born and raised by monsters from Heracles' past.[52]

50. E.g. S. *El.* 5; cf. Aeschyl. *P.V.* 566, 580, 589, etc.

51. In the epic tradition 'sacker of cities' is an honorific epithet, and Heracles bears it in the context of Hesiod's version of the Deianeira story in the *Catalogue*, frag. 25. 23 Merkelbach–West.

52. Cf. also the expression θρέμμα Λερναίας ὕδρας of the Hydra in 574 and δεινῆς Ἐχίδνης θρέμμα in 1099, of a similar monster (the Hydra is itself identi-

In the next line the chorus asks how Heracles could see the sun of another day, 'glued to the most fearsome apparition of the Hydra', mangled by the 'black-haired' Centaur's 'seething spurs' (835–50). Here all the elements of the myth become lurid, supernatural powers. Nessus is not even mentioned by name, but is simply the 'black-haired one' (837), as Achelous in the first *stasimon* is the monstrous 'apparition of a bull', φάσμα ταύρου (509). This same periphrasis describes the Hydra in its deadly revenge, a 'fearsome apparition', δεινότατον ὕδρας φάσμα (836–7), a phrase which has been needlessly emended and is, in any case, supported by 509 and by a closely parallel use of this word in Euripides.[53]

Phasma is also related to φαίνω, 'appear', and hence to the sinister meaning of that root and of the idea of light 'making visible', 'showing to the light', throughout the play. Hence at the end of the next antistrophe another invisible power, and one more potent still, is 'manifested visibly' as the 'active force', the *praktor* (861–2): Κύπρις ἄναυδος φανερὰ τῶνδ᾽ ἐφάνη πράκτωρ.[54] It is these 'silent' powers (cf. *anaudos*, 862) which have caused the immense 'roars' of pain (cf. 805 and also 773, 787, 904). Heracles, who has defeated his visible and physical enemies, is defeated by these less tangible foes, Eros and Kypris (cf. 441–2, 448–9, 861–2), the ghostly figures of his violent past, and the 'blind infatuation' which ravages him, the ravager of cities (τυφλῆς ὑπ᾽ ἄτης ἐκπεπόρθημαι, 1104).

These metaphorical and symbolical links between present and past are not an artificial superposition, but the expression of a terrible vision conveyed through the plastic power of myth and symbol: they present the demonic hold that a primitive past, the

fied with an *echidna* at 771). For the interpretation of 574 see A. A. Long, *GRBS* 8 (1967), 275–8, and for the implications of the phraseology, see my article, 'The Hydra's Nursling: Image and Action in the *Trachiniae*', *AC* 44 (1975), 612–17.

53. E. *Cretans*, frag. 82. 23–4 Austin, where 'the bull is so called because it is uncanny, strange, mysterious': H. Lloyd-Jones, *YCS* 22 (1972), 266. Cf. also Pindar, *Ol.* 8. 44, of a prophetic apparition. Murray, p. 116, speaks of the 'dream-like effect of horror unseen or not quite seen'. See also Easterling, p. 65; Letters, pp. 77–9 and 185; and F. M. Pontani, 'Lettura del primo stasimo delle Trachinie', *Dioniso* 12 (1949), 236.

54. Cf. 250–1 where Lichas calls Zeus the 'agent' (*praktōr*), a statement which, as Easterling, p. 61, says, is 'patently ironical' in the light of the true, if not ultimate, *praktōr*, Kypris.

primitive strata of human existence, have on a world from which they are banished, but not fully exorcized. This past may be viewed historically, psychologically, phylogenetically: it is the peculiar power of the myth that it allows all the possibilities. Something apart from, yet also interwoven with, human responsibility, it is analogous to those dark forces which elsewhere in Sophocles shadow human life: the family curse in the *Antigone* (cf. *Antig.* 582–603), the oracles in the *Oedipus Rex*.

The interpenetration of contemporary and mythical levels might suggest Euripidean influence (one thinks of the *Alcestis* and the *Hercules*, to name two plays closely related to the *Trachiniae*). But Sophocles has allowed the mythical material to speak in its own terms with a direct factuality which is characteristically his own.

III

The gap between Heracles and Deianeira, between myth and contemporaneity, between heroic exploits and the fifth-century *oikos* or gynaeceum, is also an aspect of a gap between an older and a newer world. Heracles' civilizing energies cannot, ironically, be confined within the tame and stable domesticity of Deianeira's house. His very prowess, though engaged in the service of civilization, links him with those savage monsters which he combats.[55] Neither protagonist crosses this gap, and both are its victims. Heracles is destroyed by his wife's love and wish to preserve the house of which he is the father; Deianeira is, as Kirkwood says, 'involved in the unmanageable sweep of events',[56] caught in a realm where she has no valid point of entry, and so destroyed.

This clash of values is analogous to that in the *Ajax* between the hero and his half-brother on the one hand and Tecmessa and especially Odysseus on the other.[57] But in the *Trachiniae* the clash centers not so much on the place of the old, individualistic heroic ethic within the *polis* as on the questionableness of that ethic for civilization in general.

In the long scene between Deianeira and Lichas, the first really dramatic scene in the play, Sophocles has made the contrast as

55. See Adams, p. 108.   56. Kirkwood, *Study*, p. 50.
57. See B. M. W. Knox, 'The *Ajax* of Sophocles', *HSCP* 65 (1961), 21ff.; Gellie, pp. 20–1, 27–8.

striking as possible by echoing the scene in the *Agamemnon* where Clytaemnestra receives Cassandra and her handmaidens from Troy.[58] Deianeira's understanding and gentleness are at the opposite extreme from Clytaemnestra's smouldering hatred. In Deianeira Sophocles' audience would recognize the humane spirit of the fifth century at its best, the compassion for the weak and helpless exemplified in the Odysseus of the *Ajax* or the idealized Athenian ruler Theseus in works like Euripides' *Suppliants* and *Hercules* or Sophocles' *Oedipus at Colonus*. The woman whose situation she recalls, however, is a figure whose raw power, violent passion, immense hyperboles are in touch still with the rougher energies of a harsher, heroic age.

For Lichas the captive girls are merely the prizes of war at a time when the sack of cities is an everyday affair. Deianeira sees them as deserving of 'pity' because of their 'misfortunes' (242–5):

Deian. These women, in the name of the gods, whose are they, and who are they? For they are pitiable (*oiktrai*) if their misfortunes (*symphorai*) deceive me not.
Lich. When he sacked Eurytus' city, Heracles set these apart, for himself and the gods a select possession (*ktēma*).

For Lichas, as for Heracles, they are a piece of 'property' (245), proof of the hero's worth and his prowess. For Deianeira they are individuals. In 307ff. she turns to the mute Iole, as Clytaemnestra turned to the mute Cassandra, to inquire – but in gentle, not imperious tones – who she is, who is her mother and father, whether she is married or not (ironical, of course, the last question in the light of Iole's real reason for being there). With a fine sensitivity she can appreciate the added mental suffering of a noble mind, for she pities Iole most of all the group 'to the degree that she alone knows how to understand too' (ὅσῳπερ καὶ φρονεῖν οἶδεν μόνη, 313). Her desire to learn the captives' names is not idle curiosity nor yet suspicion, but part of the same civilized desire to individualize and sympathize. Lichas curtly replies that he did not ask any questions (317): οὐκ οἶδα· καὶ γὰρ οὐδ' ἀνιστόρουν μακράν. A true companion of Heracles, he 'did his work in silence': σιγῇ τοὐμὸν ἔργον ἤνυτον (319).

58. See Perrotta, pp. 496–7; and Kapsomenos, pp. 68ff., especially 77–9, who pushes the parallels too far.

Through this scene with Lichas, Heracles and Deianeira meet vicariously, and they meet in terms of the values which each embodies. Through them the older heroic values of violence, egoistical passion, superior force as its own standard confront a more 'modern' and civilized ethic of compassion and imaginative self-extension to other's *symphorai*. When Lichas explains the reasons for Heracles' sack of Oechalia, his lie speaks a kind of truth.[59] Heracles avenges an insult, and was right to do so (260–73). He is punished, as Lichas sees it, not for killing *per se*, but for using guile (274–80). Heracles' values, like Lichas', are all externalized, Iliadic. His punishment too is based upon the values of a 'shame culture', being sold into slavery. That disgrace, like the killing itself, is a matter of externals, and Heracles returns after his exile 'pure' or 'cleansed' (*hagnos*, 258).

The truth about Heracles, which comes out at the end of this scene, gives an even more telling indication of his values. The deception of Deianeira, Lichas admits, was all his own idea. Heracles himself 'gave no orders of concealment, nor did he deny it' (480). That a hero like Heracles should bother to lie to his wife about such a matter is inconceivable. The inner realm of feelings and emotional pain does not count for him. It is Lichas, not Heracles, who worries, as he says, that he 'might give pain to (Deianeira's) breast' (481–2). Near the conclusion of the play Hyllus tries to talk to Heracles of Deianeira's *intentions*: her 'error' was not committed willingly (*hekousia*, 1123) and her aims were noble, he says (χρηστὰ μωμένη, 1136). Heracles fulminates that his only concern is the *act* of the killing (χρηστ(ὰ)...πατέρα σὸν κτείνασα δρᾷ;, 1137).[60]

The clash between the outside world of Heracles and the domestic life of Deianeira contrasts not only action and emotion, but also heroic achievement and the pull felt increasingly in the late fifth century toward private life.[61] Behind the figures of Deianeira stand the quieter graces of stable, settled life, a life

59. See T. Zielinski, 'Excurse zu den Trachinierinnen', *Philologus* 55 (1896), 509 and Reinhardt, pp. 51–2.
60. See Kirkwood, *Study*, p. 226. In 667 Deianeira fears that she has 'done great evil from good expectations'.
61. See J. H. Finley, Jr, 'Politics and Early Attic Tragedy', *HSCP* 71 (1966), 10. For a different view of the play's relation to fifth-century individualism, with the focus on Heracles rather than Deianeira, see Ehrenberg, p. 391.

which could cultivate the emotions and the arts which develop them, the arts which Pericles in the Funeral Speech and Euripides in the *Medea* envisage as a special quality of the new Athenian spirit. This spirit prides itself less on martial energy or the heroic *arete* of Homer and Tyrtaeus than on the elegance and refinement of culture which flower within its walls, the ἴδιαι κατασκευαὶ εὐπρεπεῖς which bring 'pleasure' (*terpsis*) to the citizens (Thuc. 2. 38. 1). Over against military competence and energy stand 'love of beauty' and 'love of wisdom' in a fine balance between *oikeia* and *politika*, personal and public concerns (Thuc. 2. 40. 1–2).

From the perspective of Deianeira's world figures like Achelous, Nessus, the Hydra, are troglodytic survivors, as it were, of a ruder, outgrown past. Yet from the perspective of Heracles' world such creatures embody still untamed and destructive forces which need to be subdued. The great speech in which Heracles lists his achievements (1089ff.) has a grandeur and a pathos which convince us of the necessity of his strength and the value of his services. Deianeira's femininity is esteemed for its gentleness and tenderness; but at the same time it destroys a hero who, for all his faults, is a great benefactor of civilization.

If, then, one leaves aside the approach through psychology and character study and seeks to appreciate Deianeira and Heracles typologically, that is, in terms of the kinds of action and qualities of life they embody, the balance between them would appear more even and the admiration for Heracles as 'best of men' should be taken more seriously. The fifth-century *polis* is not so secure that it can dispense with the heroic energies and the sheer physical strength needed to defend it. For all its aspirations toward perfection of feeling and thought, Periclean Athens thrives in the midst of the brutal reality of war, the 'harsh teacher' (*biaios didaskalos*, Thuc. 3. 82. 2). The graceful youths on the Parthenon frieze wrestle Centaurs on the metopes. Pericles' ideal vision of an Athenian hegemony of the spirit (Thuc. 2. 38–41) is balanced by a need for vigor 'without softness' (*aneu malakias*, 2. 40. 1) and courage in the face of death (2. 39. 4; 2. 43. 4–6).

If Deianeira, then, wins our sympathies for the quieter pursuits of a refined sensibility, the bestial figures in the background and the heroic energies needed to subdue them are reminders of the savagery which civilization always has to combat, a savagery to which, through its very combat, it may itself revert. Here again Thucydides supplies an instructive analogy. From the heights of 'the love of beauty and wisdom', *philokalia* and *philosophia* (2. 40. 1), he plunges us suddenly into the degradation and lawlessness (*anomia*, 2. 53. 1) consequent on the plague. Men die 'like cattle' (2. 51. 4), neglect even the hallowed customs of funeral rites (2. 52. 4), and lose the restraining sanctions of law (2. 53), the basis of all civilized society.

IV

The tensions between ruder and more civilized values posed by Heracles' 'heroism' are symmetrical with the tensions between the creative and destructive power of the house posed by Deianeira. The house which should welcome the returning husband shelters the deadly poison of his enemy. The woman who should protect this basic unit of civilization transmits the power of the 'beast'.

Not only do bestial elements infiltrate Heracles' house to destroy it, but Heracles himself is the destroyer of a house. He swore to 'enslave (Eurytus) along with child and wife' (ξὺν παιδὶ καὶ γυναικὶ δουλώσειν ἔτι) and made no empty boast' (257–8). Heracles' egoistic destruction of another's house tumbles his own in ruins. The ruin of his house is not merely a domestic and personal tragedy, as in the *Alcestis*, but, as in the *Oresteia*, implies the larger sweep of man's confrontation with the non-human world.[62]

From the very beginning the house is the focal point of the different value systems of the two protagonists. The setting of the prologue frames the theme: the house empty of the husband, whose life 'takes him into the house and out of the house, always in service to someone' (34–5). So Heracles lives. But Deianeira, deserted at home, feels all the anxieties of her bondage to the house. Her whole world is the house, which is also the inward world of her emotional life – the only life she has – love and fear. Her tragedy ends, as it began, 'in loneliness within the house' (δωμάτων εἴσω μόνη, 900; cf. 934, 950).

Her passivity, her almost uncomprehending remoteness from

62. See Reinhardt, pp. 65–6. On the importance of the house in the play see Pohlenz, p. 201; Hoey, pp. 14ff.

the meaning of events, even when the great battles are being fought over her (cf. 21–4, 524–5), her naiveté about Nessus' charm, her utter ignorance of Heracles' world, her recurrent images of birth and the natural cycle (28ff., 42) all mark the distance between their two worlds.[63] Shut in the house, Deianeira is informed of Heracles' actions and whereabouts only by the vaguest hearsay which manages to filter down to her (cf. 40ff., 65ff.). The real facts are remote and difficult for her to obtain. Even the obvious idea of sending out Hyllus for news comes from the nurse, not her own initiative (52–60). The scene with Lichas dramatizes her distance from such factual exactitude. This distance is not only a precondition of the plot: it is also a reflection of her life-situation. She dwells in a world of emotions, not events, a world of unsure communication with the 'outside' and thus deprived of objective verification of the *erga* which determine its course.[64] Hence Deianeira is ruled by the feelings which she harbors within, the desperation of which she can only speak 'in secret' (cf. 533–5). Her brooding isolation is the necessary complement to the Centaur's poison and Heracles' lust in encompassing her ruin and her lord's.

The distance between the two protagonists is not only a matter of cleavage between inner and outer space or female and male roles. It also involves the contrast, as in the *Electra*, between *logos* and *ergon*.[65] Deianeira's situation (though not her character) is very like that of Electra. Both women are isolated, virtually imprisoned, in the house. Both are at the mercy of the false reports, the manipulated and manipulative *logoi* devised by the men who come from the 'outside'. Both are totally given over to the feelings

63. On the problem of Deianeira's passivity see Adams, p. 114 ('too sad and too submissive for this world'): Kitto, *Greek Tragedy*, pp. 309–10, who finds 'this complete passivity...surprising in a woman who has such a fineness of mind...and such an understanding of life'; Masqueray, p. 5; Perrotta, p. 476 with note 1; Reinhardt, p. 66, who speaks of her 'Hausgebundenheit'; Waldock, pp. 90–6 ('absurd', p. 94); Gellie, p. 215 ('remarkable pallor of personality').

64. On the 'unsureness of communication' see Gellie, pp. 62–3. For the effects creating the impenetrability of reality to the *logos* see U. Parlavantza–Friedrich, *Täuschungsszenen in den Tragödien des Sophokles*, Untersuch. zur antiken Literatur und Geschichte 2 (Berlin 1969), pp. 26–9.

65. See Thomas M. Woodard, '*Electra* by Sophocles: The Dialectical Design', Part 1, *HSCP* 68 (1964), 191ff., and my essay, 'The *Electra* of Sophocles', *TAPA* 97 (1966), 531ff.

which become their whole life in these narrow, enclosed limits. Both reach out in love to the long-awaited male figure arriving from the 'outside', but in both cases (though in very different ways) that juncture of inner and outer proves destructive rather than fruitful.

Communication between the two realms of the *Trachiniae*, that is, between the house and Heracles' male world 'outside', takes the form of spatial movement, which, however, is a metaphor for contact of a broader nature. In the prologue, for instance, Heracles' life 'sends' him 'in and out' of the house (34–5), and he has 'gone off' to parts unknown to Deianeira (βέβηκεν, 41; ἀποίχεται, 42; ἔστειχε, 47). For all her efforts and her yearning, Deianeira cannot reach out of the house to Heracles, nor can Heracles succeed in reaching her. The bed on which he will be carried up to Oeta is brought out of the house. The bed of longed-for union becomes a separate bed of pain and death for each protagonist. In a play full of Odyssean echoes the motif of the bed carried outside the house is a harsh inversion of the immovable bed of the *Odyssey*, ultimate token of recognition between husband and wife in a restored house. Heracles himself never enters the house. Each protagonist remains frozen in his or her own space, inner and outer, and does not succeed in crossing the barrier between the two areas.

The son who embodies the strongest bond between the two traverses the void between them, but does not succeed in bringing them together. The failure of his movements from inner to outer corresponds to the larger failure of this most basic of all mediating roles in the house, the child between parents. Orphaned of both parents, Hyllus bears the full brunt of the destruction of the house (941–2).

Hyllus initially stands on Deianeira's side, within the house. Corresponding to him on Heracles' side without the house is Lichas. Both Hyllus and Lichas are emissaries of reconciliation between outer and inner worlds. Both effect just the opposite of their assigned task: they are the instruments of the mutual destruction of the husband and wife, widening the initial breach to hopeless proportions. Hyllus goes from Deianeira to Heracles, witnesses his father's terrible suffering, and brings back the news that sends the mother to her death. Lichas performs the same journey in reverse. Going from Heracles to Deianeira, he brings back to Heracles the gift from wife to husband which destroys him.

Yet Hyllus' mediation between Heracles and Deianeira is not totally negative. He also teaches Heracles something about the civilizing power of the house, the love and loyalties of its bonds. Hyllus is a child of the new, more sensitive age, the true son of Deianeira. He possesses the flexibility to revise his earlier judgment of her guilt,[66] a flexibility lacking in his father's harsher character. Hyllus' demonstration of Deianeira's loyalty is lost on Heracles, but Heracles will use Hyllus to found a new house out of the shattered remnants of the two houses which he has destroyed. Emphasis thus shifts from possessiveness to recreation, from the egocentric, archaic hero who insists that Hyllus abjure his mother and be his father's son entirely[67] to a hero who founds and restores, albeit with the same harshness as that with which he destroyed.

If the ambiguities of Heracles' civilizing functions center on his relation to the 'outer' world of the beasts and monsters, those of Deianeira center upon the house. Her life-giving and life-sustaining functions as the keeper of the house are heavily underscored in her language, with its sexual and seasonal metaphors (28, 30–2, 204) and her talk of the rhythms of life and death (144ff., 307ff., 546–9). Yet her house also contains, 'hidden' or 'well locked up' (579), the poison of the Centaur, a reminder of the explosive sexuality which is the bonding force of the house. The gentle, faithful Deianeira comes to speak with bitter irony of her 'reward for keeping the house' (*oikouria*, 542), takes to 'secrecy' (*lathrāi*, 533) and acts done 'in darkness' (*skotōi*, 596), and finally 'in the house in secret' (κατ' οἶκον ἐν δόμοις κρυφῇ, 689) smears the robe with the poison which she has kept in the 'recesses' of the house (686). At the end, however, she will 'hide' herself away in the house in a different sense, when she has shaken free of the 'beast' and dies with heroic resolve.

The wool with which Deianeira anoints the robe is a part of the domestic security of the house: it comes from the κτησίου βοτοῦ (690), the flock which forms part of the possessions of the house.

---

66. 734–7, 807–12, 1114–42.

67. Cf. 1064–9, 1124–5. Note Heracles' possessive insistence on 'mine', ἐμός, ἐμοί, 1158, 1204–5, 1238–9.

The robe, of course, has its proper place within the house. Fashioned and stored by women within the house under the wife's direct supervision, it falls under the household stewardship for which Deianeira comes to see herself so bitterly rewarded in 542 (*oikouria*, 'reward for tending the house'). But of course this domestic gift with which Deianeira seeks to reach beyond the enclosed realm of her house, its very 'recesses' (686), transmits the virulent power of the beast-world.

'What is in the house', τά γ᾽ ἐν δόμοισιν (625), becomes increasingly ominous as those bestial powers are 'revealed' (cf. 608, 862). Early in the play Deianeira, believing Lichas' story, innocently says that she will make ready everything 'within' (τἄνδον, 334). But later, as she hands over the robe, she speaks of her vow, 'to show him with full justice to the gods a new sacrificer in a new robe' if ever she should see him 'safe within the house' (ἐς δόμους...σωθέντα, 610–13).[68] When Lichas accepts the robe with the promise to 'fit upon (Heracles) her trust of words' (623), Deianeira replies, 'Go then, for you fully understand how stand the things in the house' (ἐξεπίστασαι τά γ᾽ ἐν δόμοισιν ὡς ἔχοντα τυγχάνει, 624–5).[69]

The ambiguity of Deianeira's language does not necessarily mean that she is guilty, but she is not entirely innocent either.[70] As she reaches into the dark recesses of the house and her own beast-haunted past, something of those dark elemental forces enters her world and darkens her limpid discourse and innocence with tragic complexity. The ambiguity of her language reflects the now clouded nature of her house and her life. Something of the Centaur's duplicity – *parphasis*, if that is the right reading at 662, *doliomutha*, 839 – speaks through her. Her language too enters into

68. Both πανδίκως and καινός sharpen the tragic irony. For the latter see 867 and Jebb *ad* 613. πανδίκως echoes Deianeira's premature joy at 294–5. See Kirkwood, *Study*, p. 257.

69. The irony of 624 is enhanced by the repetition of ἐπίστασθαι: cf. 543, 582, 626.

70. See Beck, *passim*, pp. 146–8; Bowra, pp. 127–8; Letters, p. 200; Waldock, pp. 98–100; Whitman, p. 115 with n. 37 on p. 266; also Richmond Lattimore, *Story Patterns in Greek Tragedy* (London 1964), pp. 32–3. Most interpreters agree that we are not to think of Deianeira as intentionally killing Heracles (*contra*, I. Errandonea, *Mnemosyne* 55 (1927), 145–64, especially 156ff.). Compare the situation in Antiphon 1. 20 and 1. 26. Ovid, too, in his version of the story, insists on her innocence (*quid tradat nescia, Met.* 9. 155).

Charles Segal

the pattern of double-meaning and deceit which had begun with the appearance of Heracles' emissary on the stage.

The tragic ironies of Deianeira's effects upon her house appear clearly in the choral passage, ode and *kommos*, which stands between the news of Heracles' sufferings and the description of Deianeira's suicide – that is, at the point when the two principals of this house are destroyed. After the concentrated account of Nessus' wiles (831–40), the chorus turns to Deianeira. She acted 'when she saw great harm for the house' (προσορῶσα δόμοισι βλάβαν, 842). But her attempt to defend the house from 'harm' has just been proven ruinous. Birth and nurture, which had earlier characterized her maternal concern and protectiveness (31, 148–50, 308, etc.), now recur inverted to describe the poison 'which death begot, which a glittering snake nurtured' (834). The prior cause, Iole, the 'new bride', brought forth, 'yes brought forth, an Erinys for the house' (892–5).

The destruction of the house appears also through a number of other metaphors which have to do with the infelicitous juncture of male and female worlds and the disastrous results of Deianeira's attempt to move from her 'inner' into Heracles' 'outer' world. When she sends Hyllus out of the house to search for Heracles, she uses a metaphor of commerce – that is, of travel and activity in the 'outside' world. 'Depart now, my son, for when one learns of good fortune it is a purchase of gain (κέρδος ἐμπολᾷ) late though it come' (92–3). Yet this commercial metaphor recurs in a literal sense to describe events in Heracles' realm which undermine the house: the 'sale' of Heracles to Omphale (252, 276) which is part of the excuse alleged by Lichas for Heracles' sack of Oechalia, with its destruction of another house. More significant still is Deianeira's later commercial metaphor, now in an embittered and cynical mood, when she sees herself receiving Iole into her house as Heracles' concubine, 'as a captain who has taken on freight, a merchandise of insult to my heart' (φόρτον ὥστε ναυτίλος | λωβητὸν ἐμπόλημα τῆς ἐμῆς φρενός, 537–8).[71] The echo of 92–3 adds to the bitterness. It is just afterwards that she makes her second attempt to reach out of the house to Heracles with the robe, and her parting words to Lichas also recall that scene at

71. We may add also the ominous associations of ships and sailing in 537–8, 560–1, 656

the end of the prologue (χώρει νυν, ὦ παῖ, 92; στείχοις ἂν ἤδη, 624).

Related to the destructive outward movement of the commercial metaphor is a sea-metaphor. In her first confrontation with the truth of Heracles' actions Deianeira dismisses the injury done her with the phrase, 'Let it flow by with the breeze' (ῥείτω κατ' οὖρον, 468), an evocation of the fresh, open world which her generosity deserves. But Hyllus uses the same metaphor, and the same word, in his parting curse to his mother as she enters the house for the last time: 'Let her have a fine breeze (*ouros*) as she creeps off far from my eyes' (815–16). The metaphor which expressed her willingness to receive Heracles back into the house recurs to seal the house's doom. The point of the repeated metaphor is not that Deianeira should stay within the house, but that this house cannot unify itself. The inner, womanly realm cannot bridge the gap to the outer, male realm; and attempts to do so, as reflected in these image patterns, only bring about its destruction. What 'sails in strong on favoring breeze' (ἔμπεδα κατουρίζει, 827) is, as the chorus sings prophetically, Heracles' death (828–30).[72]

At the very center of the house stands the hearth, also closely associated with the inner world of the women who tend it. In this play the motif of the hearth undergoes a series of inversions analogous to those of travel and the sea-breeze discussed above. At the news of Heracles' approach the women utter cries of joy at the hearth (ἐφεστίοις ἀλαλαγαῖς, 205) to salute the reunion of husband and wife and the renewal of marriage (cf. *mellonumphos*, 207). But twice the altars where Heracles dons the poisoned robe are referred to as a 'hearth', once by Deianeira herself in presenting the robe to Lichas (ἐφέστιον σέλας, 607) and once by the chorus (νασιῶτιν ἑστίαν, 658). Immediately after this second passage the chorus speaks of 'sacrifice' (*thuter*, 659; cf. Deianeira's 'new sacrificer in a new robe', 613), and then alludes to the beast's 'ointment' and 'persuasion' which will 'melt' Heracles (661–2, reading Blaydes' συντακείς). The saving, domestic fire of the 'hearth' thus merges with the fires that activate the poison;

---

72. On the verb and the metaphor of 827 see Kamerbeek *ad loc.*, who also notes the connection with *ouros* in 815 and the link with the literal voyage of Heracles in the previous ode (656).

the gift intended to bring the hero back within the house destroys the house utterly.

When that destruction is complete, the hearth returns in a context of centrifugal movement, away from the house, just the opposite of the movement which Deianeira hoped to attain. At the news of her suicide the chorus wishes for a breeze that would come to their hearth and remove them from the sight of Heracles' agonies (εἴθ᾽ ἀνεμόεσσά τις | γένοιτ᾽ ἔπουρος ἑστιῶτις αὔρα..., 953–4). Here the conjunction of the hearth-figure with the breeze-image emphasizes the shift from shelter to destructiveness as the distinction between inner and outer realms breaks down.

V

Like other Sophoclean heroes, Heracles is harsh or 'raw-minded', *omophron* (975). And yet this harshness is also inseparably connected with a towering heroic strength. Some interpreters hold that the *Trachiniae* presents the 'destruction' of the myth of Heracles,[73] that he is 'barely sufficient and credible as the hero who commanded the love of Deianeira',[74] that his great deeds remain 'insufficient to reinstate the sublime traditional figure'.[75] This view is, I think, only partly correct. What we have is not simply the 'destruction' of a mythical hero, but a tragic 'self-alienation', to use Reinhardt's word.[76] In terms of the physical action of the play, the 'best of men', as he is repeatedly called (177, 488, 811) is destroyed by a woman and weeps womanish tears (1062–3, 1070–5). The hero of physical strength is punished through his body. In his affliction he becomes all body in the most negative sense, until at the end we have a glimmer of *psyche* (1260). His civilizing conquests benefit a future that he will not see. This reversal is his equivalent of Deianeira's destruction of her house. His outer world and the values that go with it are destroyed, just as are Deianeira's inner world and its values.

Heracles' case is more complex. On the one hand we admire his resolve in meeting his death, and we discern here the true Heracles,

73. So Murray, *passim*.
74. Lattimore (above, note 70), p. 60.
75. Letters, pp. 188–9.
76. Reinhardt, p. 69: 'in seiner Qual sich selbst entfremdet'.

the great hero of legendary exploits. On the other hand it is impossible not to sympathize with Deianeira. When Heracles passes over her noble and piteous end without a sign of interest, let alone commiseration, his behavior is callous, but it is also the expression of the divinely ordained destiny which now grips him entirely. In that perspective, Deianeira's fate, moving as it is, is left in the background. Heracles has a place within a heroic world which, as Bowra says,[77] is 'difficult to relate to the fifth century', and, we may add, to that more human sensibility embodied in Deianeira. We may compare the Heracles of Pindar's poem on *nomos*, a hero whose violence we must, despite ourselves, accept because it is part of an all-powerful, but none the less impenetrable, reality, a compelling world-order whose justice we cannot easily discern in the acts themselves.[78] Within the Sophoclean corpus we may compare also Ajax, who leaves Tecmessa and Eurysaces to their fate, Antigone who abandons Ismene and Haemon, the aged Oedipus who curses his sons and leaves the city he once ruled to its doom. Heracles' heroic world and Deianeira's human warmth and tenderness are mutually exclusive. Sophocles seeks not to vindicate the one against the other, but to dramatize the tragedy of their irreconcilability and their mutual destructiveness.

Even amid the brutal roars of his pain Heracles retains a heroic grandeur. When he catches sight of Hyllus out of the smoky flames he tells him not to flee, 'not even if you should have to share death with me as I die' (μηδ' εἴ σε χρὴ θανόντι συνθανεῖν ἐμοί, 797–8). Here he simultaneously confronts his own death and appeals to a heroic ideal which he assumes will claim the young man's total devotion. Hyllus, whose report of these details makes them the more moving, ends his account with a vehement denunciation of Deianeira and a eulogy of Heracles, 'the best of all men upon the earth, another such as you will never see again' (811–12).

Almost as great as Heracles' physical suffering is his mental anguish at his present helplessness (1012–14, 1044–52, 1070–5, 1089–1104). Take me, he asks Hyllus, 'where no mortal will see me' (800). He is ashamed that others should 'see' him weep

77. Bowra, p. 135.
78. See Martin Ostwald, 'Pindar, *Nomos*, and Heracles', *HSCP* 69 (1965), 109–38. In Pindar, however, as Ostwald excellently observes (pp. 126, 130), that violence is to be reconciled with justice in a mood of faith that goes beyond anything in the *Trachiniae*.

(1073). Even in the terrible scene of his agony and violence there is an intimation, dim though it is, of a larger destiny: he must not die here (μηδ' αὐτοῦ θάνω, 802). He undertakes the painful journey (cf. 804–5) across the water to Trachis. Later, but still before his *anagnorisis* of the oracles, we see him at his worst: he calls himself 'nothing' (1107–8) and thinks only of the sweet revenge of killing Deianeira with his own hand (1108–11). But even in the midst of this 'nothingness' he calls himself the child of 'the noblest of mothers' (1105), 'named the son of Zeus who has his place among the stars' (ὁ τοῦ κατ' ἄστρα Ζηνὸς αὐδηθεὶς γόνος, 1106). The language of this last line on the one hand suggests the distance between the present and the legendary Heracles, but on the other hand it looks away from this scene of brutalizing pain to celestial horizons and vast perspectives. It reminds us of the picture of Heracles spanning continents in the parode (100–1) and the breadth of setting, celestial and astral rhythms, which describe the toils of Heracles throughout that ode (94–6, 130–1, 132). We recall too the first mention of Heracles in the play as he appeared to the young Deianeira in her distress, a resplendent rescuer, 'of Zeus and Alcmena the glorious son' (ὁ κλεινὸς ἦλθε Ζηνὸς 'Αλκμήνης τε παῖς, 19).

The oscillation between Heracles' greatness and his 'nothing-ness', between heroism and bestiality, comes to rest when Heracles hears the name of Nessus. Suddenly his suffering, hitherto direc-tionless and confused, takes on a meaning. There is a sharp cry of pain, ἰού, ἰού (1143), followed by the strong simple phrases in which he grasps his fate (1144–7):

I am gone, destroyed. Light I have no longer. Alas, I understand at what point of misfortune I stand. Go, my son, your father is no longer. Call all the seed of your kindred...

Understanding is all. 'I know', *phrono* (1145), strikes a new and important note. His is a tragedy of 'late learning', like Deianeira's and Hyllus' (710f., 934).[79] Heracles' next thoughts are not of himself, but of his clan, to be summoned by Hyllus whom he addresses with what is perhaps the second echo of Deianeira's parting injunction (cf. χώρει νυν, ὦ παῖ, 92 and ἴθ', ὦ τέκνον, 1146; 624).

79. See Whitman, pp. 104ff.; Torrance, pp. 301–2.

Heracles' moment of illumination suggests an even more famous passage in Sophoclean tragedy, the finale of the *Oedipus at Colonus*:

My children, you no longer have a father in this day. Perished are all my fortunes (1611–13).

The two heroes and the two situations are obviously very different. Oedipus has his illumination from the beginning, Heracles discovers his only abruptly at the end.[80] The former has a calm, expectant solemnity; the latter a harsh, thunderous violence. And yet both share a personal insight into a god-given destiny that sets them aside from all other mortals and confers upon them a special, guiding authority (though in the case of Heracles a violent authority) in the last scenes of their life.

'Call all the seed of your brothers', Heracles commands (1147), 'so that you all may learn the final utterance of the oracles that I know' (ὡς τελευταίαν ἐμοῦ | φήμην πύθησθε θεσφάτων ὅσ' οἶδ' ἐγώ, 1149–50). Not only does Heracles have a sense of larger continuities of blood which contrasts with Deianeira's fearful isolation at her end, but he has intimations of the divine forces in the background of his life and of his death, as his expression τελευταίαν φήμην θεσφάτων, 'ultimate oracular utterance', implies.[81] His concern is now with what of himself can survive among men, and that is not only his 'blood' (i.e. his children, 1147), but also the true 'tale' of 'report' (*pheme*, 1150) of a mysterious end.

These verses, with their triple stress on the finality of the moment, on the oracles, and on Heracles' personal and privileged understanding (*oida*, 1150; cf. *phrono*, 1145), confirm the hero's place apart in a special understanding. In his response to the name 'Nessus' (1141) Heracles shows the same heroic energy and decisive speed that marked his success against the living Nessus in Deianeira's narrative (565–8).[82] We glimpse the old heroism

80. See B. M. W. Knox, *The Heroic Temper*, Sather Classical Lectures 35 (Berkeley and Los Angeles 1964), pp. 148ff. The comparison of the violent Heracles of the *Trachiniae* to the aged Oedipus will perhaps shock some readers, but it is more compelling than might at first appear. Oedipus too has no saintly mildness at the end. See Waldock, p. 88: 'There is no blasphemy in comparing the last phase of this drama with the last phase of the *Oedipus Coloneus*, for Heracles, too, has his part assigned, he too is semi-sacred from now on.'
81. For these associations of φήμη see LSJ *s.v.*, 1.
82. The parallel is nicely observed by Kirkwood, *Study*, p. 118.

which could defeat the beasts. Yet the difference is precisely that this Nessus is dead. The enemy is now within Heracles himself, and his heroism unfolds not in action, but in understanding.

This understanding includes the hidden purport of the oracle: 'I thought I would fare well (*prattein kalōs*), but it was nothing other than my death, for those who die have no more toil' (1171–3). The lines call up the entire course of the hero's life of 'toils', *mochthoi* which 'have stood over him' and from which he now sees the long-sought 'release' (*lysis*, 1170–1). The repetition of the word 'toils', *mochthos* (1170, 1173) sums up the dominant quality of Heracles' experience of life.

This recognition of the oracle's meaning is tantamount to a broad pronouncement of the uncertain end of all human effort. Only 'those who die win no more toil' (1173). 'Success', 'happiness' – *eu prattein* or *kalōs prattein* (1171) – has been a *leitmotif* of the play.[83] Here Heracles discovers its precariousness. The hero of violent physical action comes, near his end, to a spirit of reflective generalization.

The oracle which Heracles here unravels has occurred twice before (168, 821–30), and the second time the chorus had already interpreted it as Heracles does, i.e. death (828–30). Yet it is a far different thing when the one who has borne these 'toils' and longed always for that promised 'release' (cf. 654) is himself able to accept the finality of the actual 'release'. What for the chorus was mere guesswork is now, on the lips of Heracles himself, the fulfilled certainty of Zeus.[84] That earlier 'release' which Deianeira attempted (554) and the actual 'release' which Heracles brought her by main force (21) are revealed as superficial and delusive beside the bleak truth of the 'release' which Heracles has to face. Illusory too are the hopes uttered earlier for the cessation of 'toil' or 'suffering' (*mochthos, ponos*, 117, 654, 829), for in human life 'toil' has no end. Death itself is the ultimate 'toil' or labor.

Heracles' insight into his own destiny and the necessary shape of his life at the end does not make him gentler. He is still the harsh, imperious hero who expects to be obeyed completely (cf. 1204–5,

83. See 57, 92–3, 192, 230–1, 293–4, 297. See also Easterling, p. 58.
84. I disagree, therefore, with Adams, p. 126, who thinks that the chorus' guess about the oracle in 828–30 must 'ruin Heracles' subsequent realization that the oracle meant his death'.

1238–9), ready to invoke the terrible threat of a father's curse (1202, 1239–40). Piety or impiety is a matter of what 'pleases (his) heart' (1246). Like Achilles with Priam in the *Iliad*, he knows that he can be stirred to an outburst of violent anger (1176), and he warns Hyllus against awakening his pain and the vehemence it would bring (1242).[85] Yet the wrath never breaks forth completely.

The scene between Hyllus and Heracles at the end is important in a play which is much concerned with fathers' treatment of their children, a subject of which Zeus' treatment of Heracles is the test case (cf. 139–40, 1265–9). Heracles' treatment of Hyllus is no less problematical. The 'favor' or 'gratitude' (*charis*) established between them is far from secure (1217, 1229, 1252). The obedience demanded is absolute ('obedience to a father is the noblest law', 1177–8; cf. 1183ff., 1224, 1350–3). The 'instruction' of the son by the father is harsh (1245), and the 'pieties' which he is taught are ambiguous (1246). Yet there are hints, albeit faint, of a gentleness too. The marriage of Hyllus and Iole (and I do not believe that προσθοῦ δάμαρτα of 1224 can mean merely concubinage:[86] cf. 406, 428–9) is a necessity dictated by Heracles' sense of the future (cf. his reference to his descendants and the oracle in 1147–9). But in the lighting of the pyre he has more latitude. He does not force Hyllus to do it, as he might have. Where he can yield, he does.[87]

Once the pyre and the marriage of Hyllus and Iole are assured, there is something like calm about Heracles. His last iambic lines are heavy with the solemnity of final things:

> παῦλά τοι κακῶν
> αὕτη, τελευτὴ τοῦδε τἀνδρὸς ὑστάτη.

This is my rest from ills, the final end of this man (1255–6).

When he heard the name of Nessus he proclaimed the 'final utterance' of the oracles, τελευταίαν ἐμοῦ φήμην (1149). With τελευτή...ὑστάτη in 1256 his knowledge of his 'end' is consummated. The 'release from toils' which Heracles expected (1171) proves to be but a small 'rest' or 'pause' from ills (1256).

85. *Iliad* 24. 560, 569–70.
86. So J. K. MacKinnon, 'Heracles' Intention in his Second Request of Hyllus: *Trach.* 1215–16', *CQ* n.s. 21 (1971), 33–41, especially 39; accepted by McCall, p. 161, n. 20.   87. See Bowra, p. 142; Adams, p. 131.

'The last end of this man', 1256, would have made a fitting close for Heracles and a suitable exit line. But Sophocles gives him five final anapaests (1259–63):

> ἄγε νυν, πρὶν τήνδ' ἀνακινῆσαι
> νόσον, ὦ ψυχὴ σκληρά, χάλυβος
> λιθοκόλλητον στόμιον παρέχουσ',
> ἀνάπαυε βοήν, ὡς ἐπίχαρτον
> τελέουσ' ἀεκούσιον ἔργον.

Come, my hard soul, before this disease stirs again, put on a stone-studded bit of steel and cease your cry, accomplishing as something of joy a deed done by constraint.

Nearly every word in this passage is important. The hero of physical strength, addressing his soul or *psyche*, becomes a hero of inner strength. The last 'deed', *ergon*, is a spiritual as much as a physical effort. The darker, more complex 'joy' (*epicharton*) of this final act contrasts with the outward, premature, misplaced joy of the sacrifice, performed 'with happy spirit' (ἵλεῳ φρενί) 'rejoicing (*chairon*) in the adornment of the robe' (763–4).[88] The hero who roared like a beast (805) now calls upon what is most human in him, his *psyche*, to keep silence.[89]

This heroic silence is part of a carefully prepared development. Heracles, previously 'unweeping' (*astenaktos*) in his sufferings, wept like a girl (1070–5). But after recognizing the oracles, he instructs Hyllus to prepare the pyre 'without weeping', *astenaktos* (1200). Emphasizing that such freedom from lamentation is a distinctive sign of his heroic character (εἴπερ εἶ τοῦδ' ἀνδρός, 1200–1), he redeems the lamentation of the earlier scenes (note the repetition of *astenaktos* in 1074 and 1200). The imperious hero who warned against 'sharpening (his) mouth' in anger (τοὐμὸν ὀξῦναι στόμα, 1176) and by his condition imposed a frightened silence on others (ἴσχε δακὼν στόμα σόν, 976–7) now enjoins silence on himself.[90]

---

88. Cf. also the premature χαίροιμ' ἄν of Deianeira, 293–4. Also 129 (*chara*), 201 (*chara*), 228 (*charton*), 1246 (*terpein*).

89. The *psyche* is not, of course, the Socratic 'self', but even before Socrates the word connotes the specialness of the human spirit in its capacity for tragic decision, suffering, and heroism; cf. Pindar, *Pyth.* 3. 61; S. *Ajax* 154 and *Antig.* 175–7. See in general W. K. C. Guthrie, *A History of Greek Philosophy*, vol. 3 (Cambridge 1969), pp. 467–8; E. A. Havelock, 'The Socratic Self as it is Parodied in Aristophanes' *Clouds*', *YCS* 22 (1972), 5–9, 15–16.

90. Ovid, *Met.* 9. 163–5 reverses the Sophoclean presentation of Heracles' heroism by having the hero begin in silence and only later break into a cry.

The metaphor of the 'bit' or 'bridle' (*stomion*, 1261) bears on the central ironies and inversions of the play. The word implies control over beasts, especially horses. In these last lines Heracles has become a true tamer of beasts.[91] In his weakness and 'nothing-ness' (1107–8) he conquers the equine Nessus more truly than he did in the full vigor of his strength. His weapon is now not an arrow armed with a poison from the realm of beasts and monsters, but the bit of his soul. The victory is inward and spiritual and is expressed in a metaphor taken from man's civilized and civilizing arts.

This 'bit' of the soul's restraints answers the 'deadly deceptive-speaking seething spurs' of the Centaur's drug (φόνια δολιόμυθα κέντρ' ἐπιζέσαντα, 839–40). That poison and all that it sym-bolized – the lust, bestiality, violence of Heracles – appropriately appeared in a metaphor which implied an inversion of the positions of man and beast. The 'seething' of the poison's 'spurs' on Heracles in 840 describes the physical, external effect of the venom 'foaming up' on contact with the heated skin, and we may com-pare the 'foaming up' of the venom-dipped wool on the ground in 702, ἀναζέουσι θρομβώδεις ἀφροί. But this 'seething' is appro-priate also to the *inner* ferment of Heracles' violence and lust. 'Seething' often describes a state of emotional agitation (cf. *O.C.* 434, Hdt. 7. 13. 2). Hence it once more correlates the physical effects of the poison's 'disease' and the beast-imagery which accompanies it with the inward state which the poison symbolizes (see above, section II). But the 'bit' at the end marks a state of calm and rest (cf. *paula*, 1255). Now in 1261 it is Heracles who wields the curbs. Heracles' inward victory subdues what the poison stands for and sets right the earlier inversion of man and

One thinks also of the dramatic effect of the silences of Aeschylus (cf. Aristoph. *Frogs*, 911–26).

91. The metaphor of the 'bit' carries vivid associations of the reversal of man and beast in A. *Ag.* 238 and 1066; S. *Antig.* 477–8. Cf. also S. frag. 785 N² = 869 P; *PMG* frag. adesp. 1037. 16–18 (Page). It is instructive to compare Sophocles' imagery with Pindar's in the latter's myth of Bellerophon, another monster-destroying hero. When Bellerophon conquers his 'beast', Pegasus, the literal bridle (*chalinos, Ol.* 13. 65) becomes the figurative 'philter' or 'drug' (*philtron, Ol.* 13. 68; *pharmakon*, 85). The drug itself, given by the civilizing Olympian goddess, Athena, is 'mild' (*praü, Ol.* 13. 85); and the horse is subdued. In Sophocles the pattern is just the reverse: the equine figure triumphs, and the literal 'drug' or 'philter' becomes the figurative 'spurs' imposed on the beast-taming hero (*kentra*, 840).

beast. The monstrous 'disease' was previously the mysterious force of Eros within Heracles himself or a subhuman power which 'devoured' him like a ravening beast. Now the *nosos* has become a tangible foe (1260), a simple physical reality, which the hero's endurance and strength of soul can face and conquer (cf. the juxtaposition of *nosos* and *psuche*, 1259–60).

The metaphor of the bit in 1262 caps a whole series of metaphorical inversions of the civilized arts. Deianeira describes the action of the poison upon the tuft of wool in similes relating to the working of wood (699–700) and the cultivation of the vine (703–4). The latter simile suggests that Heracles the 'farmer' is destroyed by the 'land' he plows (cf. 32–3; *Antigone* 569). The robe itself was glued to Heracles' back like the work of a carpenter (ἀρτί-κολλος ὥστε τέκτονος, 768). Deianeira's verbs of 'fitting', *prosarmozein* and *harmozein* at 494 and 687, likewise suggest the joiner's craft.[92] She preserves the Beast's instructions as if written on a tablet of bronze (682–3). Now at the end the figure of the 'stone-set bit' (λιθοκόλλητον στόμιον) shows man's civilizing craft at work on its deepest and most significant levels, within the *psyche*. Here Sophocles gives us just the glimmer of a double vision of Heracles which Euripides developed far more richly and in much greater detail in his *Hercules Furens*: on the one hand the figure of the traditional myth, the hero of the dodecathlon; on the other hand the tragic hero who emerges from a primitive world of subdued monsters to become fully human himself, the hero of the inward labors, the ψυχὴ σκληρά (1260).

Though the point is not essential for my interpretation of the play, it follows naturally from the view suggested here that Sophocles means us to think of Heracles at the end as moving toward his apotheosis. Yet the poet has handled this subject with the greatest delicacy and restraint. It is inconceivable that the ending of the myth could not have been present in his and his audience's minds.[93] The figure of the 'hero god' had been cele-

92. See *Odyssey* 5. 247–8. For the sinister associations of the word at 494 see Jebb *ad loc.*

93. For the evidence, archaeological and literary, associating the pyre on Oeta with Heracles' immortality see Robert, pp. 597–8; M. P. Nilsson, 'Der Flammentod des Herakles auf dem Oite', *ARW* 21 (1922), 310–16 (cult of Heracles on the summit of Oeta from at least archaic times); Angelo Brelich, *Gli eroi greci* (Rome 1958), pp. 193–4.

brated by Pindar in glorious lyrics (*Nem.* 3. 22 and *Nem.* 1. 33–72). Sophocles himself was to give the divinized Heracles a prominent role at the end of the *Philoctetes*. It is true that the *Trachiniae* makes no explicit mention of the apotheosis, but a number of expressions can be read as hints, particularly 1208–10 and 1270.[94]

What is most important and most typically Sophoclean, however, is that the tragedy unfolds fully on the human plane with no supernatural solution to mitigate it, even though we are never allowed to forget the supernatural background. Heracles faces his destruction by a woman and a beast without the reassurance that he will be reborn as a god on Olympus. He says repeatedly that he expects only to die (1040–3, 1172, 1203); and his death is all that is necessary. Even his recognition of the oracles only confirms him in his awareness of the finality of his plight and steels his resolution for the end.

On the other hand the will of Zeus, remote and obscure, has been hovering over the entire play. The building of the pyre and the motif of the oracles must have suggested to the audience that higher order of reality, obscure though it remains to all the human actors, Heracles included.[95] The deification remains veiled in the darkness which surrounds Zeus and his will in this play. Zeus, like Aphrodite, is the hidden, but ever-present 'agent' (*praktor*, 251, 862). Yet the spectators can still enjoy something of the privileged perspective of the gods. They can catch in Heracles' closing accents the traces of a figure proving himself worthy of Olympus.[96]

The abruptness with which the motif of the pyre appears

94. For the relevance of the legend of the apotheosis to the play see most recently H. Lloyd-Jones, *The Justice of Zeus*, Sather Classical Lectures 41 (Berkeley and Los Angeles 1971), pp. 126–8. Among those who have strongly opposed the idea that we are to think of the apotheosis are Ehrenberg, p. 390; Galinsky, pp. 51–2; Heinz, pp. 288–9 with note 5; Reinhardt, p. 74; Schiassi (above, note 28), pp. xxiii and 180–1 (*ad* 1259–63); Whitman, p. 120; Dain–Mazon (above, note 19), p. 7.

95. For this double perspective on the apotheosis with more or less stress on the discrepancy between the myth and the play see especially Bowra, pp. 159–61; Gellie, p. 77; Kirkwood, *Study*, pp. 67–8; Letters, pp. 192–3; Méautis, pp. 290–1; Moore (above, note 14), p. 77, n. 155; Pohlenz, p. 208; Zielinski (above, note 59), pp. 493–9. Seneca destroys this carefully balanced tragic perspective by beginning his *Hercules Oetaeus* with the hero awaiting apotheosis.

96. Adams, p. 130, puts the case at its strongest: 'Before our eyes the son of Zeus sheds his mortality, and with it all the thoughts and feelings of a mortal.'

supports this view. Why should Sophocles introduce a detail that could only seem irrelevant and puzzling if we are to banish all further thoughts of Heracles' future? Linforth, who argued strongly against the relevance of the apotheosis to the action, observed, 'There is absolutely nothing in the play itself which would lead the audience to expect that Heracles would die from any cause other than poison.'⁹⁷ The play, he felt, 'comes to an end with a scene which has no organic connection with what precedes'.⁹⁸ The logical conclusion from this line of argument, however, is not that the apotheosis is entirely suppressed, as Linforth thought. In that case Sophocles would have done better to omit the pyre altogether and end the play in some other way. To call the pyre scene 'an afterpiece in which (Sophocles) yields to the obligations of history'⁹⁹ and then to say that we are not to think of the apotheosis is illogical. Those very 'obligations of history' imply recognition of the divinized hero who became an object of worship. Both in the *Ajax* and the *Oedipus at Colonus* Sophocles shows no aversion to reminding his audience of the special cult status achieved by his heroes.¹⁰⁰

Heracles' final lines, I suggest, show the hero being purged of the bestiality with which he has struggled all his life. The hero is now ready for apotheosis. The inward basis for that apotheosis replaces the clear assurance of the actual event. Apotheosis does not, of course, mean sainthood. There is no sweetness and light in this end. Attaining Olympus, Heracles becomes in death as remote from ordinary humanity and human values as he was in life.

Heracles himself endures his suffering in at least partial ignorance of his future. He expects that only death awaits him, and this expectation is crucial to the heroic quality of his endurance. He has intimations of a large destiny; he knows that he has met his end in the way that Zeus ordained, and he knows that he must die by burning on the pyre. But all this tells him only that his life has some coherent shape, that it is not meaningless. He does not know what that shape is nor that it has any extension after death.

The lesser figures who surround him see even less than he. To

97. Linforth, p. 262.
98. *Ibid.* p. 261.
99. *Ibid.* p. 262.
100. See *Ajax* 1171–9 and Peter Burian, 'Supplication and Hero Cult in Sophocles' *Ajax*', *GRBS* 13 (1972), 151–6.

the chorus and to Hyllus all is darkness, and that very ignorance is a potent source of the tragic element in the play. Heracles' sense of his destiny by no means dissolves his participation in this tragic element, but gives him a heroic status above the others. This movement at the very end makes it difficult to regard the *Trachiniae* as, ultimately, a humanist statement.[101] Perhaps it is not useful to categorize the play in such terms. But it is important to do justice to the closing movement in Heracles.

VI

Heracles' heroism traverses the arc between Cenaean and Oetean fire. Before the flaming altars at Cenaeum Heracles is utterly subjected to the beast-world of his past. When he asks to be 'ferried' across to Trachis, he is recalling the fatal 'ferrying' of Nessus which that 'beast' here avenges (cf. *porthmeuson*, 802 and *porthmoi*, 571). But that movement across the sea away from Cenaeum is the first step out of this beast-world and the first glimmer of reason and purpose in the midst of the chaos and wild pain caused by those fires.

The pyre on Mt Oeta which completes Heracles' destiny answers the perverted sacrifice which celebrated his impure victory early in the play. The fire which kindled the poison of the beast and reduced Heracles to almost bestial status gives way to a fire which is to mark his passage to the gods. Even if one does not accept the apotheosis, this fire at the end is still part of a divinely appointed destiny. Its associations are with the gods, not with the beasts.[102]

The flames at the altars of Cenaeum are the reverse of a true sacrificial fire.[103] Instead of serving as the instrument of an up-

101. See Easterling, p. 68; H. A. Mason, 'The Women of Trachis', *Arion* 2, no. 1 (1963), 62ff.; on the question in general W. R. Johnson, 'The Counter-Classical Sensibility and its Critics', *Calif. Stud. in Class. Antiqu.* 3 (1970), 123–51.

102. Méautis, p. 286, rightly points out the contrast between the flame of the pyre and 'cette autre flamme du désir, de la luxure qui l'a brûlé pendant toute sa vie', but he gives that contrast an irrelevant and misleading turn: 'Après la flamme de l'Œta vient la claire lumière de la résurrection' (p. 290). This light is neither so bright nor so clear.

103. Cf. also the chorus' prematurely joyful reference to fire in 212 where they invoke Artemis *amphipuron*. The sacrifice at Cenaeum seems not to have occurred in the early epic version of the legend, 'The Capture of Oechalia', but is already present in Bacchylides 16: cf. Robert, pp. 569 and 595 with

ward mediation between man and god, they achieve a downward mediation between man and beast. The 'bloody fire' with which these offerings blaze (φλὸξ αἱματηρά, 766) suggests the venomous 'blood' of the Centaur which in fact accomplished the victory of the Beast. The sacrifice of bulls (*tauroktonei*, 760) for which these altars are aflame recalls that other bull, the tauriform Achelous, lurking behind the action (φάσμα ταύρου, 509). This Cenaean fire comes from the wood 'of the fat oak' (πιείρας δρυός, 766), and its smoke is a murky cloud which 'sits' upon the earth (προσέδρου λιγνύος, 794) instead of rising to Olympus.[104] The anointed tuft of wool disintegrates into something like the powder which results 'at the cutting of wood' (ἐν τομῇ ξύλου, 700). On the other hand the oak which will supply the wood of the Oetean pyre (1195) is Zeus' tree. The 'many-tongued oak' at Dodona in 1168 reminds us of its divine associations. Heracles also closely connects Zeus and Oeta when he introduces the pyre (1191).

On Oeta, Heracles commands, there must be no lamentation (1200), whereas the scene at Cenaeum is characterized by the most fearful cries and by a brutal violation of the 'sacred silence' or *euphēmia* befitting a sacrifice. There Heracles hurled Lichas from the cliff, and 'the whole crowd cried out with groaning' (ἅπας δ' ἀνευφήμησεν οἰμωγῇ λεώς, 783).

At Cenaeum, Deianeira shows her husband 'as a new sacrificer (θυτῆρα) in a new robe' (613), for he is a 'sacrificer' who ends by becoming the victim, burned and 'devoured'. On Oeta Heracles will participate in a kind of 'sacrifice' where he will be, in a sense, again the victim, burnt on the pyre. The motif of sacrifice helped introduce the Oetean pyre, for Hyllus knows the summit, having been there often 'as a sacrificer' (ὡς θυτήρ γε, 1192). At Cenaeum, however, Heracles 'was called sacrificer' (ἔνθα κλῄζεται θυτήρ, 659) in a context which stresses the power of the beast and his own subjection to the brutalizing fires of the poison. On Oeta the inversion of sacrificer and victim leads him upward toward the

n. 3. Sophocles, however, gives the sacrifice greater prominence by adding such details as the hundred bulls instead of Bacchylides' more plausible nine. For a more detailed discussion of sacrifice and its function in the play see my 'Mariage et sacrifice dans les *Trachiniennes* de Sophocle', *AC* 44 (1975), 30–53.

104. See Pindar, *Isth.* 4. 65–6; S. *Antig.* 1005–20. For the upward mediation of sacrificial fire and its smoke see Marcel Detienne, *Les jardins d'Adonis* (Paris 1972), pp. 73ff.

divine powers, away from the downward pull of the beasts. Here the burning of his body will have just the opposite meaning from its consumption by the fire-kindled poison at Cenaeum. These fires, far from causing the 'disease', will cure it (1208–9), even though Hyllus finds the idea hard to accept: 'How would I cure your body by burning it?' (καὶ πῶς ὑπαίθων σῶμ' ἂν ἰῴμην τὸ σόν;, 1210).

Closely related to the motif of fire is light. It follows a similar pattern, from a destructive to an ultimately creative role. Heracles and to some extent Deianeira perish of the light. But both also follow a path which leads to the light, from the caliginous altar flames at Cenaeum to the pyre on Oeta, from the Centaur's lies about the poison 'hidden' in the house to the truth.

As the play begins, night dominates. It is night which guides the rhythms of Deianeira's grief (29–30). In the parode it is night which has the active, controlling role in directing the alternations of human time, 'bringing to birth' and 'putting to rest' the sun (94–6). Night colors the emotional life presented in these first scenes; it is, Deianeira says, the time of a woman's fears (149–50). As we have already noted, night, the snaky part of Achelous and the Hydra have the same epithet, *aiolos*, 'dappled', 'shimmering' (94, 132; 11, 834). The poison must be applied in darkness (606ff., 689), amid talk of hiding shameful things 'in the dark' (596–7). The poison and its donor are repeatedly called 'black' (cf. 573, 717, 837) and the spear which won Iole is 'dark' (κελαινὰ λόγχα, 856).

In the first half of the play there can be no victory over the darkness because light is also destructive. In her misguided elation over Heracles' return Deianeira cries out with joy at the 'rising daylight', literally 'rising eye', of this report (ὄμμ' ἐμοὶ φήμης ἀνασχόν, 203–4). The phrase, however, has an ironic ring, for it suggests the violent and deadly alternation of night and day in the parode (94ff., especially 103). 'Day' in general has an ominous significance in the play (609, 660, 740, 944–6). Iole is 'too bright in *eye* (κατ' ὄμμα) and form' (379), and what is looked at 'with the eye' proves destructive (746–7, 997–8; also 272). It is by 'keeping her eye shadowed in hiding' that the Nurse observes Deianeira's pitiful end (λαθραῖον ὄμμ' ἐπεσκιασμένη, 914), the dark opposite to the 'rising eye' of her joy in 203–4. The 'infatuate madness' (*atē*) which ruins Heracles, we recall, is 'blind' (1104).

Words relating to 'appearance', generally from the root φαν-, are important and sinister. The very first line contains the 'appearance' (φανείς) of an 'ancient saying' which proves grimly true (cf. 943–6, 1169–73). Heracles 'shows forth' his promised offering at Cenaeum (εὐκταῖα φαίνων, 239), and Deianeira has a 'visible joy' (τέρψις ἐμφανής, 291), but in both cases the baleful effects of light upon the robe reverse the ostensibly happy implications of brightness.

Heracles' 'appearance', so eagerly awaited (186, 228), becomes intertwined with the more ominous 'appearances' of Eros (433), of the Centaur's poison revealed to the light (608), and of Aphrodite (863). In the last two passages repetition heavily underscores the ambiguity of these 'appearances': φανερὸς ἐμφανῶς (608); φανερὰ τῶνδ' ἐφάνη (863). The coming fate (*moira*) shows forth (*prophainei*) treacherous and great infatuation (849–50). The Hydra's venom is something 'made visible', an 'apparition' (*phasma*, 837), like the bull-shaped Achelous (509). All that the light has to reveal so far is the working of human passions and bestial black magic. The process cannot be reversed: Deianeira cannot make 'undone' what has been 'shown forth' to the light (τὸ φανθέν, 743–4).[105] When something does 'dis-appear', it is to 'reveal' destructive powers: such is the 'dis-appearance' of the tuft of wool in 676, ἠφάνισται.

Concealment and revelation are closely interwoven into this ambiguous shifting between darkness and night.[106] Though she, like the chorus, disapproves of secrecy (596–7, 669–70, 384), Deianeira had kept 'hidden' (*kekrummenon*, 556) the Centaur's blood. She is constrained by the threat of a 'hidden bed' (κρύφιον λέχος, 360) to speak to the chorus 'covertly' (*lathrāi*, 533) and to anoint the robe 'in secret' (*kruphēi*, 689). But when she next 'conceals', it is to die for this very act (κρύψασ' ἑαυτήν, 903). What is then 'revealed' to the light is the 'wretched body' of Heracles, ruined by her 'secret' plan, the body which he will 'reveal from its coverings' for all to 'behold' and 'see' (1078–80):

105. Cf. also Deianeira's *phanesomai* in 666 and her scruples about 'unclear' or 'obscure' zeal for action in 669–70 (προθυμίαν ἄδηλον ἔργου). We may recall again the φάσμα of 509, 837.
106. On the motif of secrecy see Kirkwood, *Study*, pp. 232–3.

δείξω γὰρ τάδ' ἐκ καλυμμάτων.
ἰδού, θεᾶσθε πάντες ἄθλιον δέμας,
ὁρᾶτε τὸν δύστηνον, ὡς οἰκτρῶς ἔχω.

While he is still in the grip of his maddening pain, Heracles cries out to 'Zeus' beam of light' (Διὸς ἀκτίς, 1086) to destroy him. Here too the light can only fulfil a destructive purpose, and the phrase recalls in fact the beam of sunlight which activated the venom (ἀκτῖν' ἐς ἡλιῶτιν, 697; cf. ἄπυρον ἀκτῖνός τ' ἀεὶ θερμῆς ἄθικτον, 685–6). Deianeira's invocation to Zeus' lightning introduced her first statement of the invincible power of Eros (437). But with the clear 'appearance' of the oracles (*prophanton*, 1159 and 1163; *phano*, 1164) and with the 'flash of the torch' on Oeta (1198), 'the crag of Zeus' (1191), light begins to take on other meanings. The sufferings which began with the 'altar's flash' (ἐφέστιον σέλας, 607) will conclude with a 'flash' of a conflagration in a very different setting (λαμπάδος σέλας, 1198). When Heracles perceives the meaning of the oracles, his 'light', he says, 'is no longer': φέγγος οὐκέτ' ἔστι μοι (1144). And yet he begins to have a 'light' of another kind. 'Since these things are clear (*lampra*)', he begins (1174), as he goes on to describe, with new decisiveness and firmness, what he must ask of his son. The adjective which earlier described the destructive allurement of Iole's beauty (*lampra*, 379) now characterizes Heracles' clarity of vision. That 'brightness' also characterized the sun's 'blazing fire' (λαμπρᾷ στεροπᾷ φλεγέθων, 99), part of a pitiless cycle of birth and death (94–6, cf. 203–4), and the light which activated the venom (ἀλαμπὲς ἡλίου, 691). After being a tool of the 'beast', light is now (1174) evocative of new knowledge and the will of the gods.

Some of the relationships so far indicated in this movement from Cenaeum to Oeta can be presented diagrammatically as follows:

Cenaeum	Oeta
Beast (Nessus, Achelous, Hydra)	Man, god, hero
Heracles as destructive power (victim of Nessus and Eros)	Heracles as civilizing power (defeat of Nessus)
Destroyer of house of Eurytus	Preserver of house (marriage of Hyllus and Iole)

145

Fire of poisoned robe (Nessus, lust, 'heat' of passion)	Fire on Mt Oeta
'Ferrying' by Nessus (571)	'Ferrying' from Cenaeum to Trachis (802)
Bestial roaring (805, etc.)	Restrained silence (1259–63)
'Spurs' of Nessus' poison (840)	'Bit' of soul (1261)
Sacrifice at Cenaeum (bulls, blood, sweat)	'Sacrifice' on Oeta
(Heracles 'devoured' as victim)	(Heracles burnt as 'victim')
'Fat oak' and smoky flame at Cenaeum (766, 794) (wood metaphor for tuft of wool, 699f.)	Oak and olive at Oeta; Prophetic oak at Dodona
Destructive light	'Flash of flame' on Oeta (1198)
Physical 'brilliance' of Iole's beauty (379)	'Brilliance' of truth of oracles (1174)
Fire of 'disease'	Fire that will cure (1208–10)
Death (mortal realm, victory of Nessus and Hydra)	Life (apotheosis; Olympus; ultimate defeat of Nessus, Hydra, and 'beasts').

VII

In the course of the play we have witnessed Heracles' identification with the beast-world of his past. That identification carries with it the breakdown of the principle of differentiation, the basic principle of civilization itself. The violence in Heracles is itself the expression of the fusion of man and beast into what René Girard calls the 'monstrous double'.[107] In the collapse of the fundamental divisions which constitute and protect the civilized order and affirm man's humanness, polar opposites unite, and the undifferentiated state of the resulting fusion is itself the sign of disorder and violence. To cite Girard,

Le principe fondamentale, toujours méconnu, c'est que le double et le monstre ne font qu'un. Le mythe, bien entendu, met en relief l'un des

107. René Girard, *La violence et le sacré* (Paris 1972). The passage cited below is on pp. 223–4. For a lucid account of Girard's theory see Carl Rubino's excellent review, *MLN* 87 (1972), 986–98.

deux pôles, généralement le monstrueux, pour dissimuler l'autre. Il n'y a pas de monstre qui ne tende à se dédoubler, il n'y a pas de double qui ne recèle une monstruosité secrète. C'est au double qu'il faut donner la précédence, sans toutefois éliminer le monstre; dans le dédoublement du monstre c'est la structure vraie de l'expérience qui affleure. C'est la vérité de leur propre rapport, obstinément refusée par les antagonistes qui finit par s'imposer à eux mais sous une forme hallucinée, dans l'oscillation frénétique de toutes les différences. L'identité et la réciprocité que les frères ennemis n'ont pas voulu vivre comme fraternité du frère, proximité du prochain, finit par s'imposer comme dédoublement du monstre, en eux-mêmes et hors d'eux-mêmes, sous la forme la plus insolite, en somme, et la plus inquiétante qui soit.

At this level we can understand in a new light the phantasmagoric or 'hallucinatory' quality of the mythical figures behind the play: it conveys the atmosphere of dissolution and horror in which bestial and human merge into the undifferentiated state of violence and disorder, what Girard calls the 'frenetic oscillation of all the differences'. Heracles' rape of Iole merges with Nessus' rape of Deianeira; the heat of his own desire becomes one with the heat which releases the power of the monster's poison. These identifications, then, are not to be understood only in psychological terms or as a rationalization of a mythical fantasy. They also express the conflicts and ambiguities inherent in the nature of man and the nature of civilization, in man's relation to his own violence, his own bestiality.

Heracles' last speech, with its 'bit' imagery and its heroic tone, heralds the restoration of the forcibly disrupted barrier between beast and man, between violence and civilization. When Heracles no longer struggles against his death, but accepts it and views it in the framework of the sacrificial imagery which so dominates the play, he also performs the ritual function of the 'victime émissaire', the scapegoat whose sacrifice absorbs and once more sacralizes the violence which he has released when he became the beast's 'double'. By his voluntary death he channels that violence back upon himself.

The play thus enacts in microcosm the process of *catharsis*, the *catharsis* of violence, which all tragedy effects. The action is symbolic of the tragic ritual as a whole. The last act of violence will be enclosed within a re-established ritual context, the burning of Heracles' body at Zeus' shrine on Oeta. Here the violence let loose promiscuously among men will become once more sacred, the property of the gods. But a human life must pay for that resacralizing of violence. The ritual substrate does not at all swing clear of the pattern of choice and responsibility. Heracles, who let that violence irrupt into the human world by becoming one with his bestial 'double', now becomes the victim of that violence, both in the figurative and the ritual sense.

If we may think of Heracles at the end as approaching his apotheosis, the hero passes through the three basic conditions which constitute the 'differences' on which the civilized order rests: beast, man, and god. After confounding the first two, he would emerge into the third through a process of purgative suffering which itself throws into relief the 'differences' between man and god and, of course, between god and beast.

VIII

The diagram of the play's implicit dynamics set forth above could also be organized in terms of spatial movement. Here, as in every extant play of Sophocles (even the *Electra* is not an exception), relation to place embodies and symbolically contains the entire course of the action. Heracles, as we have seen, moves from the smoke-filled plain or shore (ἀκτή, 237, 752) to the summit of Oeta *via* a passage over water which he effects only with the greatest pain (800–6; cf. *molis*, 805). Deianeira has her spatial movement too, but of course her range is much smaller. The opening scene sets up the contrast: Heracles is off on perilous adventures traversing a far-flung geography and battling exotic monsters; Deianeira repeats an unchanging round of grief and anxiety (27–31, 103–11).

The spatial associations of Deianeira are not with the 'lofty crag of Zeus', but with house and also meadow. In a lovely passage early in the play she compares the sheltered life of maidenhood to a protected place untouched by heat, rain or wind (144–7), a place rather like Hippolytus' 'untouched meadow' of virginity (*Hipp.* 73–87). The delicacy and wistfulness of the image are all the more striking because of her comparison of herself in the prologue to a farmland plowed and sown by her husband. It symbolizes a life 'free from toil' (ἄμοχθον βίον, 147). Even the wishful meadow of 144–7 is soon to be invaded by the elemental forces of nature and sexuality. Its freedom from 'the god's heat' (θάλπος θεοῦ, 145) gives way to the heat of lust (368) and the heat (686) which sets the poison to work (*ethalpeto*, 697).

Over against this sheltered meadow stands the 'meadow of cattle's summer pasture' where Lichas arrives (186), a real meadow in the 'outside' world, a place filled with thronging, excited crowds (186). Here, as in 32–3, images of place – tilled or fallow land, remote or accessible meadow – express a contrast between male and female desires, between a harsh male sexuality and a woman's longing to escape the cycle of sexual maturity, birth, ageing. When she grasps the news of Heracles' return Deianeira exclaims 'O Zeus who hold Oeta's uncut meadow' (200). This is the first reference to Oeta in the play, and it comes from Deianeira, not Heracles, in a context celebrating the return of the hero, ostensibly, to the 'inner', domestic realm. In her adjective 'uncut' (*atomos*) Deianeira seems to assimilate this place of remote male figures and patriarchal cult to her own enclosed meadow of maidenhood (144–50).

As Deianeira moves nearer to the truth of Heracles' world and its violence, however, Oeta changes its aspect and shows something of its mysterious and violent qualities. She begs Lichas to be open, entreating him 'in the name of Zeus who sends the lightning down the lofty glens of Oeta' (436–7):

$$\text{τοῦ κατ' ἄκρον Οἰταῖον νάπος}$$
$$\text{Διὸς καταστράπτοντος.}$$

The splendid and powerful lines come as a surprise from the hitherto soft-spoken Deianeira. They express not only the power and elevation of her spirit, but also her movement away from that sheltered meadow nostalgically evoked in 144–50). We do not know yet how closely associated will be Oeta and fire (the lightning of 437). The lofty, celestial aspect of Oeta will emerge only at the end (cf. 1191). Here its violence dominates the context, and Deianeira speaks of Eros in the next lines (441ff.).

The 'life free of toil' which Deianeira's meadow symbolizes is to be achieved by Heracles in connection with the remote crags of Oeta, but in a sense very different from hers (cf. *mochthos* in 1170 and 1173). Cenaeum is his point of juncture between the toils of his past and the 'toilless life' he anticipated. In spatial terms Cenaeum is the midpoint between Deianeira's 'meadow' of maidenhood and the 'meadow of Oeta' where the real meaning of those prophecies is fulfilled. For Deianeira this middle ground is the house itself. Its 'recesses' (686) are the dark hiding place of Nessus' poison, but its inner chambers will also be the scene of Deianeira's noble death.

Deianeira thus returns to her starting point, and this movement is characteristic of her associations with the circularity of nature's rhythms, the cycles of birth and death. Heracles moves to Oeta, away from the house, toward Zeus. This spatial contrast between the two protagonists is part of a larger contrast between them which could be described, somewhat crudely, as that between immanence and transcendence.

Twice in the parode the cyclical patterns of nature or of human vicissitudes are broken by the hoped-for intervention of a god. The ode opens with the recurrent cycles of night and day, life and death (94–6); but over against this stands 'some god's' rescue of Heracles from the death threatened by the 'circling' (*strephei*, 117) course of his journeys (113–21). The antistrophe ends with the circling movements of the stars (*kuklousin, strophades*), reflective of the alternation of joy and pain for men (129–31). The epode returns to the ever-moving rhythms of day and night (μένει γὰρ οὔτ' αἰόλα | νὺξ βροτοῖσιν..., 132–3; cf. 94), but the passage ends with hope in Zeus, ambiguous though it is (139–40).

Of this transcendence, in all its mystery and its harshness, Oeta is the symbol.[108] We have already traced the gradual emergence of Oeta early in the play, first as a peaceful place, an 'uncut meadow' (200), then, as the violence of lust begins to make itself visible, as a remote peak where Zeus hurls his lightning (436–7). When the violence of Nessus' revenge is about to break forth, we get a last peaceful glimpse of rock and sea in the landscape around Trachis, with 'Oeta's crags' towering in the distance (633–9; πάγους Οἴτας, 634–5); but in the next scene the mountain is lost amid the

108. For the importance of Oeta and its 'meadow' see Linforth, p. 263; McCall, p. 146. J.-P. Vernant's observations, 'Hestia-Hermès: sur l'expression religieuse de l'espace et du mouvement chez les Grecs', *Mythe et Pensée chez les Grecs*² (Paris 1966), pp. 97–143, especially pp. 120ff., could easily be extended to this play. Here again the fixed and free, circular and linear movements come together only for their mutual destruction: cf. 607, 620. See also above, note 32.

smoke of Cenaeum. Only at the end does Oeta's full significance become clear, as it is gradually intertwined with Heracles' fate and his special destiny as the son of Zeus. Heracles begins his specific instructions to his son about his burial with the question, 'Do you know Zeus' highest crag of Oeta?' (τὸν Οἴτης Ζηνὸς ὕψιστον πάγον, 1191).[109] Deianeira's invocation of 'Oeta's upland meadow' (ἄκρον Οἰταῖον νάπος, 436) initiated the destructive movement of the play and marked her first fatal step toward Heracles' 'outer' world; Heracles' description of the Oetean height closes the violence and initiates a calmer movement.

When Heracles mentions Oeta in 1191 he envisages the mountain in all its majestic height, not as a 'meadow' (200) or a 'glen' (436), as Deianeira describes it. He speaks with the authority of one who will now venture into those remote fastnesses. Regardless of the possibility of the apotheosis, he has a definite and clear direction, upward in a vertical rather than a horizontal or circular movement. The oracle which he recalls in his moment of tragic illumination also belongs to mountains (ὄρειοι Σελλοί, 1166–7).

This new definiteness about place in relation to his special destiny characterizes other Sophoclean heroes in their last moments on stage: Ajax going to 'the washing place and meadows by the shore' (654–5); Oedipus in the *Tyrannus* discovering his special tie to Cithaeron (*O.T.* 1391ff.) and in the *Coloneus* leading Theseus to the Broken Road where he disappears from human view (*O.C.* 1586ff.). In the *Trachiniae*, immersed as it is in brutality, lust, and pain, Zeus' lofty mountain is an important presence, a calm if mysterious eminence towering above the wracked lives of this world.

IX

Between the transcendence toward which Heracles moves and the cycles of birth, procreation, and death to which most of human life is bound and in which Deianeira has already perished there is an unbridgeable gap.

Some scholars would bridge the gap through Heracles' orders about the marriage of Iole and Hyllus. Bowra finds here 'an un-

---

109. I agree with Campbell, Jebb and Kamerbeek that Wakefield's conjecture, ὑψίστου, though accepted by Pearson in the OCT, is unnecessary.

suspected trait of tenderness and justice'.[110] Others, taking the opposite view, have seen here only the male possessiveness of a self-centered hero who wants to control his hard-won mistress even after his death, keep her in the family as it were:

Let no one except you ever take her who once lay at my side (1225–6).[111]

The note of egotism and possessiveness cannot be evaded. Heracles is not remade. There is no new tenderness. He remains aloof and imperious to the end, ennobled in his endurance and decisiveness, but not softened.[112] He is still imbued with the harsher qualities of Sophoclean heroism.

Yet to see here only narrow selfishness is as mistaken as it is to see kindliness or altruism. We cannot speculate on Heracles' motives when we are given no basis for such speculation. Sophocles does not tell us what is passing through Heracles' mind. We cannot treat him as if he were a real person and not a figure in a play.[113]

Whatever his motives, the *results* of his act are in accordance with history. His line must not die out; the mythical tradition makes Hyllus and Iole the founders of an important race, and Heracles' commands assure that those traditions are fulfilled.[114] Heracles is here the representative of larger continuities which require the founding of a new house out of the shattered remnants of the two houses destroyed. He must override, sternly and even menacingly (1238–40), the sensitivity and scruples of Hyllus.[115]

110. Bowra, pp. 192–3. Similarly Pohlenz, p. 203, finds it 'ein versöhnender Zug, wenn Herakles an sie [Iole] denkt und für ihr Wohl wie für das seines Hauses sorgt'. Méautis, p. 287, goes even further, and with less justification.

111. So MacKinnon (above, note 86); Kitto, *Poiesis*, pp. 170–2; Kamerbeek, pp. 246–7 (*ad* 1225f.); Ehrenberg, p. 390.

112. See Schmid–Stählin, pp. 382–3; Perrotta, pp. 521–2; H. Weinstock, *Sophokles* (Wuppertal 1948), p. 24.

113. Gellie, p. 75, goes too far, however, when he remarks 'We are judging not a character in poetic drama but an entry in Pauly-Wissowa.' On the other hand Gellie's warnings about analyzing a hero's motives in his excellent chapter on 'character' (pp. 201ff.) are applicable here: cf. especially p. 211 on Ajax' *Trugrede*.

114. See Apollod. 2. 7. 7 and Frazer's note *ad loc.* in the Loeb Class. Library edition (London 1921), 1. 269. Indeed, in one version (schol. *ad Trach.* 354 = Pherecydes *FGrHist* 3 F 82a) Heracles seeks to win Iole for Hyllus, not for himself. For the myth and its variants see Perrotta, 523–4 with n. 4; Pohlenz, 1. 203 and the note at 2. 89; Waldock, p. 90, n. 1; Masqueray, pp. 12–13.

115. A similar view of Heracles' orders about Iole is taken by Adams, p. 132; Letters, p. 189; Waldock, pp. 88–90. I am essentially in agreement though I do not accept all the details of their various interpretations.

We sympathize with Hyllus; but the gods, typically remote and inscrutable, are on Heracles' side.

Earlier in the play Iole was a touching example of the instability of human happiness (283–5, 298–303). Heracles has now passed through and beyond those vicissitudes. When he speaks of Iole here, he is cool and objective, with no trace of that passion which generated the whole tragedy. He asks merely, 'Do you know the maiden, Eurytus' daughter?' (1219). The question carries the same tone of authoritative and somewhat mysterious knowledge as his first request, 'Do you know the highest crag of Zeus' Oeta?' (1191). Heracles does not even attempt to offer reasons. His own will suffices (1245–6). We are not meant to draw closer to this figure. Hyllus intuitively, albeit reluctantly, acknowledges the commanding power of his father's vision. Indeed his initial resistance, as Reinhardt pointed out, only strengthens the effect of Heracles' certainty.[116]

The contrast between human understanding and divine purposes in the clash between Heracles and Hyllus continues to the very end. Hyllus reproaches the gods for neglecting their children (1264–74), an ironical qualification of the chorus' confidence earlier in Zeus' 'counsels' for his children (139–40). He concludes, if the final lines are his, with an implicit incrimination of Zeus:

You have seen great deaths freshly done and many sufferings newly fashioned, and nothing of this which is not Zeus.

Hyllus had made a similar statement earlier. When all was chaos and pain and he felt his utter helplessness in the face of his father's agony, he said with deep bitterness, 'Such are the gifts of Zeus' (τοιαῦτα νέμει Ζεύς, 1022). There is no lack of justification for his bitterness, but it appears now in a larger context. Over against it stand the massive figure of Heracles, whose knowledge and acceptance of the oracles enable him to bear his last suffering with dignity, and the oracles themselves, the decipherment of which seems to calm Heracles' violence. Heracles does not curse the gods, but determinedly takes the necessary steps for the closing act of his life.

The gulf between Heracles and Hyllus, between a glimmer of meaning and chaotic, uncomprehended suffering, remains im-

116. Reinhardt, p. 72.

153

passable. If the last line, 'Nothing of this that is not Zeus', suggests some larger perspective of the gods where all this violence and waste might make some sense, it also depicts the bitterness of the human participants before the dark cloud of their ignorance.[117] That bitterness is no less if the chorus rather than Hyllus speak these lines.

If Zeus, the oracles, Heracles' instructions about the pyre and the marriage of Hyllus point toward some 'higher' dimension of the tragedy, there lurks still the 'lower': the demonic invisible powers of the beasts, Centaur and Hydra, the 'form of the bull' (509), the 'deathly wraith', and poisonous 'apparition' of Nessus and the Hydra (831–4) which surface for a moment almost as an evil dream or a phantasmagoric mockery of a more rational order.

But it would be wrong to judge the play in terms of light or darkness, optimism or pessimism. The play, like most of Sophocles, is not a statement of solutions, but a dramatization of tensions in which the brutality of Heracles, the victories of the bestial elements, the cruel end of Deianeira, the moral revulsion of Hyllus at his enforced marriage with Iole, must have their due along with the oracles,[118] the implications (as I believe) of apotheosis in the pyre, the glimmers of Heracles' true heroism at the end. As the last line says, it is all Zeus: of Zeus are the wasteful death of Deianeira and the agony of Heracles, but also the oracles and the promise of a larger destiny on Oeta.

If anything can be predicated of this Zeus it is comprehensiveness, remoteness, and opacity.[119] Were one to seek Sophocles'

117. See Kirkwood, *TAPA* 210–11 and *Study*, p. 278; Easterling, p. 68; Gellie, pp. 255–6 and 259–60 for approaches along these lines.

118. For this function of the oracles see Bowra, pp. 150–1; Kitto, *Poiesis*, pp. 188–99, especially 188–91; Lesky, pp. 215–16; Schiassi (above, note 28), p. xxi. Of course the oracles also have an immediate dramatic function too, the creation of suspense and foreboding; see Reinhardt, pp. 49–50; Kirkwood, *Study*, pp. 78–9.

119. For the darkest interpretation of this opacity see Whitman, pp. 106ff. ('evil unmitigated by any sort of victory and resulting directly from the most moral action possible to the protagonists', p. 106); Biggs, p. 229 (Zeus 'seems to stand for nothing more than a universe that endowed man with mind and will, only to put these at the mercy of his biological drives'); Torrance, p. 304 ('But for the individual sufferer... there is no justice in heaven... The result is a play of the darkest imaginable colors'); Kitto, *Poiesis*, pp. 186–8; Moore (above, note 14), p. 60 ('the terrible closing lines of the *Women of Trachis*'). Pohlenz, p. 207, could still find 'die Forderung, sich in Gottes Willen zu fügen,

celebrated 'piety' here, one would have to search for it in this vision of Zeus and the divided perspective which it entails. Such 'piety' is far less a confident religiosity or a consoling faith than the strength to face the darkness of the universe, the mystery of evil, and to recognize that the equilibrating forces of the world may not be totally congruent with human purposes or human ideas of justice and order.

X

Despite the importance of Zeus, the *Trachiniae* remains essentially a human tragedy, governed by the two interlocking and mutually destructive reactions of Heracles and Deianeira. Though the two figures never meet on stage, a number of devices emphasize this interlocking. When Hyllus brings the fatal news from Cenaeum, for instance, the chorus divides its lament equally between the two protagonists (821–40, 841–62). Heracles' false 'vow' (239–40) is answered by Deianeira's 'vow' (610), also false, about the robe. At the beginning she cannot 'put to sleep her tears' (107); Heracles, tormented by the robe, calls for sleep (1005, 1051) and seems, at the end, to have put to sleep his suffering (cf. 1242). Both, in their pain, ask for pity (535, 1032), and both 'roar' in their suffering (805, 904).[120] Deianeira sheds a 'pale dew of tears' (χλωρὰν τέγγει δακρύων ἄχναν, 847–8); Heracles' 'disease' devours his 'pale blood' (χλωρὸν αἷμα, 1055), and he weeps like a girl (1070–5). Her death, like Heracles', is accompanied by 'disease', *nosos* (852, 882). The instrument of her suicide is the 'weapon's point' (αἰχμὰ βέλεος, 883), like that with which Heracles won Iole (860), and she strikes the same place on her body that the robe attacked on his.[121]

This interlocking, however, goes deeper than verbal parallels. Each character fulfils a typical Sophoclean pattern of annihilation in his or her most central values.[122] But both, in different ways,

mag er auch unbegreiflich sein'. Bowra, p. 157, is less sanguine: 'We may still ask why the gods destroy Heracles. To this in the last resort Sophocles gives no answer. He may well have had no answer to give.'

120. The parallel is noted by Hoey, pp. 16–17.

121. *pleura*: 681 and 833 for Heracles, 926 and 931 for Deianeira: see Easterling, p. 66.

122. Bowra, p. 161: 'Both are struck at the root of their lives'; also pp. 130–1, 144; see also Kirkwood, *TAPA* 208; Reinhardt, p. 70.

come to recreate and realize those values in a profounder and truer fashion than before. The tragedy lies as much in the destruction of values as of bodies.

The inversion and recreation of values for Heracles have been sufficiently discussed: when physically destroyed he becomes a truer conqueror of beasts. The reversals for Deianeira are equally abrupt. She is cursed by her husband as the slayer of her child's father (1126) and by her son as the mother who is no mother (736, 817–19). Her devotion to the creation and nurture of life, to the things she has cherished most as wife and mother, comes to serve their opposite (cf. 834, 842, 893–5). Endowed with the soul of a Penelope, she executes, unwittingly, the deed of a Clytaemnestra or a Medea. It is in language which recalls Aeschylus' Clytaemnestra that her husband describes her deeds (cf. 1051–2, 1057).[123]

Like Heracles, Deianeira has her heroism too, and the language of the play points up the strange paradox of her tragedy, that a wife who destroys her husband, a woman who kills Heracles, is in some sense a heroic figure. Her courage to search out and face the truth suggests the heroic determination of the hero of the *Oedipus Rex*.[124] Like Heracles, she has her heroic silence (813–15; cf. 1259–63); like Heracles, she does not want to be seen in her suffering (903; cf. 800 and 1073); and like Heracles she has her 'endurance', woman though she is (898):

καὶ ταῦτ᾽ ἔτλη τις χεὶρ γυναικεία κτίσαι;
Did a woman's hand dare (endure) to lay such a foundation of acts?

When she sees the probable outcome of her acts, she determines to do on her own impulse what Heracles asks Hyllus not to be afraid of doing, 'join him in death', συνθανεῖν (720 and 797). Her isolation at the end is even more terrifying than Heracles'. Though he is set apart by his special knowledge of the oracles, he can cry for the gathering of his sons (1147–50) and has the company of Hyllus and his retinue on his march to Oeta's summit.[125] Yet there is

123. See Bowra, p. 140, and above, note 58.
124. 'In this quest for truth is the germ of the *Oedipus Rex*', remarks Whitman, p. 117. Parlavantza-Friedrich (above, note 64), p. 31, and Beck, pp. 18–19, find part of Deianeira's tragic fate in an 'absoluten' or 'unbedingten Willen zur Klarheit'.
125. For this contrast between Deianeira and Heracles see Reinhardt, pp. 64–5; Gellie, p. 74.

a kind of isolation for Heracles too. The sons he calls for will not be there; and his terrific pain, as well as his emergent heroic status, continues to distance him from his ceremonial, helpless escort. He is far less close to the members of this final procession than is Oedipus in the finale of the *Coloneus*.

The tragedy of Deianeira is without issue and without hope. Her last and noblest act passes virtually unnoticed by the man for whom she has suffered so long and patiently. Her failure is total. A moment's misjudgment in a crisis wipes out years of faithful, unblemished devotion. Like Jocasta in the *Oedipus Rex* and Eurydice in the *Antigone* her death is an ending and nothing more. Heracles' has the sense of a future. Out of the depths of his agony he draws a new kind of heroism, and one more worthy of his extraordinary physical strength. This is not a new Heracles, nor quite a development of the old, but an actualization of what was in the rude hero all the time. Journeying from Cenaeum to Oeta, he traverses the path from an archaic, epic heroism to a heroism that is fully tragic. For these reasons he is, in the final analysis, the 'hero' of the play, whatever significance that term may carry.

Yet without the total and bleak annihilation of Deianeira the heroic quality of Heracles' final lines would stand out less forcefully. Correspondingly, her tragedy of immanence would be less poignant without the opposite pole of Heracles' larger destiny and more public setting. His independence, pride, and strength at the end intensify the cruelty of Deianeira's silent, unwitnessed death. Greek values were neither kind nor fair to women, and Sophocles is brutally honest in reflecting them.

The perfect complementarity of the two tragedies recalls the relation of the two protagonists of the *Antigone*. The two opposites, Creon and Antigone, destroy one another as do Heracles and Deianeira. But the complementarity of the protagonists of the *Trachiniae* is the more painful since it underlines the separation between those who belong together. Deianeira seeks union with Heracles, but she can only bring to tragic completeness their inherent polarity.

Part of what Pohlenz has called 'the tragic condition of all humanity visible behind the individual fates' in the play[126] lies in this confrontation of polarities: the enduring, patient wife and

126. Pohlenz, p. 206.

mother and the violent, heroic male; the bestiality and the nobility in man; the stable and the dynamic; the inward and outward realms of action, house and nature, plain and mountain. Each figure calls out what is darkest and what is noblest in the other; each puts the other to the fullest, final test. But the two sides cannot join into a life-giving whole. On impact they fragment into mutually exclusive and destructive parts. Each figure realizes his heroic strength not only in isolation from the other, but at the furthest possible remove, Deianeira knowing that son and husband curse her, Heracles utterly ignoring the generous and noble aspect of Deianeira's end. Yet the last glimpse we have of each onstage is an image of a great soul in the gesture which expresses and validates for eternity its most valuable and permanent strength and its most tragic contradiction: Deianeira withdrawing in noble silence to die on a marriage-bed once fought over by lustful monsters; Heracles, dying of the Centaur's poison, clamping the bit of silence on his 'firm soul' as he journeys to the unspoken destiny awaiting him on 'Zeus' highest crag' (1191).

It is only in death that both achieve their freedom from the bestial, elemental forces which surround their lives. In so doing they realize their full, tragic humanity. Deianeira, finally, refuses to be victimized by the sexual drives which have played the major role in her life, refuses to be made use of by the blind forces of nature. Heracles too rises above the beast-world into which his instincts pull him back.

Here, as in the *Ajax*, death is the last freedom permitted to man. Ajax escapes time and change, process and decay, only through negating them by death. That is the darkest side of the tragedy of the *Trachiniae*, as of the *Ajax*. But over against it must be set the manner of the death chosen. The noble deaths of Deianeira and, in foreshadowing, of Heracles are of a piece with those of Ajax and Antigone. Here is the full and ultimate meaning of Deianeira's 'ancient tale' in the play's opening lines:

You would not find out if a mortal's life is noble or base until he meets his death (2–3).[127]

127. I gratefully acknowledge a faculty summer research grant from Brown University in 1972 which facilitated the completion of the preliminary research for this study. I also thank Professor C. J. Herington for valuable comments and Mrs Robert E. Eisenauer for her usual care and accuracy in typing a difficult manuscript. This study is dedicated to the memory of Ann and Adam Parry.

On 'extra-dramatic' communication of characters in Euripides[1]

H. P. STAHL

THE title of my paper is intended to emphasize two things. By 'extra-dramatic', I want to indicate that the scenes to be considered do not participate in the dramatic action proper of the tragedy in which they appear, and so in some sense can be said to move outside the plot; but, at the same time, I also want to suggest that the dramatic structure of the plays can in each case provide a useful point of reference for a methodical comprehension of the phenomenon I have in mind.

I have chosen the term 'communication' because it can signify a close human relationship that finds expression through exchange of words, as for example in dramatic dialogue. 'Communication' does not entail any restriction regarding the kind of persons who communicate. In the Euripidean passages the persons involved frequently address each other as *philoi*, but the common English translation, which is 'friend', would unduly limit my reader's expectations. For the observations which follow are in no way tied to a particular word or a particular bond between human beings. Even *philos* and *philia* (which, unlike our 'friendship', can indicate not only the ties between friends, but the familial relationships of father and son or brother and sister as well) are too narrow terms. With regard to my special subject, I should therefore not use 'friendship', or, if at all, in an extended sense, meaning any close human relationship.

Before closing in any further on the target of this paper, I would first like to outline the complex background against which Euripides has set it off. One ingredient of this background is for

1. Part of this article (translated into English by W. Zukowski and reviewed by the author) was a *Habilitationsvortrag* ('Zum "ausserdramatischen" Motiv der Freundschaft bei Euripides'), held before the Geisteswissenschaftliche Fakultät der Westfälischen Wilhelms-Universität zu Münster (Westfalen) on 19 June 1964.

instance the *philia* mentioned above, in its traditional and common Greek sense. For the characters whom we shall consider, *philia* is one of the basic relations that tie them to their environment, a notion immanent in their thinking and inseparable from their set of fundamental ideas.

In presenting a simplified sketch of the environmental relations so basic to the characters in the play, I must paradoxically start out with a negative statement: it would be wrong to attribute to characters in a Euripidean play a complete (or even halfway complete) understanding of the world and their position in it. The world proves utterly incomprehensible to them. The more they strive intellectually to understand it, the more elusive it becomes. This is true of all facets of life, but of the gods above all. And it is especially true of those gods who seem to lend man a helping hand. Thus, Orestes says in reference to the sooth-saying god Apollo (*I. T.* 570ff.):

Nor are the gods whom we call wise less deceptive than winged dreams.

And three lines later he mentions

the man who, though not imprudent, followed the bidding of seers, and is undone: how undone to those who know!

'Those who know': Orestes, of course, in the first place refers to himself and his experience of the god's deceptiveness, but the phrase also encompasses the spectators who have witnessed his experience.

Since trust in and reliance upon divine guidance no longer seem justified, men are obviously left to their own faculties. This is implicit in Orestes' allusion to the prudent man who despite his good sense confides in the prophecies of the god. Since, however, the events which involve men are capable of many interpretations, it is increasingly doubtful whether man can accomplish plans of his own. If the course of events (*ta pragmata*) appears to form a movement of its own, the possibility of influencing it is withdrawn. In this area, too – as in that of divine guidance – a point is reached where man resigns action. What wonder that, when unexpected good fortune comes, *Tychē* is hailed as the guide – Tyche, which is the whim of chance and by definition incalculable? (*Ion* 1512):

Oh you who have already brought about change for countless mortals, so that they experience suffering and afterwards good fortune – Tyche, what a plumb-line of life we have followed...!

'Plumb-line' and 'chance' in a single statement: clearly, the concrete experience of life can only be expressed by a paradox – the intellect must keep silent.

Where in a world thus constituted is there room for the man of action, for the dramatic deed? There can be none. Studies of Euripides' dramaturgy confirm that he sought increasingly to withdraw from his characters the possibility of action.[2] The people of his plays become passive; external action is replaced by internal reaction. Viewed from the angle of their dramatic structure, the plays reveal that humanity is always a step behind events (a development which can equally well be illustrated from the historical account given by the poet's contemporary Thucydides).

But if the conduct of the gods, as well as the course of events, is inaccessible to human understanding, where can a man find his bearings? On what can he depend? On other men, his neighbors, his friends? Basically, this question must be answered in the negative, since disappointment rather than a justification of the confidence bestowed is the usual outcome of such reliance, as must be stated once more. Medea's despairing question, when she finds herself betrayed by her husband, recurs frequently in altered form (*Medea* 516):

Why, oh Zeus, have you given to men unmistakable criteria for detecting false gold, yet men have no mark ingrown on their bodies by which the villainous can be recognized?

And the murderer of a child entrusted to his protection addresses his victim's unfortunate mother with the words (*Hecuba* 957):

Alas, there is nothing on which we can rely – neither glory, nor, when we prosper, that we shall not fare ill. The gods themselves confuse and thoroughly disorder our lots to the end that we will revere them because of our inability to attain knowledge.

The dissembler expresses ideas which are thoroughly in accord with the experience of Euripides' dramatic characters. His lament

2. H. Strohm, *Euripides: Interpretationen zur dramatischen Form*, Zetemata 15 (München 1957), p. 152.

over the fact that in life there is nothing reliable seems to mark him out of all as the trustworthy man *par excellence*. How could anyone see through him or even unmask him?

There are numerous examples in Euripidean tragedy of bitter disappointment over betrayal by a supposed friend. A discriminating investigation[3] has even shown that the baffling enemy need not at all be a particular individual – as was the case with the infanticide just mentioned – but that Euripides more and more frequently brings the anonymous masses into the play as the adversary of his heroes. But in the face of amorphous anonymity vigorous action directed toward a specific goal is an impossibility. Here again, we encounter the passivity of Euripidean characters.

To sum up: gods who lead astray; events determined by chance; untrustworthy and deceitful men; anonymous crowds – this is the world in which humanity finds itself: a room with many doors, none of which can be opened. With ample justification one may speak of a *Sinneskrise*,[4] a crisis of meaning, in Euripides.

From this background sketch of the relations between the central figures and the world around them, one fact of great importance to our subject emerges: that in the whirlpool of uncertainty and loss of direction not only a single bond like that of friendship – be it in the English sense or in the wider one of Greek *philia* – is lost, but also any close human relationship appears in jeopardy. We may already surmise that, when a Euripidean character does gain certainty of human closeness, he will not win it by any active exertion of his own powers. Rather, if such certainty comes at all, we shall expect it to do so as something which comes to pass and befalls men quite unexpectedly.

In the following pages I wish to show that, in fact, such certainty of the closeness of a fellow human being is occasionally expressed in Euripides, and I shall try to describe the manner in which the artist employs this feature to heighten and intensify the tragic aspects of his plays.

3. H. Diller, *Umwelt und Masse als dramatische Faktoren bei Euripides*, Entretiens VI, Fondation Hardt (Vandœuvres–Genève 1960), pp. 89ff.

4. K. Reinhardt, 'Die Sinneskrise bei Euripides' in *Tradition und Geist* (Göttingen 1960), pp. 227ff.

I now return to the concept of the 'extra-dramatic', and to the selection of the scenes which I wish to set before the reader.

Scholarship has been much occupied with the dramatic structure of Euripides' work (we immediately think of names like Solmsen, Zürcher, Friedrich, Strohm, *et al.*). Investigations of this sort have sometimes led to charges of excessively schematic organization of individual tragedies (especially of the so-called intrigue-dramas). Above all, one grave reproach held against our author deserves mentioning here: he has been accused of concentrating on plot at the expense of the delineation of character. That is, he has been said to disregard the unity of character and to provide the people of his plays only with such traits and qualities as are necessary to further the action – or, to put it more briefly, to make the *dramatis persona* a function of the plot.[5]

We may dispense with discussion of the truth or falsehood of theses like these (and with the more general question of the validity of such lines of interpretation), since the problem before us is not affected by them. I have nevertheless introduced them for two reasons: (1) because through them I have been led to the category of the 'extra-dramatic'; (2) because the existence of these investigations has determined my choice of scenes.

The sort of communication we will be dealing with is in a way exhibited also in the so-called intrigue-dramas – where a character in extreme difficulty finds help and support from another character, together with whom he plans the intrigue in order to surmount the emergency that now involves them together. Usually, the rediscovery of a loved one previously lost leads to a common duet of rejoicing in which the suffering of the solitary past, anxiety over the threatening future, and joy at the nearness of the one who has been found again are mingled together. However, the certainty of human closeness expressed in such scenes clearly is not without a dramatic function. Indeed, it is necessary for the course of the intrigue-drama that first a uniting bond between friends or near ones should be established or reconfirmed so they can act together for a common end. Thus, a character's discovery

5. W. Zürcher, *Die Darstellung des Menschen im Drama des Euripides*, Schweizerische Beiträge zur Altertumswissenschaft 2 (Basel 1947), p. 180: the person 'verhält sich einfach so, wie es der Fortgang oder das Ziel des Dramas erheischt'.

that he can rely upon his fellow-man could, in these instances, be regarded simply as a function of the dramatic plot.

Accordingly, I have set aside the intrigue-dramas and have chosen only scenes and descriptions which have no importance for the progress of the plot. By thus limiting the range of inquiry, I believe I have at the same time gained an advantage: in the presentation of a static situation which contains no impulse to movement in the sense of dramaturgic progress the power immanent in linguistic expression is possibly stronger, since the words serve no purpose other than description of human feeling or pure communication of inner experience.

I wish to illustrate the phenomenon I have in mind first from the *Alcestis* of 438 B.C.

In this play we find a theatrical adaptation of the old folk-tale (*Märchen*) in which a man is able to redeem himself from dying by placing the life of another at Death's disposal. To this basic plot is added the burlesque feature that Death does not even get possession of the substitute victim when all is done, since a hero of superhuman might snatches her from him in a wrestling-match at the grave.

The first, or tragic, part is what interests us in our present inquiry. The victim is Alcestis who, on her wedding-day, voluntarily pledged to surrender her life for that of her threatened husband Admetus. Years have passed since the pledge was given, and today is the day on which she must depart. We find her on her death-bed in her last conversation with her husband.

The leave-taking is movingly depicted, but remarkably static – conventional, one is tempted to say. Admetus promises never to remarry and to be both father and mother to their children. He hopes that Alcestis will often appear to him in dreams.

All these are features which could be said to be determined by dramatic necessity: for Admetus must be characterized as a good husband so that his recovery of his noble wife in the second part of the play will seem fitting. His request that his wife should wait for him in the kingdom of death until he comes to her at the conclusion of his now prolonged life can be regarded in the same fashion: the dramatic plot demands that Admetus continue to live.

Up to this point, I would agree that there can be no question of a psychological depiction of the characters;[6] indeed, I would go further and assert that there is not supposed to be any, since without the play's static first part, its second part, which is not at all static, would lose its meaning.

In the final lines of the conversation, i.e. already in the *stichomythia*, individualizing emotion, indicated once before in the antecedent lyrical passage (see 278ff.), makes its decisive appearance in the constellation we have so far observed. At the end of the almost functional discussion of Alcestis' last wishes, Admetus abruptly breaks out (380):

> Alas, what shall I do alone and without you?

Alcestis' reference to time which mitigates all things does not impede him (382):

> Take me with you, by the gods, take me below.

And suddenly the recognition (384):

> Oh God, what a wife you rob me of!

This is no longer the Admetus who was to join his wife in the underworld after an admittedly sorrowful but long life – it is the man who, later in the play (897ff.), must be forcibly restrained from throwing himself upon the corpse in the grave in order to unite himself with his wife in death.

> I am undone, my wife, if you forsake me. (386)

What is happening here? Obviously, Admetus recognizes that the death of his wife is identical with the loss of his own existence ('if you...then I'). Thus, there is a movement towards her on his part, a removal of a borderline that has been separating them.

And how does Alcestis react to her husband's new closeness, to this new dimension which can have no importance in the realm of actuality and cannot change anything about her fate?

> You may speak of me as nothing, I am no longer alive. (387)

This is equivalent to no answer at all. We get the impression that Alcestis is not being reached by Admetus at all, that she does not

6. *Ibid.* pp. 24ff.

even learn any more about the certainty of his affection. The possibility of 'togetherness' remains unfulfilled; in the sphere of high tragedy, any effect is precluded.

Ten years after the *Alcestis*, the *Hippolytus* was produced. Hippolytus, the young hunting companion of the chaste goddess Artemis, has rejected the faked proposal (invented, of course, by the old Nurse) of his stepmother Phaedra. Phaedra kills herself and leaves behind a letter to her husband Theseus, in which she accuses her stepson of having raped her.

In his first passion, Theseus, invoking his father, the god Poseidon, curses his son and prays for his death. The curse must take effect, since Poseidon has promised Theseus the fulfillment of three wishes. The confrontation of father and son over the body of Phaedra is the high point of a tragic misunderstanding. In a passage cited above, Medea lamented that there was a 'clear, infallible' test for false coinage, but not for the character of a man. Now, Theseus believes he possesses such absolute and unfailing proof of his son's viciousness. He uses the word *saphes* which was used by Medea also (925):

Alas, there ought to have been established for mortals an unfailing criterion of friends and a means of judging the hearts of men [to determine] who is upright and who is not a friend.

He means that he has previously misjudged his son's character; now, however, he imagines he possesses irrefutable certainty about what that character is (972):

Why should I still wrangle with you in words, since the corpse is present as a witness giving most certain evidence?

Can there be any evidence more manifest or more unerring than the dead Phaedra provides?

Still later, when Theseus learns that Hippolytus has been assailed by Poseidon and is at the point of death, he wishes to see him to convict him of his guilt by the new evidence of divine punishment – which, in fact, has no bearing on anything but the fulfillment of Theseus' own curse (1267).

Before the dying youth is brought forth, however, Theseus learns the truth from the goddess Artemis. Thus, when they meet again, father and son are both victims of Phaedra's revenge – or, to express it in terms of the divine powers involved, of the wrath of Aphrodite who wished to destroy Artemis' chaste young devotee.

The dying youth seems even more isolated and lonely than Alcestis. His divine patroness can do nothing to save him. The only consolation she can offer (if it is any) is to assure him that she will take vengeance on Aphrodite and for her part, too, kill a human dear to that goddess. From Hippolytus, however, she must now take her leave, since it is not permissible for the gods to be present at a man's death.

> Lightly you abandon a long communion,

says Hippolytus (1441). The brutality of divine blessedness, untouched by suffering, is illustrated by the manner in which Artemis delegates what according to our feeling should be her own task, to the mortal father: *he* is bidden to take the dying youth in his arms; the two humans are asked to extend reconciliation to one another – which, evidently, the gods cannot do.

Thus, after the goddess' departure, after the dramatic action has run its course, there remain two men united in suffering: the son absolves his father of guilt for his death; Theseus holds his dying son lovingly in his arms. The whole is, as it were, a contrast to the scene over Phaedra's body, a moment of genuine recognition. Theseus says (1452):

> Oh dearest one, how noble you show yourself to your father!

Thus, at this point the motif of human closeness recurs: 'dearest one', *o philtate*, is Theseus' address to his son. And once more he expresses his new understanding (1454):

> Alas, for your pious, noble heart!

Here, too, as in the *Alcestis*, a bridge seems to be laid between the two men, a communication established that was never reached before; but Hippolytus' answer shows that he is already in the grip of another world:

> Farewell, my father, you too, many times farewell.[7]

7. 1453, transposed with 1455 by von Wilamowitz, followed by Murray and Barrett. Though it does not matter for our present inquiry, I wish to point

Once again we see that the dying one can hardly be touched any more by the closeness of the other. Theseus says (1456):

> Do not forsake me, child, bear up and endure.

Hippolytus says:

My struggle has been borne, father, I am dead. Veil my head as quickly as you can.

As Alcestis put it,

You may speak of me as nothing, I am no longer alive.

In neither case can the dying person's situation be altered in the least by the movement of the other in his direction and the removal of the former barrier between them. To be sure, there is the growth of a certainty, even a very intimate certainty; but it remains – in the former case as well as in the present one – lost and powerless in the tragic space, devoid of any fulfillment in the realm of actuality. Its essence seems to consist only in the fact that (despite all the impossibility of fulfilment, despite its very purpose-lessness) it has been there for a moment, and that it came quite unexpectedly if one considers the isolation and loneliness that pre-ceded it.

Let us pause for a moment, before turning to another play. When we compare the structure of the two death-scenes, we discover a remarkable similarity between them. In both cases, the action of the play has reached its goal; in the dramatic course of events a resting-point has been reached. This extra-dramatic resting-point is then expanded to an entire scene of the strongest internal and (as we cannot but call it) individually molded emotion. A voice for the sorrow and suffering is found in the souls of the untragic ones, the sympathetic and new-found friends, who in this

out that there is probably no need for transposing. Commentators feel that Hippolytus' 'Goodbye to you, too' in 1453 can only follow Theseus' goodbye to Hippolytus or an equivalent to a goodbye which they find in 1454. They overlook the fact that, ever since exchanging 'goodbye' with Artemis (1437; 1440: χαίρουσα καὶ σὺ στεῖχε), Hippolytus has been wishing to take leave of his father, too (already in 1444 darkness approaches him), but has been kept from doing so because of his promise to Artemis (λύω δὲ νεῖκος πατρί, 1442) and Theseus' own repeatedly expressed desire for absolution and reconciliation. It is only consistent that, with their reconciliation established, Hippolytus presses for a last goodbye to his father before losing consciousness (ὡς τάχος, 1458).

manner are themselves integrated into the sphere of tragic experience. It is, however, precisely this unexpected display of sympathy which throws into bolder relief the isolation and loneliness of the dying tragical victim.

In both cases the internal emotion is heightened by the fact that the course of external events is changed, in the imagination of the survivor, and reshaped into unreality (a sort of contrary-to-fact movement). Admetus wishes to accompany his wife in death; Theseus bids his son bear up. Each time, this would involve a different outcome to the play than that which actually occurs.

Also common to both is the abruptness with which the survivor comes to recognize the significance for himself of the impending loss. This too is psychologically convincing. Both Admetus and Theseus knew well in advance (and, in one way or another, even approved of) what was about to happen; but only the moment of parting is able to change the event, which so far has only been imagined, to an experience which puts their own existence into question.

How much Euripides put into the extra-dramatic scene of the *Hippolytus* can be determined from the following. The *Hippolytus*, as we possess it, is the second working of the same material by our author. In the first version – as Seneca's *Phaedra*, to which Racine adhered on this point, allows us to conjecture – it is highly probable that the second encounter between father and dying son did not take place. The earlier misunderstanding-scene between father and son, which we examined above, also belongs to the new version and not the old. (On this point Seneca – and, following him once more, Racine – held to the second version.) Presumably, in place of the two Theseus–Hippolytus scenes, the first version contained two scenes between Theseus and Phaedra: in the first, Phaedra slandered her stepson; in the second, she revealed the truth before her own death.

Euripides' artistic interest in the extra-dramatic final scene can further be illustrated by a 'parallel', which at first sight may look like an opposite rather than a parallel.

As the reconciliation scene at the end of the *Hippolytus* forms a pendant to the earlier scene which contained the argument of father and son at Phaedra's corpse, so the final scene of the

Medea proves to be a dramaturgically comparable pendant to an earlier scene (866ff.). Here, however, the (fictitious) reconciliation comes first, and the quarrel last. But the human revelation of the extra-dramatic final scene is no less compelling.

Medea is still convinced that she is not to blame for what she did. Rather, she seems to feel that the guilt lies with Jason (1364) and that her horrible deed is a clear consequence of his perjury and deceit (cf. 1392). Therefore the revenging deity will not listen to his complaints (1391). Medea only ('as must be done') returned the blow he had struck at her (τῆς σῆς γὰρ ὡς χρὴ καρδίας ἀνθηψάμην, 1360; cf. 1372), and so, in her strangely consistent reasoning, she still claims to be the loving mother: the dead children are 'dearest', φίλτατα, 'to their mother, not to you' (μητρί γε, σοὶ δ' οὔ, 1397; her claim is uttered at the point of highest agitation, in the broken anapaestic *stichomythia*).

The extra-dramatic scene, this time, breathes purest, self-righteous hostility; the place of the sympathizing friend is taken by a hateful superior; the contrary-to-fact movement of wishful thinking is replaced by Medea's joyful prediction of the sufferings that will actually accompany Jason through the rest of his life ('so far, you don't have reason to lament: wait for old age!', 1396), and delight is taken in the prospect of his miserable death, which Medea regally defines as a punishment of his behavior towards her ('a bitter ending you experience of your marriage with me', 1388). As in the scenes we interpreted earlier the sympathizers would do everything to see the tragic victim live on, so Medea does everything – she even inflicts incurable wounds upon herself – to harm Jason. The message, extraordinary as it may sound, is in both cases a purely human one. We should not minimize the horrors Euripides finds inherent in human nature by saying that Medea here substitutes for the not human *deus ex machina*. We would never say so about Theseus, although he, too, could be said to fill, at least partially, the place from which Artemis, *dea ex machina*, had withdrawn.

That the *Hippolytus* II has gained a great deal by being remolded towards a new climax hardly needs to be stressed. What is of methodical interest to the present inquiry is the very fact (which is not my finding) that the final scene has been newly composed. For it provides supporting evidence for the great emphasis I place on such extra-dramatic passages as the high points of the tragedies.[8]

For further illustration of the structural features we have thus far considered, we proceed over a space of more than twenty years to the posthumously produced *Iphigenia at Aulis*.

The underlying situation is as follows: the Greek host has assembled at Aulis in preparation for a punitive expedition against Troy, because Helen, the wife of Menelaus, has been abducted by the Trojan prince Paris.

A calm keeps the army in the harbor of Aulis, and the seer Calchas discloses that the voyage cannot be continued before the commander Agamemnon has sacrificed his daughter Iphigenia to the goddess Artemis. Agamemnon, concerned for his glory, makes use of a stratagem. He sends a letter to his wife Clytemnestra, enjoining her to send his daughter to Aulis to be married to Achilles, the foremost of the Greek heroes.

All this has occurred before the play commences. In the play itself we encounter a completely different Agamemnon. He regrets his intrigue and tries to undo it by writing a second letter to his wife. The letter, however, is intercepted and opened by his suspicious brother Menelaus who confronts its author with it.

In invective and viciousness, the quarrel between the two brothers surpasses all bounds. Among other things, the fact again plays its part that there is no accurate means of testing a man's character unambiguously (expressed by the word *saphes* (333) which we have mentioned before). Agamemnon is upbraided for his unpleasant hunger for military glory and his change of heart regarding the sacrifice of his daughter, Menelaus for his jealousy as a cuckolded husband. A theme of Homeric heroic epic is deliberately debased to the level of a family row.

In the midst of the quarrel a messenger suddenly arrives with the news of Iphigenia's (*and* Clytemnestra's) imminent arrival. The coming meeting with his wife, as well as the now more concrete threat to his daughter, causes Agamemnon's collapse.

8. Perhaps it should be added that these scenes cannot at all be regarded as 'retarding moments', as the rejoicing duets in the intrigue-dramas often can, where the tension is heightened by the fact that the newly found in their happiness tend to forget the danger they are in.

And now Menelaus says (471):

Brother, give me your right hand.

Agamemnon rejoins:

I do so. For yours is the victory, and I am wretched.

Agamemnon regards his brother's gesture as a final demand for surrender, and submits because he feels himself overwhelmed by events.

Such, however, is not Menelaus' meaning. Rather, on his side, he has not felt able to avoid the sight presented to his view by his deeply afflicted brother, lamenting over the news. The motif of sudden recognition, which we have commented on before, is thus duplicated here. Menelaus feels the recognition is equivalent to a process of maturation on his part (489):

I was a young fool, until, viewing the matter from close by, I recognized what it means to kill a child.

'Viewing the matter from close by' – this is the catch-word for the experience which starts at the moment when what was long intended turns into actuality. The reality is not what man had imagined it would be.

Thus, once again, a movement takes place towards the other, and a bridge is laid between two men who were formerly separated and mutually antagonistic. A true change of heart, caused by the other person's suffering, and again a change of heart which seeks to depart from the course prescribed for the play: for if Menelaus renounced his claim to vengeance, the Trojan war would not take place.

To be sure, on this occasion the other is more manifestly being reached, he does perceive the certainty of the affection offered him so unexpectedly. Agamemnon thanks his brother – but his gratitude is joyless since the situation will remain unchanged. For there will be others who also know of the oracle. The ambitious Odysseus and the common soldiery as well (here we encounter the anonymous crowd in the role of antagonist), they all will refuse to abandon the campaign and forgo their chance for glory, but will exact the sacrifice by force.

Thus, another feature of the scenes we interpreted earlier is seen to have been retained. The certainty of the other's sympathy cannot be transformed into practical help or effective action. On the contrary: on the one hand, the sympathy itself was communicated in a renunciation of action (i.e. in Menelaus' renunciation of the campaign) – and on the other hand the two brothers, despite their new fellowship, have no means by which to oppose effectively the threatening crowd. The circle is closed; the course of the play has returned to the point it had already reached at the scene's beginning. Since external events have not been changed, the scene has been, so to speak, 'extra-dramatic'.

I wish to give a final example from the same tragedy.

Later in the play, Achilles, the involuntary bridegroom, rebels against the sacrifice of Iphigenia – not because he pities the girl, but because the generals have misused his name: Achilles' honor ought not to be stained by a maiden's murder!

Achilles speaks out against the sacrifice in the assembly. But he is shouted down and almost stoned by the furious host (above all by his own troops), reviled as a woman's slave. At this time, he unexpectedly takes the betrothal seriously – in his own peculiar fashion: with the aid of a few loyal followers, he proposes to defend Iphigenia against overwhelming odds, even though the struggle is hopeless from the beginning.

At this moment, however, and in Achilles' presence, Iphigenia announces her decision to offer herself voluntarily as a sacrificial victim. In doing so, she – after all the human (and only too human) motives which have been mentioned up to this point – reaches out for the heroic motive suggested by her father and makes it her own. In passing, I should remark that, although Iphigenia is not unaffected by the hero's presence, there is no thought here at all of any stirring of passion in her for Achilles such as Racine delineates. She intends to liberate Hellas and to prevent Greek wives and Greek marriages from being dishonored by barbarians (1374ff.).

Objectively considered, in view of all that has preceded, such an interpretation of the expedition is plainly absurd. Subjectively, it makes possible the heroic self-fulfillment of a young woman who does not share the base motives of her environment. One is tempted to ask whether, for the dramatic deed (a very passive 'deed' in this case, anyway), a state of illusion is needed.

And how does Achilles conduct himself? (1404):

Agamemnon's daughter, a god would make me blessed, had I your hand in marriage!

And again:

Desire to be your husband grips me more, since I have seen your nature.

As in the three scenes we considered earlier, the bridging of the antithesis of 'I' and 'Thou' is connected with a process of recognition, a sudden insight into the situation and nature of the other: 'since I have seen your nature'. Achilles asks Iphigenia for her hand, he wishes to rescue her from death and Aulis and to take her home as his wife.

The change of heart – from the earlier motive of insulted honor – again threatens to disrupt the outcome of the drama; for if Achilles did as he intends, the Trojan war would – again – not take place. As in the other scenes, reality is transformed into unreality in the soul of the new sympathizer and reshaped in a sort of contrary-to-fact movement.

The point which my investigation has just reached calls for an interruption. For the result affords one of those rare cuts through the history of Greek literature, which, without resulting in cheap clichés, can reveal a surprising continuity.

What I wish to introduce here is an 'extra-dramatic scene' from the *Iliad*. When Achilles' wrath against Agamemnon has made him withdraw from fighting, the Greeks suffer such heavy losses that they send an embassy to Achilles' tents, consisting of smart Odysseus, fatherly friend Phoenix, and square fighter Ajax. The scene (truly a 'scene' in the dramatic sense, with three subtly characterizing addresses by the envoys and three answers spoken by Achilles) is 'extra-dramatic', because the envoys return as empty-handed as they arrived and nothing has changed in the external situation. But internally the conversation moves through the different environmental relations by which a Homeric hero is defined, and even up to that borderline on the other side of which the negation of the heroic ideal is located. Even the closest friend, Phoenix, is far too conventional (Achilles will blame him for this attitude) ever to cross this border (in this respect, there can be no parallel to the Euripidean close one). But the hero of heroes himself performs the contrary-to-fact movement so characteristic of the Euripidean scenes. Achilles, denouncing war and honor (equal portions and equal honor fall to coward and brave man, 9. 318f.), picks up the plot and leads it on into unreality: he will go home, marry (but not Agamemnon's daughter), enjoy his father's possessions. For Troy's wealth 'is to me not of equal worth with my life' (401), which, once lost, cannot be regained (408). Therefore he chooses the long life rather than *kleos esthlon* or *aphthiton* (412ff.).

If Achilles' intention became reality, the Trojan War would have to be discontinued ('I would advise you others, too, to sail home', 417f.). Of course this will not happen, and thus the main effect the scene leaves us with is our insight into Achilles' soul: even the deathbound warrior and Homeric hero *par excellence* can have an almost Euripidean difficulty in finding his bearings. Having read book 9, we will never forget his doubts and his desire to live on – in whatever situation we may find him later. The fact that he has once seriously considered the unheroic alternative to his glorious destiny (and that in terms of a free choice), illuminates his existence as that of a human being in a way similar to that we found in Euripides' extra-dramatic scenes.

I return from Homeric Achilles to his Euripidean 'bride'. Naturally, as before, the unexpected certainty that one has a new friend can have no effect on actuality; it can only be communicated and expressed in its tragic 'thereness'. Iphigenia says (1418):

Yet you, my friend (*o xene*), do not die or kill anyone on my account. But allow me to save Hellas, if I am able.

Of all the scenes with which we have dealt, this seems to me to express in purest form the tragic dilemma which the certainty of human closeness often involves for Euripides: for only by relinquishing her life does Iphigenia gain her new friend – or rather, her bridegroom. In case she wished to make use of this friendship to prolong her existence, she would have to destroy its necessary conditions and thus forfeit the friendship itself.

To sum up: in all the uncertainty and unreliability of the surrounding world, the certainty of another human being's closeness can fall to the lot of men in Euripides – but it cannot be counted on. Pentheus for example, in the *Bacchae*, dies friendless, killed by the human being supposedly closest to him: his own mother. If closeness or friendship occurs in the cases we have considered, it does so unexpectedly and without being able to alter the tragic situation. It is like a flash of light, a recognition (though hardly accomplished) that a sympathizer is there; full of restraint, it is hardly more than a gesture, certainly not a consolation. Its occurrence is basically as accidental for the character visited by it as is the deliverance in the untragic chance-dramas. Still, despite all the ambiguities which adhere to it as to all environmental relations in Euripides, it renders one thing unmistakably clear: that the one whom the new friend is no longer able to help is a human being, and, indeed, one in utter loneliness, about to meet the extreme situation of annihilation. In this may lie its poetic function.

This emphasis on human tragedy is brought about by the use of dramaturgic resting-points. Of course, as I have sought to show, while the external events of the drama have come to rest, the two communicating characters pick up the plot and, in a contrary-to-fact movement, lead it on into unreality. Because of the fact that the play's course is continued internally, within the souls of the participants, one may speak even here of a dramaturgy – an internal dramaturgy as it were. It is for this reason that in the title of my paper – 'On "Extra-dramatic" Communication of Characters in Euripides' – I have put the word 'extra-dramatic' in quotation marks.

The infanticide in Euripides' *Medea*

P. E. EASTERLING

In many respects Euripides' *Medea* is not a problematic play. It is a singularly bold, clear-cut, assured piece of writing, the concentration and dramatic intensity of which are readily felt by reader or audience and command the respect even of those who find the subject matter repellent or who cavil at the Aegeus scene and the dragon chariot. But its starkness makes it deeply disturbing; and this unease is reflected in the critical literature on the play. The language, though consistently powerful, lacks the rich expansiveness of *Hippolytus* or *Bacchae*, almost never allowing us to range in imagination away from the immediate painful situation; it is typical that one of the most prominent of the recurring images is of Medea as a wild beast.[1] Then there is the striking absence of a cosmic frame of reference: we are given no sense of divine motivation or sanction or control. Medea is admittedly grand-daughter of the Sun, but the fact has no theological significance: its function is to symbolize her sense of her heroic identity and – at a different level – to motivate the final scene. The most uncompromising feature of all is Euripides' handling of the story, his design which makes the murder of the children the centrepiece of the play.

This horrific act is something from which we naturally recoil. 'No sane person', we say, 'would do such a thing', and indeed Euripides' many imitators have tended to present Medea's behaviour as that of a madwoman.[2] Or 'no civilized person would do it'; Sir Denys Page, for example, writes, 'The murder of children...is mere brutality: if it moves us at all, it does so towards incredulity and horror. Such an act is outside our experience, we – and the fifth-century Athenian – know nothing of

1. 92; (103); 187ff.; 1342f.; 1358f.; 1407.
2. Cf. W.-H. Friedrich, 'Medeas Rache' in *Euripides*, ed. E.-R. Schwinge (Darmstadt 1968), p. 209.

it.'[3] Doubts have been felt in particular about Medea's great speech at 1021ff. in which she wrestles with her conflicting feelings of injured pride and love for her children: is Euripides merely playing with our emotions through a rhetorical handling of the situation, exploiting the dramatic effectiveness of Medea's debate with herself rather than having an eye to what a person would really do in such circumstances?[4] Or conversely, is this conflict in Medea's soul the real high point of the drama, of more tragic importance than the violent act itself?[5] Or is it possible, as has recently been suggested, that we retain some sympathy with Medea right through to her final triumph, so that the final scene is the real climax of the play?[6] Clearly an important question to be faced by any critic who wishes to interpret *Medea* is whether Euripides is exploring the realities of human behaviour or creating only an illusion of reality out of a sequence of essentially melodramatic actions.

'Real life' in drama is not, of course, the same phenomenon as real life outside. Distortion or suppression of documentary fact and neglect – within certain limits – even of probability are part of the dramatist's stock-in-trade which we accept at the same time as believing in the truthfulness of his situations. Thus it is no fundamental failure on Euripides' part that he abandons probability in his treatment of the chorus. It is highly unlikely that these respectable ladies of Corinth would really have stood ineffectually by when Medea announced her intention to kill their king and princess and then her own children. In real life they would have taken steps to have Medea taken into custody, or at the very least would have gone to warn the royal family and Jason. But we accept their inactivity because these women are not at the centre of the play: they are peripheral figures whose role is not to do and suffer but to comment, sympathize, support or disapprove. The advantages of providing Medea with a sympathetic and understanding audience within the play far outweigh any loss of

3. D. L. Page, *Euripides, Medea* (Oxford 1938), p. xiv.
4. 'She has her struggle with her maternal feelings – a theatrical struggle rather than a psychologically convincing one', H. D. F. Kitto, *Greek Tragedy*, 3rd ed. (London 1961), p. 195.
5. Cf. M. Pohlenz, *Die griechische Tragödie*, 2nd ed. (Göttingen 1954), vol. 1, pp. 255ff.
6. So W. Steidle, *Studien zum Antiken Drama* (Munich 1968), p. 165.

naturalism. A much graver breach is committed by Seneca, when he makes Medea after killing the children toss the corpses down to Jason.[7] The whole motivation of the mother who murders her children is unintelligible if she is willing to surrender their corpses to the husband whom she is punishing. Similarly, in Corneille's *Médée* there is no conviction at all in the scene where *Jason* thinks of killing the children to punish Medea.[8]

It is worth considering how Euripides manipulates the story in order to force us to take Medea seriously. The barbarian sorceress with a melodramatic criminal record who could so easily be a monster must become a tragic character, a paradigm, in some sense, of humanity. The Nurse's opening speech alludes briefly to that record: Medea is in exile for persuading the daughters of Pelias to kill their father, but there is no suggestion that she is shunned or feared by the Corinthians; the Nurse says she 'pleases' them (11f.) and the friendly words of the chorus (137, 178ff.) imply that she is an accepted, even a respected, figure. According to a scholiast on Pindar (*O*. 13. 74) Medea served the Corinthians by stopping a famine in their city; but Euripides makes no explicit mention of a story which on the face of it looks ideally suited to his purpose, for the good reason that it would introduce distracting complications into the scene with Creon. Unlike Seneca and Corneille, he clearly wanted to avoid giving the situation even the vaguest political dimension: there are to be no outside pressures on Creon, and he is to have no obligations to Medea for past services. So Euripides with fine sleight-of-hand contrives to imply that Medea's status at Corinth is one of some dignity, but without explaining why; later it becomes clear that she has a reputation as a wise woman, but the picture that is very lightly sketched in (for example in the scene with Aegeus) is as close to that of a respectable religious authority as to that of an outlandish witch.[9]

Medea as foreigner is another theme which is delicately handled by Euripides. At the most superficial level the fact that she is a barbarian from Colchis must have helped a Greek audience to accept both her past crimes and her expertise as a powerful

7. If modern editors are right in so interpreting 'recipe iam natos parens' (*Medea* 1024).

8. *Médée* V. v.

9. Cf. D. J. Conacher, *Euripidean Drama* (Toronto 1967), pp. 186–7, 190.

sorceress, but we should be rash to conclude that it offered them an adequate explanation of the child murder. If Medea is to be seen as a distinctively oriental type ('because she was a foreigner she could kill her children'[10]) why does Euripides make her talk like a Greek, argue like a Greek, and to all appearances *feel* like a Greek? It is hard to believe, particularly in view of the astonishingly crass words he gives to Jason at 536ff., that Euripides was seriously imputing moral superiority to the Greeks, implying that only a foreigner could or would murder her own kin. On the contrary, he seems to exploit the theme of Medea's foreignness in order to emphasize her vulnerability and isolation and also to make a searching analysis of the nature of civilization and barbarism, a deep preoccupation of this play, to which we shall return.

Similarly, the record of Medea's past crimes is used – initially at any rate – more to arouse than to alienate the audience's sympathy. Euripides does not suppress the murder of Apsyrtus (166–7) or the killing of Pelias (9), though he is careful not to dwell on the grisly details of dismemberment and boiling. The subdued recall of these past horrors no doubt foreshadows the violence to come; but one of its main functions is to make clear that Medea has sacrificed literally everything for Jason, thus emphasizing his special ingratitude and her special defencelessness: she has not merely abandoned her family, she has betrayed them for Jason's sake. Nor does Euripides allow any character to raise the question of the legal relationship between Jason and Medea. None of them suggests[11] that Jason was perfectly entitled to abandon Medea without bad faith because as a foreigner she could not be his legitimate wife. Like other dramatists in other plays[12] Euripides permits himself a certain vagueness in legal matters, relying on the fact that the story is set in the heroic age, not in fifth-century Athens, however strongly the social comment may strike us as contemporary. This is one of those questions which in real life would be crucially important, but which it suits a dramatist to suppress. The essential situation is perfectly clear-cut:

10. Page (n. 3 above), p. xxi.

11. Although at least one critic has done so (G. Murray, in the introduction to his translation (London 1910), pp. viif.).

12. E.g. Sophocles on the edict in *Antigone*. Cf. D. A. Hester, *Mnemosyne* 24 (1971), 19–21.

Jason and Medea are to be regarded as permanently pledged,[13] so that when Jason abandons Medea he *is* breaking faith (and even he does not deny it).

Euripides has taken pains, therefore, to present the situation in such a way that we are obliged to take Medea seriously. The structure of the first part of the play and the detail of these early scenes seem to be aimed at the same objective, the audience's full response to Medea as a tragic character.

The prologue from 46ff., the entry of the children, can fairly be described as a 'mirror scene', a tightly self-contained presentation in miniature of the course that the action is going to take. It has very little direct connection with the immediately following scene, beyond the fact that the chorus ask the Nurse to coax Medea out of the house and she does actually emerge at 214, the beginning of the first episode; its main function seems rather to be prophetic, like the short scene in *Hippolytus* where the old servant reproves Hippolytus for his neglect of Aphrodite (88–120). Here the Nurse three times expresses her fear for the children's safety at their mother's hands (90ff.; 100ff.; 116ff.), having already glancingly introduced the theme in her opening speech: 'She hates the children and takes no pleasure in seeing them. I am afraid she may make some new [i.e. sinister] plan' (36f.). Medea's own curses reinforce this sense of foreboding: 'O cursed children of a hateful mother, may you perish with your father, and the whole house go to ruin!' (112ff.). And the children themselves appear, fresh from their games, to impress their significance on the audience. From the start, then, it is made clear that this is not just a quarrel between man and wife, but a family drama in which the future and even the safety of the children are at stake. Medea herself is presented in all the alarming violence of her passion, but framed by the sympathy of Nurse and chorus, and therefore to be seen by the audience as a victim, even if also as a potential criminal.

When Medea comes out to talk to the chorus all the wildness has gone and she develops her arguments with complete composure. The focus of the dramatic interest is now this commanding personality in a sequence of encounters, first with the chorus, then with three men who in different ways have power to affect her life.

13. The theme of their oaths is given repeated stress: 21ff.; 160ff.; 168ff.; 208ff.; 438ff. (and the whole *stasimon*); 492ff.; 1392.

With the chorus she is at her most frank and open, winning their whole-hearted support with her account of the miseries of a woman's life. At this stage the audience, too, must readily give her their sympathy, but complications already begin to arise. How much, we may ask, of what she says to the chorus is special pleading, designed to make them promise to keep her secret? As always with Medea it is hard to be sure; and here we meet for the first time the subtle complexity of Euripides' character-portrayal. At least her description of the constraints on women is deeply convincing, but when she complains of her special lack of resource as a foreigner with 'no mother, no *brother*, no kinsman' to support her (257f.) we perhaps remember that it was she herself who caused her brother's death and betrayed her family. These words lead straight into her plea for collusion on the part of the chorus if she finds some way of punishing her husband: 'for woman is fearful and timid in other respects and a coward when it comes to looking on steel, but when her marriage is treated with contempt there is no bloodier purpose than hers' (263ff.). We are left in no doubt that this is a formidable woman; and, despite all that she has said in this scene about the limitations of the feminine role, it is clear that she herself is capable of overcoming them. When she makes her famous claim (250f.) that she would rather stand three times in the battle line than bear one child she wins our respect – she is talking, of course, about the emotional hazards of being a mother, not just about the physical pain and danger of childbearing – but even so, not many women would say what Medea says; these words may come back to our minds at the end of the scene with Creon.

With the king we see the full exposure of Medea's cleverness, her *sophia*. Creon is explicit that he is exiling her because he fears what her cleverness may devise to harm his family; Medea's response is a dazzling virtuoso display of the very quality he fears. First she argues that her cleverness could not possibly be used to harm *him*, next exerts extreme emotional pressure by appealing to his feelings as a father,[14] and finally makes a disarmingly modest

14. E. Schlesinger, *Hermes* 94 (1966), 42, makes much of Creon's remark at 329 that his children are dearer to him than anything else in life. This is certainly important, in that it gives Medea her cue for exploiting Creon and keeps the theme of children in the foreground, but can we say that it actually gives her the idea of killing her children?

request: just one day's grace, time for making the necessary arrangements for going into exile. But as soon as he has left and Medea has got her way there is a striking change of tone: now we see all the contempt of the clever person for the fool. 'Do you think I would have fawned on that man if I had not had some profit or plan in mind?' (368f.). Now in a highly professional way she discusses the possible modes of murder she might choose: shall it be fire, or sword, or poison, her speciality? This could easily be bloodcurdling for bloodcurdling's sake as in Seneca and Corneille, who both make much of her gruesome rites and incantations. In Euripides the effect is less gothic; indeed a main function of this detail seems to be to emphasize Medea's cleverness: in her own view of herself her magical skill is part of her heroic *arete*.

This speech at 364ff. (and particularly the last section from 392) illuminates a most important aspect of Euripides' Medea. She sees herself not just as a woman wronged, but as a great personage in the heroic mould of an Ajax or an Achilles: she owes it to herself and to her high pedigree to allow no enemy to triumph over her. The grand-daughter of Helios must face the test of courage: νῦν ἀγὼν εὐψυχίας, language that an Ajax or an Achilles might perfectly well use. In this context Medea standing in the battle line becomes fully intelligible. The scene ends on a less grandiose, more sinister, note: 'We are women, helpless when it comes to good deeds, but skilled practitioners of all kinds of evil' (408f.).[15] There is a clash here between Medea's self-image as a hero of the old style braving a great ordeal and her awareness of the destructiveness of thwarted female passion. We see very clearly that her cleverness is a potent force for evil as well as for good. The tragedy is that she does stand out above the limited or shabby people around her, does have a sharper moral awareness and far greater distinction and force of personality, yet the audience cannot help but shudder at the ruthlessness of her anger and passion for vengeance.

In her first scene with Jason, Medea is at her most sympathetic, because here we are allowed to see the full extent of the provocation she has been suffering. Jason is a status-seeker, embarrassed by his barbarian wife who refuses to go quietly, anxious to have her

15. The rhyme (ἀμηχανώταται...σοφώταται) adds to the sonorousness of this ending.

out of the way but insensitive enough to talk about exile being a hardship, crassly patronizing in his offer of material help. Medea's theme is simple: 'I saved you';[16] and she is right. All her past acts of betrayal were committed in the cause of Jason and her love for him; and now he is guilty of the greatest betrayal of all, the breaking of those dearly-bought oaths. The only extenuation would have been if their union had been childless: but they *have children* (παίδων γεγώτων at 490 carries the strongest possible emphasis). Jason's answer only confirms our sense of his outrageousness. He is sophistical in his argument that it was Cypris, not Medea, who saved him, ludicrously arrogant when he recalls the benefits he has conferred on his wife by bringing her to civilized Greece from her benighted barbarian home, patently self-deceptive[17] when he pretends that his only interest in the new marriage is the welfare of his existing family. Once more the importance of children is made very prominent, particularly at 565, when Jason implies that he needs a family more than Medea does. Medea's final taunt turns into a sinister threat which recalls the concluding lines of the two previous scenes: we are reminded that she is still planning revenge, though the encounter with Jason has done nothing to further the action in any practical sense and Medea still has no idea where she can go when she has punished her victims.

Then Aegeus arrives unexpectedly to answer her need. Aegeus is merely passing through Corinth on his way from the Delphic oracle to consult Pittheus, his old friend who is king of Troezen. The casualness of his arrival has been criticized from Aristotle[18] onwards, but as with Io's visit to the Caucasus in *Prometheus Bound* such casualness is readily acceptable to an audience provided that the scene itself is dramatically significant, and provided that it is seen to be part of a structural pattern. Here there is a clearly discernible design: three contrasting visits to Medea, of which the third offers a close parallel to the first.[19] Both the scene with Creon

16. 476; 515: powerful use of ring-composition.
17. The chorus are not deceived (578; 637ff.); and Jason's words to the princess (reported by the Messenger at 1151ff.) suggest that he was enjoying his role as royal bridegroom.
18. *Poetics* 1461 b 21. At least Euripides has warned us to expect *someone* to arrive (390–4).
19. Cf. D. W. Lucas, *The Greek Tragic Poets*, 2nd ed. (London 1959), p. 197.

and the scene with Aegeus show Medea using her wits to get what she wants from a person in authority; but whereas Creon was all suspicion and misgivings Aegeus is full of honourable and rather naive trust. Medea is equal to either situation; and the most interesting link between the two scenes is in her choice of persuasive argument. With Creon it is his feelings as a parent she exploits, with Aegeus his longing to be a parent. Once more her cleverness succeeds: she now has a refuge in Athens, and she can afford to make a detailed plan of vengeance.

Her speech at 764ff. is the most remarkable in the play. It starts with her triumphant exultation and her plot for the murder of the princess and Creon, then leads without preparation into the terrible revelation that she intends to kill her children. Her own explanation makes the best starting point for a discussion of this speech. She sees the murder of her children as a means of *punishing her enemies*. The deed will be 'most unholy', but she will do it because her enemies' laughter is not to be tolerated. The penalty that is worse than death for her enemy Jason will be to have no children, neither Medea's nor any borne to him by the princess. And so 'let no one think me cowardly or weak, or peaceable, but of quite the opposite temper: dire to my enemies and kindly to my friends. For it is such people who live in the highest esteem.' This is the kind of language with which she exults in her success over Aegeus: 'now I shall win the victory over my enemies' (764–7), language that recalls the end of the scene with Creon with its image of the heroic Medea facing the 'test of courage'. These are all words that belong to the traditional code, in which the laughter of enemies is the ultimate disgrace and harming enemies and helping friends is the duty of a hero. But Medea's appropriation of the code seems hideously out of place in a situation where the enemy is her husband and the means of punishing him is to be an act of bloodthirsty treachery followed by the murder of her own children.

The essential relevance of the scene with Aegeus must be its stress on the value and importance of children. Euripides does not make clear exactly when Medea arrives at the details of her plan, and we cannot say that the encounter with Aegeus gives her the idea to kill the children; it is enough that after the scene with Aegeus she has the idea very fully worked out: this will be Jason's

consummate punishment, to be robbed of his future. Her announcement comes as a surprise, but it is not factitious: the
prologue's prophetic warnings and the prominence of the theme
of parents and children in all three of Medea's encounters have
effectively prepared the way.[20] This technique is perhaps subtler
than the version preferred by Seneca, an episode in which Medea
sees how much Jason loves his children and says 'Now I have
him.'[21] Euripides' Medea does not need to be shown evidence of
Jason's fatherly love: she simply knows that even a man as selfish
and coarse-grained as Jason, who for the moment is quite absorbed
in his young bride and his new social status and content for his
whole family to go into exile, can still be profoundly hurt by the
loss of his children.

Even more than the scene with Aegeus it is the child murder
itself that has caused the greatest critical unease. Perhaps this is
because society so much abhors the murder of children that it
refuses to regard it as anything but the rarest and most outrageous of deviations. Hence the attempt to explain Medea's act
as something quite outside the experience of civilized people. In
general we tend not to look on murder as such with the same
disbelief; and it comes as a surprise to find from modern statistics
that a large proportion of murder victims are in fact children –
nearly one-third of the total in the United Kingdom between 1957
and 1968,[22] nearly half in Denmark in recent times[23] – and that
the killers are predominantly their parents. Often the killing of
children is accompanied by suicide on the part of the parents, but
one parent may kill a child or children as a means of hurting the
marriage partner. May it not be that in *Medea* we find Euripides
exhibiting the same psychological sureness of touch as in his studies
of Phaedra and Electra and Pentheus, or as in the scene where
Cadmus brings Agave back to reality?[24]

Medea is trying to achieve the punishment of Jason; the death
of the princess and Creon is not enough, because through her

20. Cf. D. Ebener, *Rheinisches Museum* 104 (1961), 224.
21. *Medea* 549–50: 'sic natos amat? | bene est, tenetur, uulneri patet locus'.
22. Cf. E. Gibson and S. Klein, *Murder 1957 to 1968* = *Home Office Research
Studies 3* (London 1969). I am grateful to my colleague Mrs A. M. Morris for
a criminologist's view of the problem of child murder.
23. Cf. T. Harder, *Acta Psychiatrica Scandinavica* 43 (1967), 197ff.
24. Cf. G. Devereux, *J.H.S.* 90 (1970), 35ff. for a study of this scene.

children Medea can still be hurt or insulted (by the 'laughter of her enemies'), if *they* are hurt or insulted. With them alive and in his care Jason can still look to the future through them. There is no question of Medea's admitting to a wish to punish the children: she calls them 'most beloved' (795) and her deed 'most unholy' (796): only in the prologue does she curse them and the Nurse say she 'hates the children' (presumably because they represent her vulnerability to Jason). Indeed she thinks she is being loyal to her dear ones and winning glory by her actions (809f.), heroic language which a psychologist would probably describe as an 'altruistic' and 'protective' rationalization of the child murder. It seems that very often the parents who kill their children convince themselves that the children would in their own interests be better dead.[25]

The scene of false reconciliation between Medea and Jason makes magnificent theatre; it also has a subtle importance in its relation to the rest of the play.[26] It emphasizes the link between the two stages of Medea's revenge by showing the children who are to be victims of the culminating deed innocently bearing the poisoned gifts which will make them the agents of the first murder, with Jason as their accomplice. From 894ff. the children are the focus of the action; and seeing them in Jason's embraces and hearing his confident words about their future, Medea twice breaks down, though each time she resourcefully contrives to explain her tears in a sense which furthers her deception of Jason. The episode has a complex function: it confirms our awareness of the children's importance to Jason and at the same time prepares for the moving passage (1029ff.) where Medea imagines the future that the children will never have. Moreover her self-mastery here, according to Steidle's persuasive analysis,[27] foreshadows the success of her resolve in the following scene. Certainly it must now seem clear to the audience, as it does to the chorus, that the children are bound to die: 'Now no longer have I any hope left for the children's lives, no longer. They go already to their deaths' (976ff.).

Now Medea learns that the first part of her plan has worked

25. Harder (n. 23 above), pp. 235ff.
26. Cf. A. Lesky, *Die tragische Dichtung der Hellenen*, 3rd ed. (Göttingen 1972), p. 307; Steidle, *Studien*, pp. 156f.
27. See n. 26 above.

and the children have been allowed to stay in Corinth; she must
say goodbye to them, ostensibly because she is going into exile,
but we know that she confronts the essential issue. Time is short,
and without the death of the children her revenge will not be
complete; but can she face the deed? The speech at 1021ff. in
which she expresses the struggle between her maternal love and
her desire for revenge has been tirelessly discussed:[28] is it the
tragic climax of the play, showing Medea caught in a conflict on
the outcome of which we hang in suspense, or is the inevitability
that she will kill her children strongly felt all through the speech,
and the climax reached only in the final scene? Recent critics
have been particularly concerned with the structural question and
also with the apparent inconsistency of Medea's motivation.
Within the space of a few lines she moves from the statement that
she will take the children with her into exile (1058) to the assertion
that there is no escape: they are certain to be killed in Corinth, and
she must therefore do the deed (1059–64).

The detail of the speech suggests that despite a certain rhetorical
formalism of manner Euripides keeps close to observed patterns of
human behaviour. The reality of Medea's love for her children is
evoked in her very precise recall of the hopes she used to cherish
for their future and hers (1024–35) and in her response to the
extraordinarily powerful appeal of their bright eyes and soft skin
(1070–5). But the reality of her obsessive need to triumph over
her enemies is also made inescapably clear (1049–55; 1059–60),
the need to hurt Jason as deeply as anyone can ever be hurt, which
has been fully explored earlier in the play, both in the betrayed
wife's passion for vengeance and in the heroic self-image which
makes Medea a far from ordinary but none the less convincing
and tragic figure.

Euripides needs to make us believe in Medea's maternal feeling
not because we are to think there is a real hope that she may
change her mind for good, but in order to achieve the full depth
of tragic seriousness. The deed she contemplates is so horrific that
we cannot accept it unless we are given evidence that it has cost
a profound struggle. Comparison with Seneca illustrates very well
the difference between tragic and melodramatic treatment of the
situation. Seneca's Medea carries conviction only as a raving

28. Cf. A. Lesky (n. 26 above), pp. 311f.

madwoman, whose moments of maternal feeling (938ff.) show none of the Euripidean Medea's precise awareness of what children mean to a mother. In any case, her softer emotions soon give way to visions of Furies accompanying the dismembered Apsyrtus, to whom Medea sacrifices one of the children, keeping the other to be killed in full view of Jason and the citizens. With her intended victim at her side she expresses a fleeting sense of remorse, but this is soon lost in the joy of gloating over Jason; of the child's presumed agony she seems (like Seneca) to be unaware:

> quid, misera, feci? misera? paeniteat licet,
> feci. uoluptas magna me inuitam subit,
> et ecce crescit. derat hoc unum mihi,
> spectator iste. (990–3)

Euripides' master-stroke in this speech is Medea's announcement at 1059ff. that there is no going back: the poison must have done its work by now and the princess must already be dead. We can assume that the treacherous murder of the princess and Creon will in reality mean danger for the children from the outraged royal family (as Jason later confirms, 1303ff.). Medea's reaction, when she faces the fact that the murder must have happened, is to treat this danger as inescapable, although a moment earlier she has been speaking of taking the children away with her. She is filled, in fact, with a sudden sense that she is caught in the tide of events and has no longer any choice. This is the atmosphere of sudden urgency in which we are told that the murder of children is often committed: the parent becomes convinced of a threat to the children that clinches the feeling that they would be better dead.[29] Such an interpretation seems much more relevant to Medea's case than any of the others that have been put forward, of which the latest is that the children were too young to accompany their mother in a hasty escape.[30]

The sense of urgency is brought to a desperate climax in Medea's speech after the Messenger has told his story and urged her to fly. There is no word now of triumph over her enemies or of her own situation at all beyond her need to steel herself: her whole concentration is on the children. She must act 'as swiftly

29. Cf. Harder (n. 23 above), especially p. 237, and L. Bender, *Journal of Nervous and Mental Disease* 80 (1934), 41.
30. Steidle (n. 6 above), pp. 159ff.

as possible', 'without delay'; since they are bound to be killed, she who loves them must be the one to do the deed, not some 'other more hostile hand' (1239ff.). The murder itself is represented by means of cries from the children and the chorus, but without any word from Medea; nowhere is there any hint of the gloating of Seneca's Medea as she raises the knife: 'perfruere lento scelere, ne propera, dolor' (1016).

The gloating (but never over the children) is to come in the stark final scene where Medea triumphs over Jason from the chariot, prophesying an evil death for him, refusing to let him even touch the children's bodies. The brute fact of Jason's loss moves us now; but it is Medea who speaks with prophetic authority. Clearly she has the role of the 'god from the machine' who so often in Euripides makes the final dispositions. This is one of the most alarming features of the play, the fact that there is no comparatively distant and objective divine figure to speak with the voice of authority, relating these events to real life through their link with some cult or institution and thereby restoring a sense of normality after the frightful extremes of the action. Medea makes a link between this story and a festival at Corinth (1381ff.); but she offers no relief whatever from the horror of the situation.

The powerful effect of this final scene depends on Euripides' use of the supernatural device of the dragon chariot, which transforms Medea's status from that of runaway criminal to something outside ordinary human experience. It was a bold dramatic experiment, but Euripides was justified in making it, granted that the effect could be adequately and not absurdly represented on the Greek stage. There has been criticism of the contrast between this very blatant use of the supernatural and the realistic tone of the rest of the action,[31] but some kind of miraculous device was needed if Euripides was to contrive a final confrontation between Jason and Medea in which Medea should at last have her triumph. The whole plot in fact rests on unrealistic data which we accept without qualm: for example, Medea's relationship to Helios (a frequently stressed motif which helps to prepare for the chariot)

31. R. Lattimore, for instance, regards the chariot as 'preposterous', merely a 'taxi to get from Corinth to Athens' (*The Poetry of Greek Tragedy* (Baltimore 1958), p. 108).

and the remarkable nature of her magical power. Yet throughout
we are invited to take Medea seriously as a real human being, and
even this final scene is perfectly consistent with the rest of the play
in its handling of her motivation; it is only the spectacle of her
in the chariot, high above Jason, taking with her the children's
bodies that he may not touch, that makes her seem to have been
transformed, in Murray's words, 'into a sort of living Curse...
Her wrongs and her hate fill the sky'.[32]

The sense that Euripides seems to be making out of all this is as
comfortless as the conclusions to which he points in *Hippolytus* or
Bacchae. What a vulnerable thing is civilization, when man's
passions are so powerfully destructive. When he makes the
insensitive Jason praise Greek society and values and when he
gives the barbarian witch the ideals of a traditional Greek hero he
is surely suggesting that there is no safe dividing line: civilized
life is always most precariously poised, continually threatened
from within.

One of the play's recurrent themes is that of song and the Muses:
it comes in that curious passage at the end of the *parodos* where
the Nurse meditatively wonders why poets have not devised songs
to cure human miseries instead of accompanying their pleasures
(190ff.); in the first *stasimon* when the chorus reflect how poetry
has always represented the man's side of things (421ff.); most
prominently in the great passage in praise of Athens after the
departure of Aegeus (824ff.). Athens, city of the Muses, the ideal
of civilized splendour, where *Sophia* and the Loves are in harmony:
is this merely a fine compliment to an Athenian audience, or is it
related more intimately to the deeper meaning of the play? All
these passages draw attention to the ambivalence of human
intelligence and creativity, which is potentially a source of beauty
and harmony, but liable, too, to break out in destructive violence
under the influence of passion. Medea in her *sophia* exemplifies
this ambivalence: we see her great expertise and intellectual power
turned, because of her betrayed love for Jason, to destructive – and
self-destructive – ends. And her heroic sense of identity is used to
bring out the tragic nature of what she does and suffers.

32. Murray (n. 11 above), pp. xif.

The *Medea* of Euripides

B. M. W. KNOX

IN 431 B.C. Euripides competed against Sophocles and Euphorion with three tragedies, *Medea, Philoctetes* and *Dictys*, followed by a satyr play, *Theristae*; he was awarded the third prize.[1]

But his *Medea* left a deep and lasting impression in the minds of his Athenian audience; comic parodies,[2] literary imitations[3] and representations in the visual arts[4] reflect its immediate impact and show that the play lost none of its power to fascinate and repel as the centuries went by. It struck the age as new, but like all innovative masterpieces, it had its deep roots in tradition; it looks back to the past while it gropes for the future. In it we can see what Euripides took over from his predecessors and contemporaries, how he transformed what he learned from them, and what he invented and was to refine and develop as his own unique tragic vision in the last twenty years of his long dramatic career.

He had been fascinated by this story from the very beginning. His first offering in the Dionysiac contest (in 455 B.C., only three years after the staging of Aeschylus' *Oresteia*) included the *Peliades*, the story of Medea at Iolcos, her deceitful promise to rejuvenate old Pelias, its king, and the king's death at her hands. Some time

1. Cf. the *hypothesis* attributed to Aristophanes of Byzantium. Sophocles came in second.

2. Cf. Ar. *Th.* 1130; *Ra.* 1382; Eupolis, *Demoi* K 90; Strattis, *Medea* K33–5 (apparently a full-length travesty); Plato K30; Eubulus K26; Alexis K176; Philemon K79. Cantharus K, I, p. 764 *Medea.*

3. W.-H. Friedrich's 'Medeas Rache' (*Vorbild und Neugestaltung, Sechs Kapitel zur Geschichte der Tragödie* (Göttingen 1967), pp. 7–56, now reprinted in Wege der Forschung LXXXIX, *Euripides*, ed. E.-R. Schwinge (Darmstadt 1968), pp. 177–237) is a brilliant comparative study of later versions of the *Medea* which works backwards ('Von Grillparzer zu Euripides') to an illuminating discussion of all features of the Euripidean original.

4. L. Séchan, *Études sur la tragédie grecque dans ses rapports avec la céramique* (Paris 1925, repr. 1967), pp. 396–422; D. L. Page, *Euripides, Medea* (Oxford 1938), pp. lvii–lxviii; A. D. Trendall and T. B. L. Webster, *Illustrations of Greek Drama* (London 1971), pp. 96–7.

later (we do not know the date – it may have been before the *Medea* or after it)[5] Euripides produced the *Aegeus*, the story of Medea at Athens, married to old Aegeus, its king, and her unsuccessful attempt to engineer the death of his son Theseus. In 431 B.C., twenty-four years after his first production, he staged the play we have, the story of Medea and Jason at Corinth.

We know that the version of the myth which he used in this play was not imposed on him. The many variants of the legend which can still be found in ancient mythographers and commentators as well as in the fragments of lost epics show that he had a wide freedom of choice.[6] One account had Medea kill her children unintentionally (she was trying to make them immortal and something went wrong with the formula); in another the children were killed by the Corinthians in a revolt against Medea, whom they had appointed queen of Corinth, and in yet another Medea killed Creon, left her children in the temple of Hera, and fled to Athens – whereupon Creon's kinsmen killed the children and spread the rumor that Medea had done it. At least two of these versions (and probably more besides) were available to Euripides, but he made his own by combination, addition, selection. In it, Medea, far from being queen of Corinth, is a refugee there. Deserted by her husband, Jason, she is to be deported, but she kills Jason's bride, the bride's father, Creon, king of Corinth, and her own children, whose bodies she leaves in the temple of Hera Akraia before she departs for Athens. And it seems to be suggested by the evidence that the murder of the children by Medea herself is Euripidean invention.[7]

5. There seems to be a consensus that the *Aegeus* was produced before the *Medea*: see, for references, A. Lesky, *Die tragische Dichtung der Hellenen* (Göttingen 1972), p. 305, n. 27. There is however no external evidence for the date except vase paintings (on which see T. B. L. Webster, *The Tragedies of Euripides* (London 1967), pp. 79–80, 297–8). But the argument from vase-paintings assumes too much; how do we know that the representations, frequent after 430, of Medea at Athens were not inspired by the *Aegeus* of Sophocles? Or of some other dramatist? Or by no dramatist at all? The fragments themselves are insignificant and dates based on metrical statistics are in this case quite worthless.

6. See the discussion in Page, *Euripides, Medea*, pp. xxiff.

7. I am convinced by Page's demonstration (pp. xxxff.) that Neophron's *Medea* is later than that of Euripides. (For a survey of the controversy see Lesky, *Tragische Dichtung*, p. 301; Lesky agrees with Page.) K. v. Fritz, *Antike und moderne Tragödie* (Berlin 1962), p. 386 (reprint of an article published in

Out of the old stories available to him, Euripides created a new one; a version more shocking, more physically and psychologically violent than anything he found in the tradition. What is even more remarkable is the way he handles it. How was he to present such a shocking series of actions to an Athenian audience in the theater of Dionysos?

There were several possibilities open to him. He might have made Medea a Clytaemnestra figure – a magnificent criminal whose violence represents the primitive past of the race, posed against the civilized, rational values of male democracy, represented, in this case, by Jason. He might have created a version of the story in which Medea was punished for her crimes, and so shown the working of the justice of the *polis*,[8] represented by Creon,

1959), believes that Neophron's careful motivation of Aegeus' appearance was known to Euripides but deliberately avoided by him ('mit einer gewissen absichtlichen eigenwilligen Nichtachtung') for a purpose. This argument is developed by H. Rohdich, *Die Euripideische Tragödie* (Heidelberg 1968), pp. 51ff. Euripides' Medea does not even offer to interpret the oracle Aegeus has received from Delphi; Neophron's Aegeus says he has come to Corinth expressly to ask her to do so. Euripides' purpose in abandoning the plausible motivation for Aegeus' entrance provided by his precedessor was, according to Rohdich, 'to protect his Medea from the suspicion that her *sophia* was something extraordinary and superhuman...His Medea remains completely in the realm of the human' (p. 52). But this seems to load the Euripidean passage with more weight than it can bear. It needs no superhuman wisdom to interpret the oracle given to Aegeus; everyone in the audience would have understood at once the patently sexual purport of it. And there was sufficient reason why Medea should *not* interpret the oracle. The birth of Athens' patron hero Theseus was to follow from Pittheus' misinterpretation of it (Plutarch, *Theseus* 3); if Medea explains to Aegeus that he is not to have sexual intercourse before returning to Athens, he will never get to Troezen and Aethra. (One wonders, in fact, what Neophron did about this.) According to E. Schlesinger, 'Zu Euripides' Medea', *Hermes* 94 (1966), 47, Euripides wants the audience to think that Aegeus did not go on to Troezen but returned at once to Athens (to be on hand for Medea's arrival). 'Euripides gibt ja deutlich zu verstehen, dass er mit einer anderen Sagenform arbeitet.' It is true that Euripides presents us with an Aegeus already married, that Medea promises to cure his sterility by *pharmaka*, and that the chorus' farewell to Aegeus can be interpreted (though it need not be) as a hint that he will go directly to Athens. But the exploits of the young Theseus on his way from his home in Troezen to Athens were so central to Athenian patriotic saga, so familiar to the audience (cf. Bacchylides, Dithyramb 18; Euripides, *Hippolytus* 976ff. for example) that it is hard to imagine Euripides 'working with a different version of the saga' which had Theseus born elsewhere than Troezen.

8. In the *Medea* of Carcinus there seems to have been a trial: Medea used the argument κατὰ τὸ εἰκός (Arist. *Rh.* 1400 b 9).

or of Zeus, announced by a god from the machine – Hera, perhaps, would have been appropriate, or that old standby, Apollo. He might have presented us with a Medea who murdered her children while insane, like Ino (who is actually referred to in the play) or one who murdered in cold blood but was then consumed by ever-lasting remorse, like Procne. But he did none of these things; what he did was, like the endings of so many of his plays, unexpected.

The prologue introduces the situation swiftly – a wife aban-doned with her children for a royal bride in a foreign city. Medea will take no food, listen to no comfort, no advice: she will only weep and rage. But it soon becomes clear that she is no passive sufferer. 'I am afraid', says the Nurse; 'she is planning something dreadful.' As the action develops we begin to feel the brooding menace of the unseen figure behind the stage-door; she is planning suicide or revenge and the Nurse fears for the children's lives. Soon we hear Medea's desperate cries from inside the stage-door, her curses, her wishes for death and general destruction.

This is no ordinary woman wronged: in fact the stage situation may have reminded the audience of a play they had (probably) seen some years before[9] – the *Ajax* of Sophocles. There too we hear the hero's desperate and terrifying cries from inside the stage building,[10] where, like Medea, he lies, refusing food;[11] there too a woman fears for the protagonist's child (and has had it taken away to safety).[12] And there are many other resemblances. Both Ajax and Medea fear more than anything else in this world the mockery of their enemies;[13] for both of them a time-limit of one day is set,[14] both in a set speech explore the possible courses of action open to them and, rejecting alternatives, decide, the one for suicide, the other for revenge.[15] And these similarities are enforced by some striking verbal parallels between the two plays.[16]

9. On the date of the *Ajax* see now Lesky, *Tragische Dichtung*[3], p. 180, n. 2.
10. S. *Aj.* 333, 339, 342–3.
11. E. *Med.* 24 κεῖται δ' ἄσιτος; S. *Aj.* 323 κείμενος, 324 ἄσιτος.
12. S. *Aj.* 531, 533, 535.
13. E. *Med.* 383, 404, 797, 1049, 1355, 1362; S. *Aj.* 367, 382, 454, 961, 969 etc. The four resemblances between the two plays discussed above are noted by A. Maddalena, 'La *Medea* di Euripide', *RFIC* (1963), 137–8.
14. E. *Med.* 355 ἐφ' ἡμέραν μίαν; S. *Aj.* 756 τήνδ' ἔθ' ἡμέραν μόνην.
15. E. *Med.* 364–409; S. *Aj.* 430–80.
16. E. *Med.* 974 ὧν ἐρᾷ τυχεῖν (vengeance): S. *Aj.* 685 τοὐμὸν ὧν ἐρᾷ κέαρ, 967 ὧν γὰρ ἠράσθη τυχεῖν (suicide). E. *Med.* 93 ὥς τι δρασείουσαν: S. *Aj.* 585

These resemblances are not coincidence. Medea in fact is presented to us, from the start, in heroic terms. Her language and action, as well as the familiar frame in which they operate, mark her as a heroic character,[17] one of those great individuals whose intractable firmness of purpose, whose defiance of threats and advice, whose refusal to betray their ideal vision of their own nature, were the central preoccupation of Sophoclean tragedy. The structure and language of the *Medea* is that of the Sophoclean heroic play. This is the only extant Euripidean tragedy constructed according to the model which Sophocles was to perfect in the *Oedipus Tyrannos* and which through the influence of that supreme dramatic achievement and its exploitation by Aristotle as a paradigm became the model for Renaissance and modern classical tragedy – the play dominated by a central figure who holds the stage throughout, who initiates and completes, against obstacles, advice and threats, the action, whether it be discovery or revenge.[18] Other Euripidean tragedies are different. *Hippolytus* is a drama with four principal characters.[19] Hecuba, who is on stage throughout the *Trojan Women*, is no dominating figure but a passive victim, as she is also in the play named after her, until she turns into a revengeful Medea-figure at the end. Pentheus, Heracles and Andromache are victims rather than actors. Electra in her

δρασείοις, 326 ὥς τι δρασείων κακόν. (This is a rare verb: in S. only here and *Ph.* 128, in E. only here and *Ph.* 1208, not in Aeschylus, in paratragic passages Ar. *Pax* 62, *Vesp.* 168.) Compare also E. *Med.* 47–8 and S. *Aj.* 552ff. (children unconscious of the sorrows of their elders), E. *Med.* 173ff. and S. *Aj.* 344ff. (the chorus feels that the protagonist's passion will be calmed by their presence).

17. Maddalena, 'La *Medea*', pp. 133–4, draws attention to Medea's concern for τιμή. 'Disonorata: ἀτιμάζω ο ἀτιμάω è la parola greca che indica l'offesa all'onore: è la parola usata da Omero nell'*Iliade* a dire l'offesa recata all'onore di Achille: è la parola usata da Sofocle nell'*Aiace* a dire l'offesa patita da Aiace. È anche la parola usata da Euripide nella *Medea*. Diversi e simili sono l'Achille omerico, l'Aiace sofocleo e la Medea di Euripide: diversi nei fatti ma simili nell'animo.'

18. W. Steidle, *Studien zum antiken Drama* (München 1968), p. 152, n. 1: 'rechnet man die Chorverse ab, so umfassen ihre [d.h. Medeas] Äusserungen mehr als ein Drittel des Stücks, was ihre ungewöhnlich beherrschende Rolle hinlänglich deutlich macht'. V. di Benedetto, *Euripide, Teatro e Società* (Torino 1971), p. 31: 'La *Medea*...è dominata dal principio alla fine, in una misura che non trova riscontro in nessuna delle tragedie euripidee a noi pervenute, dalla personalità della protagonista.'

19. Cf. B. M. W. Knox, 'The *Hippolytus* of Euripides', *YCS* XIII (1952), 3–4 (in German translation Wege der Forschung LXXXIX (Darmstadt 1968), 238–9).

own play comes nearest to Medea in stage importance, but she cannot act without Orestes, and in the *Orestes* he shares the stage with *her*. *Phoenissae* has no central character at all and *Ion*, *Iphigenia in Tauris* and *Helen* are plays of a different type, in which the 'incurable' tragic act is avoided.[20] The *Medea* is the only Euripidean tragedy (in the modern sense of that word) which is tightly constructed around a 'hero' – a central figure whose inflexible purpose, once formed, nothing can shake – a purpose which is the mainspring of the action.

And Medea is presented to the audience in the unmistakable style and language of the Sophoclean hero.[21] These have been isolated and discussed elsewhere;[22] all that is necessary here is to demonstrate their presence and function in the *Medea*. She has the main characteristic of the hero, the determined resolve, expressed in uncompromising terms – the verbal adjective *ergasteon* (791) 'the deed must be done', *tolmeteon* (1051) 'I must dare'; the decisive futures – especially *kteno* 'I shall kill' – this word again and again. The firmness of her resolve is phrased in the customary Sophoclean terms *dedoktai* (1236), *dedogmenon* (822) – 'my mind is made up'. She is deaf to persuasion – she will not hear (*akouei* 29). She is moved by the typical heroic passion, anger, *orge* (176 etc.), wrath (*cholos* 94 etc.). She exhibits the characteristic heroic temper daring (*tolma* 394 etc.), and rashness (*thrasos* 856 etc.): she is fearful, terrible (*deine* 44 etc.) and wild, like a beast (*agrios* 193 etc.). She is much concerned, like the heroes, for her glory (εὐκλεέστατος βίος 810): she will not put up with injustice (οὐδ' ἀνέξεται 38), with what she regards as intolerable (οὐ...τλητόν 797). Above all, she is full of passionate intensity, that *thumos* which in her case is so marked a feature of her make-up that in her famous monologue she argues with it, pleads with

20. Cf. B. M. W. Knox, 'Euripidean Comedy', in *The Rarer Action, Essays in honor of Frances Fergusson* (New Brunswick 1970), pp. 74ff.

21. In 431 B.C., of course, the only Sophoclean hero-plays we can be certain Euripides knew are the *Ajax* and *Antigone*. The characteristic mood, language and situation of this type of drama were however already present in the Aeschylean *Prometheus Bound* and in any case stem from Homer's *Iliad*. (Cf. B. M. W. Knox, *The Heroic Temper* (Berkeley and Los Angeles 1964), pp. 45–52.) The case for Sophoclean influence on the *Medea* is strengthened by the fact that no other extant Euripidean play deploys the full armory of Sophoclean heroic situation and formula.

22. *Heroic Temper*, pp. 10–44.

it for mercy, as if it were something outside herself. Like the heroes she feels that she has been treated with disrespect (*etimasmene* 20, *atimasas* 1354 etc.), wronged (*edikemene* 26 etc.) and insulted (*hubriz'* 603 etc.). Her greatest torment is the thought that her enemies will laugh at her (*gelos* 383 etc.): like the Sophoclean heroes she curses her enemies (607 etc.) while she plans her revenge. She is alone (*mone* 513) and abandoned (*eremos* 255 etc.), and in her isolation and despair she wishes for death.

Like the Sophoclean tragic hero she resists alike appeals for moderation and harsh summonses to reason. She is admonished (*nouthetoumene* 29) by her friends, but pays no more attention than a rock or the sea-waves. She is begged to 'consider' (*skepsai* 851) but to no avail: she cannot be persuaded (*peithesthai* 184) or ruled (*archesthai* 120). The chorus beg her as suppliants (*hiketeuomen* 854) to change her mind, but to no effect. To others her resolution seems to be stupidity, folly (*moria* 457 etc.) and self-willed stubbornness (*authadia* 621):[23] she is like a wild animal, a bull (92 etc.), a lioness (187 etc.).

As in Sophoclean heroic tragedy, there is also a secondary figure whose pliability under pressure throws the hero's unbending will into high relief. It is not, in this play, a weak sister, like Ismene or Chrysothemis, but a man, like Creon in the *Antigone*; in fact he has the same name, Creon; he is king of Corinth. He comes on stage his mind made up: he has proclaimed sentence of immediate exile for Medea. She must leave at once: he is afraid of her. Her eloquent appeal falls on deaf ears: his resolve, he says, is fixed (*arare* 322). She will never persuade him (οὐ γὰρ ἂν πείσαις ποτέ 325). But she does. He yields, though he knows that he is making a mistake, and gives her one more day.

However, the structure of the *Medea* does differ from that of the Sophoclean hero-play in one important respect: the hero (like Clytaemnestra in the *Agamemnon*) must conceal her purpose from everyone else in the play, except, of course, the chorus, whom (unlike Clytaemnestra) she must win over to her side. Consequently, a characteristically Sophoclean scene is missing: the two-actor dialogue in which the heroic resolve is assailed by persuasion or threat or both – Ismene to Antigone, Creon to Antigone,

23. On this word cf. Friedrich, *Vorbild und Neugestaltung*, pp. 51–2 (Wege der Forschung LXXXIX, *Euripides*, pp. 233–4).

Chrysothemis to Electra, Tecmessa to Ajax. But there *is* a speech in the *Medea* which rolls out all the clichés of the appeal to reason, the summons to surrender which, in Sophocles, all the heroes have to face. It is typical of Euripides' originality, of the way he makes things new, that this speech is delivered by Medea herself.

It is her false declaration of submission to Jason, her fulsome confession that she was only a foolish emotional woman, the speech that lures him to his doom. 'I talked things over with myself', she tells him, 'and reproached myself bitterly.' As she reports her self-rebuke she pulls out all the stops of the Sophoclean summons to reason. 'Why do I act like a mad woman? (*mainomai* 873) and show hostility to good advice?' (τοῖσι βουλεύουσιν εὖ 874). 'Shall I not rid myself of passion?' (*thumou* 879). 'I realize that my judgment was bad (*aboulian* 882)...I raged in pointless anger (μάτην θυμουμένη 883)...I was mindless (*aphron* 885)...I confess I was full of bad thoughts then...but have come to better counsel now (κακῶς φρονεῖν τότ'...ἄμεινον...βεβούλευμαι 892–3). My anger has subsided' (μεθέστηκεν χόλος 898). And later, when Jason accepts her apologies, she says, 'I shall not disobey you' (*apisteso* 927). 'What you did was best for me' (*lōista* 935).[24]

Jason is understanding and sympathetic. 'I congratulate you on your present frame of mind – and I don't blame you for things past. Anger is something you have to expect from a woman...But your mind has changed for the better' (ἐς τὸ λῷον 911). As he turns from Medea to his sons, Euripides puts in his mouth a subtle variation on a Sophoclean theme – the threat to the hero that he will realize the need for surrender, in time (γνῶναι...χρόνῳ).[25] 'You have realized what the best decision is', he says to her,

24. Rohdich, *Euripideische Tragödie*, p. 59, n. 78, draws attention to almost all the words cited above and characterizes Medea's speech as one 'die den Nützlichkeitsaspekt der intellektuell fundierten σωφροσύνη auch terminologisch gänzlich übernommen hat'. His Jason represents 'die vom Intellekt kontrollierte, auf den Nutzen gerichtete σωφροσύνη' – the fifth-century sophistic claim to intellectual mastery of the world ('in ihm steht die sophistische Idee intellektuell geführter Weltbewältigung auf der tragischen Bühne', p. 58) which is to be revealed as a mere illusion by Medea's action ('ist der Triumph des Untragischen nur verblendender Schein', p. 59).

Rohdich's theory of Euripidean tragedy is an attractive one, brilliantly presented: but in this case the fact that the 'terminology' of *Nützlichkeit* is employed also against Prometheus and the Sophoclean heroes suggests that it has older sources than the fully developed sophistic claims of the late fifth century. 25. *Heroic Temper*, pp. 25–6.

'though it took time' (ἔγνως...τῷ χρόνῳ 912). He has swallowed bait, hook, line and sinker: the way is now prepared for the murders that will wreck his life.[26]

This speech is part of Medea's grand design; these formulas of dissuasion masquerading as terms of submission are the instruments of her revenge. As if this were not a sufficiently daring adaptation of the patterns of the heroic play, Euripides presents us with another. There *is* one person who can and does pose a real obstacle to Medea's plans, who can effectively confront her with argument – Medea herself.[27] In the monologue she delivers after she hears that her fatal gifts have been delivered into the princess's hands by her children, she pleads with herself, changes her mind, and changes again and then again to return finally and firmly to her intention to kill them. When the children look at her and smile, she loses her courage. 'Farewell, my plans!' (1048). But then she recovers. 'Shall I earn the world's laughter by leaving my enemies unpunished? No, I must dare to do this!' (1049–51). Then a sudden surge of love and pity overcomes her again and she addresses herself to her own *thumos*, her passionate heroic anger, as if it were something outside herself. 'Do not do it. Let them go, hard-hearted – spare the children!' (1056–7). But her *thumos* will not relent: the children must die. In this great scene the grim heroic resolve[28] triumphs not over an outside adversary or advisor but over the deepest maternal feelings of the hero herself.

This presentation in heroic terms of a rejected foreign wife, who was to kill her husband's new wife, the bride's father, and finally her own children, must have made the audience which saw it for the first time in 431 B.C. a trifle uneasy. Heroes, it was well known, were violent beings and since they lived and died by the simple

26. On Jason's 'Blindheit' with regard to Medea see K. v. Fritz, *Tragödie*, pp. 349ff.

27. Cf. D. J. Conacher, *Euripide in Drama* (Toronto 1967), p. 195: 'Medea herself is really the only one capable of resisting Medea.'

28. Cf. Schlesinger, 'Euripides' Medea', p. 30, on the conflict in Medea's monologue as

'der Widerstand des Glückstrebens des gewöhnlichen Menschen in ihr gegen das Los das ihr zugefallen ist, Taten von übermenschlichem Ausmasse zu vollbringen, heroische Taten im griechischen Sinn des Wortes. Im Grunde wird hier in der Sprache der zweiten Hälfte des 5. Jhs. nichts anderes gesagt als das, was im Monolog Hektors in X und in Achilleus' grosser Rede in I ausgesprochen ist.'

code 'help your friends and hurt your enemies' it was only to be
expected that their revenges, when they felt themselves unjustly
treated, dishonored, scorned, would be huge and deadly. The epic
poems do not really question Achilles' right to bring destruction
on the Greek army to avenge Agamemnon's insults, nor Odysseus'
slaughter of the entire younger generation of the Ithacan aris-
tocracy. Sophocles' Ajax sees nothing wrong in his attempt to kill
the commanders of the army for denying him the armor of
Achilles; his shame springs simply from his failure to achieve his
bloody objective. But Medea is a woman, a wife and mother, and
also a foreigner. Yet she acts as if she were a combination of the
naked violence of Achilles and the cold craft of Odysseus, and,
what is more, it is in these terms that the words of Euripides' play
present her. 'Let no one', she says, 'think me contemptible and
weak, nor inactive either, but quite the opposite – dangerous to
my enemies, helpful to my friends. Such are the qualities that
bring a life glory' (807ff.). It is the creed by which Homeric and
Sophoclean heroes live – and die.[29]

She is a hero, then, but since she is also a woman, she cannot
prevail by brute strength; she must use deceit.[30] She is, as she
admits herself, a 'clever woman', *sophe*, and this cleverness she
uses to deceive everyone in the play, bending them to her frightful
purpose. Creon is tricked into giving her one day's grace; she
knows that his initial bluster hides a soft heart[31] and fawns on

29. Cf. Lesky, *Tragische Dichtung*[3], p. 306, 'einen Satz alter Adelsmoral';
Schlesinger, 'Euripides' Medea', p. 53, 'Das ist die gewöhnliche Sprache der
Heroen. Ihr θυμός verlangt nach κλέος, nach dem εὐκλεέστατος βίος, und dies
ist nach griechischem Empfinden eine durchaus edele Haltung.'
30. Cf. K. v. Fritz' brilliant analysis (*Tragödie*, pp. 361ff.) of lines 407–9.
Women are not capable of ἐσθλά – 'die grossen, die herrlichen Taten, die
Heldentaten, die von jedermann bewundert werden' – their position in life
makes that impossible. But they understand κακά – 'die krumme Wege'. Jason,
by breaking his oath, has descended to such means, and by them he will be
defeated. But Medea speaks also of her τόλμα and εὐψυχία:
'Auch darin enthüllt sich also eine Umkehrung der traditionellen Wertungen
und Begriffe. So wie hinter den ἐσθλά, die Iason vollbracht zu haben
scheint, seine κακία zum Vorschein kommt, so verbirgt sich hinter den κακά,
die Medea vollbracht hat und noch vollbringen will, ihre τόλμα, ihre
εὐψυχία, in gewisser Weise ihre πίστις, alles Dinge, die eigentlich zu den
ἐσθλά gehören, die in der Tradition als dem männlichen Geschlecht vorbe-
halten gelten.'
31. Cf. K. v. Fritz, *Tragödie*, pp. 395ff. (with a defense of the last two lines
of Creon's speech, athetized by some critics).

him (her own term, *thopeusai* 368) to gain time. Aegeus is tricked into promising her asylum in Athens: tricked is the word, for if he had realized that she intended to destroy the royal house of Corinth and her own children he would never have promised her protection. She knows this, and that is why she binds him by a solemn oath. And Jason she takes in completely by her assumption of the role of repentant wife: she showers him with such abject self-abasement, such fawning reiteration of all the male Greek clichés about women (she even says: 'A woman is female – it's her nature to weep' 289)[32] that one wonders how Jason can believe it. But she knows her man. 'That's the way a sensible woman *should* act', he says, γυναικὸς ἔργα ταῦτα σώφρονος (913).

And so the poisoned gifts are taken to the new bride; Medea, when she hears that they have been delivered and accepted, successfully resists the temptation to spare the children, and then, after savoring at length[33] the Messenger's frightful description of the poison's effects, she kills her sons. Her revenge is complete when Jason comes to save them; she holds their bodies in the chariot sent by her grandfather Helios, and, safe from Jason, taunts him with the wreck of all his hopes, his childlessness. The end of the play sees her leave to deposit the children's bodies in Hera's temple and then go off to Athens.

She triumphs.[34] She will always suffer from the memory of what she did to the children, as she grudgingly admits to Jason (1361–2),[35] but she has her full and exquisite revenge. 'These children are dead', she says to him, 'that is what will torment you' (1370). And she escapes the consequences of her action, goes safe to Athens.

This is very unlike what happens to most Sophoclean heroes. Ajax triumphs in a way, but he is dead, and Oedipus wins a kind of victory, but he is blind, and Antigone's victory comes after she has hanged herself. This complete success of Medea is connected with another feature of the way she is presented which is also in

32. γυνὴ δὲ θῆλυ. 'The neuter θῆλυ is contemptuous here' (Page, *ad loc.*). Cf. S. *Tr.* 1062 γυνὴ δέ, θῆλυς οὖσα κοὐκ ἀνδρὸς φύσιν.

33. 1133–4 ἀλλὰ μὴ σπέρχου, φίλος, | λέξον δέ.

34. Cf. W. Steidle, *Studien*, pp. 166–7; H. Diller, *Entretiens sur l'antiquité classique* VI (Genève 1960), p. 32.

35. Cf. Steidle, *Studien*, p. 167, n. 90: 'Wie wenig die moralische Seite des Muttermords eine Rolle spielt, zeigt der geringe Raum, der ihr gewidmet ist.'

sharp contrast with the Sophoclean hero. She is quite sure, from start to finish, that the gods are on her side.

All the Sophoclean heroes feel themselves, sooner or later, abandoned by gods as well as men: their loneliness is absolute, they can appeal only to the silent presence of mountains, sea and air.[36] But Medea from her first appearance has no doubts that the gods support her cause. She appeals to Themis (ancestral law) and Artemis (woman's help in childbirth!) to witness Jason's unjust action (160); she calls on Zeus, who, she says, knows who is responsible for her sorrows (332), swears to avenge herself in the name of Hecate[37] 'the mistress I revere above all others, my chosen helpmate' (395ff.). She asks Jason if he thinks the same gods by whom he swore fidelity no longer reign in power (493): appeals again to Zeus (516) and calls exultantly on 'Zeus, the justice of Zeus and the light of the Sun' (764) as she sees her plans for revenge ensured by Aegeus' promise of shelter in Athens. After the murder of the children she is still confident, in her confrontation-scene with Jason, that Zeus is on her side (1352) and makes plans to deposit the bodies of her sons in the temple of Hera Akraia (1379). When Jason appeals to the avenging Erinyes and blood-retribution (*Erinus...Dike* 1389f.) she dismisses his claim to divine protection with scorn: 'What god or spirit listens to *your* prayers?' (1391). She never wavers from her faith that what she does has divine approval.[38] She can even say, to the Messenger who brings the news from the palace which seals the fate of the children:

36. *Heroic Temper*, pp. 33–4.

37. This invocation of Hecate is often cited as part of the evidence that Medea is presented throughout as a sorceress, a 'witch'. Cf. Page on line 364: on line 367 he cites *Ion* 650 (which must be a misprint for 1050) but that passage is an invocation of Kore in her aspect of *Einodia*, not Hecate, and asks her aid for Creusa's plan to poison Ion. (For 'witchcraft' and poison see below, pp. 211ff.). But there was an aspect of Hecate which had nothing to do with sorcery or poison but rather with the home and woman's functions in it. An effigy of Hecate stood in front of every house door (A. fr. 742 Mette, Ar. *V.* 804, *Ra.* 366), women asked Hecate's advice as they left the house (Ar. *Lys.* 64), and played games with their daughters in her honor (*ibid.* 700 – 'hausliche Kult der Hekate' says Wilamowitz *ad loc.*); women called on her in childbirth (A. *Supp.* 676ff. Ἄρτεμιν δ' Ἑκάταν γυναικῶν λέχος ἐφορεύειν). Hecate is obviously an ambiguous figure and Medea's devotion to her cannot be interpreted as an attitude typical of a sorceress unless reinforced by the context (which it is not).

38. Cf. also 22, 169, 209, 1372.

'These things the gods and I, with my evil thoughts, have contrived' (ταῦτα γὰρ θεοὶ | κἀγὼ κακῶς φρονοῦσ' ἐμηχανησάμην 1013–14).

'The gods and I' – she sees herself as their instrument and associate.[39] And the play gives us no reason to think that she is wrong: on the contrary, it confirms her claim in spectacular fashion. All through the play appeals are made to two divine beings, Earth and Sun. It is by these divinities that Aegeus is made to swear the oath that he will protect Medea from her enemies once she reaches Athens; it is to Earth and Sun that the chorus appeals at the last moment, begging them to prevent the murder of the children, and Jason, in the last scene, asks Medea how, with her children's blood on her hands, she can look at Earth and Sun. 'What Earth will do we shall not be told',[40] but Helios, the Sun, is clearly on Medea's side. Not only are the poisoned gifts sent to the princess an inheritance from Helios (and the poison acts like a concentration of the sun's fire) but, more important, it is Helios who sends Medea the chariot on which she escapes to Athens. 'In the gods' name', says Jason, 'let me touch the soft skin of my sons' (1402–3). But *his* appeal to the gods has no effect; 'Your words are wasted' (1404) Medea tells him, and draws away in her chariot as Jason appeals again to Zeus. The chorus ends the play with lines which appear in our manuscripts at the end of several other Euripidean plays; some critics have thought them inappropriate here,[41] but they are obviously and squarely in their right place.

> Zeus on Olympus has many things in his store-room:
> the gods bring to pass many surprising things.
> What was expected is not fulfilled.
> For the unexpected the gods find a way.
> So this story turned out.

Medea's appearance as a heroic figure, as the murderer of her children who escapes the consequences of her actions, apparently with the blessing of the gods, must have seemed to the audience

39. It is typical of Jason's blind misunderstanding of his situation (and Medea's) that he can call her, in the teeth of the evidence, ἐχθίστη γύναι | θεοῖς (1323–4).

40. H. D. F. Kitto, *Greek Tragedy*[3] (London 1961), p. 199.

41. 'Here they seem a little inapposite', Page *ad loc.*; 'Die Schlussverse des Chores...haben hier bestimmt nichts zu suchen', Lesky, *Tragische Dichtung*, p. 309.

surprising beyond description. Euripides himself, like the gods, has many things in his store-room; he has defied expectation and found a way for the unimagined.

II

But he has another surprising thing in his store-room: Medea's final appearance. She has been on stage since near the beginning of the play; she leaves only towards the end, when she goes through the palace door to murder her sons. When she enters again, to face Jason, she is on the chariot sent by Helios, her grandfather, high up in the air. This last detail is not clearly stated in the text, but no other stage arrangement would explain why Jason cannot reach her, and must beg her to let him touch the bodies of his sons. She must be either on the roof of the stage building (but that would present mechanical difficulties) or in the *mechane* – her chariot swung out over the stage area on a crane.[42] In either case, she is high up and out of reach. But this is the place reserved in Attic tragedy for gods; this is not, as the chorus of the *Electra* says, the pathway of mortals (οὐ γὰρ θνητῶν γ' ἥδε κέλευθος 1235–6). And as the scene progresses, this hint that she has become something more than mortal is confirmed. Her situation, action and language are precisely those of the divine beings who in so many Euripidean plays appear at the end in power[43] to wind up the action, give judgment, prophesy the future, and announce the foundation of a religious ritual.[44]

42. Cf. Page, *Euripides, Medea, ad* 1414; Séchan, *Études*, p. 416, n. 7; Steidle, *Studien*, p. 166.

43. Cf. M. P. Cunningham, 'Medea ΑΠΟ ΜΗΧΑΝΗΣ', *CP* XLIX (1954), 152: 'Medea appears aloft in the place and after the manner of a *theos*. She appears as a *theos* appears; she acts as a *theos* acts and she says the sort of thing a *theos* says.'

44. The argument which follows in the text assumes that the appearance of a *theos* on the *mechane* was a spectacle familiar to the audience of 431 B.C., though it is of course true that all the extant examples of this phenomenon are dated (some certainly, the others probably) later than the *Medea*. (The first version of the *Hippolytus*, however, probably had a *deus ex machina* – cf. Webster, *Tragedies of Euripides*, pp. 65, 70 – and may have preceded the *Medea*.) It seems unlikely, in view of the exact correspondence of all the features of Medea's final appearance with the functions of the *deus* in the later plays (see below, pp. 207ff.) that this can have been the first use of this device. The *mechane* itself was used in the Aeschylean *Psychostasia* and possibly in his *Carians or Europa* (cf. T. B. L.

From her unapproachable position on high she interrupts and puts a stop to the violent action of the human beings on the lower level (Jason is trying to break down the palace door) and in this she is like Apollo in the *Orestes*, Athena in the *Ion* and *Iphigenia in Tauris*, the Dioscuri in *Helen*, and Hermes in the *Antiope*.[45] She justifies her savage revenge on the grounds that she has been treated with disrespect and mockery (1354–5), like Dionysos in the *Bacchae*; in this she is like Aphrodite in the *Hippolytus* prologue, Athena in the prologue to the *Troades*. She takes measures and gives orders for the burial of the dead (her own sons 1378ff. and the princess 1394)[46] like Thetis in the *Andromache*, Athena in the *Suppliants* and *Erechtheus*, Hermes in the *Antiope* and the Dioscuri in the *Electra*. She prophesies the future (the ignominious death of Jason) like Thetis in the *Andromache*, Athena in the *Suppliants* and *Ion*, the Dioscuri in *Electra* and *Helen*, Apollo in *Orestes*, and Dionysos in the *Bacchae*.[47] She announces the foundation of a cult (for her own children in Corinth 1382ff.) like Artemis in the *Hippolytus*, and Athena in the *Iphigenia in Tauris* and *Erechtheus*.[48] She announces her departure and destination (1384ff.) like the Dioscuri in *Electra* and Apollo in *Orestes*.[49]

And Medea speaks in phrases which recur in the pronouncements of the gods from the machine. 'Why are you trying to break down the doors with crowbars?' she asks Jason. 'Stop!'

Webster, *Greek Theatre Production* (London 1956), p. 12) and the appearance of a god at the end of the play to bring a conclusion occurs in the Aeschylean *Prometheus Bound* and (probably) in the lost *Danaides*.

45. Cf. D. L. Page, *Greek Literary Papyri* (Cambridge, Mass. and London 1942), p. 68. One may compare also the end of the *Erechtheus* of Euripides (C. Austin, *Nova Fragmenta Euripidea* (Berlin 1968), p. 36) where Athena intervenes to prevent Poseidon from destroying Athens by earthquake.

46. 1394 θάπτ' ἄλοχον. This is, in its context, a savage, exultant rejoinder to Jason's reproaches, but it is also a regular feature and formula of the address of the *theos*. Cf. E. *Andr.* 1239–40 γόνον | θάψον; E. *Erechtheus* (Austin fr. 65, v. 67) θάψον νιν; E. *Antiope* (Page, *GLP*, p. 68) ὅταν δὲ θάπτῃς ἄλοχον; E. *El.* 1278–80 μητέρα...Μενέλαος...Ἑλένη τε θάψει; E. *I.T.* 1465 οὗ καὶ τεθάψῃ κατθανοῦσα.

47. An unidentified divine figure seems to have prophesied at the end of the *Phaethon*: cf. J. Diggle, *Euripides' Phaethon* (Cambridge 1970), pp. 44ff., 53.

48. According to a papyrus *hypothesis* of *Rhadamanthys* (Austin, *Nova Fragmenta Euripidea*, p. 92, no. 14) Artemis ἐπιφανεῖσα orders the foundation of cult (τιμάς) for the Dioscuri.

49. Cf. also E. *Ion* 1616 ἕψομαι δ' ἐγώ (Athena); E. *I.T.* 1488 συμπορεύσομαι δ' ἐγώ (Athena); E. *Hel.* 1665 πέμψομεν (the Dioscuri).

(*pausai* 1319). 'Why are you directing a pursuit?' Athena asks Thoas at the end of the *Iphigenia in Tauris*. 'Stop!' (*pausai* 1437). So Apollo to Menelaus in the *Orestes* (*pausai* 1625). This is not the only command Medea issues from the *mechane*: like the gods she is prone to imperatives. She dismisses Jason. 'Go!' she says to him 'and bury your wife' (*steiche* 1394). So Athena in the *Ion* dismisses Ion and Creusa: 'Go!' (*steicheth'* 1616) and the Dioscuri in *Electra* send Orestes on his way to Athens with the same word: 'Go!' (*steich'* 1343).[50]

Medea shows the same merciless, even vindictive attitude to Jason that characterizes the Euripidean gods. 'The children are dead. This is what will give you pain', she says to him, using the same word *dēxetai* (1370) Artemis uses in the *Hippolytus* when she rebukes Theseus: 'Do my words pain you?' (*daknei* 1313). Like Artemis she holds out the prospect of more suffering to come. 'Listen to what comes next – you will cry out in even greater agony' says Artemis (1314) and Medea tells Jason: 'You are not sorrowing yet. Wait until you are old' (1396).[51] A statement of Artemis about the ways of gods with men sums up what Medea might have claimed: 'Those who are evil we destroy, children and home and all' (1340–1). Except that Medea's more exquisite revenge is to leave Jason alive and alone amid the ruin of his hopes for his sons and his marriage.

Medea is presented to us not only as a hero, but also, at the end of the play, by her language, action and situation, as a *theos* or at least something more than human. She does not start that way, but that is how she ends. Ends, that is to say, in *this* play:[52] she is going to Athens, as she tells us, and what form she will assume there we are not told. It is not likely that Euripides' audience was worried about that point: they must have been sufficiently taken

50. Cf. also E. *Ion* 1572 χώρει, Κρέουσα; E. *El.* 1289 χώρει; E. *I.T.* 1448 χώρει; E. *Or.* 1678 χωρεῖτε; E. *Antiope* (Page, *GLP*, p. 68, v. 81) χωρεῖτε; E. *Andr.* 1263 ἀλλ' ἕρπε; E. *Hel.* 1663 πλεῖ.

51. Compare Medea's 'Too late!' νῦν σφε προσαυδᾶς, νῦν ἀσπάζῃ, τότ' ἀπωσάμενος (1401–2) with Dionysus' ὄψ' ἐμάθεθ' ἡμᾶς, ὅτε δὲ χρῆν, οὐκ ᾔδετε (E. *Ba.* 1345).

52. Cf. Cunningham, 'Medea', p. 159: 'Although this final appearance of Medea involves an illusion that she is a *theos*, we are also reminded that it is not a true apotheosis...She is going off to Athens to live with Aegeus there.'

aback by the appearance of Medea, the murderer of her sons, in the 'habiliments of the goddess', assuming the attitude and using the language of the stage *theos*.

It is very hard to imagine what it meant to them (and what it should mean to us), for there is no parallel to it in Attic drama. Peleus in the *Andromache* is told that he will become a *theos* (1256) and given a rendezvous for his apotheosis (1265ff.), but it does not take place on stage. Helen, at the end of the play which bears her name (1667), is given a similar assurance (not fulfilled on stage) and in the *Orestes* she actually appears on the right hand of Apollo, on her way to rejoin Castor and Polydeuces in the heavens (1631ff.), but she does not say anything. There *are* two cases in which a human being at the end of the play performs one of the functions of the *deus ex machina*. Eurystheus, in the *Heraclidae*, on the point of death gives instructions for his burial (1036) and reveals a Delphic oracle which gives his buried corpse protective powers for Athens in future wars (1032ff.). (However he expressly forbids a cult of his grave 1040–1.) In the *Hecuba*, the blinded Polymestor prophesies the transformation of Hecuba, the deaths of Agamemnon and Cassandra (1259ff.). These are faint and partial approximations but there is nothing remotely comparable to Medea's full exercise of all the functions of the *theos* and her triumphant god-like departure through the air.

The effect of this investment of Medea with all the properties and functions of stage divinity must have been to bring home to the audience the conviction that Medea is not merely an individual woman wronged and revengeful; she is, at the end, a figure which personifies something permanent and powerful in the human situation, as Aphrodite clearly does, and Dionysos also. These two were Olympian deities, worshipped in state cult and portrayed in temple-sculpture, but the Greek imagination created many other *theoi*, was apt, in fact, to see a *theos* in every corner. 'All things are full of gods' said Thales, and from Hesiod on through the fifth and fourth centuries, Greek literature presents us with *theoi* who represent almost every phase of human activity and circumstance – Poverty, Plague, Reputation, Force, Helplessness, Ambition, Time and Sorrow, to name just a few. A sentence of Menander gives a clue to what lies behind this proliferating theogony: adding a new *theos* to the unofficial pantheon – Shamelessness

(*Anaideia*) – he says: 'Whatever has power is now worshipped as a god.'[53]

Medea, in her last appearance, certainly has power but it is not easy to define exactly what she represents. There is a *theos* in Aeschylus which bears some resemblance to her: the house-destroying *theos* of the *Seven against Thebes* (τὰν ὠλεσίοικον θεὸν οὐ θεοῖς ὁμοίαν 720–1). But this *theos* is almost immediately (723) identified as an *Erinys*, and that will not do for Medea; in fact, as a spiller of kindred blood she should be their allotted victim, as Jason vainly hopes she will be (1389).[54] Revenge – *dike* in the simplest sense – certainly has something to do with it, but she is more than Lesky's 'Dämon der Rache';[55] there would have been no need to give her the style and appurtenances of a *theos* for that – as seems clear from the figure of Hecuba in the last scenes of the play which bears her name. Perhaps the appearance of this ferocious incarnation of vengeance in the place of an Olympian god is meant to reinforce in the audience's mind that disconcerting sense of the disintegration of all normal values which the play as a whole produces, to emphasize visually that moral chaos which the chorus sang of earlier:

The spell cast by sworn oaths has faded; respect for others no longer remains anywhere in Greece, it has taken wing up to the sky (439ff.).

But Medea as *theos* must also represent some kind of irresistible power, something deeply rooted in the human situation, as dangerous as it is universal. It has something to do with revenge for betrayal but its peculiar ferocity must stem from the fact that before she was a hero and through her action became a (stage) *theos*, she was a woman.

It is clear from Medea's very first speech that this strange drama,

53. A. Koerte, *Menandri quae supersunt. II* (Leipzig 1959), fr. 223 τὸ κρατοῦν γὰρ νῦν νομίζεται θεός.

54. ἀλλά σ' Ἐρινὺς ὀλέσειε τέκνων. It is true that the chorus, at the height of its frenzied appeal to Helios to prevent the murder of the children, uses language which is generally thought to describe Medea as an Erinys: ἀλλά νιν...κάτειργε κατάπαυσον, ἔξελ' οἴκων τάλαιναν φονίαν τ' Ἐρινύν (1258ff.). The words ἔξελ' οἴκων, however, seem rather inapposite if the object is Medea herself, and would make more sense as a wish to clear the house of the spirit of vengeance. So the scholiast understood it: αὐτήν φησι τὴν δαίμονα, οὐ τὴν Μήδειαν. ὑπείληπται γὰρ τῶν τοιούτων κακῶν αἰτία εἶναι ἡ Ἐρινύς. Cf. A. *Ag.* 1571f.

55. *Tragische Dichtung*³, p. 309.

which uses Sophoclean heroic formulae to produce a most un-Sophoclean result, is grounded in the social reality and problems of its own time. There can be no doubt, to anyone who reads it without prejudice, that the *Medea* is very much concerned with the problem of woman's place in human society. I do not of course mean to revive the idea, fashionable in the early years of this century, that Euripides is a 'feminist'.[56] Even though tradition has it that speeches from the *Medea* (in the translation of Gilbert Murray) were read aloud at suffragette meetings (a careful selection, no doubt), it is not likely that Sylvia Pankhurst would have admitted Medea to membership in the League. Euripides is concerned in this play, not with progress or reform,[57] but (just as in the *Hippolytus* and the *Bacchae*) with the eruption in tragic violence of forces in human nature which have been repressed and scorned, which in their long-delayed breakout exact a monstrous revenge. The *Medea* is not about woman's rights; it is about woman's wrongs, those done to her and by her.

III

This aspect of the play is usually ignored or dismissed – on the grounds that Medea is atypical: she cannot be considered as a figure relevant to the problems of Athenian society because she is an oriental barbarian and also a witch.[58] 'Because she was a foreigner', says Page, 'she could kill her children: because she was a witch she could escape in a magic chariot.'[59] The second

56. L. Bloch, 'Alkestisstudien', *Neue Jahrbücher*, Band 7 (1901), 30: 'In seinem Herzen, stand er auf der Seite des damals gerade in mächtiger Bewegung aufwärtsstrebenden Geschlechtes.' Bloch refers with approval to Ivo Bruns' 'feine und richtige Beobachtung' (in *Frauenemancipation in Athen* (Kiel 1900), p. 9) 'dass Euripides die an Zahl noch geringe fortschrittliche Partei der athenischen Frauen in den Chorliedern der "Medeia" zu Worte kommen lässt.'

57. Cf. K. J. Reckford, 'Medea's First Exit', *TAPA* xcix (1968), 239: 'This is not to say that Euripides is acting as the women's champion...or writing social criticism or pleading for some reform.'

58. W. Schmid, *Geschichte der griechischen Literatur*, Band iii (München 1940, repr. 1961), p. 360: 'den lässt der Dichter noch wissen, dass sie als Barbarin eine Tat verüben konnte, der eine Griechin nicht fähig gewesen wäre und dass die Täterin eine Zauberin ist, d.h. er stellt sie ausserhalb des Kreises normaler griechischer Weiblichkeit'.

59. In view of the total disagreement with Page's overall conception of the *Medea* expressed in this article, it seems only fair to acknowledge at this point my deep indebtedness to his masterly commentary on the text.

half of this magisterial pronouncement kills two birds with one stone; in addition to denying the play any relevance to Athenian society it also disposes of the awkward questions raised by Medea's appearance as the *theos* on the machine – she is just a witch on a glorified Hellenic broomstick. Since Page gives no other evidence that Medea is a witch, what he seems to mean is rather: 'since she can escape in a magic chariot, Medea is a witch'. But supernatural winged chariots are hardly an identifying mark of witches: they are properties, in Greek mythology, of gods, of Apollo, of the Attic divinity Triptolemos, above all of Helios, the sun (who is, of course, Medea's grandfather). And yet Medea as a witch or sorceress appears as a regular feature of most discussions of the play.[60] There are of course passages in ancient literature which present us with lurid pictures of Medea as a figure resembling our conception of a witch. In the following lines, for example, she addresses her prayer to Hecate:

For thee, my hair flowing free as is the custom of my race, I have paced the sacred groves barefoot. I have called down rain from dry clouds, driven the waves to the sea-bottom...changed the order of the seasons ...brought wheat to harvest in the winter time.

Another poet gives us a detailed description of the witches' brew she cooks for old Aeson:

60. This is especially true of critics writing in English and French. See, for example, G. M. Grube, *The Drama of Euripides* (New York 1941, repr. 1961), pp. 152–4; A. Elliot, *Euripides' Medea* (Oxford 1969), on lines 395, 1317; D. W. Lucas, *The Greek Tragic Poets*[2] (New York 1959), p. 199: 'a genuine witch'; Conacher, *Euripidean Drama*, pp. 188–9; Cunningham, 'Medea', p. 153; Reckford, 'Medea's First Exit', pp. 333, 374; L. Méridier, *Euripide*, t. 1 (Paris 1926, repr. 1965), p. 119: 'une magicienne redoutable' etc. The evidence is surveyed in C. E. S. Headlam's edition of the play (ΕΥΡΙΠΙΔΟΥ ΜΗΔΕΙΑ (Cambridge 1904)) as an appendix, 'Medea as a sorceress' (pp. 105–7). Headlam's conclusion is that 'Euripides...in his play wisely keeps this occult power somewhat in the background and it greatly conduces to the dramatic effect that his heroine impresses us as a woman, not as a witch.'
In recent German (and more rarely Italian) literature the normal, human aspects of Euripides' Medea have been emphasized (see Rohdich, *Euripideische Tragödie*, pp. 44–6, for citations and discussion). Rohdich himself speaks of 'das Bemühen des Dichters seine Medea der ihr vom Mythos her anhaftenden Monstrosität zu entkleiden und als normale Frau für den Zuschauer verbindlich zu machen' (p. 41). This goes too far in the opposite direction; Medea is not a 'normale Frau' but an extraordinary one, as her presentation in heroic terms makes clear.

And all the while the brew in the bronze cauldron boiled and frothed white: in it were herb-roots gathered from Thessaly's lonely vales...and hoar-frost taken at the full of the moon, a hoot-owl's wings and flesh, a werewolf's entrails also, and the fillet of fenny snake, the liver of the stag.

But the first of these passages is from the *Medea* of the Roman dramatist Seneca[61] and the second from the *Metamorphoses* of Ovid.[62] It is in fact in the Roman poets of the first centuries B.C. and A.D. (Horace, Virgil, and Lucan) that something resembling our conception of a witch first appears, to give literary shape to the medieval witch of Christian times who serves the Devil instead of Hecate but claims the same powers to raise the dead, curse, blight, transform, and prophesy. From the contents of Ovid's cauldron to that of Shakespeare,

> Finger of birth-strangled babe
> ditch-delivered by a drab
> make the gruel thick and slab,[63]

there runs an unbroken line. But it does not go back as far as the fifth century B.C. The term 'witch', with its medieval overtones of black magic, ugliness and malevolence, has no place in a description of Euripides' Medea.

There is, however, one incident in Medea's career, well-known to the fifth-century audience, which, though it does not justify the anachronistic use of the term 'witchcraft', does associate her with the use of magic – her deliberately unsuccessful attempt to rejuvenate old Pelias by cutting him into pieces and boiling him in a pot. Interestingly enough, this is not magical practice, but a deliberate murder which uses other people's belief in magic to mask its real nature. Still, it is at any rate a magical context for Medea and it was a popular story; Sophocles dramatized it in his *Rhizotomoi*[64] and it was the subject of the *Peliades* at the very beginning of Euripides' career as a dramatist. It would therefore have been very easy for him to emphasize this aspect of Medea's action: the material was familiar, needing only an emphasis on

61 Lines 752ff. (excerpted).
62. 7. 262ff. Translated by Rolfe Humphries, *Ovid's Metamorphoses* (Bloomington, Indiana 1957).   63. *Macbeth* IV.i.30ff.
64. The three surviving fragments (A. C. Pearson, *The Fragments of Sophocles* (Cambridge 1917), pp. 534–6) contain in their 14 lines more of the atmosphere of sorcery than can be found in the 1420 lines of Euripides' play.

the dramatist's part to bring it to the surface of the audience's memory and cast a baleful spotlight on Medea the sorceress. But he hardly mentions it, and when he does, it is in the blandest of terms; it is described simply as a murder – 'I killed Pelias, the most painful way to die, at the hands of his own daughters' (486ff.) – without any of the sensational details. In fact, when one thinks how naturally a scathing reference to this episode would have fitted into Jason's desperate invective at the end of the play,[65] it seems as if Euripides was doing his best to avoid the subject altogether.

And in any case, in the play Euripides wrote, Medea has no magical powers at all: until she is rescued by the god Helios, and is herself transformed into some kind of superhuman being, she is merely a helpless betrayed wife and mother with no protection of any kind. She has only two resources, cunning – and poison.

Perhaps it is the use of poison which has led so many critics to use the word 'witch'. For the only fifth-century Greek word for 'witch' the dictionaries can suggest is *pharmakis*, which means of course a woman who deals with love-charms, drugs and poisons. This certainly applies to Euripides' Medea,[66] but it has nothing to do with witchcraft. Love-charms, drugs and poisons are the age-old last recourse of the unloved or vengeful wife, in fifth-century Athens, modern Egypt, nineteenth-century India or for that matter Victorian England,[67] everywhere in fact before the scientific detection of poisons made these things too dangerous (for the poisoner) to use. And Medea is not the only *pharmakis* in Athenian literature. Deianira in Sophocles' *Trachiniae* tries to win back her husband's love with a love-charm which, like Medea's gift to the princess, is a poisoned robe (and has the same effect on its victim).[68] The stepmother, in Antiphon's speech, gives her

65. Jason mentions her betrayal of her father and murder of her brother (1332–4) but then proceeds directly to the murder of his own sons.

66. Cf. Rohdich, *Euripideische Tragödie*, p. 48: 'Auch hier zeigt sich Euripides bemüht...die das Normale übersteigenden Fähigkeiten Medeas auf die Kenntnis der φάρμακα zu beschränken.'

67. Cf. Friedrich (*Vorbild und Neugestaltung*, p. 37, Wege der Forschung LXXXIX, *Euripides*, p. 216): 'Denn die "Weisheit" mit der sie ihre Widersacher zugrunde richtet, ist nicht göttlicher als die der Locusta, der Brinvillière und der Giftmischerinnen unserer Tage, die mit Pflanzenschutzmitteln und Pralinen arbeiten.'

68. The messenger speeches describing the effects of the poison in both plays have often been compared: see, e.g., Page, *Euripides, Medea*, p. xxvi, n. 4.

husband a love-charm (drinkable this time) which kills him; the prosecution claims that was exactly what she intended.[69] The Athenian princess Creusa (no barbarian witch this one) uses in Euripides' *Ion* a poison just as magical as Medea's[70] to try to kill the boy she thinks is her husband's bastard son. All three of these ladies use poison, intentionally or not, to redress the balance of their unequal struggle with their husbands – but no one dreams of calling them witches.

Of course Greek men did not approve of such feminine initiatives but they did not invest them with the supernatural and diabolical associations of the modern word 'witch'. In any case, the particular function of the medieval witch – cursing, producing barrenness in women, a murrain on the cattle, disease and death for whole families – was in the ancient world not the province of specialists but the normal recourse of ordinary individuals. This is all too clear to anyone who studies the hate-filled inscriptions known as *defixiones*, which show, from the fifth century on, ordinary persons, in Greece and elsewhere, solemnly recording on tablets of lead or pieces of broken pottery their spells for the painful destruction of their neighbors and business rivals. 'I call down on Androtion a fever to recur every fourth day until he dies' runs one of the milder specimens – scratched on a fifth-century Athenian potsherd.[71]

Medea then, in the body of the play, has no supernatural powers or equipment: all she has is a very powerful poison – but this merely puts her in the same class as Deianira and Creusa.

---

69. Antiphon, 1. 14ff.

70. E. *Ion* 1003ff.

71. M. P. Nilsson, *Geschichte der griechischen Religion*³, vol. 1 (München 1967), p. 801 (with illustration). Theocritus' jilted girl Simaetha (Idyll 2) is a literary example of such private initiative. She is not a 'witch'; she is (to quote Gow's characterization) 'poor...perhaps an orphan, presumably bourgeoise; she is not a ἑταίρα (41). Her position appears to be that of several young women in the New Comedy' (A. S. F. Gow, *Theocritus* (Cambridge 1965), vol. II, p. 33). For an act of sorcery performed by a whole community see the inscription from Cyrene (R. Meiggs and D. Lewis, *A Selection of Greek Historical Inscriptions* (Oxford 1969), 5ff.): κηρίνος πλάσσαντες κολοσὸς κατέκαιον ἐπαρεώμενοι πάντες συνενθόντες καὶ ἄνδρες καὶ γυναῖκες καὶ παῖδες καὶ παιδίσκαι. τὸμ μὴ ἐμμένοντα τούτοις τοῖς ὁρκίοις ἀλλὰ παρβεῶντα καταλείβεσθαί νιν καὶ καταρρὲν ὥσπερ τὸς κολοσός. A. D. Nock (quoted by Meiggs and Lewis *ad loc.*) says of this extraordinary procedure that the community 'reinforces the magical potency of the curse with a magical act, identical with the practice of what we regard as anti-social black magic.' (The inscription is dated to the fourth century B.C. but the ceremony described may be as old as the seventh century.)

These are of course not the parallels cited by the proponents of Medea the witch. They cite Circe and Hecate. But Hecate is a great goddess and of course Circe is a goddess too, as Homer plainly tells us.[72] The Medea of the body of the play is not comparable in any way with these powerful figures.

But if to call Medea a witch falsifies the situation, she is also, according to many modern critics, a barbarian, an Oriental, and therefore equally irrelevant to the problems of Greek society. This case is most eloquently argued by Page. 'She is just such a woman as his audience would expect a foreign princess to be. She has nearly all the features of the type – unrestrained excess in lamentation, a readiness to fawn on authority, the powers of magic, childlike surprise at falsehoods and broken promises...It was natural then that Medea should be unrestrained in the expression of her sorrow, like a Phrygian or a Mysian...she was like a wild beast in her grief and anger. And then in a moment she changes her mood and cringes before the King...a second time...before Aegeus, a third time before Jason. Respect for authority was the primary cause. The Oriental was accustomed to despots whose word was law...Broken promises Medea finds it...difficult to forgive...The contrast of truthful barbarian and lying Greek had long been a commonplace.'[73]

The case could not be more eloquently stated, but it is flawed. Medea is indeed unrestrained in the expression of sorrow, but the comparison should be – 'like Ajax, Odysseus, Achilles, Heracles'.[74] She is compared to a wild beast, but so, sooner or later, are all the Sophoclean heroes.[75] The way she fawns on Creon, Aegeus and Jason has nothing at all to do with respect for authority; she is deceiving them all, and two of them she is luring to their ruin.[76] As for her 'childish surprise at falsehoods and

---

72. *Od.* 10. 136, 220, 297 etc.

73. Page, *Euripides, Medea*, p. xix; cf. Méridier, *Euripide*, p. 118: 'Il ne faut pas oublier d'ailleurs que Médée n'est pas une grecque mais une Barbare...De la Barbare elle a la ruse et la puissance de dissimulation; l'élan sauvage de sa passion, la cruauté raffinée de ses plans, l'énergie farouche dont elle en poursuit l'exécution, s'expliquent par son origine.'

74. V. di Benedetto (*Euripide*, p. 33) takes issue with Page on this point: 'almeno per questo rispetto il personaggio di Medea non è meno "greco" di Alcesti e Fedra'. 75. Cf. *Heroic Temper*, pp. 42–3.

76. Cf. di Benedetto, *Euripide*, pp. 37–8, on Medea's 'freddo calcolo e ragionata astuzia'.

broken promises', this is a trait she shares (apart from the pre-judicial adjective) with Creusa, Philoctetes, and of course the Greek chorus of the *Medea*.

Page finds that 'above all the inhuman quality of the child-murderess was a typically foreign quality. The chorus could think of only one other example in the legends of Greece – Ino' (though, as he points out in a note, 'they might have added at least Agave and Procne'). But Page does not produce any eastern stories which will serve as cogent parallels. In fact, as an example of the 'appal-ling cruelty' of 'foreign countries' he cites Astyages who 'set a Thyestean feast before Harpagos'. But the adjective 'Thyestean' gives the game away – that's a *Greek* story! – and the list of Persian atrocities which follows contains nothing which cannot be paralleled, or for that matter bettered, from Greek myth and history.[77]

'No *Greek* woman would have had the heart to do what she has done'; Page quotes Jason to sum up his case. But dramatic characters do not necessarily speak for their creator. And this speech is neatly cancelled out by one of Thoas, the barbarian king in the same dramatist's *Iphigenia in Tauris*. Informed that the captured Orestes has murdered his mother, he exclaims (using exactly the same verb as Jason – *etlē*) 'Apollo! Not even among the barbarians would anyone have the heart to do what he has done' (1174).

In any case, there is no suggestion in the play that anyone regards Medea as a barbarian, except of course, in the end, Jason. The chorus of Corinthian women fully approve of her first announcement that she plans revenge on her husband (267–8). When she makes clear that this means death not only for Jason but also for the king of Corinth and his daughter, they raise no objections: in fact in the choral ode which follows they sing exultantly of honor coming for the female sex. When she tells them that her plans have changed – she will now kill the princess, 'whoever touches her' and also Jason's sons, they cry out in

77. There is a passage in the *Andromache* which charges the barbarian races with incest (father and daughter, mother and son, brother and sister) as well as murder of kin: but the speaker is Hermione who, with her father Menelaos, kidnaps Andromache's child, forces her to leave sanctuary by threatening to kill it, breaks the promise made to spare its life, and would have murdered mother and child if not prevented.

protest: but it is only the murder of the children which appals them. Their protest brushed aside, they say only that she will be the unhappiest among women. Where they could have intervened decisively – the scene in which Medea entraps Jason by feigned humility – they remain silent. Finally, after listening to the Messenger's ghastly account of the deaths of the king and his daughter, their only comment is: 'It seems as if heaven today were bringing much evil on Jason – as he deserves!' (1231–2).

The chorus obviously feel that Medea's situation might well be their own: as far as they are concerned, she speaks like and for them, and when after the offstage murder of the children they sing their antistrophe, far from suggesting that she is a witch and oriental barbarian (and surely this was the place to make Page's point) they find a parallel in their own Greek tradition. 'Only one woman, only one, have I heard of who in time past raised her hand against her children. It was Ino, driven mad by the gods' (1282ff.). The foreignness of Medea was fixed in the legend and it suited Euripides' purpose, since it made possible the liquid fire and the chariot of the sun, but Euripides' Medea, in her thought, speech and action is as Greek as Jason, or rather, as Ajax and Achilles.

IV

But she is a woman and her first speech, that of a woman speaking to women, exploits and appeals to their feelings of sympathy. It is of course one of the most famous speeches in Greek tragedy. No more howls of despair, or threats of suicide – she comes out of the house to win the support of the chorus for her still nebulous plan for revenge. She is apologetic, conciliatory, a foreigner who must carefully observe the proprieties. But her life, she says, has been destroyed; her husband, who was everything to her, has turned out to be the vilest of men.

'Of all the creatures that have breath and intelligence, we women are the most afflicted.' We buy our husbands with our dowry – her argument proceeds – not knowing if they will be good or bad, go into a new home unprepared for the new life. If we work hard and make a success of it, we're lucky, if not, death would be better. The man, when he tires of our company, can go out for distraction; we are forced to keep our eyes steadily on one single human being. They say we live at home in safety, while *they* fight the wars – what fools! I'd rather stand in the battle line three times than go through child-bearing once.

It is magnificent rhetoric, and it wins their heart. But it is not, as has so often been claimed, *just* rhetoric. It has its vital function in the construction of the drama but it must also reflect some contemporary reality. For dramatists, especially the greatest dramatists, are not philosophers, not original thinkers; they reflect and use, dramatize and intensify the thought and feeling of their time. And in fact there are many signs that in the intellectual ferment of late fifth-century Athens, the problem of women's role in society and the family was, like everything else, a subject for discussion and reappraisal. In Euripides' *Melanippe Desmotis*, for example, someone (presumably the heroine) makes a long polemical speech demonstrating woman's moral and religious superiority to man (Page, *GLP* 112). The *Lysistrata* of Aristophanes is of course a hilarious comedy but it has a deeply serious undercurrent of feeling, and the heroine of the play, the woman who organizes her sex on both sides to stop the war, is wholly sympathetic – it is quite clear that her creator admired her. J. H. Finley long ago drew attention to the resemblances (some of them verbal) between Medea's speech and the arguments against marriage set forth (from the man's point of view) by Antiphon the sophist.[78] And one cannot help suspecting that much later, Plato, when he says in the *Republic* that to divide mankind into male and female for the purposes of public life or education or anything, except the begetting and bearing of children, is just as absurd as to divide it into the long-haired and the bald[79] – Plato may well be adapting to his own purpose, as he so often does, ideas that were first put into circulation by the sophistic radicals of the fifth century.

Even if it is conceded that the role of women in family and society was a problem under discussion in fifth-century Athens, it may be objected that it was a theme a tragic poet might well avoid, and that even if he did choose to handle it, he would never take as his protagonist a woman who butchered her own sons.

78. J. H. Finley *H.S.C.P.* L (1939), 65ff. = *Three Essays on Thucydides* (Cambridge, Mass. 1967), pp. 92–4. Cf. also Reckford, 'Medea's First Exit', pp. 336ff.

79 *Rep.* V 454C–E.

Yet this same strange combination, of infanticide and a pro-grammatic speech about the lot of women, appears in another tragedy, which was produced before 414, how many years before, we do not know;[80] its author is none other than Sophocles. His *Tereus* told the story of the Athenian princess Procne, married to Tereus, king of Thrace. She persuaded him to bring her sister Philomela from Athens to join her. Tereus, on the way home, raped Philomela, and then cut out her tongue so that she could not denounce him. But Philomela wove the story of the outrage on a piece of embroidery and so Procne learned the truth. She killed her son by Tereus (his name was Itys), cut up the flesh, cooked it, and served it up to Tereus who ate it. The gods, in pity and disgust, changed all three of them into birds, Tereus to a hoopoe, Philo-mela to a swallow and Procne into a nightingale, whose song is a perpetual mourning for Itys.

This metamorphosis almost certainly did not take place on stage (though Tereus in the *Birds* of Aristophanes complains that Sophocles gave him a beak) and in fact we have very little idea of how Sophocles treated this horrendous tale. But among the few fragments that survive there is one speech of Procne, the wronged wife, which runs as follows:[81]

Now, separated (from my family), I am nothing. Many a time I have observed that in this case our sex, the female sex, is nothing. When we are children, in our father's home, our life is the most pleasant in the world; young girls grow up in thoughtless delight. But when we reach maturity and intelligence, we are expelled, bought and sold, far away from the gods of our fathers and from our parents, some to barbarians, some to houses where everything is alien, others to houses where they meet with hostility. But all this, when one night has joined us to our husband, we must acquiesce in, and pretend that all is well.

80. The date of production of Aristophanes' *Birds* (414) is the *terminus ante quem*. T. B. L. Webster, *An Introduction to Sophocles*[2] (London 1969), p. 4, dates it before 431 on 'external evidence' which (pp. 176–7) turns out to be its resemblance in theme and (reconstructed) 'diptych form' to the *Trachiniae*, which he also dates before 431. W. Buchwald, *Studien zur Chronologie der attischen Tragödie* (Königsberg 1939), pp. 35ff., also puts it before *Medea*: it was the model for Medea's murder of her sons. Others, basing their proposals on 'contemporary allusions', have dated it nearer to 414. There is no certainty, or even probability, here: 'Keine der angeführten Datierungen kann Sicherheit beanspruchen' (Lesky, *Tragische Dichtung*[3], p. 262).

81. Pearson, *Fragments of Sophocles*, p. 583. I follow Jebb's interpretation of the difficult opening lines.

We do not know the context of this speech but its content is astonishingly close to Medea's opening address to the chorus, and it is made by a woman who, like Medea, but in even more gruesome circumstances, kills her child to punish her husband. The attribution of such sentiments to two such similar characters by two different playwrights suggests that the lot of women was, in late fifth-century Athens, very much a question of the day, and also a subject that fascinated the tragic poets.

Even those who recognize that Medea's speech is not merely the rhetoric of an oriental witch but a reflection of Athenian social conditions, usually tamp down its explosive potential by explaining that since women in fifth-century Athens (unlike women today) were confined to the home, children and servants, excluded from active social, economic and political life, some such protest was only natural in the work of an intellectual dramatist. Though this view of woman's lowly position in fifth-century Athens has been doubted by influential scholars in recent years,[82] it seems to me, on the whole, to be fairly close to the truth. But what is no longer true is the implied comparison which makes our own society look extremely advanced in this matter and permits smug and carefully qualified understanding of Medea's protest as a historical curiosity. For our own complacency about the freedom of women in modern industrial democracy has been exploded by the literature of the militant women's movement of the last decade. In fact, almost everything the play says about women's position in society is still relevant (except perhaps for the dowry, but that is still an important matter in France, Italy and, above all, in Greece), and the startling universality of Euripides' play is clear from the fact that it says some things that do not seem to have occurred to anyone again[83] until Simone de Beauvoir wrote *Le Deuxième Sexe*.

Medea's speech wins over the chorus but now she has to deal with Creon and his sentence of immediate expulsion. He is afraid of her and one thing which contributes to his fear is the fact that, as he says himself, she is a clever woman (σοφὴ πέφυκας 285).[84]

82. A. W. Gomme, 'The Position of Women in Athens', *CR* 20 (1925), 1–25 (reprinted in *Essays in Greek History and Literature* (Oxford 1937)); H. D. F. Kitto, *The Greeks*[2] (Harmondsworth 1957), pp. 219–36.

83. With the startling exception of Geoffrey Chaucer; cf. n. 85.

84. σοφὴ πέφυκας καὶ κακῶν πολλῶν ἴδρις. This phrase is taken by many proponents of Medea the witch as evidence for their case. But, though 'wise

'Clever' is not an adequate translation of *sophe* – but then, there isn't one. It is a word which in the fifth century was used to describe not only the skill of the artisan and the poet, not only the wisdom won by experience and reflection, but also the new intellectual, enlightened outlook of the great sophistic teachers and the generation they had taught. This is why Creon fears her; it is on this point that she must reassure him, and she does. She admits that she is *sophe* – an intellectual, a person of great capacity – but points out that it has not done her any good. She speaks in generalities but it is clear enough what she is talking about. Men distrust superior intelligence in general but they really fear and hate it in a woman. *Sophos*, a clever man, is bad enough, but *sophe* – a clever woman!

This is not the first time, Creon – it's one of many – that my reputation thwarts and harms me. No one who has his wits about him should have his children taught to be unusually clever (*sophous*). They will be called lazy, indolent, and, worse than that, they'll win the jealous hatred of their fellow-citizens. If you offer new and clever ideas to fools, they'll think you good for nothing, not clever. And then again, if the city at large ranks you above the recognized intellectuals, *they*'ll be your bitter enemies. This is what has happened to me, exactly this. I am clever; some hate and envy me; others find me withdrawn, others just the opposite, and still others offensive. I am not so clever.

These lines have sometimes been seen as Euripides' bitter reflections on his own isolation as an advanced and intellectual poet. There is much truth in this view, but the lines are also Medea's, the complaint of a woman of great intellectual capacity who finds herself excluded from the spheres of power and action.

She wins her one day's delay from Creon and tells the chorus her plans; so far, they do not include the murder of the children. The chorus evidently approve, for they plunge straight into the great ode which celebrates the new day coming for the female sex.

> The waters of the sacred rivers run upstream;
> the right order of all things is reversed.

woman' meant 'witch' in seventeenth-century English, the Greek word *sophe* has no such connotation. The *sophia* Creon fears is the craft that rescued Jason from his pursuers at Colchis and brought death to Pelias: these are *kaka* in the sense defined by v. Fritz (cf. n. 30). Medea of course deliberately misunderstands his drift, but the charge she is evading is not 'witchcraft'. And her argument, after all, is soundly based. Her *sophia* has brought her to her present state, a woman abandoned in a hostile country.

Now it is *men* who deal in treachery:
now covenants sealed in heaven's name are worthless.

So much for Jason's betrayal. But they go on.

Legends now shall change direction,
Woman's life have glory.
Honor comes to the female sex.
Woman shall be a theme for slanderous tales no more.

The songs of poets from bygone times shall cease
to harp on our faithlessness.
It was not to our minds that Phoebus, lord of melody,
granted the power to draw heavenly song from the lyre:
for if so, we would have chanted
our own hymns of praise
to answer the race of man.

Time in its long passage has much to tell
of our destiny as of theirs.

This is an extraordinary passage. All the songs, the stories, the whole literary and artistic tradition of Greece, which had created the lurid figures of the great sinners, Clytaemnestra, Helen, and also the desirable figures (from the male point of view) of faithful Penelope and Andromache – all of it, Hesiod's catalogues of scandalous women, Semonides' rogues' gallery of women compared to animals, is dismissed; it was all written by men. The chorus has suddenly realized the truth contained in the Aesopian story of the man and the lion who argued about which species was superior.[85] Shown as proof of man's dominance a gravestone on which was carved a picture of a man downing a lion, the lion replied: 'If lions could carve sculptures, you would see the lion downing the man.'

Xenophanes had remarked that if cows, horses and lions had hands, could paint pictures and carve statues, they would have made gods looking like themselves. It took Euripides to apply the revolutionary implications of that statement to the relation be-

85. Hausrath Hunger 264: cf. Babrius 194 (Crusius) and Chaucer, *Wife of Bath's Prologue* 692ff.

Who peyntede the lioun, tel me who?
By god, if wommen hadde written stories
As clerkes han withinne hire oratories
They wolde han written of men more wikkidnesse
Than all the mark of Adam may redresse.

223

tween men and women. 'Legends now shall change direction; woman's life have glory' sings the chorus, but the future tense is unnecessary. Euripides' play itself is the change of direction.[86]

For though he has spared us no detail of the hideous revenge Medea exacts from her enemies, he has presented that revenge in heroic terms, as if she were not a woman but an Achilles or Ajax. She has no doubts about the rightness of her course – her one moment of hesitation she dismisses as cowardice. Like Achilles in his rage against Hector she surpasses the bounds of normal human conduct: Achilles wishes that his spirit (*thumos*) would drive him to strip Hector's flesh from his body and eat it raw and does treat his enemy's body shamefully. Medea kills her sons to make Jason a lonely childless man. The one is as heroic, and tragic, as the other.

But Achilles relents. Medea does not. Her final words to Jason are full of contempt, hatred and vindictive triumph: her rage is fiercer than the rage of Achilles, even of Ajax: it has in the end made her something more, and less, than human, something inhuman, a *theos*.

But this was only to be expected. For Ajax and Achilles have run their full course as men in the world of men, earned their share of glory, used to the full the power and skill that was theirs, before their time came to die. But Medea is a woman: no matter how great her gifts, her destiny is to marry, bear and raise children, go where her husband goes, subordinate her life to his. Husband, children, this is all she has, and when Jason betrays her the full force of that intellect and energy which has nowhere else to go is turned against him.

One passage in their last confrontation is revealing. 'Did you really think it right to kill them', he asks her, 'just because of what goes on in bed?' (*lechous* 1367).[87] And she answers: 'Do you think that is a small suffering for a woman?' It is a great suffering – for she has nothing else. It was to this marriage that she devoted all the courage, skill and intellect she possessed – to save Jason in Colchis, to murder Pelias, for his sake, in Iolcos; to this marriage

86. Cf. I. Caimo, *Dioniso* 6 (1937–8), 4: 'in realtà l'inno che celebra la donna e suona per contro l'ignominia all'uomo è già qui nel suo nucleo primordiale'.

87. Cf. Rohdich, *Euripideische Tragödie*, pp. 59ff.: 'Die Antithese: λέχος und Affekt'.

she has devoted all her energy, all her power. She could have been a queen, and who knows what besides, in her own country; she gave it up for her marriage. And when that was taken away from her the energy she had wasted on Jason was tempered to a deadly instrument to destroy him. It became a *theos*, a relentless merciless force, the unspeakable violence of the oppressed and betrayed which, because it has been so long pent up, carries everything before it to destruction, even if it destroys also what it loves most.[88]

88. The text of this article was delivered to the editors in June 1974.

On the Heraclidae of Euripides

ALBIN LESKY

(translated by H. VON HOFE)

THIS drama, severely criticized years ago by A. W. Schlegel,[1] is, in spite of its apparently simple structure, one of the most problematic of the extant plays. There is a correspondingly large amount of secondary literature, and since there is such a thorough bibliographical survey of this secondary literature in the works by G. Zuntz and R. Guerrini mentioned below, a reference to them here will suffice. There are, however, two inquiries in particular which, we feel, serve, in their radically opposite positions, as the standard-bearers of the much debated issues. Both modified previously extant theses, but they did so in such an impressive way that anyone who wishes to approach the questions anew must begin with them.

One of these inquiries is the 'Exkurse zu Euripides *Herakliden*',[2] which Wilamowitz wrote in his Greifswald period and which he adhered to in essence throughout his work.[3] Long before him, G. Hermann[4] assumed that the *Heraclidae* had been shortened by the loss of one episode, which he conjectured came at the end of the play. It was an important step when A. Kirchoff[5] decided that this loss occurred inside the play after line 629. But while both scholars suspected an accidental lacuna, Wilamowitz showed that such a precisely circumscribed damage could not conceivably have come about by chance. He argued that the drama had been revised, and that in the revision an episode (following line 629) with the report of Makaria's death and a second strophe-pair were

---

1. A. W. Schlegel, *Vorlesungen über dramatische Kunst und Literatur* (Ausgabe Bonn 1923), p. 121.
2. U. von Wilamowitz-Moellendorff, 'Exkurse zu Euripides Herakliden', *Hermes* 17 (1882), 337 = *Kl. Schriften* I (1935), 82. Further references 'Exkurse'.
3. U. von Wilamowitz-Moellendorff, *Glaube der Hellenen* I (1931), 299.
4. In A. Matthiae, *Euripidis tragoediae* (Leipzig 1813–24), vol. VIII, p. 257.
5. A. Kirchhoff, *Eur. Trag.* (Berlin 1855), vol. II, p. 496.

sacrificed. Wilamowitz did write in the above-mentioned inquiry (p. 353): 'Scholars often assume that Greek dramas have been reworked; in most cases the proof is a pitiful failure'; but he nevertheless impaired his major thesis with the attempt to show in detail traces of a revision in various passages of the play. It is of course obvious that the question of the loss of a report of Makaria's death is not affected by whether or not one agrees with him in the particulars.

This question was debated later in different ways, but on the whole the viewpoint of Wilamowitz seemed to have prevailed: 'fabula misere mutila' stands in Murray's Oxford text.

The article of G. Zuntz, 'Is the *Heraclidae* mutilated?',[6] brought about a complete reversal. He also has predecessors, but his work, with its concise and impressive argument, presents so sharp an attack on the revision hypothesis that it became the established view and it was generally accepted that the *Heraclidae*, as we now read it, aside from minor interpolations, retains its original extent.

The author of these pages, from the first edition of his *Tragische Dichtung der Hellenen*[7] on, advocated the position that this is in no way a conclusively solved problem, and took fully into account the possibility of the shortening of the play by a revision. Recently R. Guerrini has concerned himself with the drama in a series of articles,[8] and in so doing has once again taken up the position of Wilamowitz. The present writer here attempts a reconsideration of this group of problems, partly because the state of research seems favorable to it, and partly because he is now convinced that an observation which he published – still with great hesitation – in the third edition of his *Tragische Dichtung* is in fact of decisive importance to the entire question.

6. G. Zuntz, 'Is the *Heraclidae* mutilated?', *Class. Quart.* 41 (1947), 46. Just recently Harry C. Avery wrote in his article on the *Heraclidae*, *Am. Journ. Phil.* 92 (1971), 539, which has a different goal than ours: 'I take it as essentially proven that the text we now possess of Euripides' *Heraclidae* is substantially the same, except for minor error resulting from transmission, as the text which was used in the first production early in the Peloponnesian War.'

7. A. Lesky, *Tragische Dichtung der Hellenen* (Göttingen 1956), p. 175; compare the third edition (Göttingen 1972), p. 356.

8. R. Guerrini, 'I "frammenti" degli Eraclidi di Euripide', *Studi Classici e Orientali* 19/20 (1970/71), 15; 'La morte di Euristeo e le implicazioni etico-politiche degli Eraclidi di Euripide', *Athenæum* n.s. 50 (1972), 45; 'La morte di Macaria (Eurip. *Heraclid.* 819–22)', *Studi It.* 45 (1973), 46.

In the treatment of our problem one circumstance usually stood in the foreground: five fragments have been handed down to us which are more or less attested to be from the *Heraclidae* without having any place in the play as we now read it. The verses are so conveniently assembled at the end of the drama in the Oxford text that it is unnecessary to print them again here. Wilamowitz did not hesitate to use three of the fragments in the reconstruction of the section he thought had been deleted by the reviser. He posits an excited debate on the sacrifice of the maiden and on the propriety of such a sacrifice; he attributes fr. 854 to this debate, where there is talk of the terror and glory of being sacrificed (σφαγῆναι). He places fr. 852N., which gives the command to honor one's parents, at the end of the report of Makaria's death. In answer to his own question, whether it was a messenger or Demophon who brings this report, he decides it was the latter, since he is the person who could properly appreciate the maiden's act. Wilamowitz takes fr. 853N. as decisive evidence, as he puts it, that Euripides wrote thus. In these words there is reference to the fundamental precepts that men should honor the gods, parents, and the common customs of Greece. In this fragment Iolaos is supposedly talking to Demophon, which justifies the form of address. In Murray's edition the verse from Aristoph. *Equ.* 214 is printed in addition as fr. 851N.: τάραττε καὶ χόρδευ' ὁμοῦ τὰ πράγματα, which, according to a comment of the scholiast, is supposed to be a parody ἐξ Ἡρακλειδῶν Εὐριπίδου. There is no possible connection here. Wilamowitz attributes the supposedly parodied verses to the Kopreus scene, which according to him had another form than the one handed down to us. Every point in this remains questionable. Finally, little importance can be given to the verse which speaks of the honor due to the parents (fr. 949N.). Stobaios attaches it to verses 297f., which he quotes.

Pohlenz[9] and Zuntz, among others, have argued strongly that the fragments here briefly surveyed do not provide conclusive proof. They advance two arguments in particular. First, the theme 'Thou shalt honor thy parents' has, according to them, no place in the *Heraclidae*, and secondly they appeal to the fact that the transmission of quotations in the *florilegia* is not to be depended on. Indeed, fr. 853N. is attributed to the *Antiope* by Trincavelli

9. Pohlenz, *Griechische Tragödie*, 2nd ed. (Göttingen 1954), vol. II, p. 144.

and fr. 854 is quoted by Stobaios as coming from the *Heracles*. It has no bearing there, so that Nauck's conjecture 'Ηρακλεί⟨δαις⟩ is very likely. It is probably less important that only the first two verses of fr. 852 are attributed in the manuscripts of Stobaios (S, M, A) to the *Heraclidae*, while in the excerpt from Orion's *Antholognomicon* there is no attribution at all. 'Orion' gives three additional verses, which, just like the first in Stobaios, begin with ὅστις δέ and possibly do not belong together with the first two at all. If one takes these two verses in themselves, then the masculine would not necessarily exclude an attribution of them to the *Heraclidae*, since it could be explained by a general formulation of the maxim.

R. Guerrini has recently made the attempt, in the first of the articles mentioned in footnote 8, to show that the doubtful verses do come from the scene which Wilamowitz had assumed was removed by a reviser. It must be recognized that Guerrini has brought together with painstaking scholarship everything that may be adduced for the inclusion of the fragments in the *Heraclidae*. Above all, he attempts to secure the place of the motif of the honor due to parents, since reference is in fact often made to Makaria's great father (539, 562, 626). But it is still questionable whether or not there is a passable bridge from such passages to fragment 852. Guerrini stresses the fact that this fragment is ascribed indirectly a second time to the *Heraclidae*, since in Stobaios immediately following it verses 297f. from our play are attested to with the lemma ἐν ταὐτῷ. Nor does he pass over the fundamental uncertainty of gnomological attributions. Zuntz[10] is able to produce an example which may rouse our suspicions: *Heraclidae* 745–7 and 865f. are attributed to the Κρῆσσαι in Stobaios. Like Wilamowitz, Guerrini too sees in fr. 853N., with its three commandments, the formal quintessence of the drama and compares verses 236ff. with the τρισσαὶ ὁδοί with them. The apparent parallels are at first striking, but on closer inspection differences between the argument *ad hoc* and the general maxim become recognizable. For the address τέκνον in fr. 853N. in the context which he (like Wilamowitz) assumes, he can refer to line 381 of our drama, where Iolaos addresses Demophon ὦ παῖ. For fr. 854N. with τὸ μὲν σφαγῆναι δεινόν he cites the fact that

10. Zuntz, 'Is the Heraclidae mutilated?', *Class. Quart.* 41 (1947), 46 n. 9.

Makaria speaks of the δεινὸν σφαγῆς in one passage (562f.) precisely when she is thinking of her father with pride.

A more complete defense of the doubtful fragments is not conceivable, and yet one can only say of them what Guerrini himself states of fr. 854: 'anche qui ci sembra impossibile stabilire con esattezza in quale contesto i versi potessero figurare'. We end indeed in uncertainty: it would be going too far to assert that, in a scene of which we know nothing, there was no conceivable context for the doubtful verses; on the other hand, there is so much uncertainty about them that they are not able to carry the weight of proof that a scene formerly existed but was later deleted. With respect to the problems associated with the *Heraclidae* it was definitely not advantageous that these fragments were given so much emphasis. In this case nothing remains but to practice that which is so seldom practiced by philologists, the *ars nesciendi*, and to leave these doubtful fragments in the background of the discussion of our problem.

One must look elsewhere for a solution to the problem of revision. Here we indeed give a decisive importance to the much discussed lines 819–22 and take pleasure in agreeing with Guerrini in the third of his articles mentioned in footnote 8.

After the third *stasimon* the servant of Hyllos comes and tells of the battle which has just been won. At first Hyllos had attempted to determine the outcome of the battle by means of a duel with Eurystheus, but the latter refused to take part in such a duel. Now the battle of the armies had become inevitable.

> μάντεις δ', ἐπειδὴ μονομάχου δι' ἀσπίδος
> διαλλαγὰς ἔγνωσαν οὐ τελουμένας,
> ἔσφαζον, οὐκ ἔμελλον ἀλλ' ἀφίεσαν
> λαιμῶν βροτείων εὐθὺς οὔριον φόνον (819)

Defenders of the view that the structure of the scenes in the play as transmitted to us was intact believed in all seriousness that Euripides himself reported the death of Makaria here in this form. It is regrettable that Pohlenz[11] is among these. It was possibly under his influence that Zuntz took the authenticity of the verses into account in his essay in *Classical Quarterly* (p. 52), but in his excellent book *The Political Plays of Euripides*[12] he took another

11. Pohlenz, *Griechische Tragödie*, vol. II, p. 146.
12. Here quoted from the first edition (Manchester 1955), p. 153. A second edition was published at the same place in 1963.

position: 'A reference here to Makaria seems indeed incredible.' Here we must now follow all the consequences through to the end. The first question, whether these lines can be dissociated from the death of Makaria, can definitely be answered in the negative. It is not possible to obelize the word βροτείων, as Murray does, because in *Iph. Aul.* 1084 we read of Iphigeneia's act of sacrifice: βρότειον αἱμάσσοντες λαιμόν. Likewise, therefore, it is wrong to replace the word by a conjecture: Paley's βοτείων does not have sufficient support, and Wilamowitz[13] correctly remarked with respect to Vonhoff's βοείων that one thereby burdens the text with a factual error, since for the σφάγια one uses μῆλα. J. B. Barnes and E. B. England, following Pearson, avoided the problem by referring βρότειος to βρότος, 'blood that has run from a wound, gore' (L.S.J.) and by understanding it proleptically; but this is really just an act of despair, which one should not further discuss in light of the passage from *Iph. Aul.* For the rest, D. L. Page objected quite properly to all theses attempts which try to get around the interpretation of the word given by the situation.[14]

Thus it can only be a human sacrifice which is spoken of here, and in that case the sentence of L. Méridier[15] retains its indisputable validity: 'Cette mention énigmatique ne peut se rapporter qu'à Macarie.' But for him these are verses of Euripides in which the author wished to inform his public of the completion of the sacrifice. With the establishment of the fact that this is totally impossible we reach the next stage of our argument. Here one should not stress too much the observation that after the deletion of lines 819–23 there results the much finer connection of οἱ δ' ἅρματ' εἰσέβαινον to Ὕλλος μέν: there is another decisive argument for the assumption that the verses are a clumsy interpolation. Anyone who charges Euripides with such a lack of taste that he would allow a fact of such importance to be disposed of in these words, as if it were just one detail among others, must accuse him of a dreadful thoughtlessness also. Wilamowitz long ago[16] pointed out that the sacrifice of Makaria is in the wrong place here. The interpolated verses describe a routine sacrifice before battle,

13. 'Exkurse', p. 339.
14. D. L. Page, *Actors' Interpolations* (Oxford 1934), p. 35.
15. To line 822 in his *Belles Lettres* edition of the play (Paris 1961).
16. 'Exkurse', p. 341.

whereas Makaria's sacrifice is meant for Persephone, is supposed to propitiate the underworld powers, and is the prerequisite for the whole undertaking, for Demophon's helpful intercession and for the deployment of the army. When Makaria leaves the stage after her parting speech (line 596), no one can doubt that she goes immediately to fulfill her readiness for the sacrifice. It was gross thoughtlessness on the part of the interpolator to force this into the preparations for battle after Hyllos' offer of a duel. N. Wecklein[17] thought up a philological novel, which is not made any better by the fact that Pohlenz endorsed it. On his supposition the seers delayed the sacrifice of the maiden because they hoped it would be made superfluous by Hyllos' challenge of Eurystheus, and Hyllos himself intended to save the life of his sister in this way. All this has not the least support in the text and the sacrifice would be more than ever in the wrong place. Wecklein argues that Hyllos could not have proposed that his enemy carry off the Heraclidae in the case of his defeat if the sacrifice of Makaria had already assured the victory, but this is much too rationalistic. Méridier[18] took up this idea, but rightly mitigated it in a footnote: Hyllos could confidently propose the duel just after the sacrifice of Makaria. In truth, however, the sacrifice of the maiden and the duel proposed by Hyllos are two separate motifs; it was not the intention of the author to bring them together. It is our task to interpret him, not to compose a poem that goes beyond his.

If one does not avoid the necessary conclusions by making detours, one can see in lines 819–22 only an interpolation. Its purpose is clear. The completion of Makaria's sacrifice has to find a place somehow and somewhere, however unsuitable this place may be. The most likely of all possibilities then is that a report which the author himself once gave in a lost or deleted part had to be replaced in such a manner.

Now we come to an argument, which I at first only hesitantly

17. N. Wecklein, *Blätter für das bayer. Gymnasialschulw.* (1886), 20. Pohlenz, *Griechische Tragödie*, vol. II, p. 146, put particular emphasis on οὐκ ἔμελλον (821). It is conceivable that this means nothing more than that the priests went to work with a certain haste. But even if one wished to put a particular stress on οὐκ ἔμελλον, the words could only betray an interpolator (inept, indeed, but still capable of thinking), who was using them to cover up the fact that the sacrifice, actually long ago completed, has here been moved to the wrong place.

18. Cf. footnote 15: p. 192.

put forward,[19] but which, on renewed consideration, seems to me to be very important and which occasioned this present review of the whole problem. Fundamentally it is concerned only with the precise determination of the wording, which has till now been passed over in a manner difficult to understand. Euripides loves to achieve his effects by means of touching scenes. One need only recall the scenes of flight to an altar or the *Heracles*, where at the end of the first half of the play the hero enters his palace and his clinging children hinder his walking. What happens to Iolaos after the exit of Makaria is also touching (602ff.). The author gives clear stage directions by means of his text, as in other cases. Iolaos feels himself incapable of bearing the suffering, he can no longer remain on his feet. Now the boys are to help him, who must be thought of as being present at the altar from the beginning as κωφὰ πρόσωπα: λάβεσθε κεῖς ἕδραν μ᾽ ἐρείσατε | αὐτοῦ πέπλοισι τοῖσδε κρύψαντες, τέκνα. The wording leaves no doubt: the boys take hold of Iolaos and lead him to a place where he has a lasting seat. He is also supposed to be able to lean on something; this is in ἐρείσατε. There is a comparable passage in the *Bacchae* (684) where some of the women sit πρὸς ἐλάτης νῶτ᾽ ἐρείσασαι φόβην, in contrast to others, who are lying on the ground. Iolaos sits on a step of the altar and supports his back on it. In his deep grief he orders the boys to cover him with his clothes. The situation after the song of the chorus is a totally different one. The servant of Hyllos comes and greets the boys. But he sees neither Alcmene nor Iolaos at the altar (τῆσδ᾽ ἕδρας) where he expected to find them. Iolaos no longer sits where the boys seated him, and the servant asks, when he sees him lying on the ground (633): τί χρῆμα κεῖσαι καὶ κατηφὲς ὄμμ᾽ ἔχεις; Something else has also changed in the position of Iolaos: whereas before he had himself covered, the servant now sees that he has let his gaze drop to the ground in deep dejection. Thus his face can no longer be covered. It is difficult to understand how Pohlenz[20] could write: 'Wilamowitz himself emphasized with complete correctness that 633 connects directly to the situation from 602ff.' For the rest, Wilamowitz indeed noticed the clear change in Iolaos' position, but weakened the force of his observation because he attributed the whole passage

19. A. Lesky, *Tragische Dichtung*, 3rd ed., p. 357.
20. Cf. footnote 11.

with Alcmene's entrance to the reviser, who also, by his account, brought Iolaos lying on the ground into the text. This is forgotten today, since Wilamowitz, rightly, found no one to follow him in his assumption that this part of the play had been worked over. Naturally, scholars neglected to draw the conclusion which then became necessary. The falling and lying down of painfully affected characters is in no way an uncommon motif in Euripides; one need only read the fine observations of Jacqueline de Romilly on κεῖσθαι.²¹ But there is a considerable difference between a person's lying down, and his being placed by someone on a seat (ἕδρα) and his back being propped against an altar (ἐρείσατε). Or are the boys supposed to have laid Iolaos on the ground? Thus, something must have gone on between 602ff. and 630, which resulted in the fall of Iolaos. Now this is exactly the space between two scenes in which Kirchhoff, Wilamowitz, and his successors have set a report of the death of Makaria. It is to be hoped that no one will wish to assume that Iolaos fell to the ground during the song of the chorus! But then this fall is only understandable if some concrete cause brought it about. One can hardly think of any such cause other than the report of Makaria's death. His grief over the girl's death is now intensified; it had already been bitterly portrayed at the time of her preparation for the sacrifice. Iolaos, in despair, rejects Makaria's plea to die in his arms (564). It would be beyond his ability to be present at her death. Thus it is understandable that the report of the completion of the sacrifice throws him completely to the ground. His fall is thoroughly significant when seen in terms of the progression of the action: with it the deepest part of the κάτω ὁδός is reached; with the coming of the servant the road moves upwards again to the high point of the *reiuvenatio*.²²

21. J. de Romilly, *L'évolution du pathétique d'Eschyle à Euripide* (Paris 1961), pp. 8off. This passage of the *Heraclidae* does however require a sharper differentiation.

22. The difficulties of line 619 are unsolved: ἀλλὰ σὺ μὴ προσπεσὼν (*sed suprascr.* πιτνῶν *ut videtur* L²) τὰ θεῶν ὑπὲρ μηδ' ὑπεράλγει. Elmsley gave προπίτνων and, instead of the ὑπέρ, which evidently comes from the ὑπεράλγει, the imperative φέρε. Zuntz concerned himself with this passage in *Political Plays*, pp. 43, 44. He accepts Elmsley's φέρε, but does not take προπίτνων as referring to a fall, because: '"Do not bear what the gods send" – in what manner? Falling forward (like Iolaos)? It seems absurd.' He takes προπίτνων in the meaning 'imploring' and paraphrases: 'Let not, what the gods give, move you

For the sake of completeness we will mention two other arguments which more than once played a role in the debate over the play. The *Heraclidae* is considerably shorter than any other of the extant tragedies (one cannot count the *Alcestis* because of its special status). With respect to this Zuntz comments: 'after all, one must be the shortest'. Adherents of the revision theory have referred to the sentence in the *hypothesis*: ταύτην μὲν οὖν εὐγενῶς ἀποθανοῦσαν ἐτίμησαν. Their opponents would like to have this refer to the choral song after Makaria's exit, or alternatively they question the reliability of the *hypothesis*. Neither of the two arguments mentioned above suffices for any solution. Both can be refuted; only one must add that a multitude of evasive arguments is necessary to avoid assuming the existence of a scene with the report of Makaria's death.

It must be conceded without further ado that we do not have the means to answer the question: who gave such a report and what might he have looked like? Demophon is more probable than any messenger (since there is a long messenger speech later in the play). But one cannot even say whether it was a self-contained report, and a *kommos* is also conceivable. The motif of Makaria's request to die in the arms of women (565f.) might possibly have been somehow utilized. Here it is significant that Makaria speaks of 'women', but not of Alcmene. Some have occasionally wondered at the fact that Alcmene does not come onto the stage at all during the first half of the play; but they have failed to consider that in the scene with Kopreus, Iolaos and Demophon, just as in that with Demophon, Iolaos and Makaria,

---

to invocations (in praying to escape the inescapable) nor (in realizing this impossibility: cf. vv. 615–18) to excessive grief.' To me Elmsley's φέρε seems hardly tolerable even in this connection; for the necessary imperative I would prefer a word like στένε. This word is common enough in tragedy.

I do not wish to conceal the fact, however, that I cannot quite get rid of the idea that προπίτνων could be used for 'falling down' (to which Aesch. *Pers.* 588, admittedly, does not give complete support) and that the choral song could have come, not before, but after the report of Makaria's death. Line 621 εὐδόκιμον γὰρ ἔχει θανάτου μέρος and line 627 εἰ δὲ σέβεις θανάτους ἀγαθῶν would fit well with this. Line 626 ἄξια δ' εὐγενίας τάδε γίγνεται presents difficulties. But the present tense is not impossible even after Makaria's death; compare Schwyzer–Debrunner, p. 274, with examples from tragedy, in particular Eur. *Hec.* 695. But it must not be forgotten that what Zuntz said of Elmsley applies to every attempt at restoration: 'if Elmsley is supposed to have restored the original wording; which is by no means a certain assumption'

three actors were necessary and none was left over for the role of
Alcmene. For this reason Alcmene had to remain in the temple
with the maidens and the spectator has to accept the fact that
neither the tumult with Kopreus nor Demophon's demand of
sacrifice to Iolaos (which actually brings Makaria onto the stage)
suffices to bring about her entrance. To contradict an often
expressed assumption,[23] it is also not likely that she had a part
in the deleted scene. Its effect was directed to Iolaos and led to his
total collapse. The entrance of Alcmene at line 646 gives throughout the impression of being her first appearance in the play.
Wilamowitz should never have questioned this scene. The misunderstanding which it mischievously lets loose on the Messenger
with his joyful news is authentically Euripidean. Such scenes
begin with the error of the drunken Heracles in the *Alcestis* and
end with the almost comic scene in *Iph. Aul.*, where Clytaemnestra
greets the unsuspecting Achilles as a future son-in-law. But the
fact that Alcmene comes into the play so late does not only stem
from the lack of a fourth actor. The last part and, above all, the
end of the drama is reserved for her. The fierce resoluteness of
her words at 646ff. already reveals that Alcmene who gives the
end of the play its dark tone.

The end of the drama requires a few more words. Alcmene
has made an evil, sophistic deal with the chorus, which amounts
to the death of the prisoner. She will have Eurystheus be killed,
but have his corpse handed over to the Athenians. The chorus
is only too ready for such a transaction (1021).[24] Alcmene
urges them to speed with her last words and gives as a reason the
advantage which the Athenians will derive from the corpse of
Eurystheus. 'Then, servants, take him forth!' And then comes the
surprising line, annulling the entire transaction with the corpse:
'And when you have killed him, throw him to the dogs!' Here
one must object most sharply against every attempt at smoothing
this out by conjecture. Elmsley wished to write πυρί instead of
κυσίν in line 1050, but it does him honor that he admitted his
hesitancy: 'Sed vereor ne poetae potius quam librariorum

23. Thus already Wilamowitz, 'Exkurse', pp. 342f.

24. It is difficult to decide whether the often cited resolution of the πόλις to
spare Eurystheus (964, 967, 1012, 1019) is assumed to have been carried out
in the intervening time, or whether a passage concerning him has been lost.
The first possibility seems more likely to me.

peccatum sit'. Méridier, to be sure, admitted πυρί into the text. There is even less to be done with Housman's κόνει. This very strange ending is protected by the fact that we encounter a similar σκάνδαλον on yet another occasion in Euripides. At the end of the *Orestes* Menelaos has totally capitulated (1617): ἔχεις με. We might expect that it would now come to a compromise, but Orestes gives his ally the command to set fire to the palace. Here Apollo brings the solution to a situation from which there is no way out. Both here and there, however, it is wrong to use the conjectural planing knife to abolish out of hand anything which causes us trouble.[25] In the *Heraclidae* a bitter irony is expressed, which R. Guerrini recently effectively elucidated in the second of the articles mentioned in footnote 8: from the defense of the νόμος, under whose banner the saving of the Heraclidae from raw violence takes place, a new violence and a new injury to the νόμος arises. Perhaps, in light of this irony, Guerrini permitted the *laudes Athenarum*, which is contained in the piece, to recede into the background too much. Yet in the interpretation of this play we certainly ought not to neglect a feature which has already been ironically prepared for in the nature of Alcmene: the abolition of a νόμος which was undoubtedly much under discussion at the time the play was produced.

In the *Belles Lettres* edition Méridier printed the closing verses of the chorus directly after the last words of Alcmene. This would be possible if one accepted Elmsley's impossible πυρί with him (1050). But G. Hermann saw what was correct long ago and G. Murray accepted it in the Oxford text. A lacuna must be placed before line 1053; the ταὐτὰ δοκεῖ μοι of the one semi-chorus can only stand in relationship to the words of the other, which protested Alcmene's excess or announced counter-measures. The conduct of the chorus in the final part is not exactly that of a heroic fighter for justice; choruses are not usually accustomed to be such in tragedy. We may not, however, burden it with the reproach that with ταὐτὰ δοκεῖ μοι it agrees with the intention of Alcmene to throw the corpse of Eurystheus to the dogs.

25. For the literature on the end of the *Orestes* see *Tragische Dichtung*, 3rd ed., p. 470.

Euripides' *Hippolytus*, or virtue rewarded

GEORGE E. DIMOCK, Jr

In March 428 B.C., when Euripides' *Hippolytus* was played for the first time in the theater of Dionysus at Athens, the plague, or rather its first onset, was just coming to an end. Thucydides, one of the few who caught it and recovered, tells us what the scene in the city was like. We must remember that Athens had now for three years been fighting Sparta and her allies, and that the citizens had taken refuge within the walls. I quote from Jowett's translation (2. 52):

The crowding of the people out of the country into the city aggravated the misery; and the newly-arrived suffered the most. For, having no houses of their own, but inhabiting in the height of summer stifling huts, the mortality among them was dreadful, and they perished in wild disorder. The dead lay as they had died, one upon another, while others hardly alive wallowed in the streets and crawled about every fountain craving for water. The temples in which they lodged were full of the corpses of those who died in them; for the violence of the calamity was such that men, not knowing where to turn, grew reckless of all law, human and divine.

Particularly in the first months of this calamity, Athens was evidently in a state of demoralized terror. By the time of the production of our play, things had no doubt settled down somewhat. The stifling heat of summer had given way to the raw cold of winter twice, and there was more adequate shelter. On the other hand, something like a fifth of Athens' infantry had died of the sickness in its first two years (Th. 3. 87), and worst of all, her foremost statesman, Pericles himself, had succumbed. Athens seemed to be under a curse.

Even those rational spirits who ordinarily would have scoffed at the idea of divine interference had good reason to fear the anger of the gods. When asked, the Delphic oracle told the Spartans that they would win the war if they did their best, and that

239

Apollo would help them 'summoned or unsummoned' (Th. 1. 118; 2. 54). Perhaps not many Athenians were impressed, but when in the second year of the war the plague struck Athens and spared the Spartans and their allies, many must have been convinced. As is obvious from the first book of the *Iliad*, Apollo sends plagues. Nor was this all. At the beginning of the war the Spartans had demanded that the Athenians 'drive out the curse of the goddess' (Th. 1. 126–7). They were hoping to embarrass Pericles, whose remote ancestors had been involved in the murder of the Cylonian conspirators who took refuge at Athena's altar and image on the Acropolis. Now Pericles was dead at the height of his life and power. Could it be that the gods were bent on the destruction of Athens because of ancient sin, or for some other, obscurer reason?

It is more than coincidence that from the days of the Peloponnesian War and the great Athenian plague there survive even now two tragedies, both of which deal with the destruction of essentially innocent men, men of whom it can even be said that their goodness destroyed them. In both of these plays, furthermore, the relevance, or even the existence, of divine law is called into question, just as it was by the Athenians under the impact of the plague. One of these plays is Euripides' *Hippolytus*, the other is Sophocles' *Oedipus the King*. It looks as though both Sophocles and Euripides were concerned to find what it might mean for an essentially innocent man, or city, apparently to be doomed to destruction by the gods. Could the reality of the gods, and thus of the threatened destruction, be denied? Or if visitations like the plague indeed came from the gods, did it mean that they were unjust, or perhaps even vindictive?

Sophocles' answer seems to be that there are indeed gods and that they can and sometimes do lead the best of men into the most horrible mistakes which then lead to the most horrible suffering; but we can live with this fact if we are strong enough, as strong as Oedipus. If it is the gods' will, it is right even to be as wrong as he. 'In season, all is good', Creon appallingly says as he leads the polluted Oedipus into the Theban palace at the end of the play.

Euripides' answer, as we would expect, is rather different. We shall see that his play *Hippolytus* communicates the following: no goodness of man (or state) can prevent the forces that rule the world from destroying us, if that is the way they are tending; but that does not mean that men should stop trying to realize the height of goodness in their lives. Even in the midst of ruin, goodness brings its reward. To put it more briefly, Euripides' play *Hippolytus* is an eloquent statement of the proposition that virtue is its own reward.

The myth with which Euripides began is a variant of the 'virtuous youth' story which we see in the Bible in the story of Joseph and Potiphar's wife, and in the *Iliad* in the story of Bellerophon and Proetus' wife Anteia. In both those stories the point is that the sexually tempted young man refuses to violate a sacred bond of loyalty to a superior, and as a result eventually survives in some brilliantly successful way the wife's attempt to incriminate him. Heaven rewards him for being good. As near as we can tell, Hippolytus by contrast is always destroyed – by his horses, as his name suggests. In what appears to be the traditional Athenian version of the myth,[1] the wicked stepmother, Phaedra, tries to seduce him herself, in person, and when she fails, accuses him to his father, Theseus. Only after Theseus has brought about his son's destruction through the god Poseidon does the stepmother then willingly or unwillingly confess and kill herself. From the historical fact that brides-to-be in Troezen, across the bay from Athens, dedicated a lock of hair to Hippolytus and sang of Phaedra's fatal love for him, we may conclude that Aphrodite always had a powerful role in this version of the myth and explicitly caused Phaedra's infatuation. Aphrodite is exceedingly relevant because a Greek bride-to-be's problem was to get over her feelings of τὸ σωφρονεῖν...ἐς τὰ πάνθ' ὁμῶς, 'chastity towards all things alike', as David Grene translates line 80 of our play. In particular she had to get over her feelings of chastity towards the violation of her own body, and to accept the violation of that body.[2] The story of the destruction of an unbelievably beautiful young man because he refused to submit to the demands of Aphrodite would be of considerable help in this process. It would suggest, first, that it is better to obey Aphrodite, however painful that may be.

1. W. S. Barrett, (ed.) *Euripides, Hippolytus* (Oxford 1964), p. 11.
2. For the importance of the Hippolytus-myth in preparing brides psychologically for marriage, see K. J. Reckford, 'Phaethon, Hippolytus, Aphrodite', *TAPA* 103 (1972), 414–16.

Next, the point that it is a *man* who is punished for trying to remain chaste would satisfy some of the bride-to-be's hostility towards the male who was about to violate her and would both distance and make seem more legitimate her feelings for the chastity she was having to give up. Thirdly, the aggressive woman in the story, in an equally ambivalent fashion, suggests on the one hand that sex is desirable and that the woman need not be a passive victim in her sexual role; on the other hand, the woman too is punished for spoiling the young man and all that beautiful chastity for which the bride-to-be is now feeling a last, intense yearning. In some such way the story of Hippolytus was apparently helpful to brides-to-be at Troezen.

Euripides thought he saw, in a myth to help girls submit to marriage, a myth to help Athens and mankind in general submit to the cruelty of history. In Aphrodite he depicted the cruelty of the forces which determine our fate; in Artemis, the 'chastity towards all things alike' which is always defeated, and for which we always yearn.

In Euripides' play, Artemis has much the better of it. Aphrodite speaks the prologue and makes two things at once apparent: she is all-powerful, and she is vindictive. I here give David Grene's translation of the Greek, as I shall do throughout except where otherwise noted:

> I am called the Goddess Cypris:
> I am mighty among men and they honor me by many names.
> All those that live and see the light of sun
> from Atlas' Pillars to the tide of Pontus
> are mine to rule.
> Such as worship my power in all humility,
> I exalt in honor.
> But those whose pride is stiff-necked against me
> I lay by the heels.
> There is joy in the heart of a god also
> when honored by men.

Then later,

> But for his sins against me
> I shall punish Hippolytus this day.

What are his sins? That he 'will have none of the bed of love, nor of marriage'. Does Aphrodite complain that this threatens

242

the propagation of the species? No. She merely takes Hippolytus'
refusal as a personal affront. Further along she tells us how far she
is willing to go to satisfy her pique:

> Renowned shall Phaedra be in her death, but none the less
> die she must.
> Her suffering does not weigh in the scale so much
> that I should let my enemies go untouched
> escaping payment of that retribution
> that honor demands I have.

Then, for her exit-lines, she gloats:

> Look, here is the son of Theseus, Hippolytus!
> He has just left his hunting.
> I must go away.
> See the great crowd that throngs upon his heels
> and shouts the praise of Artemis in hymns!
> He does not know
> that the doors of death are open for him,
> that he is looking on his last sun.

Here Euripides makes the point unmistakable that if there is
a goddess of love and she operates on human principles, just such
vindictiveness as this must be characteristic of her; for no one can
doubt that the unwilling infatuation of one poor individual like
Phaedra, when it collides with the understandable shock and
horror of an innocent youth like Hippolytus, can cause all the
havoc which Aphrodite names here.

By contrast, our first impression of Artemis is meant to be an
exceedingly appealing one. Hippolytus and his companions, fresh
from the hunt, enter hymning her:

> Hail, Holy and Gracious!
> Hail, Daughter of Zeus!
> Hail, Maiden Daughter of Zeus and Leto!
> Dweller in the spacious sky!
> Maid of the Mighty Father!
> Maid of the Golden Glistening House!
> Hail!
> Maiden Goddess most beautiful of all the Heavenly Host that
> lives in Olympus!

Then Hippolytus steps forward and speaks:

My Goddess Mistress, I bring you ready woven
this garland. It was I that plucked and wove it,
plucked it for you in your inviolate Meadow.
No shepherd dares to feed his flock within it:
no reaper plies a busy scythe within it:
only the bees in springtime haunt the inviolate Meadow.
Its gardener is the spirit Reverence who
refreshes it with water from the river.
Not those who by instruction have profited
to learn, but in whose very soul the seed
of Chastity toward all things alike
nature has deeply rooted, they alone
may gather flowers there! the wicked may not.

Loved mistress, here I offer you this coronal;
it is a true worshipper's hand that gives it you
to crown the golden glory of your hair.
With no man else I share this privilege
that I am with you and to your words
can answer words. True, I may only hear:
I may not see God face to face.
So may I turn the post set at life's end
even as I began the race.

'The spirit Reverence' (Αἰδώς) makes it impossible that Hippolytus should violate anything, should do anything wrong, ever.
He is the embodiment not just of sexual chastity but of chastity
towards all things alike, and he leads a life of perfect beauty. He
is happy: he wishes only to end his life as he began. In a sense he
will have his wish.

About the beauty and desirability of this ideal, Phaedra agrees.
The difference is this: Hippolytus has it; she wants it and can't
get it, prevented by Aphrodite. In her delirium Phaedra raves
(208–11):

> O,
> if I could only draw from the dewy spring
> a draught of fresh spring water!
> If I could only lie beneath the poplars,
> in the tufted meadow and find my rest there!

and (215–22):

> Bring me to the mountains! I *will* go to the mountains!
> Among the pine trees where the huntsmen's pack
> trails spotted stags and hangs upon their heels.
> God, how I long to set the hounds on, shouting!

244

And poise the Thessalian javelin drawing it back –
here where my fair hair hangs above the ear –
I would hold in my hand a spear with a steel point.

and (228–31):

Artemis, mistress of the Salty Lake,
mistress of the ring echoing to the racers' hoofs.
if only I could gallop your level stretches,
and break Venetian colts!

No wonder she is in love with Hippolytus. The irony is that it is precisely that which makes her love him which bars her from her heart's desire: she loves his chastity.

So far, in terms of the play, Hippolytus' state is completely enviable. Can we find fault with it at any later point? Let us admit that he finds horrible the Nurse's suggestion that his father's wife is madly in love with him, and that he curses the whole race of women in consequence. Let us admit also that what little he has heard previously about women confirms him in his condemnation of them. Is this not understandable in the circumstances; understandable, as the old Huntsman said, as the drastic morality of the young (117–20)?

For an impartial estimate, let us turn to Phaedra's friends, the chorus, after Hippolytus has cruelly, though necessarily, refused her. These are the friends of Phaedra who have let Theseus curse Hippolytus and banish him; who have exposed Hippolytus to his death, in fact, rather than tell the truth and ruin Phaedra's reputation. This is what these women say of him (1120–5; 1142–50):

My heart is no longer clear:
I have seen what I never dreamed,
I have seen the brightest star of Athens,
stricken by a father's wrath,
banished to an alien land.

But my sorrow shall not die,
still my eyes shall be wet with tears
for your heartless doom.
Sad mother, you bore him in vain:
I am angry against the Gods.
Sister Graces, why did you let him go
guiltless, out of his native land,
out of his father's house?

For these women, Hippolytus is Athens' brightest star, and his calamity is not a punishment but an outrage. Frankly, I see no way to consider Hippolytus's way of life, chastity and all, as anything other than the best that man can aspire to in this play's terms.

This is the place to consider the opening scene, where Hippolytus' guilt towards Aphrodite, and therefore his tragic flaw, if he has one, is established. Superficially this is a temptation-scene like the carpet-scene in Aeschylus's *Agamemnon*, where the sinner, already doomed, is induced to re-enact his sin symbolically for the benefit of the audience. Yet, unlike the scene in *Agamemnon*, in *Hippolytus* something approaching exoneration is provided, as we have seen, by the old Huntsman's words and his implied criticism of the goddess (117–20):

> You should grant forgiveness
> when one that has a young and tempestuous heart
> speaks foolish words. Seem not to hear them.
> You should be wiser than mortals, being Gods.

Nor is this all. At an earlier stage in the scene Hippolytus actually shows a piety superior to the Huntsman's and at the same time discredits the goddess much more seriously. The Huntsman has established that the quality of arrogance (*to semnon*) is hateful, and then asks Hippolytus why he does not pay his respects to a *semnen* goddess (99). Though *semnos* ordinarily means something more like 'august' when applied to a divinity, Euripides is nevertheless concerned to demonstrate even in such a case the latent negative connotations of the word. Hippolytus is properly and naturally shocked at what he takes to be the Huntsman's inadvertent impropriety. The irony of course is that Aphrodite has in fact already shown us just how *semne* she is in demanding the lives of Phaedra and Hippolytus and the ruin of all concerned. If Hippolytus is *semnos* for not greeting Aphrodite respectfully, or for 'having none of the bed of love or marriage', he is at least a good deal less so than Aphrodite.

Yet Hippolytus is, after all, tactless. His innocence and purity make him so. Euripides does not demand of him what some modern critics do, a depth of understanding beyond his years which would allow him to respond to the Nurse's obscene proposal in a manner to reassure Phaedra. On the other hand, he is

246

not such a fanatic of *sophrosyne* as many think. Euripides makes it clear that Hippolytus would violate *sophrosyne* by breaking his oath and telling the truth if he thought that that would convince his father (1062). As it is, he prefers to keep his oath rather than to break it uselessly, as a less scrupulous man might. This is enough to satisfy Artemis (1307–9), just as Phaedra's not altogether rigorous resistance to the Nurse and her plot is enough to satisfy her (1305). Euripides does not demand miracles of his characters, and so it is that Hippolytus does not preserve an absolutely prudent tactfulness either here in the temptation-scene or later in his confrontation with his father.

Yet his heart is clearly open, respectful, and noble. It is not until he is pushed into it at the very end of the scene that he addresses contemptuous words to Aphrodite, and here the point is that the question is not really one of affability or tactfulness or flexibility at all, but of the fact that life does face us with insoluble dilemmas. Hippolytus' contemptuous words at 108–13 may be paraphrased as: 'Bring me my dinner; and then let me exercise my horses. As for your Cypris here, a long farewell to her!' – in other words, 'I don't give a damn about sex.' In the first place, as we have seen the Huntsman unsuccessfully try to explain to the goddess, this is pardonable, especially in the young. In the second place, it is true. Civilities at the shrine will not change the fact that Hippolytus does not like what Aphrodite stands for. He could not embody in his life the Artemis-ideal of chastity towards all things alike if he did. At the end of the play Artemis calls Aphrodite (1301–2),

> that most hated goddess,
> hated by all of us whose joy is virginity,

and I see no appeal from this verdict. In Euripides' view you cannot serve both Artemis and Aphrodite.

Hippolytus' flaw, then, is essentially that he is too good. Everyone in the play agrees, except Theseus, and Theseus thinks that Hippolytus is *un*-chaste, that he has raped his wife. Even the Groom who tells of the chariot-wreck is emboldened to tell the king to his face that he is wrong (1249–54):

> I am only a slave in your household, King Theseus,
> but I shall never be able to believe
> that your son was guilty, not though the tribe of women

were hanged for it, not though the weight of tablets
of a high pine of Ida, filled with writing,
accused him – for I know that he was good.

There is not even a chance that the people of Troezen, or that
Euripides, for that matter, finds Hippolytus a prig (1178–80):

Then he came himself down to the shore to us,
with the same refrain of tears,
and with him walked a countless company
of friends and young men his own age.

Prigs do not have so many friends. All this shows us that when
Euripides has Artemis tell Hippolytus at the end of the play that
the nobility of his soul (τὸ εὐγενὲς τῶν φρενῶν) proved his ruin
(1390), he intends no criticism of any kind.

On the contrary, the play makes Hippolytus a ground of
accusation against Heaven. In this article we have already heard
the chorus say that they were angry against the gods, and heard
them upbraid the Graces for Hippolytus' banishment. Lest a
chorus of women seem insufficiently representative of the community of Troezen, Euripides introduces a supernumerary chorus
of young men,[3] representing none other than the 'countless com-

---

3. There is disagreement about whether 1120–5 is sung by the regular
chorus of women of Troezen, or by a supernumerary chorus of men. The
masculine participles in 1105 and 1107 make it certain that the voice in 1102–10
at least is male. (I owe a debt of gratitude to my colleague Thalia Pandiri for
weaning me away from the scholiast's suggestion that in these lines the chorus
speaks in the character of Euripides himself. Two masculine participles are
insufficient to communicate to any conceivable audience so violent and un-
precedented a break in the dramatic illusion. Sophocles, *O.T.* 896 τί δεῖ με
χορεύειν; where the chorus speaks in its own person as Athenian citizens is
different.)

Barrett in his Oxford edition states correctly (368) the criteria for the solution to the problem and then unaccountably fails to come up with it. The
criteria are these: (i) 'secondary choruses are used only when the main chorus
will not serve', and (ii) 'their identity is always announced before they sing'.
The second criterion is splendidly fulfilled by Hippolytus' words at 1098–9:

ἴτ᾽ ὦ νέοι μοι τῆσδε γῆς ὁμήλικες,
προσείπαθ᾽ ἡμᾶς καὶ προπέμψατε χθονός.

Come, young men, my agemates in this land,
say your farewells and set me on my way.

(I have changed Grene's first line.) It is hard to imagine Euripides writing
these lines unless he wished to introduce a secondary chorus. Nor is it far to
seek where these young men came from: they have responded to Theseus'
summoning the city (ἰὼ πόλις, 884) to witness Hippolytus' crime. What use

pany of friends' referred to above, to make the same point. They make it more moderately, to be sure, but nonetheless express disappointment in the gods. Their words, in fact (1002–10), introduce the women's angrier lines:

> The care of God for us is a great thing,
> if a man believe it at heart:
> it plucks the burden of sorrow from him.
> So I have a secret hope
> of someone, a God, who is wise and plans;
> but my hopes grow dim when I see
> the deeds of men and their destinies.
> For fortune is ever veering, and the currents of life
>   are shifting,
> shifting, wandering forever.

Taking their cue from this suggestion that life may be only a meaningless flux, the chorus of women responds, at first, by praying for a mind flexible and cynical enough to be proof against the amorality of fortune (1111–19):

> This is the lot in life I seek
> and I pray that God may grant it me,
> luck and prosperity

Euripides found in this group is not difficult to imagine. It was obviously important to him that Hippolytus should be seen to be loved and admired by all the youth of Troezen, and they are referred to again in the messenger speech (1179–80) as accompanying him down to the shore. It was also presumably important to Euripides' conception that the injustice done to Hippolytus should be felt not only by the women of the community but by its men. Their disillusion is shown to be equally real, but more measured and philosophic, than the women's.

We may conclude, then, that a group representing the young men of Troezen sing lines 1102–10. They concern the difficulty of believing that the gods care for men when one considers cases like Hippolytus'. The regular chorus of women then take over with the antistrophe (feminine participle in 1111) and continue to the end of the ode. This is indicated by the fact that their prayer for moral flexibility in the antistrophe is grounded, at the beginning of the second strophe, in their inability to maintain strict principles (οὐκέτι γὰρ καθαρὰν φρέν' ἔχω) when *they* (as contrasted with the men) see what has happened to Hippolytus. This proves that the masculine participle read in several manuscripts at 1121 is wrong; Barrett is correct in reading λεύσ(σ)ω with BVCE. In any case the men must follow Hippolytus off the stage as soon as possible, and our attention must be firmly caught and held for an appreciable time by the women, in order that sufficient time may seem to elapse to contain the chariot-wreck. The messenger who will report it enters, at best, only 40 lines later. Thus it is the women who sing 1120–30 as well as 1111–19 and 1131–50.

and a heart untroubled by anguish.
And a mind that is neither false clipped coin,
nor too clear-eyed in sincerity,
that I may lightly change my ways,
my ways of today when tomorrow comes,
and so be happy all my life long.

Their reason for this prayer (given in 1120–5 quoted above) is the same one which makes the young men of the city doubt the care of the gods for men, but the women's response is the more extreme of the two. Like the Athenians smitten by the plague, the women no longer see reason to take very seriously any law, human or divine. Their words are quite reminiscent of Jocasta's in *Oedipus the King* when she is convinced that there is no truth in oracles, that nothing can be confidently predicted (*O.T.* 979):

εἰκῆ κράτιστον ζῆν, ὅπως δύναιτό τις,

best to live at random, as best one can [my translation].

It is here that Jocasta comes close to saying that there is nothing so very bad even about incest. If there is no justice, no order in heaven – if in short there are no gods – nothing matters. There is no serious right and wrong about things any more. The chorus in *Hippolytus* does not go quite so far as Jocasta, but we have already heard (1142–50) how they end their song in anger against the gods. No doubt this was the feeling of many Athenians as they looked at their noble city in the throes of the plague, marked by heaven for destruction.

Euripides does not leave things here, however. At the end of the play, through Artemis, or men's potential for reverence – they are the same – he restores meaning to life, discovering a kind of justice in it which finally seems satisfying. Banishing Hippolytus, Theseus hates him with a boundless passion (1051–4):

Hippolytus.
  Must I go at once to banishment?
Theseus.
                    Yes, and had I the power,
    your place of banishment would be beyond
    the limits of the world, the encircling sea
    and the Atlantic Pillars.
    That is the measure of my hate, my son.

Hearing of the chariot-wreck, however, his mood begins to change (1257–60):

For hatred of the sufferer I was glad
at what you told me. Still, he was my son.
As such I have reverence for him and the Gods:
I neither rejoice nor sorrow at this thing.

Theseus when he is faced with the actuality of his son's destruction, feels awe and reverence, as well he might, and Reverence (*Aidōs*) is the spirit which tends Artemis' meadow. Theseus is coming under her influence. A few lines later, even as the chorus hails Aphrodite, whose victory seems so complete, as the unique ruler of god, man, and every living creature, Artemis comes on stage to establish her claim, summoned by the awakening of her influence in the heart of Theseus.

Every Greek would recognize Artemis in Theseus' feeling of constraint and the stilling of his passion as he begins to take in the fact of his son's catastrophe; but that she will be present too in his feeling of shame when he comes to realize that his son is innocent, would perhaps not be so clear. Yet the Greek word for the two is the same: *aidōs*, indifferently 'reverence', or 'shame'; and there is obviously a connection. Euripides explicitly prepares us for this extension of the meaning of Artemis when he has Phaedra discourse on the causes of life's failure at the beginning of the play (375–87). There is laziness, and pleasure, she says, and then there is shame, *aidōs*. Shame is of two kinds: the one is harmless but the other a plague. Riddling words, but it is evident that it is the second kind of shame which she sees as the ruin of otherwise good lives and is determined to be rid of at all costs. It is the shame that keeps you from holding your head up like a free person; it is the consciousness that you are doing, or have done, or are prepared to do, something vile. Rather than suffer this shame further, Phaedra prefers to die; and rather than permit Hippolytus to make this shame known, so that it passes to her children, she is prepared to slander him and kill him. The harmless kind of shame, on the other hand, is evidently Hippolytus' kind, a feeling of almost physical repugnance at the thought of violating any sanctity, small or great. In his case at least Phaedra is wrong that it is harmless. Aphrodite, goddess of violation, does not like it. Phaedra is right, however, when she says in the Greek, if not in Grene's translation, that the distinction between the two shames is not completely clear. *Aidōs*, then, in both its forms belongs to Artemis, and once

Theseus opens himself to it in the way we have seen, Artemis pours shame upon him in a burning flood (1286–97):

> Miserable man, what joy have you in this?
> You have murdered a son, you have broken nature's laws.
> Dark indeed was the conclusion
> you drew from your wife's lying accusations,
> but plain for all to see is the destruction
> to which they led you.
> There is a hell beneath the earth: haste to it,
> and hide your head there! Or will you take wings,
> and choosing the life of a bird instead of man
> keep your feet from destruction's path in which they tread?
> Among good men, at least, you have no share in life.
> Hear me tell you, Theseus, how these things came to pass.
> I shall not better them, but I will give you pain.

This is the way we speak to ourselves when we have caught ourselves in some horrible mistake, and well expresses the apparently useless pain which shame brings.

After the poison, the balm. Once the heart is purged of passion, it is possible to realize that despite the terrible things they do to each other, men are not to blame; passion is. Love, in the shape of Phaedra's lust, Theseus' jealousy, and the Nurse's affection for Phaedra, has destroyed them all. This knowledge too comes from Artemis (1325–41):

> You have sinned indeed, but yet you may win pardon.
> For it was Cypris managed the thing this way
> to gratify her anger against Hippolytus.
> This is the settled custom of the Gods:
> No one may fly in the face of another's wish:
> we remain aloof and neutral. Else, I assure you,
> had I not feared Zeus, I never would have endured
> such shame as this – my best friend among men
> killed, and I could do nothing.
> As for you, in the first place ignorance acquits you,
> and then your wife, by her death, destroyed the proofs,
> the verbal proofs which might have still convinced you.
> You and I are the chief sufferers, Theseus.
> Misfortune for you, grief for me.
> The Gods do not rejoice when pious worshippers die:
> the wicked we destroy, children, house and all.

Nothing in this world checks passion. Where Aphrodite rules, Artemis is powerless; but that does not mean that passion is good, or that injustice is approved by the gods in general. Hearing this, Theseus understands the truth at last.

Hippolytus' problem remains. He is brought on stage a battered wreck, in such physical and moral pain that there is nothing in him of Oedipus' rage to live out his calamity. Hippolytus is utterly disillusioned and only wants someone to take a spear and kill him (1363–77):

> Zeus, do you see this,
> see me that worshipped God in piety,
> me that excelled all men in chastity,
> see me now go to death which gapes before me;
> all my life lost, and all for nothing now
> labors of piety in the face of men?
>
> O the pain, the pain that comes upon me!
> Let me be, let me be, you wretches!
> May death the healer come for me at last!
> You kill me ten times over with this pain.
> O for a spear with a keen cutting edge
> to shear me apart – and give me my last sleep!

This is the low point of the play; yet Euripides will bring us back even from here. It is possible that even a modern man in a condition like Hippolytus' might take comfort from the thought that though his goodness was indeed killing him, he was at least good. This is the kind of thought that Artemis inspires, and we should not be surprised to hear her utter it to Hippolytus (1389–90):

> Unhappy boy! You are yoked to a cruel fate.
> The nobility of your soul has proved your ruin.

The comfort this provides is suggested in the divine fragrance which Hippolytus at once senses, and which, as he tells us, lightens his pain. As of old, he senses Artemis' presence without seeing her, and in the dialogue which follows she convinces him of two things: that she loves him, and that the true cause of his disaster is Aphrodite. Therefore in spite of what Phaedra and his father have done to him, he is able, as he should, to transfer the blame to Aphrodite (1403–4):

> *Hippolytus.*
> She claimed us three as victims then, did Cypris?
> *Artemis.*
> Your father, you, and his wife to make a third.

(Grene mistranslates here, 'Your father, you, and *me* to make a third.') Hippolytus, his passion soothed and his respect for other people reawakened by the Artemis both within him and without, can see even Phaedra as a victim rather than a monster. He is heartily sorry for his father, and Theseus, for his part, would now gladly die for his son. To such a height of understanding Artemis has brought them. One flare-up of resentment remains as Hippolytus and Theseus together recall how shamefully Aphrodite has deceived them. 'If only men might be a curse to Gods', Hippolytus cries (1415), and thereby causes Artemis to try to reconcile him still further to the conditions under which we all live. ἔασον, 'Hush, that is enough', she responds (1416). First she promises that she will take vengeance for Hippolytus' suffering the next time Aphrodite loves a mortal. As one editor suggests, we may think of Adonis. I do not think Euripides meant this to be excessively vindictive on Artemis' part.[4] Experience suggests that Aphrodite's protégés are no surer of coming through life happily than Artemis' are, and there is a certain justice in this of which Euripides' audience would be more appreciative than we. We must not forget that Pericles congratulated the Athenian dead for dying at the moment of taking vengeance.

Next, Artemis promises Hippolytus that he will be remembered always (1423–30):

> To you, unfortunate Hippolytus,
> by way of compensation for these ills,
> I will give the greatest honors of Troezen.
> Unwedded maids before the day of marriage
> will cut their hair in your honor. You will reap
> through the long cycle of time, a rich reward in tears.
> And when young girls sing songs, they will not forget you,
> your name will not be left unmentioned,
> nor Phaedra's love for you remain unsung.

This compensation takes on more meaning for us if we remember the curse Hippolytus called down upon himself as the worst fate he could imagine if he should be guilty of what his father charged him with (1028–31):

---

4. Barrett comments *ad loc.* that Artemis' phrase, σῆς εὐσεβείας κἀγαθῆς φρενὸς χάριν (1419), 'brings out the justice of her revenge (lest it should seem mere spite)'.

> If I have been a villain, may I die
> unfamed, unknown, a homeless stateless beggar,
> an exile! May the earth and sea refuse
> to give my body rest when I am dead!

Now Artemis promises that his end will be the very opposite of this.

Artemis' final and most important contribution is to perform almost physically the reconciliation of father and son (1431–6):

> Son of old Aegeus, take your son
> to your embrace. Draw him to you. Unknowing
> you killed him. It is natural for men
> to err when they are blinded by the Gods.
>
> *(To Hippolytus)*
>
> Do not bear a grudge against your father.
> It was fate that you should die so.

It is true that at this point Artemis must take her leave, and that Hippolytus remarks on this (1441), μακρὰν δὲ λείπεις ῥᾳδίως ὁμιλίαν, 'You can lightly leave a long companionship.' No goddess like Artemis may look on the ugliness of death unpolluted. Nevertheless Hippolytus continues to find it worthwhile to obey her. The reconciliation continues as she inspired it, with no further condemnation of the gods. If the beauty of this reconciliation gives us a measure of comfort after the terrible things we have been witnessing, it is Artemis' doing.

A misunderstanding of the supreme moment of Hippolytus' reconciliation with Theseus has caused editors since Wilamowitz to see a problem in the text where none exists, inducing them to reverse the order of lines 1453–5. This procedure produces the following not very satisfactory sequence of thought:

> *Theseus.*
> Dear son, how noble you have proved to me!
> *Hippolytus.*
> Yes, pray to heaven for such legitimate sons.   1455
> *Theseus.*
> I weep ['Woe' Grene] for your goodness, piety,
>   and virtue.   1454
> *Hippolytus.*
> Farewell to you, too, father, a long farewell!   1453
> *Theseus.*
> Dear son, bear up. Do not forsake me.
> *Hippolytus.*
> This is the end of what I have to bear.
> I'm gone. Cover my face up quickly.

The difficulty which the change seeks to remedy and fails is, why does Hippolytus say, 'Farewell to you, too, father', when Theseus has not said, and in fact never does say, 'Farewell' to Hippolytus? οἴμοι φρενὸς σῆς, 'I weep for your goodness', certainly does not mean 'farewell' in ancient Greek, though it might make some sort of shabby valedictory in a modern language. In the manuscripts Hippolytus' ὦ χαῖρε καὶ σύ, χαῖρε πολλά μοι, πάτερ ('Farewell to you, too, father', etc.) follows immediately on Theseus', 'Dear son, how noble (γενναῖος) you have proved to me!' and the solution is immediately at hand if we only realize how happy that would make a young man with as much reverence for his father as Hippolytus has, contrary to what some critics suppose. Artemis' approval has done much to lighten Hippolytus' pain; but her approval he has always had. It is his father's absolutely unqualified admiration that makes his death a completely happy one. 'You be happy, too, father, happy a thousand times!' he cries in gratitude, and the Greek formula of farewell, so ironically and therefore fatally addressed to Aphrodite in the prologue (113), now takes on its full literal meaning, or more than that, if possible, to express what Hippolytus has gained by the very thing which caused his loss, his *aidōs*.[5]

Those who think that Hippolytus sneers at his father in their scene of confrontation may be quickly answered. The 'unaccustomed as I am to public speaking' *topos* (986–9) with its remark that orators are often unimpressive in intellectual conversation, is at least not intended as an insult to Theseus. Hippolytus merely hopes that his lack of experience in the *agora* may not be fatal to him in this less formal situation. The remark is undeniably tactless, however. What Euripides is doing here is to show how Hippolytus' innocence and purity of spirit serve merely to rouse his father's anger the more. Not only does it not occur to him that his father may consider that he is being called a nonintellectual demagogue, but he goes on to tell him truths which ought to assist his case but do not because they too are tactless. First he tells his father that he does not find Phaedra irresistibly

5. Charles Segal, in *Greek, Roman and Byzantine Studies* 11 (1970), 101–7, argues cogently for the order of the lines as they stand in the manuscripts. He ignores, however, the real happiness expressed in the words ὦ χαῖρε καὶ σύ, χαῖρε πολλά μοι, πάτερ.

256

attractive (1009–10), and then that he would certainly not be so lacking in *sophrosyne* as to lust after the crown. Monarchy itself, he naively adds, must have driven mad those who like it (1014–15). There are two quite certain indications in this scene that the tactlessness is inadvertent. First, for Hippolytus the worst thing about the whole affair is that *his father* thinks him evil (1070–1); this is the negative to which the supreme happiness of hearing his father pronounce the words, 'Dear son, how noble you have proved to me!' is the positive obverse. His father's condemnation almost makes him weep (1070), and he would certainly do so if he were observing such misfortune in another (1078–9); since it is his own case, however, and he is standing before his father, he may not indulge himself. *Sophrosyne* does not permit. Secondly, the end of the scene dramatizes Hippolytus' complete obedience to his father even when his father is so fatally in the wrong. No servant, says Hippolytus, will drive him into exile without a fight; has Theseus the heart to do it himself? 'Yes', answers Theseus (1088–9); 'and I will do it, too, unless you obey me; you will never get pity from me!' (my paraphrase). With these words Theseus turns on his heel and leaves the stage. After a prayer to Artemis and a last allusion to his father's failure to see his innocence, Hippolytus obeys with no more protest than, οἶδα μὲν ταῦτ', οἶδα δ' οὐχ ὅπως φράσω (1091): 'I know the truth, yet have no way to tell the truth' (my translation).

As the tragedy ends, Theseus sums it up in words which remind us of Athens, and in particular of Pericles' death a month or two before the festival at which our play was performed:

> Pallas Athene's famous city,
> what a man you shall miss [Grene: 'have lost']!
>   Alas for me!
> Cypris, how many of your injuries
> I shall remember.

Though Aphrodite is so often ruinous, men can be splendid as Hippolytus, and Pericles, were splendid. And now, for the very end, the chorus suggests perhaps the greatest consolation of all:

> This is a common grief for all the city;
> it came unlooked for. There shall be
> a storm of multitudinous tears for this;

the lamentable stories of great men
prevail more than of humble folk.

Euripides would have us realize what Virgil, too, knew and
Shakespeare's Enobarbus knew but failed to act on, that to 'win
a place i' th' story' for the right reasons far outshines mere
worldly success.

Euripides' *Heracles*[1]

JUSTINA GREGORY

THE recurrent problem of the *Heracles* is its apparent lack of unity. It is generally said to fall into either two or three parts, with the episode of Heracles' madness causing a decisive break in the action.[2] While some critics hold that such a lack of cohesion is fatal to the dramatic structure of the play, others maintain that the ruptures constitute the tragedy's main interest.[3] It is not only the play's structure that has been called into question; there is also puzzlement over the dominant theme. J. T. Sheppard looked to the closing lines, and proposed friendship, strength and wealth as motifs of the *Heracles*.[4] H. H. O. Chalk declares: '*Arete* is the hub of the wheel...Youth, Age and the passage of Time, Tyranny and Wealth...[are] the spokes.'[5]

There seems little doubt that the play falls into three parts, but whether this division bespeaks a lack of unity is another matter.

1. For the text I have used U. von Wilamowitz-Moellendorff, *Euripides Herakles*, 2nd ed. (Berlin 1895), henceforth referred to as Wilamowitz.

2. For the view that the play falls into two parts cf. William Arrowsmith, *The Complete Greek Tragedies*, ed. Grene and Lattimore, vol. III *Euripides* (Chicago 1959), p. 268; Gilbert Norwood, *Greek Tragedy*, 4th ed. (London 1953), p. 229; Walter Zürcher, *Die Darstellung des Menschen im Drama des Euripides* (Basel 1947), p. 90. For the view that it has three parts cf. Anne Pippin Burnett, *Catastrophe Survived* (Oxford 1971), p. 157; J. C. Kamerbeek, 'The Unity and Meaning of Euripides' *Herakles*', *Mnemosyne* 19 (1966), 3–4; H. D. F. Kitto, *Greek Tragedy*, 2nd ed. rev. (London 1939), p. 236; and J. T. Sheppard, 'The Formal Beauty of the *Hercules Furens*', *CQ* 10 (1916), 72–9.

3. Norwood (*Greek Tragedy*) condemns the play for its lack of unity, while Arrowsmith (*Complete Greek Tragedies*, vol. III) maintains that the 'material has been ordered to effect, rather than obviate, this dislocation of structure'. Wilamowitz too feels that the disregard of unity is intentional: 'Die Disharmonie seiner Heraklestragödie ist ein Abbild der Disharmonie, die für seine Überzeugung zwischen der Heraklessage und der reinen Sittlichkeit, zwischen dem Mythos und der echten Religion oder Philosophie vorhanden war' (II, 132).

4. Sheppard, 'Formal Beauty of *Hercules Furens*', p. 72.

5. H. H. O. Chalk, '*Bia* and *Arete* in Euripides' Heracles', *JHS* 82 (1962).

Moreover, while the aforementioned themes are touched on at various points in the play, none of them is adequate to explain the whole. They are not themes particularly germane to the character of Heracles: references to *philia*, the futility of wealth, the passage of time turn up in almost any Greek tragedy one cares to examine.

If one hopes to defend the structural and thematic unity of the *Heracles* it would be helpful to be able to point to some motif that spans all the episodes: a motif, moreover, that is particularly linked to the story of Heracles and that can help to account for the various modifications Euripides has made to the received myth.[6] Such a motif is perhaps to be found in the theme of Heracles' two fathers. Euripides lays considerable stress on this peculiar inheritance of his hero. Heracles' genealogy explains at once his glorious deeds and his subsequent madness, and it is unique in Greek legend.

To be sure, Heracles is not the only Greek hero to boast two fathers: Phaethon, Theseus, Helen and Ion can claim a similar distinction. Nevertheless, the circumstances of Heracles' begetting were unexampled in Greek myth. In order to seduce the virtuous Alcmena Zeus was obliged to assume the aspect of her husband Amphitryon; as a result, Amphitryon had some special share in the engendering of Heracles. Euripides' Amphitryon is far more than a mere cuckold. In the opening lines of the play he introduces himself as τὸν Διὸς σύλλεκτρον... πατέρα τόνδ' Ἡρακλέους – 'the man who shared his bed with Zeus, and the father of Heracles'. What one critic has called 'the impossible fact of the double fatherhood'[7] is introduced, then, in the first line of the play, and mentioned repeatedly thereafter (148–50, 170, 339ff., 353–4, 798ff., 1259ff.). The intention can scarcely be 'to rub in the impossibility of the legend'.[8] The story is presented as no miracle but bald fact, and the very avoidance of precise detail is an inducement to take it seriously. When Euripides has misgivings about the veracity of a myth he generally expresses them in no uncertain terms. Thus his Helen alludes dubiously to the story of her birth from an egg (*Hel.* 256f.), and the chorus of the *Electra* deny that the sun could ever have changed its course because of a mortal's crimes (*El.*

6. For Euripides' innovations in the myth see Wilamowitz, II, 109–13.

7. Victor Ehrenburg, 'Tragic Heracles', in *Aspects of the Ancient World* (New York 1946), p. 162.   8. *Ibid.*

736ff.). No such irony, no such doubts are to be found here. We can only assume that if Euripides chose to emphasize his hero's dual fatherhood it was because he saw a certain significance in it.

If we are willing to follow the development of the play as a whole in all its apparent vagaries, the significance of the dual fatherhood emerges. The theme provides a kind of counterpoint to the general movement of the play: it links Heracles' present to his past, his deeds to his birth, and thus helps to soften the unexpectedness of the episode of madness – for that episode too can be traced to the circumstances of his begetting. From his two fathers Heracles has inherited aspects both divine and human. At the opening of the play his divine inheritance seems to prevail. His family and the chorus invoke him in heroic terms; the only dissenting voice is Lycus', and Lycus seems sufficiently refuted when Heracles returns miraculously from the underworld, rescues his family and puts Lycus himself to death. In the middle of the play we are shown Heracles gone mad, transformed into something less than human. In the third part the hero, restored to his senses, must reassess his view of himself. He realizes that he is no longer semi-divine but all too mortal, no longer invincible but weak and in need of human aid. The references to Heracles' parentage seem – though somewhat imperfectly and inconsistently – to keep step with these changes in the fortunes of the hero. A review of the action of the play may help to demonstrate the function of the dual fatherhood motif, as well as to point to the more general links among the episodes.

Euripides introduces his hero by way of his family – a family so dependent on him that their very existence is threatened by his absence. They are 'conventional' people: that is, each, in contrast to the extraordinary Heracles, reminds us of other Euripidean figures. Like Iolaus in the *Heraclidae* or Adrastus in the *Supplices* Amphitryon has outlived his usefulness as a warrior, outlived men far younger and stronger than himself. Like Iphis in the *Supplices* he will try to dissuade his companion, a high-spirited young woman, from rashly throwing away her life.

Like Cadmus in the *Bacchae* Amphitryon has given much thought to the manifestation of divinity in the family. It is Amphitryon who first directs attention to the phenomenon of Heracles' dual fatherhood. He seems in fact to be engaged in a perpetual and one-

sided rivalry with Zeus; at every point he measures his own conduct against the god's and finds Zeus wanting. Thus he speaks of
what would happen 'if Zeus showed a sense of justice toward us'
(212); claims that he, mortal though he is, surpasses Zeus in *arete*
(342); and addresses his final prayer to Zeus ('but in vain', he
remarks bitterly, 501) while Megara is addressing hers to Heracles.
Later he alludes angrily to the gods' callousness (1115, reading
μάθοι), and implicates Zeus in the disaster that has struck Heracles
(1127). If the rivalry has its comic aspects (for there is no doubt
as to the origins of Amphitryon's hostility) the old man's accusa-
tions still draw attention to an important circumstance of Heracles'
existence.

It is not unusual for Euripides to balance against his old men
some younger woman, a daughter or daughter-in-law. So Alcestis
forms a counterpoise to Pheres, Macaria to Iolaus, Evadne to
Iphis and Adrastus. Amphitryon finds himself at odds with his
daughter-in-law Megara. As the play opens the pair have fled
with Heracles' children to the altar of Zeus Soter (48) in an
attempt to escape the persecutions of Lycus. Amphitryon remarks
that they are in an ἀπορία σωτηρίας (54); perhaps he is suggesting
that Zeus has failed to live up to his name. Nevertheless he is
inclined to wait and hope for the best. Megara, in contrast, draws
the most pessimistic conclusions from their situation. She presses
Amphitryon to admit that they have no grounds for hope, for she
herself would prefer an immediate death to prolonging their
misery.

The disagreement between Amphitryon and Megara never
grows into a formal *agon*, and it is in any case only temporary.
When Lycus appears and informs them that he means to burn
them alive at the altar, Megara and Amphitryon confront their
now certain death in a joint stand of dignity and courage.[9] However, their earlier disagreement has its reverberations later in the
play: the contrasting attitudes embodied in the old man and the

9. Burnett, *Catastrophe Survived*, pp. 161–2, accuses Megara and Amphitryon
of behaving like 'non-suppliants', and breaking the suppliant pattern by
abandoning sanctuary. She does not seem sufficiently to acknowledge that their
situation has changed drastically upon Lycus' entrance, and become entirely
hopeless: if they do not now leave the altar voluntarily they will be burnt alive.
Under the circumstances they can hardly be blamed for choosing a milder
form of death.

young woman will recur in the debate between Theseus and Heracles at the end. In each case the question is the same: should the shifting fortunes of human life be the occasion for hopefulness or despair? The dialogue between Amphitryon and Megara is broken off by events, so the audience must await the end of the play for an answer to the question.

Lycus is another conventional character; it has often been pointed out that he has the standard qualities of a tyrant.[10] He is as wicked and confident as Polymnestor, as brutally candid as Eteocles.[11] His estimation of Heracles is in sharp contrast to the family's: he refers insultingly to the story of Heracles' birth (148–9) and disparages the absent hero's accomplishments. Amphitryon does not deign to answer the first charge: that, he says, is Zeus' affair (170–1). But he can and will defend Heracles against the charge of cowardice. So Lycus' attack becomes the pretext for a celebration of Heracles (174–203).

The praise of Heracles is continued in the first *stasimon* – the evocation of his labors (348–435) showing the hero in his mythical aspect, in contrast to the familial context of the previous scene. When the members of the chorus lament their decrepitude (436ff.) their complaints serve to heighten the sense of the distance between those *philoi* who are unwilling or unable to help Megara and her family,[12] and Heracles with his youth and strength and loyalty. All hope rests on him, and he is not there (434–5).

But then he returns, at the very moment Megara and Amphitryon are preparing to die: he comes back from the dead to save his family. His arrival in the nick of time is a device for heightening dramatic suspense, to be sure; but it may also be a further proof of his abilities. Euripidean characters do not invariably return at the most propitious moment. Some, like Pentheus, arrive too late to stop what is happening; others, like Orestes in the *Electra*, by their

10. 'Lykos ist nicht mehr als ein gewöhnlicher Bühnenbösewicht' (Wilamowitz II, 118). Cf. Zürcher, *Darstellung...*, p. 20.

11. Like Eteocles he claims to be acting out of *eulabeia* (166; cf. *Ph.* 782).

12. For the distinction between unwilling and unable cf. 55–6. Professor John Herington has suggested to me an alternate meaning for these lines: Amphitryon might be playing on the two meanings of *philoi* ('relations' as well as 'friends') and referring to Zeus in 55, in 56 to Heracles. There is support for such an interpretation in 346 and in 430, where the family's lack of *philoi* is discussed in the context of Heracles' absence in Hades.

very arrival precipitate a crisis; still others, like Medea, themselves create the interval of time they require for their designs. In each case the timing seems appropriate to the character in question.

The arrival of Heracles signals the transition from the first part of the play to the second, from the 'suppliant action'[13] to the episode of madness and murder. The scene of Heracles' return offers the audience its only glimpse of the hero before he is stricken by madness, its only chance to test the reports of him against the actuality of his presence. In the hope of establishing some co-herence in the development of the hero Wilamowitz, followed by others, has tried to discover traces of madness in Heracles from the first moments of his homecoming.[14] Yet such an interpretation is contradicted by the text. On his arrival Heracles shows none of the conventional signs of madness, such as confusion or excessive choler.[15] He is alert to his surroundings: on noticing an ill-omened bird he takes the precaution of coming in secret to the palace (596–8). His threats against the disloyal Thebans and against Lycus are no more extreme, given his superior energy, than Amphitryon's at 232ff. or the even more debilitated chorus' at 254ff. Heracles is acting in the tradition of the conscientious king who on his return home must purge his city of hostile elements; one might compare his plans to the policy announced by Aeschylus' Agamemnon (*Ag.* 848–50) and actually carried out by Homer's Odysseus. There is no suggestion in the text that Heracles' plans are either hubristic or insane.

At the same time, however, it is made clear that violence is Heracles' natural mode of expression. His responses to Megara's account are of the simplest: anger, consternation, a vow of revenge. νῦν γὰρ τῆς ἐμῆς ἔργον χερός (565) – 'I will take this in hand', he says when he has understood the situation. Such simplicity

13. Cf. Burnett, *Castastrophe Survived*, pp. 159ff.

14. Wilamowitz, II, 129. He later abandoned his position: cf. *D. Lit. Zeit.* (1926), 853 = *Kl. Schr.* I, 466. But cf. Burnett, *Catastrophe Survived*, p. 168; E. M. Blaiklock, *The Male Characters of Euripides* (Wellington 1952), pp. 128ff.; Norwood, *Greek Tragedy*, p. 233; and Max Pohlenz, *Die griechische Tragödie*, 2nd ed. (Göttingen 1954), p. 297.

15. On conventional signs of madness in Greek literature cf. Ainsworth O'Brien Moore, *Madness in Ancient Literature* (diss. Princeton; Weimar 1924); and Josef Mattes, *Der Wahnsinn im griechischen Mythos und in der Dichtung bis zum Drama des fünften Jahrhunderts* (Heidelberg 1970).

appears characteristic: Heracles' account of his journey to the underworld is as unadorned as the rest of his discourse, laconic to the point of absurdity.[16]

Although the violence and simplicity of Heracles are suggested in the scene of his return, the dominant note is affection. 'O most beloved of men!' Megara greets him. For Amphitryon, Heracles is 'light returning to his father'.[17] A good king in his zeal to purge the city, a loving husband and father and son[18] – no shadow is cast either on Heracles' character or on his accomplishments.

As Heracles goes indoors, his children clinging to him, the members of the chorus sing in his honor. Like many another chorus in tragedy this one has tended to interpret the universe in terms of the protagonist's fortunes. During Heracles' absence the old men had been painfully aware of their own age and helplessness. Now, when he has returned and by his youthful strength saved his family from death, they proclaim youth as the greatest imaginable blessing, and they propose a change in the order of things to accord with their vision (655–68).[19] They suggest that if the gods had both ξύνεσις and σοφία in regard to men – both perception and good judgment – they would grant all good men a second youth, at once rewarding the virtuous and making them readily identifiable to all.[20] Such a proposal is to be found elsewhere in Euripides,[21] but it is particularly appropriate here because Heracles himself has just returned, in a sort of second birth, from the world of the dead.

16. The same note is struck in the *Alcestis* when Heracles describes his wrestling match with Thanatos in the fewest possible words (1140). Far from casting doubt on the reality of what is being described, these terse accounts make the point that for Heracles such exploits are all in a day's work.

17. As Wilamowitz points out (III, 124) Amphitryon's words echo Heracles' own greeting to the house a few lines earlier, at 524.

18. There seems no necessity to emend the text at 575 from γέροντι to τεκόντι as Wilamowitz, following Wakefield, has done; nor to explain the nomenclature as a symptom of madness as Murray does. Heracles seems to refer to Amphitryon within a few lines indifferently as πατήρ (at 533, 587, 619), and γέρων (at 544, 556).

19. For the relationship between this *stasimon* and the play as a whole cf. Heinz Neitzel, *Die dramatische Funktion der Chorlieder in den Tragödien des Euripides* (diss. Hamburg 1967), pp. 11–41.

20. Wilamowitz' translation of these lines, which gives *xunesis* to the gods and *sophia* to men, does not seem possible.

21. *Supp.* 1080ff.

In spite of their relief the members of the chorus are still troubled, for they see incongruities at every level of existence. Their formulation suggests that the gods do not in fact have men in mind at all; or if they do, that their judgment diverges from men's. These two possibilities had already been anticipated by Amphitryon when he remarked that Zeus must be either out of touch or unjust (347).[22] In addition to the incongruities between men and gods, there are divergences among men. A man can read the skies, but he cannot make out another man's character from his face (665–8). The notion of disparity touched on here will acquire importance from the episode of madness, for a madman's perceptions are incongruous with those of other men; and again from the last scene of the play, in which Heracles' own life will be used to demonstrate the gulf between men and gods.

The *stasimon* ends with a positive assertion of Heracles' divine origins. Διὸς ὁ παῖς (696): 'he is the son of Zeus'. Through birth and deeds he seems to have travelled a long way toward immortality.

Lycus is presently lured indoors in one of those scenes of deception which are often found in Euripides.[23] At no point is it suggested that Heracles is wrong to kill Lycus: the man is only getting his just deserts (760).[24] The righteous murder of the tyrant prompts the chorus to revert once more to the theme of Heracles' paternity (798ff.). In reasserting his dual fatherhood the members of the chorus seem to retreat slightly from the emphasis of their statement at 696, but their conclusion is essentially the same as before. The truth of Zeus' role in the engendering of Heracles has been confirmed beyond all question by Heracles' ἀλκή (805), against Lycus' slanders (148–9) and their own earlier doubts (353–4).

Yet at this very moment everything changes. Two apparitions appear, and the old men are struck by a surge of terror (816).[25] Of

22. For the *amathia* of the gods cf. *Or.* 417 and *IT* 386 (where Iphigenia refuses to apply the epithet to Artemis).

23. The device of luring someone indoors in order to murder him recurs in the *Electra*, *Hecuba* and *Orestes*.

24. For the contrary view see Burnett, *Catastrophe Survived*, p. 166.

25. *pitulos* signifies, as Wilamowitz explains *ad loc.*, the 'rhythm of disharmony' (III, 179). On the word see also Charles Segal, 'Nature and the World of Man in Greek Literature', *Arion* II, no. 1 (1963), 42.

the two Iris speaks first: to reassure the members of the chorus that they are themselves in no danger, and to set forth Hera's point of view. For Hera is presented as the ultimate source of the madness that strikes Heracles. Because this is the first and last time that Hera's motives for dispatching Lyssa will be explained, the speech deserves consideration.

In fact the explanation is only hinted at, but it is accepted so unquestioningly by characters within the play that the audience has no reason to suspect it. Iris begins by saying that she has come in search of 'one man, whom they call the son of Zeus and Alcmena' (825–6). There may be a note of doubt, a distant allusion to the complexities of Heracles' parentage in the φασίν; but Hera herself obviously considers Heracles the true son of Zeus. For that is the prime and sole explanation of her hostility. We are reminded that Hera too is related, in an oblique sort of way, to Heracles. She is the wronged wife of the story as Amphitryon is the wronged husband; but whereas Amphitryon bears Heracles no grudge, Hera hates him for his very existence. Once again a mortal outstrips a god in *arete*.

No further explanation for Hera's anger is ever given, but none seems required. Everyone in the play assumes that Hera was the agent of Heracles' undoing (cf. 1127–8, 1191, 1263–4). As for the audience, the repeated references to Heracles' parentage have in a sense laid the groundwork for this new development, and made Hera's anger seem, if no less unjust, at least less trivial and unexpected.

The origins of Hera's resentment may be plain, but its persistence is awesome. After all, Heracles has shown himself the very best of mortals: he has devoted his strength to the service of his fellow men and accorded due piety to the gods (48–50, 375–9, 849–53). There seems to be no connection between his past accomplishments and his present punishment, and this discrepancy has troubled commentators as it troubles Lyssa. Moreover, the labors should have been sufficient punishment to satisfy Hera; in the traditional version of the myth they too can be traced to her machinations. This play, however, ascribes to them a different origin. Amphitryon had expressed doubt at the very beginning whether τὸ χρή or Hera was responsible for the labors (20–1); now Iris provides an answer. As long as Heracles was busy wth his labors, she informs us, Necessity preserved him; nor would Zeus allow Hera to interfere with him (827–9). Destiny then, not Hera, was the sponsor of the labors; far from being a punishment, they have shielded Heracles from the goddess' anger and allowed him to attain an uncommon glory. So Hera has not yet had her wish in regard to Heracles. And she will be 'nowhere' (841) if she does not get her way, for it is almost a definition of divinity that its will must be done. A god's wishes may be postponed, as in the innumerable cases where justice comes slowly, or they may have a self-imposed time limit (as in the *Ajax*, where Athena's anger will last for one day only); but they may not go unfulfilled. Heracles' challenge to Hera lies not in his accomplishments but in the fact that he has escaped his due punishment so long – he has been evading it ever since she sent the serpents to his cradle (1266–8). Heracles' madness must be understood in terms not of his own guilt but of Hera's will, a will offended by his very begetting. There is a sense in which his situation can be generalized: everyone is guiltless of his parentage but pays the penalty for it all his life.

The second divinity is Lyssa, who introduces herself with a genealogy which Euripides seems to have fashioned to suit his own purposes.[26] Lyssa might have claimed kinship with the Erinyes, who are born of Gaia and of the blood of Ouranos (*Theog.* 185); or with the Moirai, the Keres, Eris and Apate, who are the parthenogenetic daughters of Night (*Theog.* 211ff.). Instead Euripides makes his Lyssa the daughter at once of Ouranos and of Night: the one a celestial, the other a chthonic divinity. Like Heracles himself, she is the product of two divergent elements.

The descriptions of Heracles' madness offered by both Lyssa and the Messenger help to place it in its proper context. His madness is a matter not of sickness[27] but of abnormality: both mind and

26. Wilamowitz, III, 184. Aeschylus takes similar liberties with Hesiodic genealogies – cf. Anne Lebeck, *The Oresteia: A Study in Language and Structure* (Cambridge, Mass. 1971), pp. 127–8.

27. E. M. Blaiklock, *Male Characters in Euripides*, maintains that Heracles' madness is merely an epileptic fit, 'a tragic example of one of these states of automatism which sometimes takes the place of an epileptic convulsion' (p. 127). However, such a theory leaves the role of Heracles' madness in the play unexplained. Mere physical illness is the least interesting of subjects for a dramatist, for it has in itself no moral significance. If Blaiklock's theory is unsatisfactory in itself his development of it is equally so. He relies on modern accounts of epilepsy for his parallels rather than on ancient ones and has a

body function in a fashion different from other men's.[28] The eyes are normally organs of perception and expression: Heracles' eyes no longer perform either role. His hearing has gone awry, for he is deaf to his family's pleas and warnings. The silence, the wild laughter described by the Messenger (930, 935) signal a divorce from *logos*. Even Heracles' breathing is no longer controlled (869). His bearing has lost the particular expressiveness of a human being and become as inscrutable as an animal's (cf. 869, where Lyssa compares him to a bull). In the final stage of his madness[29] he not only loses all sense of his surroundings but fails to respond to the most imperious human taboos. He disregards one suppliant, Amphitryon; and kills another, his own son. Methodically, 'like a blacksmith' (992) he slaughters his children and his wife. Except for Athena's intervention he would have murdered Amphitryon as well.

Amphitryon's survival is part of the myth and essential to the play's structure,[30] but it is also appropriate to Euripides' thematic purposes. His survival here, like his desire to continue living in the first episode, suggests that there is some small margin for hope even in the midst of disaster, and prefigures the choice of life over death that his son will make in the last scene.

Heracles has killed his family and brought his palace crashing down.[31] Now he lies unconscious, trussed up like an animal: a creature as abject and pitiable as he was once enviable and proud. The chorus' laments mark the change in his fortunes. Earlier the old men had found their inspiration in Apollo's Linos

---

tendency to misuse details, as when he interprets Heracles' wariness in entering the city as a display of 'the suspicious character and the persecution complex of epileptics' (p. 128). By that standard every Greek in literature who paid attention to bird omens must be considered an epileptic.

28. For a discussion of the relationship between disorder of perception and disorder of the mind see Michael Simpson, 'Sophocles' Ajax: His Madness and Transformation', *Arethusa* II, no. 1 (1969), 89–90.

29. Heracles seems to go mad in three stages. When he first suspends the sacrifice (928) he still recognizes Amphitryon and is still aware of his surroundings. At 947 he embarks on an imaginary journey to Mycenae; and after he 'arrives' there (963) begins to kill his family.

30. Wilamowitz, III, 113, points out that Amphitryon is the only character in the play who is present from beginning to end.

31. The destruction of the palace echoes the destruction of the hero. Cf. J. Wohlberg, 'The Palace–Hero Equation in Euripides', *AAntHung* 16 (1968), 149–55.

song (348ff.) and in the paean of the Delian maidens (687ff.); now they can only sing a requiem for the dead (1026). They are puzzled by Zeus' cruelty toward his own son (1086–7) – and in fact the distance and indifference of Heracles' divine father (and of the gods in general) will form a subdued contrast throughout the scene to the tenderness and loyalty of his human father (and of mortals in general).

The first thing that Heracles notices on awakening is the clear sky above him (1090) – a sign that his sanity is restored.[32] He is as ignorant of his situation as when he first arrived home, but this is a different kind of ignorance. Heracles, the ship not moored to *tuchē* (203), the lead ship who drew his children after him like small boats (631–2), now realizes that he has been in a storm (1091ff.). Beyond that he recalls nothing; as far as he can tell he is surrounded by unknown corpses (1097).

When Amphitryon comes forward Heracles recognizes him instantly. His first word to the old man is 'Father!' (1111), and Amphitryon replies: 'My child! For you *are* mine even in your trouble' (1113, and cf. also 1192). The affection that was so evident in the scene of Heracles' return has survived Heracles' murderous attack on his family. Amphitryon is a model of tact and compassion as he prepares Heracles for the revelation of what has occurred. Heracles' amnesia is complete, and at first his reactions are of the simplest: he is ashamed at being tied up (1124) and ready to blame Hera for anything that may have occurred (1128). But such attitudes are no longer appropriate. They belong to his previous proud self, and Amphitryon does not allow him to persist in them but guides him first to the realization of his own accountability (1129), then to the recognition that the corpses are his own children's (1131), and finally to the full story of the murders (1135). Heracles reacts as violently in grief and self-hatred as he had reacted in anger to the news of Lycus' usurpation. His first impulse is toward suicide; it is only Theseus' arrival that checks him.

Heracles in his madness had not recognized his family; now Theseus fails to recognize Heracles, veiled and stricken as he is. Amphitryon identifies his son in heroic terms as the giant-killer of

32. Cf. G. Devereux, 'The Psychotherapy Scene in Euripides' *Bacchae*', *JHS* 90 (1970), 41.

Phlegraia (1192–4). Theseus replies in a very different tone: φεῦ φεῦ· τίς ἀνδρῶν ὧδε δυσδαίμων ἔφυ; (1195) – 'Was ever mortal so unfortunate?' Amphitryon agrees that he knows no man (*thnetos*, 1197) who has suffered so much. The exchange sets the tone for the scene: again and again Theseus will remind Heracles of his mortality. If birth and *arete* had earlier proved Heracles the son of Zeus, his crimes have sent him back to earth again.

Like Amphitryon, Theseus is loyal to the unhappy Heracles. He has come to help him, and the first necessity, as he sees it, is for Heracles to remove the cloak he has thrown over his head. Theseus argues first that he does not care about pollution: he wants to share Heracles' ill fortune as he shared his good (1220ff.). Heracles has never before had any bad fortune worth sharing; this is the first time reciprocity has been in question. Theseus' very solicitude is another indication of how much Heracles' situation has changed.

Theseus' second argument is that Heracles' actions cannot affect the divine order in any case: 'Mortal that you are, you cannot taint what is the gods'' (1232). The remark recalls Creon's assertion in the *Antigone* that no man can pollute the gods (*Ant.* 1043–4). Such statements obviously acquire their color from their contexts. Here the emphasis seems to be on Heracles' mortality and on the distance between the divine and the mortal spheres, the indifference of the gods to matters that mortals take seriously. Heracles' misfortunes would seem to demonstrate the same point.

As the two discuss Heracles' predicament Theseus repeatedly rebukes his friend. His misfortune, he remarks, reaches sky-high (1240). Heracles must not be presumptuous or he will be punished (1244). When Heracles takes these words to heart and in discouragement reverts to the idea of suicide, Theseus tries a different approach. Now he reminds Heracles of his former glory, his obligation to live up to his reputation (1248, 1250, 1252, 1254). Heracles' past and present are in contradiction; some reassessment seems to be in order.

That is precisely what Heracles undertakes. He does not invoke the theory of ebb and flow in human fortunes that had been put forward early in the play by Amphitryon (101–6) and is implicitly accepted by Theseus in this scene (1224–5), but promises rather to demonstrate that his life has been a total loss (1255ff.). His existence was built on a bad foundation, he explains: he inherited pollution from Amphitryon and the burden of Hera's enmity from Zeus. He had to contend as an infant with deadly serpents, as a young man with the endless drudgery of the labors – and now, as his last and worst labor, he has killed his own family. Reviewing his life, he sees it as intolerable from beginning to end.

In this speech Heracles sounds for the last time the theme of his double fatherhood. Having attributed his ill luck to a bad inheritance from both Amphitryon and Zeus (1258–64), he turns to Amphitryon and adds:

σὺ μέντοι μηδὲν ἀχθεσθῇς, γέρον·
πατέρα γὰρ ἀντὶ Ζηνὸς ἡγοῦμαι σὲ ἐγώ. (1264–5)

Don't be pained, old man – I think of you as my father, not Zeus.

He has just explicitly stated, with no sense of a biological contradiction, the fact that he has two fathers. But he is aware of the spiritual contradiction involved in being simultaneously the son of Zeus and of Amphitryon, and now at last he makes a choice. At this moment of defeat and anguish he explicitly acknowledges his share of mortality, his human father. This mortality is what Theseus has been insisting on throughout the scene, and as Heracles admits the justice of the case the theme of the dual fatherhood takes its final place in the scheme of the play.

But the play is not yet at an end – Heracles still has to deal with his own bitterness and with the practical consequences of his situation. If the disaster has overshadowed his past glory it has also ruined his future. Let Hera dance, he says bitterly (1303); like Heracles himself (1133) she has triumphed in a war that was no war, defeating 'the benefactor of Greece, a man utterly innocent' (1309–10). Heracles understands that there is no connection between his conduct and his punishment. It was all a matter of Hera's will (1305).

Lycus had threatened Heracles' family with death although they were innocent of wrongdoing; Heracles all unknowingly carried out Lycus' plan. The murder itself constituted the worst of punishments for the murderer, who had done nothing to deserve such suffering. These events imply a frightening absence of cause and effect in the workings of things. The will of the gods, that traditional epic theme, has been shown to operate not even contrary to human justice, but with no reference to it at all.

Such conclusions are implicit in the play, but Heracles' reasoning does not lead him that far. Although Theseus agrees that the disaster was Hera's doing (1311–12), he is less interested in the origin and significance of Heracles' madness than in the immediate question of his friend's future. Once more he spells out his lesson: Heracles must accept what destiny has given him. The gods themselves submit to ill treatment from one another – why should Heracles, mortal that he is (θνητὸς γεγώς, 1320) expect any special privileges? But along with his homily Theseus also provides what help he can by offering Heracles asylum in Athens.

Heracles addresses himself briefly to the theoretical portion of Theseus' speech (1340–6). His words have caused difficulties for commentators; Lesky, for instance, remarks:

> The poet speaks suddenly from the mask of his hero...he denies the idle tales of bards about the immortals' adultery and hostility and raises before us an image of a god who has no wants outside himself. The whole play was motivated by Hera's wrath and in perplexity we ask ourselves whether the poet does not invalidate the presuppositions of his own work by such criticism.[33]

Heracles' words make better sense within the play than without it; there is no reason not to suppose that here as elsewhere he is expressing his own opinions rather than 'the poet's'. Heracles seems to be addressing himself directly to the two generalizations offered by Theseus at 1316 and 1317: that the gods commit adultery with one another, and that divine sons put their divine fathers in chains.[34] On the contrary, their life on Olympus is harmonious, Heracles maintains. Unlike human beings, they do not have to hurt each other to gain their desires. The gods' conduct toward human beings is a different matter: there Theseus' examples might find a distorted application to Heracles' own life. Adultery between a god and a mortal woman was responsible for Heracles' existence, and a divine father has allowed his mortal son to be tied up in chains. But these are matters that Heracles does not choose to analyze. Though he harbors a deep resentment against Hera, his fundamental faith in the gods remains unshaken, and he chooses to condemn the false stories that have been told

33. Albin Lesky, *A History of Greek Literature*, trans. James Willis and Cornelis de Heer (London 1966), p. 382.

34. G. M. A. Grube, *The Drama of Euripides*, 2nd ed. (New York 1961), p. 58.

about the gods rather than the gods themselves.[35] His need to keep faith with established religious ideas is a measure of the limitations Euripides has set on his hero and his play. But it is simultaneously an indication of Heracles' optimistic nature. Ultimately he adheres to the point of view advanced by Amphitryon at the opening of the play. He would rather be hopeful than succumb to despair as Megara did; he would rather stay alive than commit suicide.

Heracles' speculative mood does not last long. Such thoughts are *parerga* (1340), foreign to his way of life; he soon reverts to the problem of his future. His reason for rejecting the idea of suicide is characteristic: he does not want to be open to a charge of cowardice (1348). In this he is the old Heracles. But changes have taken place. He, who never wept before, now weeps (1354–5), yielding to physical weakness and grief beyond the point Theseus thinks proper (1410ff.). At last he takes his leave, leaning on Theseus. Even his posture is consistent with his acceptance of mortality. The gods, he has just informed us (1354–6), need nothing. In accepting Theseus' support Heracles acknowledges his distance from the gods and his need of mortal help.

As the play draws to an end the irony of Amphitryon's opening speech is now brought home. Amphitryon had introduced himself as an exile and an involuntary homicide; so now is his son. Amphitryon had spoken of Heracles leading his bride home to the the sound of flutes: now Heracles arranges for Megara's burial and himself departs to the sound of wailing.[36] Structurally the play has come full circle.

If there is a lingering sense of incompleteness, it is perhaps because Heracles himself seems to misinterpret his experiences. His madness has cost him his family, and his grief is presented in all its harshness. But in seeing his whole life as one continuous misfortune Heracles seems to misread its lesson. His madness has at any rate solved the dilemma implicit in his dual fatherhood: it has forced him to choose mortality and Amphitryon. (And was not this what Hera had in mind all along?) The audience knows that the labors were no prelude to his punishment, but actually

35. On the Pindar-like aspect of his position cf. Burnett, *Catastrophe Survived,* pp. 174–5.

36. Cf. *Alc.* 914ff., where the contrast between now and then, marriage and mourning, is explicitly drawn.

protected him from Hera's anger. Moreover, it can see that Heracles' actions do not accord with his pessimistic conclusions. He decides to go on living, and to make such a choice is to have found some reason to hope.

Euripides has here reversed the usual sense of the Heracles story: instead of a man becoming a hero, he has shown us a hero becoming a man. He has accomplished this shift in meaning primarily by rearranging the mythic material to make Heracles' career culminate in disaster rather than in triumph; but he has underscored it by his treatment of the motif of Heracles' dual fatherhood. At the outset Zeus' share in engendering Heracles is generally accepted, though occasionally questioned. By the middle of the play Heracles seems to have confirmed his divine inheritance beyond any doubt. With his madness and the accompanying change in his fortunes, however, his mortal heritage comes to the fore; and finally Heracles himself proclaims Amphitryon as his true father – not as a matter of historical fact, but as a matter of emotional choice. In fact, Euripides has done in this play what he has done elsewhere as well (in the *Alcestis*, for instance): he demonstrates that the extraordinary privileges of his mythical characters may bring them nothing but grief, but that there is in compensation a certain comfort, or at the very least an abiding interest, in the circumstance of being a man.[37]

37. I would like to express my gratitude to Professor Cedric Whitman, who directed the Harvard dissertation on which this essay is based, and to Professor John Herington, who gave me generous advice and assistance in revising it to its present form.

The first *stasimon* of Euripides' *Electra*

GEORGE B. WALSH

EURIPIDES' narrative choral odes continue to trouble the critics. The hymn to the Mountain Mother in the *Helen*, the hymn to Apollo in *Iphigenia among the Taurians*, the song of the wedding of Peleus and Thetis in *Iphigenia in Aulis*, and the song of Achilles' armor in the *Electra* were once generally regarded as having little or nothing to do with the plays in which they appear. They were thought to be dithyrambic, essentially non-dramatic compositions, or *embolima* of the type Agathon is supposed to have written. These odes are now better appreciated, and we have learned to look in them for clues to the meaning of his plays, but we still condemn or defend their dramatic relevance according to an Aeschylean or Sophoclean model. We want a larger definition of the function of choral song in drama, and a critical approach to Euripides' odes that will reveal their meaning without obscuring their peculiar complexity.

Euripides' narrative songs may be better understood if we compare them with another more familiar type of Euripidean lyric, which we may call the escape ode. In an escape ode the chorus sings of its own or of someone else's escape from the present dramatic situation, with great elaboration and emphasis. Such odes also characteristically insist upon a sharp contrast between the dramatic location and the scene of escape; the style of escape lyric is more ornate than that of most other Euripidean odes, and so more distinctly differentiated from the language of dialogue;[1] the mood of escape odes is generally lighter than that of the dramatic context, with happiness either celebrated or anticipated. The four narrative songs named earlier exhibit all the salient features of an escape ode, except that they are not cast in the form of an escape wish: they lack a statement in the first person optative. The most striking feature of the *Electra* ode, for example,

1. Cf. Smereka, *Studia Euripidea*, vol. 1 (Leopoli 1936), pp. 125ff.

is its contrast with the immediate dramatic context. Escape odes commonly project a change of place from the dramatic action, describing distant and happy scenes;[2] the first *stasimon* of the *Electra* adds other sorts of change. For example, it provides a contrast with the dramatic situation by turning from the present to the remote past. But this is just what an escape ode does: it creates a breach in the ongoing dramatic action. The ode shifts the focus of the spectator's attention away from the situation and events of the play, by evoking distant scenes and events of the past which differ sharply from those taking place on stage. As the chorus turns away from the stage, it tells us what is outside the reality of the play, and so it provides a foil for defining the dramatic situation itself.

On the other hand, the first *stasimon* of the *Electra*, like an escape ode or any other choral lyric in drama, is bound to the action of the play by shared themes and verbal echoes. The particular kind of thematic link joining ode and context may vary, depending on the content of the ode. In the escape ode of the *Bacchae* (lines 370–432), for example, where the escape wish is expressed as part of a statement of moral belief, the explicit link between ode and play is the chorus' condemnation of Pentheus. The first *stasimon* of the *Electra*, which is almost exclusively narrative, is related to its context in another way. The events and persons of the lyric narrative are analogous to the events and persons of the drama, and much of the meaning of the ode may be found by pursuing this analogy.

Regardless of the difference between an escape ode and narrative ode in the forms that their thematic connection to the drama may take, the basic problems in understanding them remain the same. Both types of ode are characterized by the combination of two apparently contradictory features: thematic relevance to the dramatic situation, and contrast with it. Critics tend to emphasize one or the other in arguing a case for relevance or irrelevance, but it is the combination of the two that determines the ode's dramatic function. The contrast between ode and play produces something like the *Verfremdungseffekt*. Dramatic illusion, which allows an audience to become closely involved with stage events,

2. If the play is set in Greece, for example, then the chorus looks to exotic places for release; if, as in *Iphigenia among the Taurians*, the scene of the play is remote from Greece, then the chorus yearns for familiar landscapes.

must be disturbed by an ode that offers a strikingly different illusion of reality. When the dramatic illusion is weakened, the spectator is kept at a distance from the action on stage so that he can critically evaluate what he sees.[3] The themes and images shared by the ode and the dramatic action – the implicit analogy between events and persons of lyric and stage – point to the problems that the spectator is called upon to evaluate.

Since the contrast between the ode and its context is the most obvious feature of their relationship, I shall begin with that. One of the means used to make the ode stand apart from the action is style: the lyric is highly decorated, the iambic dialogue relatively stark. The style of the first *stasimon* of the *Electra* also has a particular quality that suits the subject matter of the ode. As the chorus turns from the present dramatic situation to the remote past, the ode is given an appropriately strong Homeric flavor by epic-Ionic diction and dialectal features.[4] Its glorification of heroic times is inflated still more by the elaborate sound play of τοῖς ἀμετρήτοις ἐρετμοῖς (433), or ποτανοῖσι πεδίλοισι (460).

The ode turns to the past in progressive stages,[5] with each

3. Cf. Barrett's commentary on the second *stasimon* of the *Hippolytus* (Oxford 1964), p. 297, and for a different view, Grégoire's commentary on the third *stasimon* of the *Helen* (Paris 1950), p. 105. Even without lyric interruption, the spectator may be prevented from becoming emotionally involved with stage events: Bernard Knox, 'Euripidean Comedy', in *The Rarer Action*, ed. Alan Cheuse and Richard Koffler (New Brunswick 1970), p. 71, remarks of the action preceding the first *stasimon* of the *Electra*, that 'we are being invited, not to identify ourselves with the passions and destinies of heroic souls, but to detach ourselves and observe the actions and reactions of ordinary human beings'. The repeated use of musical imagery in Euripides' plays may have a similar effect: by reminding us that the action of the drama has been formed by the hand of a poet, it is 'part of the general technique of holding the audience at a distance' (A. P. Burnett, *Catastrophe Survived* (Oxford 1971), p. 92, n. 10). Stinton suggests that the rhetoric of *agon* scenes may also produce a 'suspension of emotional issues' (*Euripides and the Judgment of Paris* (London 1965), p. 39). *Verfremdung* should perhaps be regarded as a standard feature of Euripidean dramaturgy.

4. E.g., the initial syllables of εἰλισσόμενος, and εἰνάλιον (Seidler, *metri gratia*); the epic endings of χρυσέων τευχέων and ἀελίοιο (on -*oio* endings, cf. Page on *Medea* 135, Barrett on *Hippolytus* 848–51); φυάν (the word in tragedy elsewhere only at Aeschylus, *Niobe* fr. 273 Mette, according to LSJ); ἱππότας (apparently derived from the Homeric ἱππότα and involving perhaps a confusion between Chiron, and Peleus ἱππηλάτα, for which see Denniston, *ad* 449); σάκος; ἴτυς (in a non-Homeric sense, but still rare); ἄωρ (Hartung's suggestion for δορί in 476).

5. See O. Panagl, *Die 'dithyrambischen Stasima' des Euripides* (diss., Vienna 1967), p. 90.

strophic movement taking a further step back in time: the voyage to Troy (432–41); the Nereids seeking out Achilles at home (442–51); the fabulous arms whose decoration depicts the deeds of heroes of a still earlier period (452–75, with the second antistrophe expanding on the strophe). This temporal movement away from the dramatic situation is analogous to the geographical movement of the escape ode of the *Hippolytus*.

The scene which immediately precedes the ode's vision of the past is dominated by the poverty apparent in the stage-set of the Farmer's cottage, the home of Agamemnon's daughter. The ode, in contrast, is imbued with the splendor of light and of gold: Achilles' arms in general (443), his helmet in particular (470), and the gleaming sun which shines in the center of his shield (464f.). The lively, joyful spirit of Achilles' journey to Troy is brought home by the images of dancing: the gamboling dolphins, the 'light-footed leap' of Achilles himself, the chorus of Nereids. All of this may be vividly evoked by the dancing of the dramatic chorus itself.[6] Electra, on the other hand, has shown herself too overwhelmed by the miseries of the present even to think of dancing (178ff.):

> οὐδ' ἱστᾶσα χορούς
> Ἀργείαις ἅμα νύμφαις
> εἱλικτὸν κρούσω πόδ' ἐμόν.
> δάκρυσι νυχεύω.
>
> Nor shall I set the chorus dancing,
> nor beat and turn my foot
> with the girls of Argos.
> I pass the night in tears.

There is a more telling, but less explicit, contrast between the ode and the characters of the play in their differing values. For the Farmer, the wealth which illuminates the figure of Achilles in the ode is useful, not glorious. It can help to feed guests, and purchase medicines[7] (426ff.), but only a little is necessary for one's daily wants and in this there is no difference between the rich man and the poor man. Orestes learns from his confrontation with the

6. Cf. H. D. F. Kitto, *Greek Tragedy* (London 1939), p. 343, n. 1, on the mimetic effect of the second *stasimon* in the *Helen*.

7. Denniston (*ad loc.*) finds the mention of medicines 'curious', but it underlines the pragmatism of the Farmer.

Farmer that neither wealth nor tales of heroic deeds such as those depicted on Achilles' shield can be a criterion of nobility (373ff.):

> πῶς οὖν τις αὐτὰ διαλαβὼν ὀρθῶς κρινεῖ;
> πλούτῳ; πονηρῷ τἄρα χρήσεται κριτῇ.
> ἢ τοῖς ἔχουσι μηδέν; ἀλλ' ἔχει νόσον
> πενία, διδάσκει δ' ἄνδρα τῇ χρείᾳ κακόν.
> ἀλλ' εἰς ὅπλ' ἔλθω; τίς δὲ πρὸς λόγχην βλέπων
> μάρτυς γένοιτ' ἂν ὅστις ἐστὶν ἀγαθός;
> κράτιστον εἰκῇ ταῦτ' ἐᾶν ἀφειμένα.

> Then how may a man discriminate
> and judge the matter rightly?
> By wealth? He'll consult a poor judge there.
> By poverty? But poverty's diseased, and
> teaches a man to be base by need.
> Shall I look to battle? But who could be
> witness to another's courage
> when he faces the enemy's spear himself?
> It's best to let the question go.

Although Orestes' anti-heroic, even modern rejection of these criteria of human worth is not explicitly rebutted by the first *stasimon*, the two are evidently at odds. The ode cuts through Orestes' doubt with a vision of legendary heroism which takes for granted the importance of wealth and war, and in which each detail of the picture adds to a compelling impression of bygone splendor. On Achilles' shield, the most violent deeds are integrated in the order of the cosmos: the sun and the constellations occupy the center, the killing of monsters the periphery. In each part of the ode the gods' presence is manifest, as the Nereids accompany Achilles to Troy, and bring him his armor, and Hermes helps Perseus to slay the Gorgon. In the action of the play, Orestes has no god upon whose aid and direction he can rely, but only his dubious understanding of Apollo's oracle: ὦ Φοῖβε, πολλήν γ' ἀμαθίαν ἐθέσπισας ('Phoebus, your prophecy was stupid cruelty' (971)) is an outcry that accurately reflects the degree of confidence he feels in the god's moral guidance.

This contrast between the first *stasimon* and its context is only one facet of the ode's place in the drama. We have also to consider what themes and images are shared by the ode and the continuing action of the play, and what their significance might be. Some of the themes and images used in the ode reflect a conscious response on the part of the chorus to the dramatic situation; some anticipate events later in the play of which the chorus cannot be aware when it sings the first *stasimon*.

The meaning of the ode as it is consciously intended by the chorus may be deduced from the ode's rhetorical structure, which is not unlike that of the Pindaric epinician.[8] The first strophe celebrates Achilles' voyage to Troy, the antistrophe his enlistment as a warrior, and in both events the presence of the Nereids enhances his stature. In the second strophe and antistrophe, the heroic deeds depicted on his armor add to his brilliance. What glorifies Achilles glorifies Agamemnon in turn, as we are twice reminded that Achilles was Agamemnon's companion (440, 451 – in each case at the end of a stanza) and that Agamemnon was king of all the warriors at Troy (479f.).[9] Agamemnon becomes the *laudandus*, and everything in the ode a foil for praising him.

The rhetorical progression from the remote to the immediate, from Achilles to Agamemnon, and finally to Agamemnon's death at Clytemnestra's hands, runs parallel to a series of geographical references in the ode, in which each is successively closer to the scene of the drama: the voyage to Troy; the Nereids passing from Euboea to Pelion and Ossa; the story heard about the armor by the chorus at Nauplia.

The geographical progression, like the rhetorical one, ends in the epode, where the final link to the present situation is given. The epode connects the ode to the drama in several respects. In imagery, it replaces the brilliance of Achilles with the blood and dust of battle. Electra's actual situation, as we have seen it in the first episode, breaks in upon the romantic vision of the past: the Greek heroes are called δορίπονοι, recalling the πόνοι of which Electra repeatedly complains (e.g., 73, 120, 135). Finally, τοιγάρ (482) provides a logical connection between the ode and the dramatic situation:[10] Achilles was glorious, and so was his commander Agamemnon; Agamemnon was killed by Clytemnestra; Clytemnestra *therefore* must die, for having murdered such a hero.

---

8. For the use of Pindaric rhetoric in Euripides' lyric in general, see H. Parry, *The Choral Odes of Euripides* (diss., Berkeley 1963), *passim*.

9. Neitzel, *Die dramatische Funktion der Chorlieder in den Tragödien des Euripides* (Hamburg 1967), pp. 74f., calls this *Rangordnung*.

10. Cf. Parry, *Choral Odes of Euripides*, p. 93.

Why should this point be made after the first episode? Neitzel has suggested that the ode provides the key to Electra's motives in murdering her mother.[11] The vision of past glory represents what she has lost to Clytemnestra and Aegisthus, and so it is most effectively juxtaposed with the first episode's revelation of her humiliation and her hatred for those who have humiliated her. What the ode describes may also represent what Electra expects to gain by killing Clytemnestra and Aegisthus – the restoration of the heroic past. She seems to believe that this is both possible and desirable, and all her hopes depend on the arrival of Orestes. Thus, the ode's evocation of heroic times looks forward to the recognition scene in the following episode, when Electra discovers that Orestes is with her and that they are now in a position to win back what they have lost. If Orestes kills the man and woman who killed Agamemnon, who was in turn the commander of the glorious Achilles, then Orestes will place himself above all of them.

In Electra's eyes, Orestes is the heir to the qualities and rights she ascribes to Agamemnon. Agamemnon, for her as in the first *stasimon*, is the 'best man of Greece' (ἄνδρ' ἄριστον Ἑλλάδος, 1066). Having led the Greeks to Troy he deserved welcome and glory at home. Clytemnestra's crime consists in denying him his due, in meeting him not with the crown of victory, but with murder (οὐ μίτραισι γυνή σε δέξατ' οὐδ' ἐπὶ στεφάνοις, ξίφεσι δ' ἀμφιτόμοις, 163f.). When Orestes proves his manhood by killing Aegisthus, he asserts his proper claim to Agamemnon's heroic position, taking the crown won at Troy of which Agamemnon was deprived by Clytemnestra (88off.):

> ὦ καλλίνικε, πατρὸς ἐκ νικηφόρου
> γεγώς, Ὀρέστα, τῆς ὑπ' Ἰλίῳ μάχης,
> δέξαι κόμης σῆς βοστρύχων ἀνδήματα.[12]

It is Agamemnon's crown that Orestes wins, and so his act of vengeance recreates and completes the victory at Troy. When he kills Aegisthus, Orestes proves himself truly equal to his inherited position as the great man's son, τοῦ κλεινοῦ πατρὸς ἐκφύς (206), πατρὸς ἐκ νικηφόρου γεγώς (88of.).

Thus the first *stasimon* provides an index of Agamemnon's

11. Pp. 69ff.
12. This is essentially the Homeric view of Orestes' story: cf. *Od.* 1. 298ff.

stature, of the crime that destroyed him, and indirectly of the son who will avenge him. As Neitzel has suggested, the ode reflects Electra's attitude in these matters. But the more important question here, it seems to me, is not whether the chorus' vision of the past offers an accurate indication of Electra's motives and expectations, but how accurately its vision of the past reflects present reality as the continuing dramatic action defines it. How similar are the deeds of Electra and Orestes in the play to those of the heroes in the first *stasimon*? How are Electra and Orestes to be judged, against the standard set up by the ode? Finally, how is the ode itself to be judged as we see the results of Electra's and Orestes' attempt to imitate the model of heroic action it provides? All of these questions are posed by the analogy between Orestes and past heroes implicit in the rhetoric of the first *stasimon*. What we must consider more closely is the development of this analogy in the action of the play, as heroic achievement takes on a significance that the chorus did not consciously anticipate. Verbal cues recalling the first *stasimon* occur frequently later in the play, and mark the significant points of comparison between ode and action.

Electra expects Orestes to be an Achilles of the present, and her notion receives its first real test in the recognition scene following the first *stasimon*. Achilles, in the ode, is characterized by his 'light leap' (439), his 'swift-moving foot' (451); Orestes, as he emerges from the Farmer's hut, walks with a 'light nimble step' (549).[13] Orestes does not, however, fit the image Electra has expectantly embellished over the years. He has come in stealth, as Electra's ideal Savior never would (524ff.), and so the present begins to fall short of the heroic standard of the past.

The murders of Aegisthus and Clytemnestra are also prefigured in the imagery of the ode. In the ode, the nymphs who accompany Achilles to Troy and give him his armor turn his preparations for war into a brilliant celebration. In the action of the play, Orestes also has the nymphs for helpers, but it is because Aegisthus' rites for the nymphs give him his opportunity for stealthy killing. When Aegisthus is dead, the Messenger tells Electra (855ff.) that Orestes ἔρχεται δὲ σοὶ κάρα 'πιδείξων οὐχὶ Γοργόνος φέρων, ἀλλ'

13. The words for Orestes are λαιψηρῷ ποδί; cf. λαιψηρός of Achilles in Homer, *Il.* 21. 264, and S. M. Adams, *CR* 49 (1935), 121 on the passages in Euripides.

ὃν στυγεῖς Αἴγισθον. Perseus' slaying of the Gorgon was one of the pictures decorating Achilles' armor in the ode: Perseus has cut the Gorgon's throat (λαιμοτόμαν, 459) as Orestes does Aegisthus' and then his mother's (cf. 1223).[14] Orestes, like Perseus, must hide his eyes as he kills (1218).

If Orestes is so much like Perseus, why is Aegisthus' head '*not* the head of the Gorgon'? The relative clause ὃν στυγεῖς seems to draw a distinction between Gorgon the monster, and Aegisthus the personal enemy 'whom you hate'. It is as if the chorus were saying that the murder of Aegisthus was not merely the traditional sort of heroic achievement, but something better because it satisfies the lust for revenge. There is another meaning in this passage, however, which lies just beneath the surface and which is the opposite of what the chorus intends to say: the element of personal motivation which distinguishes the murder of Aegisthus from monster-killing is precisely what makes the murder of Aegisthus less palatable and more ambiguous morally than its heroic counterpart. This is also true of the murder of Clytemnestra.[15] Euripides debunks the glamor of violence as it is depicted in the ode not so much by changing the nature of violence itself as by revealing more of the minds of those who practice it.[16] If the slaying of the Gorgon is glorious, it is because it is morally unambiguous – a disinterested act of pure heroism. The irony of Orestes' and Electra's situation, that in imitating the ode's vision of heroic action they stray farthest from its essence, is reinforced by the echoes of the ode that come at each of the two murders later in the play.

There is one difference between the heroism of the ode and the action of the drama of which the protagonists are painfully aware.

14. The analogy between Perseus and Orestes is not original in Euripides: cf. Headlam, *CR* 15 (1901), 9ff., and *Choephoroe* 829. In the ode here, the Chimaera as well as the Gorgon prefigures Clytemnestra: each is called a λέαινα (473, 1162).

15. Since Clytemnestra's murder is also prefigured by the ode's monster imagery (cf. *supra*, n. 14), another interpretation of the passage at 856f. is possible: Aegisthus' is not the Gorgon's head because Clytemnestra's will be; Aegisthus is the lesser victim, Clytemnestra the greater. The chorus then may be saying, 'You have not killed Clytemnestra yet, but you do hate Aegisthus too and you have at least killed him. Therefore rejoice in the first murder, and look forward to the second.' For the effect of this scene, cf. O'Brien, *AJP* 85 (1964), 23.

16. This reflects, perhaps, what Jones sees as Euripides' preoccupation with 'human consciousness', *On Aristotle and Greek Tragedy* (London 1962), pp. 241ff.

In the ode, as we noted earlier, there are gods everywhere, guiding and legitimizing the deeds of heroes. In the play, the gods provide only moral riddles[17] and, as a result, the human, personal element – the motivation of Electra and Orestes at which we have just glanced – is isolated from the divine and placed in full view at center stage. At the end of the play, Electra blames herself more than the Dioscuri do, and rightly, because she knows best that she killed Clytemnestra not because Apollo demanded it but because she desired it herself (cf. 1303f.). Electra feels the strength of her personal motivation too strongly to pass the responsibility for her actions upward to a divine necessity.[18]

The images of monster-killing and divine presence in the first *stasimon*, as we have seen, provide a model of heroic action which may at first seem to represent a glorious victory for Electra and Orestes as they will triumph over their enemies later in the play. When it becomes increasingly apparent that violence in the play has none of the charm of the remote and idealized world depicted in the ode, the ode comes to serve as a background to the actions of Electra and Orestes against which the horror of what they do stands out the more sharply because it is presented as a betrayal of the heroic ideal.[19]

The ode, in this way, helps us to see the characters of the play more clearly. This process may work in the other direction as well, so that the behavior of the characters sheds some light on the meaning of the ode. The ode presents what Electra has in mind when she complains of the present and looks forward to the future: a social order determined by heroic achievement, in which the children of Troy's conqueror will regain their proper place at the summit as heroes do, by killing their enemies. When this leads to matricide, we are bound to wonder whether the ode's vision of the past was not in some way false, and whether Electra's

17. Cf. 1244ff. for the last word on this from the Dioscuri: it is possible, perhaps unavoidable, to perceive what is right and do wrong, to have a just grievance and exact an unjust retribution. Jones (*On Aristotle and Greek Tragedy*, p. 246) sees the rewarding of the Farmer as symptomatic of a larger moral paradox: that he is given wealth when he values it so little effects 'a kind of self-refutation within the Euripidean drama'.

18. Avoiding the religious terminology of the Dioscuri, she tends instead to express her moral dilemma in a personal, emotional form: Clytemnestra was 'dear and not dear' (1230).

19. Cf. Adams, *CR* 49 (1935), 121.

behavior was not so much a betrayal of heroic ideals as the pursuit of something which never existed as she imagined it and so could never be recaptured except in the distorted form it takes in the play.

Our question about how the dramatic action qualifies the meaning of the ode may be posed in yet larger terms: Adams[20] suggests that in the play 'incidentally at least, is a deliberate assault on Legend'. The first *stasimon* may be only emblematic of an entire tradition which Euripides is concerned to expose as hollow. It evokes Homeric times, and the Homeric version of the Orestes legend in which revenge is heroic and without moral ambiguity.[21]

The chorus' vision of the past suppresses moral ambiguity even in the legends of the heroes it celebrates. It does not recall – although we may – that Bellerophon, the slayer of the Chimaera (472ff.), ended his life in an exile more total than Electra and Orestes must face when they have slain their 'monster'.[22] The chorus in the first *stasimon* only sees the splendid moment of action pictured on Achilles' shield. But the flaws in Electra's heroic heritage soon emerge clearly, when the story of Thyestes and the golden ram in the second *stasimon* is explicitly presented as a monitory *exemplum*. The incident is one of φάσματα δείματα (711; so LP: Hermann proposed δείγματα), as the pictures on Achilles' shield are σήματα, δείματα Φρύγια, 'signs to frighten the Trojans'. The fearsome manifestations of the second *stasimon* are analogous to those of the first, but they are now warnings of what must be avoided. According to the chorus, Clytemnestra's crime begins with her ignoring this lesson (745f.): ὧν οὐ μνασθεῖσα πόσιν κτείνεις. Electra and Orestes follow in her footsteps, not only in mistaking what the past has to teach them, but even to the point of committing in the detail the same offenses that Clytemnestra did when she killed Agamemnon.[23]

Finally, brother and sister succeed in becoming themselves what the figures on Achilles' shield are said to be: τροπαῖα δείματ'

20. *Ibid.*

21. *Supra*, n. 12. For Homeric language in the ode, cf. *supra* n. 4.

22. For Clytemnestra and the Chimaera, see *supra*, n. 14; for Bellerophon, see *Il.* 6. 155ff., especially 200ff.

23. In particular, there is the repeated pattern of the dominant woman contriving for and acting at the side of her male accomplice. See O'Brien, *AJP* 85 (1964), 30f.

(or δείγματ') ἀθλίων προσφθεγμάτων (1174).[24] They are fearful visions, prodigious horrors whose aspect stifles their victims' cries for mercy; they demonstrate, to paraphrase Denniston's version of this passage, a rout of piteous address. Like the scenes of violence on Achilles' shield they terrify the enemy, and force him to turn away.

With this we come full circle in seeking the meaning of the analogy between the action of the play and heroic achievement as it is depicted in the first *stasimon*. Electra and Orestes follow the model of the past, and in so doing reveal the horrors that are concealed beneath the charm of the ode's narrative.

In sum, the first *stasimon* of the *Electra* serves a double purpose: its salient brighter side provides a contrast with the dramatic action – a reproach to the people on stage for falling short of the heroic ideal; its hidden, darker warnings prefigure what actually happens, an end of striving for success altogether different from what Electra and Orestes expected as their due.

If an ode as apparently pointless as the first *stasimon* of the *Electra* is in fact fully relevant to what the people on stage feel and do, we may suggest at least that an appreciation of the ode will inform our appreciation of the play. On the other hand, any explanation of an ode like this one must take account of the fact that it stands out sharply from its context. The world of the lyric represents something conspicuously lacking on stage; it is simple and paradigmatic, mythological rather than realistic, visually vivid rather than emotionally intense. This contrast between ode and play is meaningful, and points to some of the larger problems of the drama.

The poet's use of the choral ode to interrupt and to provide a contrast with the action on stage is, perhaps, symptomatic of his dramatic technique in general: he does not allow his audience the comfort of a consistent point of view.[25] The first *stasimon* of the *Electra* may be regarded as one pole of an antithesis, between an ideal world of the gods' harmony and the hero's glory, and a real

24. Cf. 456, 468f., 711. For the text, see O'Brien, *AJP* 85 (1964), 24, n. 18 and Denniston *ad loc.*

25. See Walter Jens, 'Euripides', in *Opuscula aus Wissenschaft und Dichtung* 21 (Pfullingen 1964), reprinted in *Euripides*, ed. E.-R. Schwinge (Darmstadt 1968), p. 11. See also William Arrowsmith, who observes in Euripides an 'insistence upon preserving the multiplicity of possible realities in the texture

one of human toil and conflict represented on stage. The uneasy coexistence of realistic and mythological elements in Euripides' plays has been noted before,[26] and it is important that we recognize it for what it is – a vehicle consciously designed to convey the poet's meaning.

First, the juxtaposition of dramatic realism and lyric idealism serves to disturb or attenuate the illusion of reality created by stage events. The choral ode breaks the continuity of the action and diverts the attention of the spectator from the scene of the play; it jolts the spectator from an uncritical, emotional involvement with the experiences of the dramatic characters. And, because ode and play evoke different realities, the spectator may not assume that any part of what he sees represents a single, simple reality.

When the choral ode turns the attention of the audience away from the stage, it also offers a model for understanding stage events: the world of felicity inhabited by heroes and gods. This world may seem remote from reality as the drama presents it, but the choral ode presents an image of felicity that is specifically designed to fit the requirements of the play. The lyric does not merely provide a generalized 'background' against which the people on stage stand out in contrast.[27] The poet invites us to assess both drama and lyric by playing off the world depicted in the ode against the apparently different one depicted on stage. The dramatic characters strive to realize on stage the lyric paradigm, and heal the initial breach between ode and action. Sometimes, in unexpected ways, they succeed.

of his action', 'A Greek Theater of Ideas', in *Ideas in the Drama*, ed. John Gassner (New York and London 1964), p. 18. We should do better to look for a key to the drama's meaning in this technique than to assume, as many critics have, that the lyric's images of felicity serve merely to relieve the emotions of the spectator to 'bring in...the ideal world to heal the wounds of the real' (G. Murray, *Euripides and His Age* (London 1913), p. 234), to give 'much needed relief' (Denniston, p. xxxii), to add 'a little desired sweetness to a play which will get none from any of its characters' (R. Lattimore, *The Poetry of Greek Tragedy* (Baltimore 1958), pp. 118f. on the *Medea*).

26. Pohlenz discusses what he calls Euripides' 'menschliche Handlung und kultisches Lied' (*Griechische Tragödie*[2] (Göttingen 1954), pp. 438ff.). J. C. Kamerbeek, in 'Mythe et Réalité dans l'Œuvre d'Euripide' (Fondation Hardt, *Entretiens sur l'Antiquité Classique*, VI (1960)) sees the question as more general than one of lyric and action. See also K. Reinhardt, 'Die Sinneskrise bei Euripides', in *Tradition und Geist* (Göttingen 1958), pp. 240ff.

27. Cf. Grube, *Drama of Euripides* (London 1941), p. 122.

Trojan Women and the Ganymede Ode

ANNE BURNETT

IT is usually said, either with admiration or with regret, that in *Trojan Women* nothing happens. Desmond Conacher gives this opinion an elegant expression when he speaks of the 'long passion of the Queen and her women' which is saved from being a 'mere sequence of disaster' by a faint, rhythmic pattern of hope revived and then betrayed again.[1] Others have mentioned with less sympathy the play's 'unrelieved despair', and Wilamowitz even proposed the deletion of some of Cassandra's lines because he felt they were in opposition to this overriding mood.[2] The play is described as a piece without event; it is said to have but a single tone, and to display little or no structure, a fact which Conacher would relate to its being the last drama in a trilogy.

Now certainly *Trojan Women* is different from tragedies like *Medea* or *The Bacchae*. It does not engineer a single great overturn of fortune, because the downfall of its principals has occurred before the tragedy begins (106–7; 614–15) and all that remains now is for the women to embrace their disasters and savor them as their own. The action of the play thus has a formal likeness to that of *Prometheus Vinctus*, except that here the single figure of the vanquished giant has been splintered to become three female mortals, to whom a chorus of other women adhere. Another difference is that in the Aeschylean play the principal had been humiliated at first hand by a god, whereas in *Trojan Women* an intermediate human agency, the Greek army, has brought about the ladies' degradation. And this fact leads to the second grand

1. Desmond Conacher, *Euripidean Drama* (Toronto 1967), p. 139. For a time critics gave the play 'content' by reading into it references to contemporary political events, the Sicilian expedition or the conquest of Melos; a summary of such treatments and a bibliography are to be found in A. Pertusi, 'Il Significato della trilogia troiana di Euripide', *Dioniso* 15 (1952), 251–3 and notes 2 through 6.

2. *Analecta Euripidea* (Berlin 1875), pp. 221ff.

peculiarity of the Euripidean play. There are in truth not one but two major overturns that this visible plot just fails to portray, since everything that is shown on this stage is as filled with a coming disaster for Greeks as it is expressive of the accomplished destruction of Troy.

These two cases of magnificence punished lie, one just behind, the other just ahead, of the staged action of the *Trojan Women*. Within the actual play, however, a sequence of scenes based upon other types of tragic overturn has been set up like a panelled screen. These have not always been recognized for what they are because each is a revision or a distortion of a familiar tragic movement, but if we ignore for a moment the intention of the characters and look instead at that of the poet, the outlines of each scene become clear. A future 'defeat' for Greece is described in Cassandra's proleptic 'messenger speech', and then the present 'sacrifice' of Astyanax is demanded, acquiesced in, and lamented, as a new and paradoxical meaning is poured into familiar scenic forms.[3] Strangest of all is the third panel in which a suppliant Helen is pursued and then rescued from the threat of death in a parody of a happy-ending plot. It is not a paucity of action, but rather its discordant variety, that should attract the critic's notice in this play.

A dissonance of forms serves the poet well in his imitation of his subject – war's end – but the structure of *Trojan Women* does not simply mirror chaos. There is a distinct and disturbing order here, based upon a crucial juxtaposition of opposites, for the tragedy has been constructed so that the scene in which Astyanax is taken from Andromache shall be followed immediately by that in which Helen is restored to Menelaus. The child is innocent, and he becomes the victim of premeditated Greek cruelty;[4] the woman

3. The demand is brought by Talthybius, in the role taken by Odysseus in *Hec.*, by Achilles in *IA*, by Teiresias in *Phoen.*, by Demophon in *Hcld.* Andromache takes the part of the relative in the farewell, using the traditional funerary reproach, μητέρ' ἀθλίαν λιπών, 741 (cf. Clytemnestra at *IA* 1465, λιποῦσα μητέρα; Hecuba at *Hec.* 440, μὴ λίπῃς μ' ἄπαιδ', cf. 417; Admetus at *Alc.* 368 and 388) and the familiar 'in vain did I bear you' (758; cf. Admetus at *Alc.* 880). Like the mother in *Erechtheus* she must also voice the victim's 'willingness', and this she couples with a greeting to the 'divinity' to whom the sacrifice is offered, the four-fathered Helen (768–9).
4. It is seldom noted that, shocking as the scene is, it has been considerably tempered; indeed this observation is true of all the events in the play. In the

is in some sense guilty, and she profits from witless Greek lechery. The intrusion of an unmerited and ignoble escape upon the drama of an unmerited and noble death causes a severe ethical shock, and since this shock derives from the central structural fact of the play, we must regard it as central to the experience Euripides meant to provide for his audience.

The depiction of Helen's escape, even if it were not synchronized with the atrocious death of Astyanax, would offer an affront to pro-Trojan sympathies encouraged by the focus of the tragedy. When it is set in the midst of the boy's terse drama, this unedifying release seems to represent the achievement of that sacrifice, and as such it deals a blow to the spectator's moral and aesthetic hopes. He cannot dodge its effects, for the harsh illogic of the two events is forced upon him not only by their juxtaposition but also by a terrifying disparity of tone, as if a bit of Offenbach were to interrupt the stern melodies of Gluck. Andromache's farewells to her son are sombre and magnificently bitter, so that the excess of her pathos extends our sense of the strength and flexibility of the human fiber. We admire her and think better of ourselves, but then a humiliating upset comes. In the scene that follows Helen is shallow, Menelaus is spineless, and even Hecuba shrinks from queen to harridan; the scale is mean, and the reputation of humanity is saved only by a few touches of redeeming comedy.[5]

Hecuba, whom we have known as a Job-like principal, turns from her passive agony to stand where a pursuing villain normally stands. She is playing the part of the Egyptian Herald, or of Copreus in *Heracleidae*, and she calls for blood. Meanwhile Helen,

Little Iliad (frag. 18 Kinkel) Neoptolemus himself tore the child from the arms of a nurse and threw him over the wall, and this extremely violent tradition was clearly popular, for it is represented in the decoration of a seventh-century relief pithos found on Mykonos and published by Miriam Ervin, *Arch. Delt.* 18*A* (1963), 37ff. The pithos bears witness to versions of the fall of Troy that were far more brutal than what Euripides shows, for above the major panel with the Trojan horse there are a double series of metopes showing Greek warriors who slash and stab at Trojan women and children; gushing blood is a repeated motif. All the women but Helen supplicate; she, much more elaborately dressed than the others, uses her hands to uncover a bare shoulder as Menelaus stands astonished, his raised sword paralyzed (description *ibid.*, pp. 61–2).

5. On this scene see D. Ebener, 'Die Helenaszene der Troerinnen', *Wiss. Zeit. der Martin Luther Univ.*, Halle-Wittenberg 3 (1954), 691–722, and the bibliography cited there.

one whom the Trojan women have asked us to hate, makes the ritual gesture of the sacrosanct helpless creature (1052), and though her touch evidently kindles rather more *pothos* (891) than piety in her husband, it yet has its mechanical effect. Like other champions Menelaus must judge a case before he acts, but unlike the others he has to choose between a pursuer whom the audience has learned to admire and a victim who has been described as herself a destroying monster. Clearly the poet has decided to pit the formal necessities of the traditional judgment scene against the ethical necessities of this particular moment in such a way as to make us uncomfortable with both, and the absurdity of the situation is summed up in its vacillating judge. After Hecuba, with reasons dangerously like those of Pylades at *Orestes*, 1131ff., has urged a wrong action, and Helen has begged for an undeserved mercy as if it were her due, Menelaus responds. First he flouts the formal conventions by giving his approbation to the wrong party – to Hecuba, the pursuer, instead of to Helen, the pursued (1036). This is an aesthetic outrage, but Hecuba is the figure for whom we have been taught to care, and so it is at least emotionally satisfactory. Menelaus, however, at once negates this satisfaction and also his own decision by postponing any present action against the pleading culprit (1046–8). By so doing he erases the previous debate and with it the ideas of rational human justice which are ordinarily expressed in the trial procedure. He also disappoints the clandestine hopes that have been encouraged in the audience, for Helen is not stripped or raped by the army or even attacked by the women of Troy. In spite of Menelaus' promise, the spectator knows that she will never be punished at all, and the whole affair becomes an example of that worst of tragic events, a case of blood that never gets shed, just because someone resigns a purpose that he once had held (cf. Aristotle, *Poetics* 1453b37–1454a1).

Menelaus and Helen make their exit and perhaps we may imagine that even as they go Helen sketches that famous gesture[6]

6. See the Helen metope of the Mykonos relief pithos (note 4, above). The pithos takes the tradition of this gesture well back before Ibycus (Schol. *Andromache* 630), who had been supposed to have been its inventor (so L. Ghali-Kahil, *Les Enlèvements et le retour d'Hélène*, École Française d'Athènes 10 (1955), p. 42). The scholiast at *Lysistrata* 155 had reported that the story came from the epic cycle. For other early representations of the meeting of Helen and Menelaus in which Helen is thus provocative, see Ghali-Kahil, pl. xlii, nos. 1 and 2;

which was to mean her return, not to a lynch mob, but to her husband's bed. How else, after all, did she manage, between here and the shore, to change his resolve against sailing with her (cf. 1100ff. and unanimous ancient tradition)? The passive Hecuba has made her single active move in this tragedy, and she has seen it end in the shambles of Menelaus' uxoriousness. She had looked to him to be her accomplice in violence, to act out her vengeful anger, but he is only a vulgar *erastes*. Οὐκ ἔστ' ἐραστὴς ὅστις οὐκ ἀεὶ φιλεῖ she says at last (1051), knowing now that the man she had chosen as an executioner will always be putty in this 'victim's' hands.

Such is the disorderly scene that Euripides chose as cap to the brutally efficient one in which Andromache almost thrusts her son upon Talthybius. An unnatural meeting has been contrived between serious tragedy and something almost farcical, and character, mood and tension all seem to have been sacrificed to the creation of a useless incongruity. The easy explanations of comic relief and dramaturgical irresponsibility have been offered, but there have also been reasoned attempts to read the Helen scene so as to make it conform with the apparent tenor of the opening of the tragedy. Scholars who refuse the *jeu d'esprit* explanation generally argue that the play as a whole describes undeserved suffering and that this subject is given its ultimate twist in the present episode where Hecuba is forced to violate her own honor and pride and to fawn on one of her captors, only to be humiliated and made to feel the new and excruciating pain of frustration and shame.[7]

Certainly the scene proves, as nothing has so far, that Hecuba no longer has the power of a queen. Indeed, it suggests that she does not have the character of a queen, and at the same time, by making her assert herself, it robs her of her innocence. She is not forced in this scene; rather she forces herself and her demands upon Menelaus and in so doing reduces herself to the moral scale

on a later skyphos (Boston 13186 = Ghali-Kahil, pl. xlvii) Aphrodite helps to hold back Helen's robe, so that her whole body is displayed through a transparent peplos, while Menelaus stares fixedly.

7. See for example E. Howald, *Die griechische Tragödie* (Munich and Berlin 1930), p. 157. A more complicated view is that of M. Orban, 'Les Troyennes', *LEC* 42 (1974), 22, who believes that Hecuba's action in the Helen scene is typical of a general *Ate* that fixed itself upon Troy at its founding. He speaks of her attitude towards Helen as one of 'farouche et ridicule espoir', but he maintains nevertheless that her abiding characteristic is her dignity.

of her chosen champion and her chosen prey. She makes a case against her enemy that is harmful to her own claim as well, for her charges of greed and opportunism reflect almost as much upon herself and her city as they do upon the woman she would see killed.[8] The dispute is unseemly, the judge is incompetent, and though it is easy to quarrel over just how much the queen loses in nobility, it is impossible to maintain that she is in any way enhanced as a figure of innocent suffering by her part in this mock judgment scene. Once she herself has called for blood, she can no longer be read as a pathetic anthology of war's atrocities.

Why has the poet chosen to pit his Trojan queen against Menelaus' wife and to make a scene that destroys the passive grandeur of his principal, breaks the mood of his opening episodes, and interrupts the pageant of Astyanax' death? Why has he caused Hecuba to attempt a deed that must fail, and why has he then emphasized that failure with a scene-sequence that places the corpse of a kinsman in her arms, just after she has asked for the corpse of an enemy? In tragedy events evaluate, and these events seem to discover in Hecuba some meaningful connection between her decision to challenge Helen and the fate that demands her lonely lament over the last Priamid. Since the Helen scene cannot be read as consonant with a tragedy of pure anguish and despair, perhaps we should try to reread the rest of the play, asking whether there is not some way in which the two modes interlock or communicate, some ethical or aesthetic reason for Helen's semi-comic escape. The poet has prepared a formal link between the second and third episodes, asking the spectator to pass from Astyanax to Helen by way of a short song, and surely the critic should follow by the same route.[9]

8. At 1008–9 Hecuba charges Helen with being one who fawns on *Tyche*; at 691–6 she counseled Andromache to follow her own example and allow the wave of *Tyche* to roll over her. At 1010ff. she sneers at Helen for not having killed herself rather than stay with Paris; at 699ff. she advises Andromache to live with Neoptolemus and to please him sexually if she can. At 988 she charges that Helen has given the name of Kypris to a projection of her own inner self; at 886 she proposes that everyone view Zeus as a projection of the mind of man. Hecuba's repeated charge is that Helen chose to come to Troy because of a love of luxury, but this is a predilection which Troy's luxurious inhabitants must have shared with her.

9. Wilamowitz was not of this opinion; he described the second stasimon as having almost no connection with the drama, and no internal unity at all.

II

While one young Trojan spills his blood before the Greek conquerors, the chorus sings of another, of Ganymede, who pours out wine among the blessed gods. The second stasimon (799–859) is ordinarily called by the name of Zeus' boy, but technically speaking the ode is only one quarter his, for it plays with two sets of balanced pairs. Two antistrophic systems, without epodes, display four figures of roughly equal weight, a pair of mortals and a deathless pair. The statement of the chorus, reduced to its utmost simplicity, is that while men attack Troy the gods are indifferent to the city's fate; in the first strophic pair they set two enemy Greeks in motion, while in the second, two immortals who should have been actively friendly are studied in their bland tranquillity. The twos are significant because the singers have discovered a double ingratitude and a double injury in the fact that the city which twice provided lovers to the gods has twice been conquered by the Greeks.

Such is the outline of the song; ostensibly it is a reinforced demonstration of injustice and disorder in the realm of Zeus. In fact, however, the poet has created such an odd mixture of fulness and reticence, emphasis and aposiopesis for his singers that what is urged by them as a plain case of neglect and ingratitude becomes, in the hearing, a complex and contradictory plea. The women mean to show that undeserved evils have been suffered while deserved good fortune has disappeared, but their demonstration of these claims is weakened by some curious anomalies.

To begin with, the announced subject of the first strophic pair is the double Greek attack upon Troy, the early one led by Heracles and the present one that Agamemnon leads, and so the antistrophe ends with these (damaged) lines:[10]

'Das erste [Strophe] mit einigen Komplimenten für Athen ist eine unerfreuliche Konzession an das Publikum. Nur das zweite gehört der Stimmung nach hierher: es führte den Göttern zu Gemüte, wie undenkbar sie sich gegen Troia gezeigt haben' (*Analecta Euripidea*, p. 19).

10. Murray and now Biehl cut ὅτ' ἔβας ἀφ' Ἑλλάδος from 807 and correspondingly cut φοινία and αἰχμά from 819. The result is a pair of curiously limp *clausulae* for both strophe and antistrophe, with the weakness particularly evident at 818, where the subject of this final, presumably thematic, statement must be inferred from the πυρός... πνοᾷ at 815–16. The αἰχμά of 818 prophe-

δὶς δὲ δυοῖν πιτύλοιν τείχη †πέρι
Δαρδανίας φοινία κατέλυσεν αἰχμά† (818–19).

Two times with double stroke a bloody spear broke through
Dardanian walls.

In spite of this summation, however, the chorus has not sung of the
old campaign and the new, but only of the old, preserving the
effect of doubleness by giving strophe to Telamon and antistrophe
to Heracles. Each hero makes his way through responding lines
to arrive at Troy at the same point in the stanza, so that Troy
seems to fall twice in echoing passages (806–7; 817–18) that
actually describe one and the same event. In effect, then, the
women split the ancient expedition in two, making one of its parts
represent itself while the other must stand for the unmentioned
modern, Atreid campaign. As a result, these plaintiffs who would
complain of violence and outrage unaccountably picture their
attackers in a most favorable light. The attack of their actual
conquerors is not only wrapped in silence, it is absorbed into the
earlier expedition to become an heroic exploit from the romantic
past. Agamemnon is unmentioned, obscured by Heracles;
Laomedon takes Paris' place, and Helen, the emblem of Greek
guilt, is no longer the bait, having disappeared entirely behind the
image of the superb horses that were Zeus' gift to the ancient
Trojan king.

In the second half of their song the singers offer their two
examples of divine insouciance. This time the two are really two,
not merely one divided, but there is still discernible illogic in the
lines, for the two cases are not given parallel expression. Two gods
have received the favors of two Trojan lovers and might therefore
be charged with ingratitude, but the chorus treats only one of
these divinities, singing Ganymede and Eos, not Zeus and Eos, in
their final strophic pair. In this way the women avoid making any
direct charge against Zeus, but as a result they seem to blame
the Trojan who had presumably bought heavenly favor for them.
They have missed their object, since Ganymede has no power,
either to help or harm, and when the women do turn to a god, the
figure they reproach has hardly any more weight than this once-

sies the αἰχμά at the close of strophe β and links the two systems together, so
that it is tempting to try to keep at least the substantive in 819, on the assumption that the corruption at 809 is too deep for mere surgery.

mortal boy. Eos is pretty and ineffectual, scarcely Olympian and notably unable to protect one favorite son, much less the whole population of her husband's city.

In this song, then, two legendary Greeks and two peculiarly pale immortals are held responsible for the fall of Troy. The women seem already to be stitching their history into some bit of embroidery, and only when they speak of their own ruined city do they convey any sense of actuality. Beneath their rich decoration, however, the lines carry allusions and expressions which re-evaluate the women's three subjects – Greeks, Trojans and divinities – in some surprising ways. Telamon and Heracles mingle to make a double portrait of the Greek warrior, and it is a fully heroic one, touched with the favorable colors of words like συναριστεύων (804–5), ἄνθος (809), and εὐστοχία (812). Salamis and Athens together represent Greece, the honey-rich island hanging pendant to the shore and seeming to float just beneath the Acropolis (801), and this combined city is pre-eminently sacred (802), splendid (803), and honored by the god who has given it the olive as an eternal crown (802). The attack upon Troy is thus made to come from a source embellished with traditional words of praise, at the hands of noble men (799) who are comrades in fine deeds and commanders of the flower of men. The expedition as a whole is imaged as exclusively masculine both in impulse and in composition, and it is shown to have been moved by an honorable anger that belongs to the masculine world. Heracles came ἀτυζόμενος πώλων (809–10), but to these horses we will have to return.

The women of Troy provide less detail about their own city and its defenders. The place that has fallen is represented by the 'broad-flowing' Simois (810), by the 'marine' shores of the Troad (826) and by the walls that Apollo built (814);[11] epithets

11. Neither here nor in later mentions of the walls is there any reference to Poseidon; nowhere in the play is there indication of any special Trojan cult of that god. This silence would seem to bear out Fontenrose's contention that Poseidon's concern, in the prologue, is for the physical city of Troy, and especially for its walls, but not for its inhabitants. Athena must ask a favor of him precisely because he has not until now shown any special enmity towards the Greeks; his accession marks a general Olympian shift of favor, not one that is peculiar to Athena. See J. Fontenrose, 'Poseidon in the *Troades*', *Agon* 1 (1967), 135–42 and *Agon* 2 (1968), 69ff.; the counter-argument is stated by J. R. Wilson, *Agon* 2 (1968), 66ff.

are few and neutral when they come. The city is maternal (825) but it is visualized strictly as a complex of secular buildings ('dewy' baths, 833; running tracks, 834; *melathra*, 841; *pergama*, 851) which once rose up in pride (ἐπύργωσας, 844). The coastal bluffs of the Troad are brought into the city and identified with the women there by means of the simile of the bereaved bird, and thus the whole country seems to produce a single cry (829) as it laments husbands, sons, and mothers that are gone (831–2). Troy was, by this definition, made of two components (as Greece was made of Salamis and Athens in the previous strophe), one belonging to nature, the original female water and earth, the other built up of stone by the arts of men and gods. The maternal Trojan land endures, but the masculine towers and walls are gone, and as the women tell it, there never was a male defense of Troy. The whole city seems to have been passive from the moment when the mouth of Simois received the prows of the Greek ships (810–11)[12] and the walls proved to be susceptible to flame (815). The war is subtly likened to a rape, for the singers make it the violation, by torch and lance and oar, of the Trojan stream, dewy bath and encircled inner space. The only Trojan men to be mentioned had disappeared long before the present catastrophe occurred and they belong properly to the description of heaven, not of earth. Because they are two, however, they cannot but form a Trojan balance to the Greek pair of the opening stanza. And where Telamon and Heracles, the exemplary Greeks, are all action, weapon and thrust, the two typical Trojans, Ganymede and Tithonos, are passive in their amorous lassitude, willing 'victims' of another sort of rape.

Such are the mortals, the strong enemies and weak friends, that the chorus describes, and their gods are just as paradoxical. Athena, Apollo, Zeus, Eros and Eos must stand for Olympian injustice and ingratitude here, and each of them is defined as the giver of a boon to mankind! Athena's gift of the olive for crowns is the first to be mentioned (802–3); Apollo's construction of the Trojan walls is next (814), and meanwhile the horses that were given by Zeus have been referred to (810), though their divine

12. There is an echo here of *Agam.* 695–6, as there is of *Agam.* 48ff. at 829–30; probably the desire to spur Aeschylean reminiscences influenced Euripides' decision to return to the outdated trilogy form for his Trojan dramas.

donor has not been named. Eros has sent Troy towering up (843–4, where responsion makes this come in answer to Ganymede's service at 822–3; cf. 612) and Eos is identified as the giver of the light dear to men (849). Finally, unspecified gods once gave the charm of magical immunity (859) to Troy, but that gift, according to choral complaint, now has been withdrawn. For the rest, the gods of this ode have their usual gracious and gorgeous attributes; the particular choral point is that two of them have been lovers of men and as such were the authors, not only of the happiness of their paramours, but also of certain expectations based on that happiness (857; cf. the 'high hopes' that Hecuba has been cheated of, 1252). It is this widespread Trojan hope that has now been so ungraciously betrayed, but even that betrayal is described with a phrase of dazzling charm – τὰ θεῶν δὲ φίλτρα φροῦδα Τροία – and with these words the poem ends.

This surprisingly suave verbal surface is an expression of conscious poetic intention, just as the curious organization of the poem is. They work together to convey a contrapuntal message of loveliness and joy, just where the singers mean to tell a single tale of grievous suffering. A third element in the poet's final effect is the choice of mythic material, and here the structure of the poem insists on certain telling emphases. The ode's logical four subjects, once the largest mythic selection was made, were, as has been said, two mortals and two gods: Heracles and Agamemnon in the first section and Zeus and Eos in the last. The figures of Telamon and Ganymede do not properly belong to such a system, at least not on their present scale, and their intrusion thus brands them as the bearers of the poet's particular impulse in this song. It is they who have led the ode out of its hypothetical over-schematized form and into its actual, genial design.

The negative influence of these two 'interlopers' – their displacement of Agamemnon and Zeus – has already been touched upon, and it is time to consider their positive effects. Telamon, by way of Salamis, brings Athens into the song; Athens figures all of Greece, and Athens is where all brightness and glory lie. The bereaved Trojan earth is thus caught, in the poem's sequence, between a glittering Olympian palace and an almost equally gorgeous Acropolis. Telamon affects Troy more directly than this, however, for his name urges the listener's memory back to

Hesione and Laomedon (cf. Pindar, *N.* 3. 35; *I.* 5. 26ff.), and the mention of the horses that were denied to Heracles (809–10) confirms this tendency. The famous high-stepping steeds provide an interlocking mythic motif that joins Telamon with Ganymede and indicates that Euripides is using his first, intrusive mythic hero as the herald of his second one, much as Pindar does with Amphiareus in the Sixth *Olympian*.

It is Ganymede around whom the ode was really made, and with Ganymede another figure enters, his father, whose importance is announced by a change of name. Euripides obviously knew the Ganymede anecdote as it appeared in the Homeric Hymn to Aphrodite but there,[13] as in the *Iliad* (5. 265; 20. 232; cf. Apollod. 3. 146; Diod. 4. 75; Schol. Lycophron, 1232), the father of Zeus' cupbearer was Tros. By making the parent Laomedon instead,[14] Euripides ties all the major Trojan legends into a single knot and brings into his poem a man who is like Tantalus,[15] one who has lived close to the gods and been guilty of offenses against them. This man indeed had behaved more outrageously than Tantalus did, for to his ingratitude towards the gods he had added ingratitude to Heracles, the hero who had been his benefactor.

Laomedon is introduced by name (814) simply as one whose death was identical with the skill of Heracles' archery (813–14). His death is the purpose of the expedition, which can be resumed in a single sentence which begins with the departure from Greece, touches on arrival at Troy, and ends with the blood of Laomedon (809–14). The mention of Apollo in the next few words serves as a reminder, in case any were needed, of the history of this man towards whom a great campaign was oriented. The walls of Troy are established as built by Phoebus (814; cf. 1174) and this one fact defines the king. He was one who exploited his divine stone-

13. *Hom. h. Aph.* 202–17. The Ganymede–Tithonos sequence is common to both, as are the wine, the golden cups, the beauty of the boy.

14. According to the scholiast at 822 (= frag. 6 Kinkel), the *Little Iliad* also made Laomedon the father of Ganymede.

15. See J. T. Kakridis, 'Die Pelopssage bei Pindar', *Philologus* 85 (1930), 463–77, for likenesses between the two pairs, Tantalus/Pelops and Laomedon/Ganymede. There were points of actual contact between the two tales, since Tantalus was associated with the stealing of Ganymede, either as Zeus' accomplice (Schol. *Il.* 20. 234) or as his rival (Euseb. *Chron.* 2, p. 40).

masons, an arrogant mortal who not only refused the gods their pay but threatened to tie them hand and foot, lop off their ears, and sell them into slavery (*Il.* 21. 450–5). The earlier mention of the horses had already added the next phase of the old tale to the mythic orchestration of this ode (809), fixing Laomedon's repetition of his characteristic crime as the first cause of the first Trojan war. A second time Laomedon had profited from extraordinary aid, when Heracles had killed Poseidon's monster for him, and a second time Laomedon had refused to give the promised wage, [16] and so Heracles came, 'aggrieved at the loss of the horses' (809). All of which means that in a song about divine ingratitude, the chorus has been made to lament walls that were divinely given and received with brutish human ingratitude; in a song about unjust Trojan suffering, they have been made to provide their conqueror with a just cause for his attack (cf. *Il.* 5. 642–8 and Pindar, *I.* 6. 29: Λαομεδοντιᾶν ὑπὲρ ἀμπλακιᾶν).

Laomedon, whose name need not have been mentioned at all, thus serves to undermine the womens' claims, for once he is placed at the beginning of the tale, Troy's sufferings can no longer seem wholly unjust or wholly undeserved. He blocks the effectiveness of Ganymede as well, whom the women would use as proof of a divine debt unpaid. When Croesus stood on his funeral pyre and cried out to Apollo ποῦ θεῶν ἐστιν χάρις; (Bacchylides 3. 38), he did so on the grounds of specific gifts, as yet unreturned, that he had offered to the Delphic god. So also with Pelops in the first *Olympian*, asking for aid, and with those other Euripidean ladies who are so certain of divine ingratitude, Creusa and Alcmena. These Trojan women, however, have not themselves given the gods special pleasure, nor have they offered their kin to rejoice the beds of Zeus and Eos. Only Laomedon could have made that claim, and unfortunately the women have reminded us of how well he was repaid. The horses that were refused to Heracles were the same that had been given by Zeus to the father of the stolen boy, and in the Hymn to Aphrodite they are proof of Zeus' pity (καί μιν Ζεὺς ἐλέησε 210) and of the father's joy. Ganymede was

16. This seems to have been epic material as early as the seventh century; see Wilamowitz, *Euripides Herakles*, vol. 1² (Berlin 1895), pp. 31–2. The Phrygian of *Orestes* likewise links the gift of the horses with the fall of Troy: ἰαλέμων ἰαλέμων | Δαρδανία τλάμων Γανυμήδεος | ἱπποσύνᾳ Διὸς εὐνέτα (1392–3).

to be ἀθάνατος καὶ ἀγήρως ἶσα θεοῖσιν (*Hom. h. Aph.* 214; cf. *Il.* 20. 232, ἀντίθεος and Pindar, *O.* 10. 104–5, where beauty and youth save Ganymede from ἀναιδέα θάνατον), and these two gifts of immortality for the son and horses for the father left the King of Troy rejoicing without and within:

οὐκέτ' ἔπειτα γόασκε, γεγήθει δὲ φρένας ἔνδον,
γηθόσυνος δ' ἵπποισιν ἀελλοπόδεσσιν ὀχεῖτο.

(*H. h. Aph.* 216–17).

No more he groaned aloud but felt delight inside his heart,
And off he drove rejoicing, behind the storm-swift steeds.

Such are the effects of Laomedon, but the deepest paradox of the song derives from the importance it gives to Ganymede, who might, like Tithonus, have been dismissed with an epithet.[17] Instead, the Olympian life of the lover of Zeus is pictured in detail and made the one element in the ode that endures, while armies move and cities fall. Beauty was always the boy's one characteristic (*Il.* 20. 235; *Hom. h. Aph.* 205) and the present song attempts no innovations at this point. With ἁβρὰ βαίνων (820; cf. 506) the poet gives a touch of Lydian elegance to the youthful figure, making him like the page of Croesus in Bacchylides' Third Ode (48; cf. Hdt. 1. 55); by mentioning gymnasium and race track he suggests that it was the sight of the naked boy in royal sport that roused Zeus' desire, just as Sophocles supposed, when he wrote μηροῖς ὑπαίθων τὴν Διὸς τυραννίδα (frag. 345 Pearson). And finally, with an extraordinary phrase, Euripides recalls the gift of eternal adolescence which seems to come to the boy with continuous applications of heavenly *charis*: σὺ δὲ πρόσωπα νεαρὰ χάρισι παρὰ Διὸς θρόνοις καλλιγάλανα τρέφεις (835–7).

17. Tithonus is given oblique mention as the 'child-engendering husband' who came from Troy (852–3), who was stolen away in a golden chariot (855–6), and who is now in the goddess's chamber (845). Presumably he brings with him into the poem his reputation for beauty (cf. *Hom. h. Aph.* 218; Tyrtaeus, frag. 9. 5 D), but apparently not the motif of his extreme old age, judging from τεκνοποιός. His age is mentioned first by Mimnermus (frag. 4 D), but Tithonus' chief early identification seems to have been simply as father of Memnon (Hes. *Theog.* 984f.). He is also paired with Ganymede in later times; see Schol. Ap. Rhod. *Arg.* 3. 158. Orban, 'Les Troyennes', p. 20, suggests that Tithonus is compared to Ganymede as an example of 'amour licite' against one of 'amour coupable', but there is nothing in the poem to support this idea.

Ganymede's bliss proves that Zeus has a weakness for the beauty of mortal flesh that is to all men's advantage, and that was the didactic significance of his figure.[18] There are very few surviving early representations of him in art, but those that remain express the same magnificent good cheer that marks the telling of the story in the Homeric hymn. Ganymede as cupbearer may bend one knee or approach a seated Zeus as worshippers do their heroic ancestors,[19] reminding us that his service was a form of praise, but the rape is more often depicted. Here the boy is provocative – unclothed but carrying the hoop of his childhood and the cock of his erotic vocation – while a robed Zeus firmly pursues.[20] The moment of capture is shown in all its auspicious joy in the terra-cotta statue from Olympia, as a smiling Zeus strides off towards heaven with an equally contented boy tucked under one strong arm.[21] This was the rape of Ganymede as the fifth century still knew it, a mutually satisfactory meeting that gave festive proof of easy intercourse between men and gods.[22] The boy's success was a portent, for it promised that gifts from mortals – hymns, prayers and libations as well as the person of the worshipper – could bring a god into that archaic state of 'hilarity' that meant mercy and graciousness.[23]

Woman-like, the ladies of the chorus think that Ganymede the

18. Compare the remarks of C. P. Segal on Poseidon and Pelops, 'Pindar's First and Third *Olympian Odes*', *HSCP* 68 (1964), 213: 'This very eros represents the possibility of an immediate connection with the divine'; cf. 219. Roman iconography made Ganymede an emblem of immortality; F. Cumont, *Recherches sur le symbolisme funéraire des Romains* (Paris 1942).

19. See J. A. Overbeck, *Griechische Kunstmythologie* (Leipzig 1871–84), Bd. I, Taf. VIII.

20. *Mon. Inst.* X, pl. 23; *Arch. Zeit.* (1863), pl. LV; see D.-S. *s.v.* 'Jupiter', fig. 4232.

21. The best photographs are found in Ludwig Drees, *Olympia* (Berlin 1967), plates 42–3 and Taf. XIV.

22. At *IA* 1049ff. Ganymede appears at that best of mixed parties, the wedding of Peleus and Thetis; at *Cycl.* 581ff. the context is again festive as Silenus becomes, in the monster's eye, not just a cup-bearer but a well-endowed Ganymede; here the idea of salvation is strongly present.

23. This notion is neatly expressed in the aitiological pun that derived the name Ilium from Apollo's joy at taking a Trojan bride, ἵλεων μείχθη ἐρατῇ φιλότητι (Hesiod frag. 116 Rzach = 235 M–W). For the same 'good cheer' as a result of praise, Hes. *Erg.* 338–40; *Hom. h. Dem.* 204, 274; Theognis 780; Archilochus frag. 94 West; Pindar, *O.* 3. 34; *O.* 7. 9; Emped. frag. 128 D–K; Eur. *Hel.* 1007; *IT* 271, etc.

lover should have bought advantages for his family and friends with his fleshly merchandise. They forget that such profit is almost never the result of a liaison with a god, that the mortal lover usually endures trials and often suffering, while his family or city may receive new duties – priesthoods, cults, colonial missions, crusades – at the end of the heavenly affair. Of course Ganymede's story is different from those of the other mortal lovers of the gods; it is touched by none of the shadows that ordinarily cross such tales, nor does it contain any of those motifs of warning or failure meant to teach even men like Anchises not to presume too much upon their ability to please. Ganymede knows no earthly duty and no earthly suffering, for contact with god immediately transports him to another level of existence. He is one of the handful of favorites taken up to heaven to continue their offices there, and even among these his fate is unique.[24] He is not like Ariadne, who was made divine, but neither is he like Pelops, who was sent down, or Tithonus, who had to be retired. Ganymede continues forever, immortal, ageless but not divine, his reward an eternity of service and praise, which he is allowed to offer above. This was the 'hope' held out by Zeus in his rape of the boy, not the hope of material prosperity, offered just to Troy, but the hope of immortality, extended to all men who truly pleased god. It is well termed a 'charm', but ill-chosen by this chorus of women who have lost all desire to please heaven, who have forgotten how to praise and richly intend to blame the gods for their misery.

Because a Trojan boy is engaged in an eternal exchange of graciousness with Zeus, the Trojan women feel justified in reproaching heaven with ingratitude. They insist that their catastrophe is a man-made accident, but they argue that it has come upon them because of the callous indifference of the gods. The whole balanced form of their song, however, with its echoing Ἑλλὰς ὤλεσ' αἰχμά (838) and φίλτρα φροῦδα Τροίᾳ (858), proves how deep their error goes. Ζεὺς γὰρ κακὸν μὲν Τρωσί, πῆμα δ' Ἑλλάδι θέλων γενέσθαι ταῦτ' ἐβούλευσεν πατήρ as someone,

---

24. Semele seems to be among the gods rather as mother than consort (Pindar, *O.* 2. 28); the other lovers of Eos (Cephalus, Cleitus and Orion) were not installed on Olympus or given immortality, though Euripides speaks of Cephalus as carried ἐς θεούς (*Hipp.* 455). As a reverse variant Ixion might be named as one who lost a place in heaven by attempting to become an Olympian paramour uninvited.

probably Cassandra, has said in the first play of this trilogy.[25] Zeus has not been lax; the present disaster is of his design, but the women cannot entertain this thought. It is they who have named Laomedon, but no more than he are they ready to suppose that gods who favored might also punish them. They prefer to imagine divinities who are lost in the luxury of Olympus, sunk in sensuality and unconcerned with events on earth, for that way there is no lesson to be read in the fall of Troy. Theirs is an arrogant vision, because it assumes that gods are like the worst of men, careless even of their own prerogatives. It is also a false vision, for it has been contradicted at the outset by the active gods who appeared to speak the opening dialogue.

III

In its surface effects the Ganymede Ode most directly influences our view of the Greeks, making this present campaign seem the more vicious by contrast with that other comradely crusade which had been led out from a city of temples by a demi-god. Agamemnon and Odysseus[26] are the Heracles and Telamon of today, and they are moved by treachery and ambition instead of honor and loyalty. Even within their own camp petty cruelty ruled, as the ugly plot of *Palamedes* had shown,[27] and in victory they have lost all resemblance to their lyric prototypes. The present victors have behind them two great acts of sacrilege, having seized Cassandra and killed Priam before the play began, and on these boards they descend to a ghastly mimicry of such crimes in their mock sacrifice of a Trojan boy. This act of useless savagery repeats the violence and

25. Frag. 45, in B. Snell, 'Euripides Alexandros und andere Strassburger Papyri', *Hermes Einzelschriften* 5 (1937), 1–68, where all the papyrus and book fragments are presented with commentary. Snell's division of the action into episodes, and his theories about the dénouement, are not entirely convincing; for other discussions, see Pertusi, 'Significato', pp. 255–8; T. B. L. Webster, *The Tragedies of Euripides* (London 1967), pp. 165ff. and 'Euripides' Trojan Trilogy', *For Service to Classical Studies: Essays in Honour of Francis Letters* (Melbourne 1966), pp. 207–9.

26. In accordance with the tradition of the *Iliou Persis* it is here Odysseus, not Neoptolemus, who is the author of Astyanax' death (721); he is said to have persuaded the army, however, and so all share in the guilt of the atrocity.

27. On the content of this play, see Webster, *Tragedies*, pp. 174ff. and *For Service . . .*, pp. 209–10; also Pertusi, 'Significato', pp. 258–62.

cynicism of the full-scale outrages that have already angered Athena, but it labels the Greeks now as cowards rather than *theomachoi*.[28]

On the Hellenic side, the ode stands to the whole play as foil, and the ironic effects of its romanticization of the Greeks of old are easily recognized as important to the peculiar bitterness of the tragedy.[29] Less easily appreciated are the subtler influences that emanate from the song to modify our understanding of the Trojan principals. The play is often read as if it set Greeks of complex character and fate against Trojans who have no comparable depth, flat creatures who are the pathetic objects of a violence that cannot curb itself, but to this the Ganymede Ode offers contradiction. It makes the city of the past a place of bad faith and effeminacy, impiety and arrogance, and it forces us to consider the present remnants of its population with the figure of Laomedon somewhere in our minds. The women, thanks to these self-inflicted truths, take on an ethical density that in fact ennobles the play, lifting it above any charge of diatribe or sentimentality. They are far more interesting than mere random victims could be, for they are part of a community capable of decision and error, one that has already, with heaven's help, fixed its own destruction.

The trilogy of which the *Trojan Women* is the closing act opened by establishing Trojan responsibility for the fall of Troy. Indeed the first play, *Alexander*, seems to have been a variation on the theme that the Ganymede ode so lightly suggests with its Laomedon, the theme of divine favor misunderstood and misused by men puffed up with pride. Troy, the god-built city, had received a destruction warning in the form of Hecuba's dream, but the Priamids had refused to extinguish the torch that was their son, and so the arrogance and wealth of Troy were fated to burn.[30]

28. Note Hecuba's epitaph, with its telling enjambment (τὸν παῖδα τόνδ' ἔκτειναν Ἀργεῖοί ποτε | δείσαντες 1190–1).

29. Compare the effect of the paradoxical language of the *parodos* (205ff.) where the women describe the Greece to which they expect to sail (Sparta excepted, 210–13) in terms that are curiously Pindaric and suggestive of blessedness: σεμνῶν ὑδάτων 206; τὰν κλεινὰν...εὐδαίμονα χώραν 209; σεμνὰν χώραν 214; κάλλιστον 215; ὄλβῳ βρίθειν...εὐθαλεῖ τ' εὐκαρπείᾳ 217; τὰν ἱερὰν...ζαθέαν...χώραν 219; Σικελῶν ὀρέων ματέρ'...καρύσσεσθαι στεφάνοις ἀρετᾶς 222; καλλιστεύων...ζαθέαις πηγαῖσι τρέφων εὔανδρόν τ' ὀλβίζων γᾶν (226–9).

30. *Alexander* frags. 1 and 10 Snell; cf. Schol. at Eur. *Androm.* 293; Hygin. *Fab.* 91; Pindar, *Paean* 8. 28–31 (here the vision is of a fire-bearing hundred-handed monster).

All this Cassandra knew and told, but no one could receive her information. The dangerous child had lived and in the *Alexander* he returned, the full-grown instrument of doom. The play showed how an uncomprehending Hecuba tried to kill him, when such killing would have been a miasmatic crime (though she had been directed to suppress his birth), and how he was saved to be the mortal author of the fall of Troy. Everyone who began the day by listening to Cassandra thus knew that Troy had carried in itself the seeds of its own disaster, just as Hecuba had carried the child that she failed to kill.

Even a late-comer to the theatre would have been twice reminded of the Priamid failure to destroy the destroying Paris, for Helen and Andromache both refer to it in the surviving play. Helen reproaches Hecuba with having been herself the cause of the Trojan war, saying (919–22):[31]

πρῶτον μὲν ἀρχὰς ἔτεκεν ἥδε τῶν κακῶν,
Πάριν τεκοῦσα· δεύτερον δ' ἀπώλεσε
Τροίαν τε κἄμ' ὁ πρέσβυς οὐ κτανὼν βρέφος,
δαλοῦ πικρὸν μίμημ', Ἀλέξανδρόν ποτε.

First she produced the source of all these ills
when she gave birth to Paris; secondly, the old man
ruined Troy and me as well when he failed to kill
the boy, the torch's bitter replica, called Alexander then.

This of course comes from an unfriendly mouth, but Andromache had already confirmed the tale as the accepted Trojan version of the war's beginnings (596–9):

οἰχομένας πόλεως...
δυσφροσύναισι θεῶν, ὅτε σὸς γόνος ἔκφυγεν Ἅιδαν,
ὃς λεχέων στυγερῶν χάριν ὤλεσε
πέργαμα Τροίας.

a city damned...
by heaven's brooding care, when one you bore fled Hades'
grasp
and for a loathsome bed destroyed the walls of Troy.

With a few touches the *Trojan Women* completes the saga of Paris, telling how the actions of that luxurious prince (598) plus the enticements of wealthy Troy (994–6) brought first Helen, then

31. Snell, 'Euripides Alexandros', p. 36, note 2 argues that the πρέσβυς of Helen's words cannot be Priam, but he has against him Wilamowitz and most other readers of the play. It may be noted that at 593 Priam is πρεσβυγενής.

the Greek army, and so at last the flames and slavery of this final day upon his motherland.

The Trojan trilogy, viewed as a single action, can be likened to the Aeschylean *Persians*, and the fact that the agents of punishment have been given a separate play in which to show themselves worthy of punishment, should not obscure the essential valence of Troy. The city was itself the true tragic principal, its swollen excess having set all this machinery in motion by exciting the anger of the gods. The old outrageous Troy was fully depicted for the audience of the *Alexander*, but we, because of accidents of preservation, can observe only the vanquished and desperate women who survive its fall. They have been literally cast to the ground, but even in defeat they continue to measure the heights to which their city had towered, for their pride, their materialism, and their scorn for the divine are with them still. Hecuba's cry, 'Gone is wealth, gone is Troy!' (582) sets the keynote for a persistent identification of these two concepts (reminding the irreverent modern of Shylock's 'My daughter! O my ducats! O my daughter!' at *M. of V.* II. viii. 15). Even more telling is an earlier phrase when the queen laments the loss of her former importance by saying ὦ πολὺς ὄγκος συστελλόμενος (108–9), for her language treats Trojan pride as an excessive swelling that has been reduced.[32] Troy is steadily described as a city of extraordinary wealth, pride and luxury: this is what the women have lost and what Astyanax will not grow up to exploit and enjoy.[33]

After their materialism, lack of faith stands out as the second negative characteristic of the Trojan women. They have but a grudging and uncertain sense of the divine, and they betray everywhere that lack of impulse towards prayer that shapes the Ganymede Ode. When they do address a god, it can be with ugly

---

32. Compare Hecuba's use of ὄγκος at 1158, where it means 'boast', and see also Eur. frag. 724 N τὰ μέγιστα...θεός...συνέστειλεν; Diod. Sic. 4. 20. 1, of the physique of men who live without luxury, τοῖς ὄγκοις εἰσὶ συνεσταλμένοι.

33. Trojan wealth and luxury: 497, 506, 582, 991–6, 1253; pride and tyranny: 152, 474–5, 748, 1020–1, 1169 (ἰσόθεος τυραννίς), 1277–8 (μεγάλα ...ἀμπνέουσα). There are commonplaces about the corrupting power of Trojan wealth and luxury among the *Alexander* fragments (36, 37 Snell), and a major theme of that play seems to have been the overweening pride of race that made the Priamids resent being equated with a cowherd from the mountains (frag. 40 Snell).

irreverence, as at 1060ff., where Zeus is scolded as if he had been a traitor within the city, or 1077, which is reminiscent of Amphitryon (*HF* 347). In Hecuba this rebellious tendency is so sharply marked as to become her major ethical trait. Urging the completion of the thing dearest to her – the killing of Helen – the closest she can come to prayer is the famous 'Zeus, whether you be nature's law or a projection of the mind of man' (886). Her agnostic phrasing is of course suitable to her request, which is that Zeus should aid in the killing of his own child, but certainly it makes a curious prayer, as even Menelaus notes (889). Earlier in the play, when force of habit had brought the cry 'O gods!' into her throat, Hecuba had sourly excused herself by saying, 'Those are cowardly allies that I call upon, but it is usual to name them when one's luck is bad' (469; cf. 969, where she offers herself as an ally to the goddesses who, she supposes, need her aid). Once more, at the end, she forgets herself, moans ἰὼ θεοί, then erases her unconscious piety with an arrogant, 'But why do I call upon the gods? They didn't listen in the past when they were addressed' (1280–1). Words of this sort are common in Euripidean tragedy, but they are fearful and embarrassing here because the audience has seen these same 'unlistening ones', these 'cowardly allies', in the act of planning exactly what Hecuba desires, revenge and posthumous honor for violated Troy.

In a dim and feminine form the women of this play thus reflect the 'Laomedon qualities' which had made Troy in its grandeur offensive to the gods. Hecuba in particular distills in her tired flesh the whole destiny of Troy, and in the Helen scene she shows herself a true representative of that city as it has been portrayed. The scene is marked by futility and lack of seriousness, effects produced by the action (or rather the inaction) of Menelaus, but perhaps even more by the words of Hecuba. Helen has repeated the familiar and well-loved tale of Troy, adding, with the three goddesses, the superhuman element missing in the play's other accounts.[34] She cannot quite argue that she was in any technical sense raped, and so she urges for her husband's satisfac-

---

34. On the traditions of the judgment of Paris, see F. Jouan, *Euripide et les légendes des chants cypriens* (Paris 1966), pp. 95ff., where it is argued (but by no means proved) that Euripides meant his audience to suspect Helen of misrepresenting the promises of the goddesses.

tion the violation of her normal will and *ethos* by the gods. If she is to be found guilty of a crime worthy of tragedy, she will have to be charged with having corrupted or exceeded her fateful mission; as a proper object of political vengeance, she should be accused of having broken faith or plotted against Troy; and as the victim of Hecuba's private retaliation, she should be shown to have the blood of Priamids on her hands. But Hecuba does not address herself to any of these points.

True to the tendencies of her house, the Trojan queen chooses to deny the gods any part in the origins of the war. This leaves her logically in the unfortunate position of having to give more effect than ever to the spontaneous crimes of Paris, and in her attempt to defend him and the Priamids from all responsibility, she arrives where her character has led her. The fabled wealth (993) and the opportunities for excess (1020–1) that existed only at Troy are shown to be the true causes of the war, as Hecuba concludes, with more truth than she knows, that it was the oriental splendor of the place that drew the devastating Helen out of Greece. All effective denunciation of the woman is deflected by the establishment of Troy itself as her temptation; even the traditional charge of lust is weakened, and Hecuba ends by accusing her enemy of nothing more serious than leaving her husband because she preferred the life of a capital to that of a backward town. No wonder Menelaus' determination to kill this light creature grows weaker instead of stronger, as he listens to her worldly arraignment.

In her single moment of decision Hecuba attempts to reassert something like her old power, involuntarily reflecting some of the old irreverent short-sightedness as well. She would condemn some one to an irregular death, just as she did in the morning's tragedy, and comparison of the two stage situations suggests that Euripides has purposely caused her to repeat the pattern of her behavior in the earlier play. Because a seeming slave had been successful in the games, Hecuba in the *Alexander* had joined a male accomplice to kill off the man whose victory was an insult to her pride. The murder which was to defend Priamid superiority would have been an act of sacrilege accomplished at the very altar of Zeus Herkeios[35] where the Greeks were later to kill Priam, but Hecuba was saved from committing such a crime. The stranger was her own

35. Snell, 'Euripides Alexandros', p. 48.

son, the god's chosen implement for Troy's destruction, and a timely recognition preserved him for his mother's embrace and his fated task.[36] The play thus ended with expressions of joy and relief that mingled jarringly with Cassandra's unheard prophecies of flames and desolation for Troy. Here in *Trojan Women* Hecuba would once more persuade a male accomplice to kill, and this time her object is another victor, the second instrument of Trojan fate – the woman used to draw the destroying army out of Greece. As in the previous case the deed would have been an outrage to the gods, for Helen is the child of Zeus and makes herself a suppliant, but once again a miasmatic killing is avoided. Menelaus, the would-be assassin, finds that he cannot use his sword in the crucial moment because of a rediscovered sense of Helen's flesh, and so once more a kind of recognition interrupts the intended act.

A congruence so striking ought to indicate that Hecuba was as arrogant and blind in her second assassination attempt as she was in her first. And so it does,[37] though the poet has given to each of her pursuits its own ethical stamp. The queen of the morning's tragedy acted from pride of race and class, insisting that her own family should always be triumphant, but in the afternoon her reasons are far more admirable. In the Helen scene she means to avenge herself, her city, her husband and her sons for the Trojan siege and capture. The presumption arises from the scene's position that she particularly wishes to avenge the ugly seizure of her

36. In the scene as it is represented on Etruscan urns, Aphrodite sometimes appears to work the recognition; if this was the case in *Alexander*, the similarity to Menelaus' recognition of Helen would be all the greater. Hyginus has Cassandra, like the Pythia of *Ion*, rush from the temple in time to interrupt the murder; J. O. de G. Hanson, 'Reconstruction of Euripides' Alexandros', *Hermes* 92 (1964), 171–81, combines this interruption by Cassandra with a final appearance by Aphrodite. Snell proposes an interruption by a rustic, the erstwhile protector of Paris, and Webster suggests a recognition somehow brought about by an unidentifiable old Ethiopian crone (*Tragedies*, p. 172); he, incidentally, makes Aphrodite speak the prologue and has Apollo appear at the end. Ovid, *Her.* 16. 90, reflects yet one more version, in which recognition tokens are significant.

37. See Snell, 'Euripides Alexandros', p. 66: 'Hekabe erscheint nun nicht mehr als die dumpfunschuldig Leidende. Im Alexandros hat Hekabe etwas von dem wilden Ungestüm, das Euripides schon in der Hekabe an ihr gezeichnet hatte (das in den Troerinnen immerhin auch in der Helenaszene herauskommt).'

grandson, and this ensures the spectator's sympathy. As soon as she is face to face with Helen, however, her inability to accuse the woman of any major crime shows that once more Hecuba is rashly mistaken in her victim. Indeed she seems not to know who it is she would kill, as little conscious now of Helen as Zeus' child[38] as she was before of Paris as her own.

Blindness is the telling common factor between her two attempts to kill, and it is a blindness plainly marked as culpable. Anyone may fail to perceive the intention of heaven, as Hecuba does when she chooses to attack the two key figures in a divine scheme of punishment, but only the extraordinary sinner will refuse the guidance of everyday piety. Hecuba, in her two vengeance attempts, shows an active disrespect for altar and suppliant, as well as for a victor and for one reputed to be the daughter of a god. She is deaf to Cassandra's words because of Apollo's trick, but she overlooks the gods' ordinary rules willfully, and twice her Trojan resistance to the idea that they control her fortunes brings her to the brink of a crime that would have been abominable in the view of heaven.

Hecuba is mistaken in thinking Helen the proper object for political retaliation, and she is mistaken in thinking that she herself has any vocation as the avenger of Troy. Athena plans her own punishment for the ill-disciplined conquerors, and Cassandra boasts that she herself is to be her city's champion. Hecuba of course does not credit any of this because she hears it from her daughter's throat, and many critics have been as deaf as she to Cassandra's words. The first episode is generally regarded as a grand *coup de théâtre*, a classical twin to the mad scene from *Lucia*, but Cassandra is not mad. She is the only mortal in this play who understands what the gods intend, and she insists on making sounds of joy in the midst of general complaint, not out of foolishness, but because of Athena's promise that she would 'brighten the hearts' of these former enemies (65). Cassandra celebrates this day of woe because she looks forward to events in her own doomed life that will bring victory to Troy even after its defeat (353; 460)

---

38. For Cassandra, Helen is simply ἡ Διός, 398; cf. the chorus at 1109 where she is *Dios kore*, though the women are calling for a thunderbolt to strike her ship. Andromache rhetorically denies Zeus' paternity at 766, but she substitutes other supernatural fathers for Helen, whom she would make an evil demon receiving the sacrifice of Astyanax.

and triumph to her father, even in his grave (327).[39] She looks to a 'blessed' (327) future with good reason, though for the others, to whom blessedness means material riches, all bliss is in the past (as at 1170).

Cassandra will knowingly achieve what Hecuba mistakenly attempts, for she will avenge her house, her brothers and her fatherland (359–60), not against Helen, a mere bit of bait (368), but against Agamemnon, the warrior who added crimes of his own (252–3) to the prosecution of a fated task. She will destroy her mother's enemies with her present marriage (404–5), for she herself is an erinys (457, where the other two are presumably the Aeschylean pair, Helen and Clytemnestra). Cassandra's wedding torches are repeated in the torches that set fire to Troy at the play's end (298; 343; 1295), and by an opposite progression, a spark from burning Troy will give a ghastly light to Agamemnon's couching with this concubine. The torch of Hecuba's dream is at last to be turned upon Greeks as well as on Troy, and though it destroys her it will fulfill Cassandra's need for justice, beyond her fondest desire (345). This coming 'victory' is the true achievement of Astyanax' mute submission to a parody of the traditional city-saving sacrifice.

Cassandra's pyrotechnical appearance promises punishment for the Greeks, and it announces a supernatural vengeance action that will be played out in the future, on the opposite shore of the Aegean, with Agamemnon as its fated victim. Cassandra has been chosen to join the coming storms as an agent of divine redress, and her revelation of this fact proves absolutely that Hecuba's self-appointed vendetta against Helen was quite outside the providential plan – one last recapitulation of all the superb errors of Troy.

Helen is as impervious as Ganymede and for the same reason, because the beauty of mortals can make them dear to the gods.

39. Like Wilamowitz, H. Steiger found these lines destructive of the artistry of the Cassandra scene, but he did not believe that they should be excised; he thought that Euripides had been unable to resist putting them into Cassandra's mouth because they expressed his own political beliefs; see 'Warum schrieb Euripides seine Troerinnen?', *Philolog.* 59 (1900), 369. Schmid–Stählin, 1. 3: 1, 470 reports Cassandra's boasts as being over-rhetorical and a breach of taste, but P. G. Mason, 'Kassandra', *JHS* 79 (1959), 91 observes that Euripides is using Cassandra's rhetoric as 'a balance to the sufferings of Troy and a reminder of the wider workings of providence'.

She has served on earth in a capacity not unlike the boy's, and she remains, with him, a promise of that undeserved happiness which even the fiercest of gods may give. The Ganymede Ode represents this bliss with its image of a joyful and submissive service to god, and then the tragedy reports on what men make of a promise such as this. It shows an indiscriminate group of victors and vanquished, all of whom have lost the fear of god and so the ability to serve. Praise has turned to blame; temples are pulled down, not built; piety and idealism have withered away, and retaliation and brute survival are the only values that even the best of these mortals, the women of Troy, still know. Virtue is not only impracticable, according to the world's most virtuous wife (634ff.), it is to blame for present suffering (657ff., 742–3). Only Cassandra, herself a Ganymede *manqué*, has the least comprehension of the gods' concerns; she alone praises and submits to them, and she alone knows a strange reflection of the central poem's proffered bliss.

Such failure matters absolutely to mortals, but not much to the gods. They have finished their design, and it has a dreadful beauty in spite of the materials they were forced to use. The torch that Hecuba dreamed has set fire to Troy. The war that began with the dubious sacrifice of a Greek girl (370–1) has ended with the hideous killing of a Trojan boy. And the story-tellers' cause, the abduction of Helen by a Trojan prince, has found its exact counterweight in the taking of Apollo's priestess by the conquering Greek king (357–8). The war that was imaged as a kind of rape in the second ode has spawned a multitude of violent couplings (778–9, 780–1), measuring the difference between this world that men create and another that, with the favor of the gods, they might enjoy. It is the difference between the violation of a captive enemy, and the rape of a Ganymede.

The *Rhesus* and related matters

H. D. F. KITTO

AMONG the many human problems that refuse to disappear the problem of the authorship of the *Rhesus* is by no means the most important though it may be among the most tiresome. The latest investigation, and probably the most thorough, is Professor W. Ritchie's *The Authenticity of the Rhesus of Euripides* (C.U.P. 1964). Ritchie discusses the documentary evidence that has come down to us, submits the text to a sustained and careful stylistic examination – vocabulary, syntax, and style in its many manifestations: metre, structure of the lyrics, dramatic technique. He compares the play point by point with normal Euripidean usage and arrives at the fairly confident conclusion that the play was written by Euripides, rather early in his career, somewhere between 455 and 440 B.C.

Some years earlier D. W. Lucas, reviewing another book on the *Rhesus*, wrote: 'There is a strong presumption that the play is an early work of Euripides'; but having said that, he added what oft is thought but not often so pungently expressed: 'But in spite of all, many will remain disinclined to believe that Euripides could have written a work so intellectually null, so completely devoid of the clash of argument, of ideas, and of verbal nicety and precision.'[1] True; there are many such.

An interesting situation; in fact, the situation is much more interesting than the play. Close analysis of the style, supported in this case by what documentary evidence we have, says one thing; literary or dramatic or aesthetic judgment says: 'I don't believe it.' As Coriolanus remarks, in Shakespeare's play: 'When two authorities are up, Neither supreme, how soon confusion May enter 'twixt the gap of both.'[2] The purpose of this article is to suggest that there may be a third, or at least an auxiliary approach, one that goes a little further than stylistic analysis, and may be

1. *C.R.* I (n.s.) (1951), 20.
2. III. i. 109–14.

317

a little more solidly based than what Ritchie calls aesthetic judgment.

We may agree that the style of the *Rhesus* is Euripidean, but what does that prove? Professor Ritchie himself is aware, naturally, that here we are not on very firm ground. 'Virtually the only evidence for tragic style other than that of Euripides is supplied by two poets whose styles are both marked by a high degree of individuality. It is not unlikely that other poets may have approached more closely to the manner of Euripides. For this reason we must treat similarities of style between *Rhesus* and Euripides with some caution' (p. 194). Yes indeed. As P. T. Stevens put it, reviewing Ritchie's book, 'The Euripidean style may well have been a tragic *koine*.'[3] For example, we know that in English eighteenth-century poetry there was a distinct eighteenth-century style – and, as it happens, in some respects it is not unlike the Euripidean: cool, well-kempt (for the immutable laws of Taste, unknown to the gifted but benighted Elizabethans, had at last been revealed), addicted – the lesser poets absurdly addicted – to periphrasis and ornamental epithets and adjectives:

> ...brighter than a Ray
> Shot from th' effulgent Source of Day –

meaning 'sunshine'.[4] It is a style which, at its best, is clean and effective, witty rather than imaginative; a style natural to an age of Enlightenment – and Euripides' too was that; and the cynical may find it an agreeable fancy that the Enlightenment, in poetry, promptly became 'a Ray Shot from th'effulgent Source of Day'.

The possibility, even perhaps the probability, that there was such a 'tragic *koine*' reduces the cogency of stylistic comparisons. For example, Ritchie compares certain 'inflated' expressions found both in the *Rhesus* and in Euripides. When the chorus is awakening Hector it bids him: λῦσον βλεφάρων γοργωπὸν ἕδραν (line 8). Ritchie records that ἕδραν is a favourite word of Euripides, that γοργωπός occurs four times in his extant plays, and in this phrase in the *Rhesus* it is only the periphrasis βλεφάρων ἕδρα that is unusual.[5] Yes, but it makes a difference whether the owner of

3. *C.R.* 15 (n.s.) (1965), 270.
4. From an anonymous, and very bad, poem *On the Late Queen's Sickness and Death* (1738). Reprinted in the *Week-End Book* (London 1926).
5. *Authenticity of the Rhesus*, pp. 213f.

the 'Gorgon-glaring eyes' is awake or asleep; whether the phrase makes us smile gently or laugh outright; and with that, statistics cannot cope. It is indeed true that both the author of the *Rhesus* and Euripides use inflated language. At *Rhesus* 288 the Shepherd says that he and his fellows οἰκοῦμεν αὐτόρριζον ἑστίαν χθονός; Ritchie compares this,[6] reasonably, with *Alcestis* 183f.: πᾶν δὲ δέμνιον ὀφθαλμοτέγκτῳ δεύεται πλημμυρίδι: a phrase which invites us to reflect that the flood of tears comes from the eyes, makes them damp, and soaks the whole bed. There are other such parallels; but what do they prove? Not necessarily any more than that both poets were infected with the same prevalent disease.

Similarly, Ritchie compares with great resource and thoroughness the style and technique of the lyrical passages. They are similar – but again, why not? Both Aeschylus and Sophocles, we feel, composed their choral odes under great pressure of thought and imagination; for example, they will abruptly switch, in midstanza, to a different type of rhythm, and for a dramatic reason easily apprehended. The Euripidean lyric style, on the whole, is very different: it tends to be pretty in language, easy-going in syntax, rather monotonous in rhythm; not often are we made to feel that the charming stanzas are packed with thought or passion. It is a style in which, we feel, any competent lyric poet could have written. Is it not likely that several others did?

Clearly, none of this carries much weight, nor does it pretend to, but it does, I think, reduce the weight that we can confidently place on analysis of style. Then have we nothing else that we can turn to? What about literary and dramatic judgment?

Of that, Ritchie is sceptical, and it must be admitted that he has good reason. 'On the aesthetic side one's verdict will be a matter of private taste' (p. 123). It is often, and if that is all, not much reliance can be placed on it. 'Aesthetic arguments, which are necessarily of doubtful relevance for questions of authorship, are often open to challenge and not seldom founded on misinterpretations of the poet's intentions' (p. 346). That is dismally true. Ritchie might have gone further and pointed out that there are not many surviving plays of which perfectly competent scholars have not, between them, propounded quite contradictory interpretations. So far, Ritchie's scepticism is well founded. But this

6. *Ibid.*, p. 215.

affects much more than a mere question of authorship. So far as that question is concerned, we are being offered the choice between stylistic analysis, which is subject to the uncertainties that we have just been discussing, and 'aesthetic arguments' which, as Ritchie rightly suggests, are often founded on no more than individual (or 'private') pot-shots at the poet's intentions. (A recent, and conservative, count reveals that there are on the market at least eleven quite different interpretations of the *Tyrannus*, of which at least ten must in some degree misrepresent the poet's intention. Each, of course, represents 'a point of view', and a man cannot be hanged for having a point of view, but what we want, if we can get it, is the poet's point of view. Is it possible to get it? When the remains of an ancient building are unearthed, archaeologists do not rely on 'a point of view', one opining that it was a temple, another, that it was a row of shops. They carefully consider the evidence. So should we.)

Nor is that all: so many technical faults have been found in the works of the three best Athenian tragic poets as to suggest that in sheer craftsmanship they lagged far behind their fellow artists who worked in marble, bronze, clay, or paint. But it may be that if we have misapprehended a playwright's intention we are ill-placed for judging his style and technique, and *vice versa*. If then it can be shown that aesthetic, or as I would prefer to say, literary judgment need not be so random, so dependent on private taste as Ritchie rightly says it has been, then we may find in our hands an instrument for supplementing, perhaps even correcting, the not very certain results of stylistic examination.

The argument needs a specific example. To be really cogent it would need a dozen or more; but in this world we cannot have everything, and editors have to be exigent. For various reasons I choose the *Ajax*: it was composed by an admitted master of his craft, it has often been severely criticized as a poor work of art, and it has been interpreted in the most diverse ways. Brevity may give my attempt the appearance of dogmatism; the indulgent reader will understand.

Roughly speaking, interpretation has been of three types.

(1) The play falls apart in the middle, when its hero has killed himself; what follows, the dispute about the burial, is of inferior dramatic interest, and so are the new characters who are

brought on. The most downright exponent of this view was Waldock: those Greek tragic poets used up their dramatic material at so furious a pace that they often ran out of steam too soon and had to stoke up afresh in order to reach the terminus. Others, less downright, have looked around for palliatives: the Athenians simply loved debate, the Greeks had an inordinate interest in burial, anything else you can think of. But the play sorely lacks unity.

(2) There is no real lack of unity. The second part is necessary, to rehabilitate the character of the hero. Jebb went further: 'The goal of the play is the consecration of the hero.' So too did Murray: he argued that since Ajax was one of the Attic tribal heroes, and since the centre of a hero-cult was his tomb, it would have been of extreme interest to Sophocles' audience that Ajax should receive burial.

(3) The most recent interpretation that I have seen is Mr G. Gellie's: 'The whole point of the play is that no one else can follow Ajax up to the rarefied air of the truly heroic mind.'[7] This accords very well with a current theory of Sophocles the proponent of human heroism; the question is, how far it accords with the evidence of the play.

A fourth explanation is perhaps worth a brief glance: the play is awkwardly composed because the myth itself was of a shape not well suited to dramatic presentation. If this was worth mentioning it is because the idea still survives in nooks and corners that the Greek tragic poet was hampered by having to represent a myth; as if he had his plot delivered at his front door from a van labelled *Greek Myths*. All the evidence is, of course, that the poets who were any good took all intelligent freedom in altering myth, adding or subtracting as their dramatic idea required.

In considering those main types of interpretation we should first ask and answer the simple question: What chiefly should claim our attention, what the dramatist *did* put into his play, or what he did not?

Let us take (2) above, 'rehabilitation', even 'consecration'. We have the text before us, and can read it. What is said in the last hundred verses? The two kings have decreed that the body shall be flung out, for sea-birds to eat. (It sounds vaguely reminiscent: is there not something of the kind in the *Antigone*?) Odysseus

7. *Sophocles: a Reading* (Melbourne 1972), p. 192.

opposes it. Why? I summarize what he says. (1) Do not allow the violence of hatred to push you into trampling on what is right (δίκη). I hated him more than anyone did, but I bear in mind that he was the best of us all, after Achilles. (2) It is wrong (οὐ δίκαιον) to try to injure a brave man when he is dead, I too hated him while it was decent, καλόν, to hate him. (3) You can do him no injury now, only infringe the laws of the gods. (4) He was indeed our enemy, but a man of great worth, and with me that weighs more than hatred. And remember: no man is good all the time; today's friend is often tomorrow's enemy. Rigidity, the σκληρὰν... ψυχήν, is not admirable (which is just what Haemon said to Creon, *Antigone* 700–8). (5) I ask you to permit his burial because I too shall come to this.

Agamemnon gives way, but only as a favour to Odysseus. 'For my part', he says, 'I shall always hate him, in this world and in the next.' Finally we notice – if we are in a noticing mood – how Sophocles chose to end his play: Teucer, with reluctance, feels that he cannot allow Odysseus a share in the funeral rites, 'lest it be resented by the dead man'. But why should Sophocles have decided to end his play with that, if not to suggest that in this matter of rigidity, of unceasing hatred, there is nothing to choose between Agamemnon and Ajax? Neither of them – nor Menelaus either – can understand that the vicissitudes of life demand a more intelligent and generous response than that.

All that is surely a remarkably poor performance – on the part of Sophocles – if he intended the rehabilitation of Ajax's character, his consecration as a tribal hero, or a confirmation of his unapproachably heroic mind. Odysseus does indeed assert what nobody has denied, that Ajax was the best of them all, after Achilles, and makes that one reason for not treating him as Creon treated Polyneices' body, in the other play, but it is only one reason out of several. There is no attempt to palliate his attempted crime; instead, Odysseus urges what we have already heard from Ajax himself (lines 678–82): today's friend is often tomorrow's enemy – a fact of life, and one that we must accept. If we consider his other arguments we shall notice that they bear a strong resemblance to those urged upon Creon by Antigone and Teiresias. Of heroization, not a single word. We can read what Sophocles did say; are we to neglect that in favour of what he did *not* say?

But there is much more that we must overlook if we are to accept any of the interpretations with which we began. For example, there is the way in which the first scene ends. At line 79 Athena makes a remark that some have found regrettably ungodlike: 'Is it not most agreeable to laugh over a fallen enemy?' Quite so, but it was not badly contrived if Sophocles' idea was to prompt his audience to give a little extra attention to what Odysseus does say when his enemy has gone in to continue his torturing of 'Odysseus': no exultation, but: 'I pity him, thinking as much of myself as of him; for I see that none of us who live is more than a semblance and an empty shade.' There is an echo of that later in the play, audible, if our hearing is good enough. At line 1257 Agamemnon angrily derides Odysseus for trying to champion one who 'is a man no longer, only a shade'. There was an earlier echo, at lines 1087ff. Menelaus is being vindictive towards the dead Ajax, and says: Ἕρπει παραλλὰξ ταῦτα, 'these things go by turns'. We know that; the play has reminded us of it several times, notably in the great speech written for Ajax at lines 646ff.: 'Summer follows Winter, Night follows Day...' But all that the uncomprehending Menelaus can make of it is: 'That man was always blazingly insolent; now it is my turn: his body shall be flung out.' Of course, the two kings have received great provocation, but so too had Odysseus, in the first scene. Their response to it is one that would infringe the laws of the gods and outrage humanity itself; his response is pity. Did Sophocles design that contrast in order that we should take no notice of it?

We look elsewhere. In a play so full of impressive speeches not the least impressive, and surely the most affecting, is Tecmessa's, at 485ff. The quality of the poetry, if nothing else, should compel attention. In all simplicity, she reminds Ajax, and us, of the disaster which – at the hands of Ajax himself – overwhelmed her house and reduced her, a princess, to the condition of a slave-concubine. It is a striking confirmation of what Athena had said, if we happen to remember it: 'A single day can overthrow anything human.' Shall we not be rather dull of response (perhaps because we are thinking of something else) if we do not at once reflect how immeasurably greater that was than the reverse that Ajax has just experienced, and how much more wisely she faced it than Ajax? We may then notice what she says next; it is what is said also by the chorus (lines 245–58) and by Teucer (lines 1004–23): that what Ajax has done threatens all those near him with death or enslavement or exile or shame and bitter grief. That is something that we should neither ignore nor evade.

Let us notice other facts of the play which current interpretations find either unnecessary or inconvenient. The Messenger supplies two.

He enters, evidently, with urgent news, but before delivering it he uses up a dozen verses telling us what happened to Teucer on his return to camp. Certainly we need to know that Teucer is at hand, but why should a sensible dramatist invent the information that as soon as he was seen coming he was very nearly murdered by the infuriated soldiery? What had *he* done to anger them? Nothing. Then why did they attack him? And why should Sophocles keep his expectant audience waiting? The only reason for their rage, he tells us (line 726f.), was that Teucer was brother to the madman who had plotted to destroy them all – and we have already been told, twice (lines 27 and 230–2), that Ajax had slaughtered not cattle only but the herdsmen too. It is a detail in the structure of the play, small but not inconspicuous, which deserves notice. It shows, evidently, that the army was not impressed by the unapproachably heroic mind of Ajax; it shows too that the army, like the two kings later, regarded him as a traitor and a public enemy.

Then, in his second speech, the man spends time on what we might think no business of a Messenger: he tells us, in some detail, how, twice, Ajax had spoken with arrogant self-confidence about the *theoi*, and, twice, he uses the pregnant phrase κατ' ἄνθρωπον φρονεῖν, as something that Ajax was incapable of doing. A reasonable praphrase of it would be: Remember the limitations, and the obligations, imposed on us by the fact that we are mortals, not gods.

It is the first time in the play that we have heard the words, but the idea has been with us from the beginning and remains to the end. Perhaps we remember that Athena said: 'You see how strong the gods are?', and we remember Odysseus' reply. That reply Athena commended as σωφροσύνη, 'wisdom', 'understanding'. She continued: 'A single day can overthrow anything human; therefore do not speak boastfully towards the *theoi*, and do not swell with pride if you excel other men in prowess or wealth.'

324

It is a precarious world that we inhabit, and it is well to be aware of the fact. We have seen that this is the substance of the plea made by Odysseus to Agamemnon; the great services rendered by Ajax in the past are relevant to it but subsidiary. We have seen how Tecmessa, instinctively, accepted what could not have been avoided, the ἀναγκαία τύχη, not nursing an implacable hatred for the man who had ruined her life. No such understanding, such willingness to accept, can we find in Ajax. To him, pride in his prowess was everything. As Coriolanus, in Shakespeare's play, defies 'Great Nature' and asserts that he can stand alone (V. iii), so did Ajax think that he could do without the *theoi*. Odysseus, talking with Agamemnon, deplored the σκληρὰν ψυχήν, the rigid mind; the chorus had called Ajax στερεόφρων, 'unbending' (line 926); the same fault is imputed to Creon by Haemon (*Antigone* 710–18). It is the opposite of κατ' ἄνθρωπον φρονεῖν. We have seen that the two kings, in their meaner way, are no more capable than Ajax of understanding the obligations imposed on us by our common human estate; like him, they cannot abate their hatred.

There is another feature of the play that deserves more attention than it usually gets. Why did Sophocles, three times, bring in the theme of Hector's sword and Ajax's belt? He may perhaps have meant something by it; at any rate, half of it was of his own invention, for in the Homeric story the belt had nothing to do with Hector's death; and the central idea, that of the dead reaching out to kill the living, lines 1026f., occurs in as many as five of the extant seven plays. Let us look.

In this play it is first announced in the middle of Ajax's great Summer-and-Winter speech – almost as if the two themes are connected, as of course they are. All that Ajax reads into it here is that it proves the truth of the proverb, that the gifts of an enemy never bring good. But on the third occasion, lines 1023–39, Teucer takes it much further. It is he who completes the theme by adding that the belt which Ajax had given in exchange for the sword became the instrument of Hector's death. So, the enmity of the two men, emphasized by Sophocles much more than by Homer, has at last reached its consummation. Then Teucer is made to say: 'Surely it was the Erinys that forged the sword and Hades that fashioned the belt...This, like everything else in human affairs, was directed by the *theoi*.'

325

That is the conclusion of the thrice-repeated theme. Does it not seem that Sophocles was actually *thinking*? But what about?

Of the five instances of such delayed and reciprocal action the most fully developed is the one in the *Trachiniae*: Heracles slew Nessus, and then Nessus caused the death of Heracles. But perhaps the instance most useful to us at the moment is the one we meet during the climax of the *Electra*, lines 1417–21; and if we took it more seriously than we usually do we might find that play less of 'an enigma'. After Clytemnestra's final scream the chorus is made to say: 'The dead are at work! The tide is flowing back; those who died of old are draining the blood from those who killed them.'

Neither there, nor in the *Trachiniae*, nor here in the *Ajax*, is emphasis laid on the moral 'justice' so earnestly desired by modern criticism; rather, upon 'justice' as *dike*, the way in which the universe *works*. Something done generates its recoil. The sword-and-belt theme really is akin to the Summer-and-Winter theme; each is an example of 'the way things are'. The latter theme is even more impressively stated in the *parodos* of the *Trachiniae*: 'Sparkling Night gives birth to blazing Day, and then lulls him to rest...The Great Bear circles everlastingly around the Pole.' There, far too often, modern criticism impoverishes the imagery with some such phrase as: 'The chorus tries to reassure Deianeira' – as if Sophocles had no more sense than to put into the mouths of village-maidens such astronomical splendours, for so modest a purpose. There, as elsewhere, the poet is establishing for his Greek audience, well used to such amplitude in tragic drama, the framework within which all that follows coheres and makes important sense; we, with our devotion to the tragic hero and the rest of it, instinctively remove that framework and then complain that the play is ill-constructed. In the *Ajax*, as I hope we have seen, our attention is always being drawn (unless we obstinately resist) to certain features of the universe of which we are part, notably to the fluctuations, steady or sudden, which are of its nature. *Sophrosune* or 'wisdom', κατ' ἄνθρωπον φρονεῖν, consists of the understanding and acceptance of that nature; the rigidity that does not understand and will not accept it is disastrous.

Aristotle held that of the six components of a tragedy the most important is ἡ τῶν πραγμάτων σύστασις, the organizing, or structuring, of the dramatic material. Precisely what he meant by that may be debatable, perhaps no more than the logical ordering of the events. But it seems a hint worth taking, and we have been trying to take it – including in the term 'material' everything that the dramatist laid before the attention of his audience, for example Teucer's refusal, and the sword-and-belt imagery, and the army's attack on Teucer. For it seems reasonable to suppose that the classical Greek poets, like their contemporary vase-painters (until the period of decline) did not put in irrelevant twiddly-bits; that the poet had something to 'say', and said it with the normal Greek directness and economy.

If that is so – and a similar scrutiny of other plays could only confirm it – then the σύστασις τῶν πραγμάτων is, as it were, the living skeleton within the living play. That is what the dramatist designed as the foundation of the whole structure. The alternative is to suppose that for one reason or another he was not in full control of his work. Therefore, if it really is our aim to get as close as we can to the poet's intention – not merely to say, 'Well, anyhow, that's how it strikes *me*' – then it is to the *sustasis* that we must give our first attention. That is our best chance of escaping from the pressure of received ideas of our own epoch (the tragic hero for example) and from enthusiasms of our own (such as Attic tribal heroes or the heroic mind). Though it may be hard to believe, some of these are quite unhellenic.

Another outcome of our study of this play, which again the study of others could only confirm, is that the focus of the poet's thought lies further back than we might expect; his perspective is wider. Waldock's criticism of the *Ajax* illustrates that perfectly: as a tragedy of Ajax the play ends in the middle. But I hope we have seen that Sophocles was thinking further than that: Ajax was not intended to fill his picture, not even Ajax *plus* an assemblage of other interesting, or uninteresting, characters. If we do not see them all not only in relation with each other but also in relation to the background of κατ' ἄνθρωπον φρονεῖν we have completely missed the point.

Manfully resisting the temptation of going back to Aeschylus, let us now move forward to Euripides, and so come once again within reach of the *Rhesus*.

Mr Gellie has well said: 'Perhaps, with our obsession with

personality, and the "star" system that goes along with it, we are a bad audience for Sophocles.'[8] Yes; we tend to fix our gaze on the star when we should be looking at the firmament. But if we are 'a bad audience for Sophocles', perhaps we are no better an audience for Euripides, and for similar reasons. He, even more than Aeschylus and Sophocles, has been accused of dramatic ineptitudes – in his tragedies, though, significantly, not in his non-tragic plays. His plots, it has been said, are ill-made; his characters, even important ones, are allowed to disappear and others to take their place; the character-drawing is sometimes inconsistent. Hence, it has been argued that the rather inconsequent composition of the *Rhesus*, for example the virtual oblivion that envelops Dolon, is no reason for doubting its Euripidean authorship. But the case is not quite so simple.

Good technique in drama, as in other things, is not absolute, but relative: relative to the job in hand. We have spent some time trying to demonstrate that in the *Ajax* Sophocles was thinking rather further than we normally expect, not about a 'star' but about the 'firmament'. From the one point of view his technique is poor; from the other, as satisfying as we could hope for. Now, Euripides' 'firmament' is very different from Sophocles'; much more disconcerting. Nevertheless, it is what he is thinking about, and we should consider his technique in relation to that, not to some imaginary absolute standard of the Aristotelian kind.

Certain excessively prosaic scholars of the last century were scornful of Euripides as a maker of plots: he was a 'botcher'. (It was convenient to overlook that in his non-tragic plays he reveals himself as a virtuoso.) Plays like the *Troades* were no more than a set of disconnected episodes – which no doubt is just what Aristotle thought of them. From that error we have recovered, recognizing that in this play – and comparably in others – Euripides was thinking beyond that; was building up a picture of stupidity and inhumanity which, in the end, was going to recoil disastrously on the heads of its perpetrators. But we still hear rumblings of discontent; about the *Hippolytus* for example: for who is supposed to be the central character, Hippolytus or Phaedra? and if Phaedra, why does Euripides forget her in the second half of the play? and why does he make his noble heroine

8. *Ibid.*, p. 191.

relapse into lies and treachery? Such questions are misconceived, because entirely out of scale with the play. Euripides was thinking not of individuals but of fundamentals: the play begins with one *theos* and ends with another, and if we do not see them as facts or powers in our universe with which we have to come to terms – if we can – or perish, we are nowhere near apprehending his intention, nor, therefore, of saying anything worth while about his dramatic technique.

It is complained too that his character-drawing is inconsistent; in the *Hecuba* for example we are invited to agonize over the ill-used Queen, but near the end she, with no preparation or dramatic probability, becomes just as inhuman towards Polymnestor as the Greeks have been to her. A ruinous fault, had it been part of his intention to draw a portrait of Hecuba. But since that would have contributed nothing essential to his play, and since he does exactly the same with Alcmena at the end of the *Heracleidae*, we may suspect that he was thinking further: suggesting to his audience (not unversed in political affairs) an uncomfortable fact of which recent history has given us several illustrations, that the oppressed, once liberated, are as likely as not to become oppressors in their turn. We should not allow our 'obsession with personality' to get the better of us.

Good technique is relative, not absolute. What may be good, or at least intelligent and acceptable, in one play is not of necessity good in another. Therefore the mere fact that some of these Euripidean 'faults' are found also in the *Rhesus* proves nothing in particular. We have to look rather more closely. In order to do that we will consider the *sustasis* of two of Euripides' plays commonly considered second-rate, and then at the *sustasis* of the *Rhesus*. The two plays are the *Andromache* and the *Supplices*.

The *sustasis* of the *Andromache* has been sensitively studied by Professor K. Aldrich.[9] I am content to summarize his conclusions. 'Euripides seems preoccupied with two thoughts about the Trojan war: how did it start, and what did it lead to? The aftermath is shown on the stage; the causes are learned from the reflections of the characters. The *Andromache* presents us not with the great war of the epic legends... but rather with a senseless, drawn-out melee,

9. *The* Andromache *of Euripides*, University of Nebraska Studies, no. 25, n.s. (April 1961).

demeaned by the nature of its inception, sordid in its execution, and infamous in the ramifications of its results...The war had its heroes; they are dead. Those who lived on were scoundrels...It left a trail of wreckage, from which no greatness could rise...Was this disabling of human life a necessary evil?...The characters and the chorus answer: no. A beauty-contest set it off (247–308). A wife-stealer started it (103–16). It began with a husband's misplaced jealousy (607–15). Choose any cause you will: the beginnings were as unworthy as the end was tragic' (pp. 69f.). 'Menelaus, Hermione, and Orestes all illustrate a most important feature of the play. Each serves the plot in his or her individual capacity, but all are alike in their imperviousness to reason' (p. 72). Such, in brief, is the outcome of Aldrich's very detailed study of the *sustasis* of this play. If we accept it – and it is certainly well argued – it may not make us admire the play any the more; that is immaterial, a matter of 'private taste'. What it does do is to show (unless we can disprove it) that the play was composed with intelligence, even if we think it a misguided intelligence, not with hopeless incapacity.

A few words about the other 'feeble' play; then we shall be well poised for our return to the *Rhesus*.

What we are first shown is a group of mourning mothers (of whom there must have been plenty in Athens at that time) with Aethra. Theseus arrives. At first he is coolly rational: 'Adrastus' expedition was idiotic. It turned out to be a disaster. Now he must take the consequences; they have nothing to do with *us*.' Then comes Aethra's appeal to pity, generosity, the law of nations. At once Theseus yields: he takes up the cause of the Suppliants, and is nobly backed by the Athenian people. We, perhaps, expect that such a change of front in Theseus should be fully explored and accounted for; a field-day for the amateur psychologist. Euripides has no such interest; it would only have distracted attention from his real theme. He is intent on giving us two aspects of a problem in political morality, the 'sensible' and the 'ideal' – and we may observe here that it is no part of the tragic poet's function to solve problems, only to pose them.

We come to Theseus' altercation with the Theban Herald. Obviously it is nothing like the typical Sophoclean dispute – Antigone's with Creon for instance – in which we are made to feel that the total personality of each disputant is engaged. Most Euripidean disputes seem formal; intellectualized, as it were. Of course we find them less 'dramatic' than the Sophoclean kind; but for our present purpose, that is irrelevant, since what we are trying to do is to make contact with Euripides' mind.

The Herald is made insolent, Theseus wise and noble. If that were all, it would not be much; but it is not all, by any means. The Herald gives an idealized picture of autocracy, Theseus of democracy, with a story-book picture of the tyrant. Do we say that Euripides, as a patriotic Athenian, is praising, to his Athenian audience, the democratic ways of their city? There are one or two facts to notice before we say that.

Some shrewd criticisms of democracy are put into the mouth of the Herald, criticisms that Plato was to make later, weaknesses made plain by Thucydides: the danger that a large assembly, many of whom are inexperienced in public affairs and are unable to detect spurious reasoning, may be hoodwinked by wily and dishonest politicians, who are clever enough to put the blame on others when things go wrong; the danger that such an assembly may decide in haste and repent at leisure; the danger too of *elpis*: 'If only he saw that Death was in his vote...', but he always thinks that he himself will escape unharmed. So is 'spear-mad Greece' being destroyed. – To this, the speech made by Hermocrates to the warring Sicilian cities (Thucydides 4. 59ff.) affords an interesting parallel. – Euripides is hardly inviting his audience to subside into complacency. Still less when it hears, this time not from the Herald but from Theseus, that there are three classes in a city: the rich, who are useless, eager only to get more wealth; the poor, who are dangerous, because they are consumed by envy and are encouraged by evil and crafty leaders to speak hatefully of the rich; and the 'middle' class, who alone are reliable citizens (lines 238–45).

Other observations on war and its causes are made during the play, and Euripides seems indifferent who makes them. 'Wretched mortals! Why do you lay your hands on spears and slaughter each other? Stop! End the misery. Keep watch on your cities peacefully, among peaceful men. Life is brief; pass through it quietly, not in wretchedness.' That is Adrastus (lines 949–54). 'Mankind is stupid! We throw away the blessings of peace and begin wars.

A city tries to enslave a weaker city, a man a weaker man.' That (once again) is the Herald (lines 491–3). 'You have ruined your city because you were led astray by young men; some eager for fame, provoking wars unjustly, corrupting the citizens; one wishing to be General; another hoping for power, that he may misuse it; another, to make money out of it, thinking nothing of what the people will suffer.' That is Theseus, speaking to Adrastus (lines 250–7). Some critics have opined that Euripides was thinking here of Alcibiades. That may be true, but it is only a guess, and a guess that is worse than a waste of time, since it drags down Euripides' thinking from the general to the particular. Throughout the play, as also in the *Andromache* (if we accept Aldrich's interpretation), he is thinking of war as an evil thing, arising out of evil motives.

Though not all wars; not, for example, the war that Theseus now undertakes, though only when his appeal to reason has been utterly rejected by the Herald. And we should notice here that Euripides is no sentimentalist but grimly realistic. Although Theseus is fighting from the highest motives, he is given no easy victory over the unjust Thebans. The battle is a stubborn one, with slaughter on both sides. Idealism demands a heavy price.

Is it odd, merely a concession to tradition, that Adrastus should deliver a funeral oration over the Seven? Perhaps. Yet Euripides was in the habit of thinking, and of inviting his audience to think too. Moreover, Adrastus praises only five of the seven; he says nothing about Amphiaraus or Polyneices, presumably because the virtues of the former were unchallenged, and to praise Polyneices would only have been a misguided *tour de force*. He may therefore have been suggesting that men fighting in an unjust and stupid cause are not necessarily fools or villains.

Finally, when the desolate scenes of mourning and wild grief are over, Euripides produces Athena. She is rather disconcerting. Gods sometimes are, in these plays. It is disconcerting, in the *Agamemnon*, that Artemis will not allow Agamemnon to do what Zeus has sent him to do unless he will first kill his own daughter. (Some of our ideas about the Greek gods do not seem to have been shared by the Greek tragic poets.) Athena forbids Theseus to hand over the ashes of the dead to the Argives without a *quid pro quo*; and the comfort she gives to the bereaved is the prophecy of a war of revenge in the next generation. The first is usually explained by

332

reference to current international politics, the second by the fact that the victorious war of the Epigoni was so famous. That may be. Yet did Euripides really imagine that something said by him in a play produced in Athens would have any noticeable effect among the Argives? and was legend so much his master that he felt bound to pursue it to the end? We have been following the play with some care up to the present moment; we have had continuously before our eyes the group of mourning mothers; we have witnessed the passionate grief of Evadne and the bleak sorrow of Iphis; we have heard Thesesus dissuade the mothers even from looking upon their dead: the sight is too ghastly. Can we banish all that from our minds as soon as Athena speaks? Is she not brought in to suggest with a freezing impersonality that politics and folly will continue; that Athens should insist on some payment for her recent services to the Argives; and that there will be another war, this time a victorious war of revenge – though even a victorious war deprives mothers of sons and turns wives into widows? If the strong current of the play carries us along to such a conclusion as that, then we may say that the play ends with the sign: *Da Capo*.

We have been looking at the *sustasis* of the *Supplices* and (vicariously) of the *Andromache*, two of Euripides' 'feebler' plays, and emerge with one or two conclusions not very different from those that we brought back from our study of the *Ajax*, notably that the reason for our dissatisfaction is usually that we expect the dramatist to have attempted, not very successfully, what he had no intention of doing. Thus, one critic has complained that 'the character of Theseus is not tragic in any sense of the word' – as if that meant that the play is a failure. The same critic assumed that at least part of Euripides' purpose was to send 'a political message to Argos' and therefore found that the message was wrapped in confusion and inconsistencies. But all such assumptions need to be proved, not taken for granted, and the only way of proving them is to study the facts of the play. Doing that, we arrive (once more) at the conclusion that the Greek tragic poet was thinking rather more deeply than we had at first supposed, and thinking, in this case with passion, about matters which not only were of importance to him and his audience, but are of no less importance to ourselves too. Further, that he usually communicated that thinking with some clarity and force – once we have cleared away what obscures our own vision. So fortified, we will return to the *Rhesus*, to see what the *sustasis* of that play will do for us.

The action of the play falls into three distinct parts. In the first, Hector is the chief character, until he is joined by Rhesus; the second deals with the exploit of Odysseus and Diomedes; the third consists of the lamentations over Rhesus uttered by his mother the Muse – and with sundry other matters. It will not disturb us if we find no close, Aristotelian, connection between one episode and the next, provided that each, in turn, relates to some unifying conception; and we should not forget that the prologue has been lost.

Our poet, taking the Homeric *Doloneia* as his main 'source', naturally strikes out for himself. He lays his scene in the Trojan, not the Achaean, camp. That means that he not only may, but must, invent most of the material for the first part of his play. He decides to make other changes. In the Homeric story Rhesus arrives before Dolon sets out. Dolon has seen Rhesus and his Thracian army, so that the Achaean marauders can extract that information from *him*. In the play, Dolon leaves before Rhesus comes; therefore a new method must be devised for giving the vital news to Odysseus and Diomedes. Again, in Homer it was in the Trojan camp that the night-fires were burning; naturally, since they had encamped for the night on the field, ready to resume their attack at dawn. In the play, the fires are transferred to the Achaean camp. That was necessary for the plot, though no reason is given why the Achaeans had a greater fire that night than ever before in the war (line 81). Conceivably, that was explained in the prologue; so far as the play is concerned, it remains a mystery.

From this point the play begins, and continues for some time in lively fashion, except that we would like to know why nearly everyone is shown to be almost devoid of commonsense. – But we should not be impatient. Trojan sentinels, who are the chorus, noticing those unusual fires, do their duty and awaken Hector; that is to say, they conjure the sleeping king, in resounding tragic diction, to λῦσαι βλεφάρων γοργωπὸν ἕδραν. As soon as he is awake and hears the news he knows what they mean: the Achaeans are preparing for flight. He would have destroyed them during the past day, he says, 'with this slaughtering hand of mine', if night had not intervened and if the σοφοί and the μάντεις had not dissuaded him from continuing in the dark. But now (he says) they are running away; we must attack at once, in full force. We will kill or enslave every man of them.

The chorus-leader points out that so far nothing is known for certain, but that makes no impression on Hector. Fortunately Aeneas arrives and tells Hector not to be a fool: trying to cross palisaded trenches in the dark, to drive chariots across narrow bridges, is madness. Better to send a spy, to find out what is going on. The chorus agrees with Aeneas, and Hector crumples up. We shall find that he usually does, when somebody talks sense to him.

Who will volunteer? Dolon is willing to undertake the dangerous mission, πρὸ γαίας, to discover what is going on in the Achaean camp. Hector gladly welcomes the noble offer. But Dolon reflects that κέρδος added to an ἔργον doubles the χάρις: what will his reward be? Homer had dealt with the question of a proper reward, but briefly; our poet does much better. Hector makes four distinguished offers; all are set aside by Dolon, for stated reasons. 'Then what *do* you want?', says Hector. – 'Achilles' horses.' – 'I too had set my heart on them, immortal horses given by Poseidon to Peleus. But you shall have them.' – 'I accept; I shall have received the most glorious reward for my courage.'

It is a lively passage. The critic must beware of 'guying' what he is criticizing; still, it does sound rather like an auction. Is it intended to be satirical?

The chorus remains entirely solemn: it lauds the bravery of Dolon, and prays that the *Dike* of the gods may watch over him – who however cannot take his leave without telling us in detail how he will insert himself into his wolf-skin, how far he will go as a quadruped, and when and where he will again become δίβαμος, 'biped'. Finally he asserts that he will return in safety and bring with him the head of either Odysseus or Diomedes, to prove that he really has been into the enemy camp. – We note the tragic irony, though without overestimating its subtlety. In the *stasimon* that follows the chorus sings earnestly: it spends a whole stanza invoking Thymbrian and Delian Apollo; it prays that Dolon may return safely, and later, when Hector has vanquished the Achaeans, ride in glory behind the immortal horses; and finally it speculates whom Dolon will slay: may he bring back the head of Agamemnon and capture Menelaus alive!

We know that we have seen the last of Dolon, but what are we expected to think and feel about it? To smile would be heartless; to weep, difficult; to shake a grave head over the coming doom of a foolish boaster, a bit elementary; yet the chorus takes it all very seriously. Perhaps the best thing is to wait and see.

The Shepherd arrives with good news for Hector. Our dramatist's presentation of Hector's character seems consistent: once again he jumps to a conclusion and is wrong; rude as well: 'Stupid fellow! Do you think I have time to listen to good news about your sheep? You know where my father's palace and throne are: take your news there!' However, the man persists; he gives his description, with tragic diction richly dight, of the nocturnal event that he has just seen: the approach of an irresistible army, rank upon rank uncountable, and making considerable uproar, πολλῇ ἠχῇ, with the terrifying bells hanging from the harness of the horses of Rhesus; and in the midst of it all, in a chariot drawn by horses whiter than snow, Rhesus, standing like a god, with a Gorgon emblazoned on his shield. It is true that a verse quoted from a lost prologue in the first Argument gives Rhesus, and the Shepherd, the benefit of a full moon; even so we have to agree with the Shepherd when he says that it is no small thing to plunge an army, by night, into wooded country full of wild animals when you know that an enemy is encamped hard by. What is the point of this remarkable passage? Parody? burlesque? No doubt that will appear later.

That great news Hector takes coldly. 'Rhesus is no friend of ours. While we were being hard pressed he held aloof; he comes only now, when we have no need of him, like a man who took no part in the hunt but turns up in time for the feast.' 'True', says the chorus-leader, 'but you should welcome anyone who offers help.' – 'We need none; tomorrow, victory is ours.' – 'Are you so certain about tomorrow?' – 'Quite certain.' – 'Wait and see; you never can tell.' – 'Well, since he has come, let him come as a ξένος, but not as an ally.' The chorus-leader thinks that ἐπίφθονον; the Shepherd adds that the very sight of Rhesus will terrify the Achaeans – and once more, Hector's firm stand collapses.

This is followed by the second (and last) *stasimon*. There are two stanzas of welcome for Rhesus, son of the Strymon and the Muse, who comes to Troy as Zeus Phanaios, as Zeus Eleutherios. (Perhaps it was not an entirely happy thought to explain the unusual method by which the River impregnated the Muse, 'eddying in watery form between her unsullied breasts', but let that pass.) In the remaining two stanzas the chorus wonders if Troy will ever again enjoy day-long festivals, when the enemy has been driven back. Then it apostrophizes Rhesus: 'Come! Confront and slay Achilles! Nobody can stand against you. Slay Achilles! No Argive shall return home.' Then, a direct address of welcome to the great King, as he makes what must have been a stupendous entrance, in his golden equipment and with bells clashing on his horses, 'Ares in person'.

It seems clear that our poet has been intent on raising Rhesus to the very pinnacle of majesty. Was that the reason why he decided to send away Dolon first, that nothing should interrupt the *crescendo* that began with the Shepherd's story and reaches its climax here? But in the scene that now begins – Hector's reception of Rhesus – we can hardly help feeling that Rhesus, after all, is no more than garishly painted cardboard. Politeness compels us to suppose that this is what the poet intended. Was it his purpose to write a burlesque on legendary heroism? That would indeed explain the literal absurdity of the Shepherd's narrative, also perhaps the way in which the Dolon episode has been handled. Perhaps we should adopt it as a provisional hypothesis.

Hector now receives Rhesus. We have the promise of a dramatic scene: the meeting of two vainglorious men, each utterly confident that he can end the war tomorrow. What does the poet make of it? Rhesus congratulates Hector on his imminent victory: 'I am late, but in time to join you in the destruction of the Achaeans.' Hector's reply is uncompromising reproach. 'It was I who with martial aid raised you from a local chieftainship, ἐκ μικρᾶς τυραννίδος, to the kingship of all Thrace; in return for which, in spite of embassies and rich gifts and many pleas, you were willing to see my realm destroyed.' In reply to that, Rhesus explains: 'Just as I was setting out for Troy, long ago, Scythians invaded Thrace...a fierce war, but in the end successful...then, the toilsome journey to Troy...No, I have not been wallowing in

337

luxury, as you have said.' He concludes, with no excess of tact, by telling Hector that he, Hector, has been struggling, day by day, for nine years, to no effect, but that he, Rhesus, will vanquish the Achaeans in a single day and go back home the next. No need for Hector to lift a finger.

So much for that. Our poet now writes a stanza for the chorus: 'Loyal ally! friend sent by Zeus! May your words provoke no *phthonos*; but no Achilles or Ajax can compare with you.' The dialogue is resumed. No more is heard of Hector's resentment. Indeed, Rhesus now proposes that when they have driven out the invader he and Hector, jointly, should ravage all Greece, to teach them a lesson. Hector may be silly, but not silly enough for that: the invitation is declined; upon which Rhesus comments: 'It seems to me that you are content to suffer, and do nothing in return.' Hector takes no offence, but offers Rhesus the command of the left wing, the right, or the centre. Rhesus would prefer to do it all on his own, 'but if you would think it a disgrace to have no part in the final victory after struggling for so long, put me opposite to Achilles'. But he is not fighting. 'Then who is next best?' Ajax and Diomedes are mentioned, and the crafty Odysseus. Rhesus chooses Odysseus: he loathes and despises craft; and when he hears of some of Odysseus' exploits he boils over with contempt; he will take him alive, crucify him, and leave his body for vultures to eat. Hector makes no comment, but brings this first part of the play to an end by taking Rhesus to the sleeping-quarters assigned to him and his army.

This might be a moment to pause and look back. The successive scenes have been quite lively in themselves. Long-winded rhetoric, smart logic-chopping, have been mercifully absent, but is not the continual foolish boasting becoming a little monotonous? Except for Aeneas and the Shepherd, everyone is infected by it – Hector, Dolon, Rhesus, even the chorus. From time to time the chorus has injected a little common sense into the proceedings, but even the chorus gives way when it looks forward to seeing Dolon come back with the severed head of Agamemnon and with Menelaus a captive. Further, must we not say of the chorus that its lyrical contributions do nothing to enlarge the ambit of the play? It is entirely uncritical of the preposterous Dolon, its enthusiasm for Rhesus as an invincible god incarnate, although it seems to be shared by Rhesus, will hardly be shared by any audience; and when, once, it seems to strike a more resonant note, when it hopes that Zeus will avert *phthonos* from Rhesus' words, we know that the bell is cracked, because we know that Rhesus is going to be killed merely because he is there – and has horses well worth the stealing. Once or twice the idea of burlesque has occurred to us, but surely good burlesque needs more gusto and more variety than we are finding here. There is perhaps a theoretical possibility: that the rest of the play is going to contrast the modest courage of the Greeks with the absurd overconfidence that prevails on the other side. That would be at least an idea, though a second-rate one, but we know already that nothing of the kind is in prospect.

For the second part of the play the dramatist has set himself a nice problem: how to present, on the stage, the exploit of Odysseus and Diomedes. He manages quite neatly to get his chorus off-stage to permit the entrance of the two Achaeans. Those two are at once nicely contrasted: Diomedes adventurous, Odysseus bold enough but cautious: 'Have we not done enough for one night by killing Dolon, stripping him of his armour, and getting the password out of him?' Diomedes would go looking for Hector, to kill him – or Aeneas, or Paris, but Odysseus dissuades him – and now Athena appears; not to set us thinking about the wretched Dolon or indeed about anything else; only to help the story forward.

Nothing in the play is less Euripidean than the way in which the poet uses Athena, both here and in the *finale*. She is a mere mechanical contrivance, a 'god of convenience', signifying nothing. To be sure, in his later, non-tragic plays Euripides uses the gods lightly or satirically, as many another Greek poet did, but what we have to accept here is that 'the *theos*' has not given it to Odysseus and Diomedes to kill Hector or Paris (line 397), and (lines 634f.) that Diomedes, eager to kill Paris when he is seen coming, may not act πλέον τοῦ πεπρωμένου; 'It is not θέμις that he should be killed by you.' In other words, he is on someone else's list. Professor Ritchie is able to take all that quite seriously: 'The sufferings of men are to be traced back to the caprices of the gods; the human figures of the drama become little more than puppets of the divine will. One is reminded of Euripides' treatment of his theme in Hippolytus'...and of Athena in the *Aiax*, where Athena 'has visited Ajax with madness to punish a personal slight' (pp. 124f.). But if we are to accept the *Rhesus* as Euripidean it is better *not* to be reminded of such other plays, in which the *theoi* are the very opposite of 'caprice' and the characters the very opposite of 'puppets'. One is much more forcibly reminded of Aristotle's one reference, in the *Poetics* (1454 b 2–6), to the gods: that they are a handy dramatic device – Aristotle's own *theos* having disappeared into the furthest reaches of metaphysics.

Athena's role here is only to help the playwright. Having announced what is 'fated', she tells the two men what, in Homer, they had learned from Dolon: that Rhesus has come, and that if he survives the night he will infallibly overrun their camp and burn their ships the next day. Since on this point she corroborates what Rhesus himself has said, we are evidently expected to believe it. She also tells them, thereby corroborating the Shepherd's story, that he has marvellous horses which shine in the dark, whiter than swans, horses well worth having.

Now the dramatist has to allow time – theatre-time – for the two men to do their bloody work, off-stage. His solution was to bring in Paris, looking for Hector; but he encounters Athena instead. She, pretending to be Aphrodite, assures him that nothing is amiss.

Once again, as when Hector and Rhesus first met, our poet creates a potentially dramatic situation, this time in the comic vein, and then fails to do much with it, for it is over almost as soon as begun. Nor is he much happier in what follows. Having got rid of Paris, Athena uses her divine powers to speak to Odysseus and Diomedes. She tells them to 'lull to rest their whetted swords', θηκτὰ κοιμίσαι ξίφη, because Rhesus lies dead and the horses are in their possession. (Presumably the two men knew that already, but the audience must be told.) However, her next remark is more to the point: the Trojans are on the alert; they had better make their escape.

That, perhaps, was awkward; what follows is better contrived. The chorus re-enters, excitedly looking for the supposed thieves. Soon Odysseus and Diomedes also re-enter – not of course with the horses; we are to forget about them. (Or perhaps Odysseus enters alone and we are to picture Diomedes waiting with the horses off stage. The busy, naturalistic action of this part of the story was awkward material for the Greek stage.) Knowing the password Odysseus is able to fool the chorus and get away safely. And now, what next?

Lyrical dialogue. The chorus wonders who the bold intruders can be. Suspicion falls on the wily Odysseus, and the passage ends with the chorus fearing what Hector may do to them for their apparent negligence. Now there enters one of Rhesus' men, a wounded charioteer. In a vividly confused story he tells of the nocturnal slaughter. Who did it, he cannot say, but he is sure that it must have been 'friends'. That suspicion ushers in what the poet has devised as the climax, or at least the ending, of this second part of his play. It is by no means badly done, but let us recognize it for what it is: an ancient anticipation of the modern who-dun-it. For Hector enters, in a natural fury with the sentinels who were so negligent as not to see the 'enemy spies' either coming in or going out (οὔτ' ἐξιόντας is a clever touch.) They shall be scourged and then beheaded. They of course protest their innocence, and are unexpectedly supported by the Charioteer. He makes argument to prove that the criminal is none other than Hector himself: he desperately wanted the horses; no enemy could possibly have made his way into the camp unseen; Hector with his Phrygians was encamped just in front of them; above all, the Achaeans could not possibly have known that Rhesus had even arrived, 'unless some god had told them' – a clever detail, and one which ought to apprise us that the poet's theology was not really very profound.

Hector naturally repudiates the accusation; he suspects the hand of Odysseus. But the Charioteer is not in the least impressed; for him, Hector is the criminal, and, if we accept Norwood's explanation of the otherwise feeble lines 875ff., he cries, 'Perish the dastard! It is not merely with my tongue that I assail you. Justice!' and makes to kill him, but either is overpowered or faints from his wound, and then is taken to Hector's house.

So ends part II of the play, in excitement and suspense, though not very much. It has little connection with Part I: what we were shown there of the character and mental equipment of Hector and Rhesus has nothing to do with the fact that two daring Achaeans made their way into the Trojan camp and, with supernatural prompting, murdered Rhesus; and the heroic lunacy of Dolon, although it was so piously endorsed by the chorus, means no more to the dramatist, or to us, than that before killing him Odysseus got the password out of him. However, now the Muse descends to inaugurate part III, and we are entitled to expect that she will supply something – let us call it an 'idea' – which will give the play some cohesion, some sense of direction, which at the moment it urgently needs. Such extravagant hopes are soon dashed.

For the Muse, mother of Rhesus, the poet writes: (a) a short introductory speech, (b) two lyric stanzas, (c) two fairly long speeches. In (a) she introduces herself: one of the Sisters, the Muse, 'who receives honour among the cultured' (σοφοῖς). It was Odysseus that killed Rhesus – no news to us, but Hector and the chorus must be told – 'and he will be punished for it as he deserves' – which we have to take on trust. The two lyric stanzas hardly do justice to the grief of a bereaved mother. In the first she mourns for five verses, then gives us information that would have been of great interest had we known it earlier: it was against the will of his parents that Rhesus went to Troy. (That is explained later.) The second stanza duly curses Diomedes, Odysseus and Helen.

The Muse passes at once to the first of her two long speeches. They are worth reading: we should not know otherwise what real ineptitude is.

She begins by apostrophizing the son of Philammon, Thamyris, who has been in her thoughts both during his life and since his death. That may seem rather remote, but we have not yet understood. We know, of course, that he, a mortal, challenged the Muses to a contest in song, and that they, to punish his hybris, blinded him. The Muse recalls that, but adds what we did not know: the hybris of Thamyris had a second consequence – the birth of Rhesus: τεκεῖν μ' ἔθηκε τόνδε δύστηνον γόνον. It happened like this. – The spot chosen for the contest was Mt Pangaeum. For a reason not explained the Muse, *this* Muse, had to make the journey alone, apart from her Sisters, and on the way she had to cross the Strymon. (We remember from Aeschylus that the crossing of the Strymon was disastrous to Xerxes' army; we would not expect a Muse to be inconvenienced by a mere river, but we should be wrong.) Crossing the river she 'entered Strymon's procreant bed', λέκτροις φυταλμίοις – as if that were the most natural thing in the world. Hence, Rhesus.

We noticed earlier that our poet was a little heavy-handed in his treatment of the divine copulation; here, even more so. It is as if he could leave no stone unturned, in order to stumble over it. She continues for a few verses almost in the style of New Comedy: feeling shame before her Sisters, and for her own un-wedded state, she gave her baby to Strymon, and he gave it for rearing to the river nymphs. Reaching manhood, Rhesus was King of Thrace and first among men. – If we ask, What about Hector's uncontested statement that he had raised Rhesus ἐκ μικρᾶς τυρραννίδος, the answer seems to be that we should not recollect things said earlier in the play.

Now we are told why his parents had forbidden Rhesus to go to Troy: she knew that it was his doom, πότμος, to be killed there, if he answered Hector's repeated request. – From his point of view it was a pity that she had not passed on that information to Rhesus; but of course it would have spoiled the play.

What we next have to assimilate is that the whole distressful episode was contrived by Athena; Odysseus and Diomedes were no more than her tools: οὐδὲν δ' 'Οδυσσεὺς οὐδ' ὁ Τυδέως τόκος ἔδρασε δράσας. Why Athena should have been so anxious to have Rhesus killed the Muse does not seem to know; at least, she does not explain it. Perhaps that should not surprise us: the Muse, naturally, had not been able to read that part of the play in which it was explained – that Athena wanted to save her Achaeans from imminent destruction. The Muse can think only of Athena's base ingratitude: the Muses have done so much to make Athena's city glorious – to assist which argument Musaeus is made to have been Athenian – and her reward is that now she has her son's dead body in her arms.

It must have been with unconscious humour that the poet now makes the chorus-leader turn to Hector and say: 'You see, Hector? The Charioteer was quite wrong in reviling us for the murder.' 'I knew it was Odysseus', says Hector; 'but I did nothing wrong in asking him to help us; he owed us that. I regret his death, and I will pay him rich funeral honours.' 'No', says the Muse; 'He will not go into the dark earth.' She goes on to explain that she has a recondite claim on Persephone's favour; she will ask her to release from the Underworld the spirit of Rhesus. She, the Muse, can never again behold her son, but his spirit will live on in the recesses of Mt Pangaeum as an ἀνθρωποδαίμων, a Βάκχου προφήτης, 'a god revered by those who know' – and they evidently include our playwright, since he has made a special study of the legends and ritual observances of Thrace. The Muse now observes that as she, now, is singing her lament over Rhesus, so later will she and her Sisters sing the lament over the son of Thetis; 'And Athena, who killed you, my son, will not be able to save him from death' – a remark that might seem to be merely spiteful. She adds that it is better not to have children, and upon that she disappears. The play now returns briskly to the matter in hand. 'Dawn has come, Hector; it is time to be up and doing.' Hector gives his orders, says once again that he is sure victory will be theirs before sunset, and the play is over.

We surveyed the often-impugned *Ajax*, the *Supplices*, and, vicariously, the *Andromache*, and came away with two ideas: that we can best make contact with a dramatist's mind by beginning with the study of his *sustasis*, and that when we do that with a competent Greek dramatist, we are apt to find that faults in technique attributed to him are illusory, that the focus of his dramatic thinking lay further back than we, nowadays, instinctively expect. We have tried the same method on the *Rhesus*. Must it not be our conclusion that its author had no idea at all, beyond that of making a play of some kind out of the Dolon–Rhesus episode? In the last resort it is to the choral odes that we would turn for signs of some unifying intention: this chorus, in its two *stasima*, can do nothing but echo, even amplify, the foolishness of Dolon and the emptiness of Rhesus.

I have just said, 'the idea of making a play out of the Dolon–Rhesus episode'; but what kind of play? It has been debated if the playwright intended something like a satyr-play, or a burlesque or a comedy. Some few passages do suggest something of the kind, but a stealthy massacre is no proper material for burlesque or comedy, nor should such a treatment of the story culminate in a scene of mourning, unsuccessful though that scene is. As for that scene, it has been pointed out that Euripides too had the habit of ending with an aetiology. True, but he knew where to draw the line. His aetiological references were always brief, and to something familiar to his audiences; this one is far from brief, familiar only to τοῖς εἰδόσιν, and the poet has made it hard to believe that the Rhesus whom we have seen and heard talking will be successfully transmogrified into an ἀνθρωποδαίμων and prophet of Bacchus. The self-conscious learning that pervades the third part of the play destroys any emotional impact, if such were intended, and is not even relevant to what has gone before.

The prevailing poverty of thought, and consequently of dramatic tension, is betrayed not only by the monotonous, and ultimately useless, character-drawing of Hector, Dolon and Rhesus, and by the wooden 'theology', but also by the avidity with which the author seizes upon anything that turns up, as he makes his way along: the 'auction' scene, Dolon's disguising, the Shepherd's tale of nocturnal splendours and din, the deceiving of Paris by Athena–Aphrodite, the who-dun-it passage; each of them, it may be, interesting enough for the moment, but adding up to nothing at all. 'Intellectually null': now that we have looked at the *sustasis* of the play, we can surely find no fault in Lucas' judgment, unless we think it an understatement. It is not merely that the play fails as a tragedy; it fails on any level. No play should so often require us to forget what has gone before, or lead us to expect what does not happen. We remember what Aristotle said about Euripides (1453 a 29f.): that he made every kind of mistake yet was the most tragic of the poets. What he meant by τραγικός was something like 'emotionally disturbing' (as we shall see later), but in this respect too nothing can be less Euripidean than the *Rhesus*. Perhaps it has become clear that it makes no appeal whatever to the *mind*, but does it stir our emotions either? Does it make us grieve for Dolon, feel pity – or anything else – for Rhesus, or weep with the Muse, when she tells us about Thamyris and Musaeus, about her conjugal encounter with the Strymon, and the disgraceful ingratitude of Athena? The style, diction, syntax may resemble those of Euripides; if we venture to look deeper – as perhaps the Alexandrian scholars did not – we find that we are looking at nothing but a blank wall.

It is true that Professor Ritchie, with perhaps an excess of benevolence, finds that 'the feelings of the audience are directed against the Greeks, especially against Odysseus, while the Trojans and their allies are sympathetically treated' (pp. 87f.). Really? It would have been a strange way of arousing sympathy with the Trojans to represent them all, except Aeneas, as distinctly foolish; and with their ally, to give Rhesus that absurd speech about crucifying Odysseus. As evidence for the other half of the proposition Ritchie refers to lines 710–22, where the chorus is very bitter about one of the past exploits of the wily Odysseus – which Greeks in general seem to have admired – and to lines 906–9, the stanza in which the Muse briefly curses Diomedes, Odysseus and Helen. But there is such a thing as dramatic, as well as linguistic, style. If Euripides, or any other sensible dramatist, had intended his audience to be moved to sorrow, or indignation, by the Muse's cursing, he certainly would not have led up to it by the who-dun-it passage, and he could not have followed her subsequent speech with the dry comment of the chorus-leader: 'You see, Hector...?' The cursing is no more than routine, and much the same can be said of the other passage, lines 710–20. Shall we propose the contrary, that our poet is trying to arouse our lively apprehensions on behalf of the Greeks, since he is always telling us that they are going to be slaughtered tomorrow? That would not work either: we know that they were not. He is not trying to engage our emotions at all, or, if he was, he had no notion how to do it. Euripides *did*.

When was the play written? The fourth century has of course been suggested by several scholars. Ritchie, summarizing his very careful survey of the documentary evidence, concludes (p. 58) that if the play is not genuine Euripides, the early fourth century is the only plausible date. We certainly must not assume that no fifth-century tragic poet ever wrote a third-rate play – and had it accepted for performance. Still, with the disputable exception of the stylistic evidence, nothing in the play suggests a fifth-century date, and everything in it fits very comfortably into what we know of fourth-century drama, whether from the scanty remains of it or from the *Poetics*. It may be worth while to consider this a little further.

Aristotle gives us a fair amount of information about the tragic drama of his own time, and much of what he says about tragedy in particular, as distinct from poetry in general, shows that he is in tune with the fourth century and out of tune with the fifth.

One of his basic requirements is that Tragedy should observe τὸ φιλάνθρωπον: what we, as members of the human race, think right and proper. That is not very far from the eighteenth-century concept of Natural Justice, even Poetic Justice, except of course that Aristotle is not sentimental about it; the sufferer must suffer beyond his deserts, otherwise there is no cause for pity and fear. Nevertheless he must have fallen into some grave error, to make his suffering explicable. If there were no ἁμαρτία then his suffering would be μιαρόν, 'abominable' – a word that Aristotle uses twice in the critical chapters 13 and 14.

That doctrine of ἁμαρτία has become canonical, but in two respects it has little relation with the practice of the fifth-century poets. The tragic thinking of those whom Aristotle calls 'the old poets' (1453 b 27–9) was not bounded by τὸ φιλάνθρωπον, nor restricted to the ἁμαρτία of one man (or even of two, or three) and its consequences to him (or them). As we saw, perhaps, from our brief study of the *Ajax, Supplices* and *Andromache*, the real concern of 'the old poets' lay further back; it extended beyond τὸ φιλάνθρωπον to the human condition itself, to what the Greeks often called the δίκη τῶν θεῶν. That Greek phrase is commonly translated 'the Justice of the Gods', which is well enough – if we know that δίκη is not necessarily 'Justice' and that 'gods' can be a misleading translation of *theoi*. We are on much safer ground if we understand the δίκη τῶν θεῶν as meaning something more like 'the way in which our world operates'. A good example – though there are many others – would be King Pelasgus, in Aeschylus' *Supplices*. He, through no fault of his own, is suddenly caught in a dilemma from which, as he says, there is no issue except through disaster. From Aristotle's point of view that makes no sense; it is μιαρόν. But his view is too small. The first word in Aeschylus' play is Zeus, and as many scholars have said, the idea of Zeus dominates the play, and presumably the whole trilogy too. The ill-used maidens appeal to Zeus the champion of the oppressed. How comforting, to know that the oppressed do have a divine champion! But that is not the way in which it works out, in this trilogy. Zeus does nothing to help them. Fleeing from oppression, they turn the screw on the helpless King – and it seems probable that he loses his life in the war that follows; the maidens are compelled to submit, but only to murder their hated suitors; and for that murder (it seems) they have to make some kind of atonement. That is the way in which Zeus works in this trilogy – and, as Aeschylus says in the course of the play, the mind of Zeus is an abyss which no human thought can plumb. The moral violence that began with the Suitors in Egypt rolls on; it engulfs the King; it provokes murderous retaliation which (it seems) must in its turn be paid for. (The philosophical structure of *Hamlet* is very similar.) τὸ φιλάνθρωπον cannot cope with this. We could wish that our world were arranged more comfortably; unhappily, it is not. That is the kind of situation that can and does arise in our world, and the fifth-century tragic poets had the toughness of mind to face it. Greek drama, we often say, was 'religious drama'. Yes, but 'religious', in a Greek context, is a dangerous word. That drama was 'religious' not in the sense of being doctrinal, devotional, theological, but of striving to present the way in which the world operates, of exploring the δίκη τῶν θεῶν.

By the fourth century that wide background had entirely vanished. Now, at best, tragic drama was only ethical. Consequently the *theoi* have become no more than a dramatic convenience, as Aristotle says, and as the *Rhesus* exemplifies with its purely mechanical Athena. Serious thinking about serious matters had migrated from the poets to the philosophers. What was left to the poets was what philosophy cannot make its aim: emotional excitement and aesthetic gratification of one kind or another. Fifth-century tragedy had of course provided these in abundance, but so much more; now there is nothing else, except (for Aristotle) ethical propriety. Hence his fundamental theory, that tragedy arouses pity and fear, and allays such emotions by *catharsis*. Nowhere in the *Poetics* does he give a hint that tragedy is 'religious', in any sense of that word. Indeed, so far does he go in the direction of emotionalism that in his discussion of the tragic πάθος he lays it down that the act of violence is not really τραγικόν unless it occurs between kinsmen. That, and only that, will produce the necessary thrill of horror. But he insists that the horror should be kept under control, and he reprobates 'the old poets' for not controlling it. Medea's murder of her children was μιαρόν, abominable. Aristotle was always logical, and here his logic leads him to the conclusion that the best type of tragedy is that exemplified by the *I.T.*, a play that has all the dramatic virtues except that of being a tragedy. Could anything show more clearly how foreign the fifth century had now become?

But Aristotle was not writing as a philosopher theorizing *in vacuo*. On the contrary, he has his contemporary theatre very much in mind. Thus, he tells us, twice (1453 a 17–21 and 1454 a 9–13), that the best of the 'modern' poets use a much smaller range of myth than the older ones. He explains, and he approves: they now use only the myths of those families 'whose lot it was to do and suffer fearful things'. That shrinkage on the tragic horizon which we have been considering is reflected, necessarily, in a shrinkage of usable myth. Thought is no longer any business of the tragic poet; pity and fear are everything.

And what of those 'modern' poets who were not of the 'best'? He tells us. There were those who relied only on spectacular effects (1453 b 7–11). Were none such written in the fifth century? We cannot deny the possibility, but it seems unlikely. About a second type of play we can be more positive; the play with the double ending, the soft option, 'now, by some, considered the best'. Aristotle is almost as disdainful of those as of the super-spectaculars: 'Those are thought best only because of the flabbiness, the ἀσθένεια, of the audiences. The poets give the audiences what they want.' Presumably Aeschylus and Sophocles had done that too, and Euripides also, though with rather less applause. That ἀσθένεια τῶν θεάτρων had not yet set in.

The times have changed indeed; we seem to be in a different world, so far as drama is concerned – and maybe some of the other arts too. It is in a world of this kind, with its much more unexacting audiences, that the *Rhesus* might have done quite well, though not brilliantly. What was wanted now from drama was entertainment, whether clever and sophisticated, or just sensational, or emotionally relaxing; laced, perhaps, with ethical decency, and not hostile to the intellectual discussion, in passing, of this or that; but essentially entertainment. How interesting, to be given a close-up of Hector, Dolon and Rhesus; to see the intrepid Greek spies in action; to hear of the Muse having a surreptitious baby who was to become an ἀνθρωποδαίμων!

Naturally, it makes no sense, no *real* sense, but who expected real sense from a tragic poet now? If we must believe that Euripides was the author, I would suggest that he wrote it at the age of fifteen or so, πρὶν φῦσαι φρένας, as you might say.